INSIDE THE IRA

Dissident Republicans and the War for Legitimacy

ANDREW SANDERS

EDINBURGH
University Press

© Andrew Sanders, 2011, 2012

First published in hardback in 2011 by
Edinburgh University Press Ltd
22 George Square, Edinburgh EH8 9LF
www.euppublishing.com

This paperback edition 2012

Typeset in 11/13.5 Goudy by
Servis Filmsetting Ltd, Stockport, Cheshire, and
printed and bound in the United States of America

A CIP record for this book is available from the British Library

ISBN 978 0 7486 4696 8 (paperback)

The right of Andrew Sanders to be identified as author of this work
has been asserted in accordance with the Copyright, Designs
and Patents Act 1988.

Contents

Acknowledgements

No such work can be undertaken without the help of a number of individuals.

Firstly, I wish to thank my editors, Nicola Ramsey, Eddie Clark and James Dale at Edinburgh University Press, who have always been at hand with salient advice.

The basis for this book was my 2008 PhD thesis, completed at the Queen's University of Belfast. The original thesis was read and re-read multiple times by my supervisors, Professor Richard English and Professor Graham Walker. I was fortunate to work with two outstanding scholars and I take great pleasure in thanking them both sincerely.

I also want to make special mention of my undergraduate supervisor and great friend Ian Wood. It is not an exaggeration to say that without him, none of this would have happened.

I would also like to offer thanks to other faculty and staff at the School of Politics, International Studies and Philosophy at Queen's University Belfast, particularly Paul Bew, Margaret O'Callaghan, Aine Egan and Joanne Canavan. My PhD external examiner, Michael Cox, also deserves mention in these acknowledgements. The initial research and writing of the thesis was made possible by a stipend from the Department of Employment and Learning, and I also thank Catherine Coll for her assistance in my application for the funding. A Sir Thomas Dixon travel scholarship funded a research trip to America which enhanced that particular section of the project.

In Seattle, I wish to acknowledge Father Thomas Murphy, Jennifer Schulz, Kan Liang and Theresa Earenfight at Seattle University and George Behlmer at the University of Washington.

In the various libraries I cannot thank enough those who provided me with assistance. At the Linen Hall Library in Belfast, Kris Browne, Ross Moore and Alistair Gordon; at the UCD archive in Dublin, Seamus Helferty; the staff at the American Catholic History Research Center and University Archives, Catholic University of America, Washington, DC; in Boston, the excellent archive at the Burns Library; the staff of the Tamiment Library at New York University, especially Marion Casey; the staff at the Public Record Office of Northern Ireland.

I am also indebted to the following people for a variety of reasons: Richard O'Rawe, Gerard Hodgins, Anthony McIntyre, Danny Morrison, the late Sammy Duddy, Shaun McKeown, John Bunting, Brian Hanley, Roy Johnston, Ian McBride, Marianne Elliott, Robert St Cyr, Mary McGlynn, Joseph Skelly, Lieutenant General Sir Alistair Irwin. Additionally, I wish to thank those, both credited and uncredited, who agreed to interviews. For obvious reasons, certain interviewees have to remain anonymous. Sadly, their war is still not over.

Friends internationally were also integral to the completion of this work: Caoimhe Nic Dháibhéid; Colin Reid; Máiréad Collins; Pavlos Koktsidis; the Calo family; Simon McDade and Olga Beagon; Kellie Smith and Richard Forbes-Simpson; Antony Small; the Langrell family; Mike Evans; Billy Weydemeyer; the Peters family in Milwaukee; Douglas Byrd and family; the Richardson family; Andrew Wilson; John Daly and the IAHC; the Dobbie family; the Marroni family; the Budzynski, Guerin, Martin, Cunningham, Lynn, Irwin and Sanders families.

I also wish to thank my family: Stuart, Barbara, Sarah and Duncan Sanders, and especially Heather.

Notes

I have deliberately varied the use of both Londonderry and Derry.

Unless otherwise defined, the use of IRA is in reference to the Provisional IRA.

Martin Melaugh's CAIN website, www.cain.ulst.ac.uk, provided information that benefited this project considerably, particularly Malcolm Sutton's 'Database of Deaths'. I have used this alongside *Lost Lives* as sources of information on the victims of the troubles. Thanks also to Pat Lyons for permission to cite statistics about voter turnout.

I also used the www.ark.ac.uk website for information on Northern Ireland Elections and http://electionsireland.org/index.cfm for other electoral information.

Abbreviations

32CSM	32 County Sovereignty Movement
ABC	American Broadcasting Company
AP/RN	*An Phoblacht/Republican News*
BCBL	Boston College Burns Library
BICO	British and Irish Communist Organisation
BT	*Belfast Telegraph*
CBS	Columbia Broadcasting System
CIRA	Continuity Irish Republican Army
CPNI	Communist Party of Northern Ireland
CPSU	Communist Party of the Soviet Union
CRA	Civil Rights Association
CSJ	Campaign for Social Justice
DUP	Democratic Unionist Party
FBI	Federal Bureau of Investigation
IAUC	Irish American Unity Conference
ICA	Irish Citizen Army
IICD	Independent International Commission on Decommissioning
IMC	Independent Monitoring Commission
IN	*Irish News*
INAC	Irish Northern Aid Committee (also known as Noraid)
INLA	Irish National Liberation Army
IPLO	Irish People's Liberation Organisation
IRA	Irish Republican Army
IRLA	Irish Republican Liberation Army
IRSCNA	Irish Republican Socialist Committees North America
IRSM	Irish Republican Socialist Movement

IRSP	Irish Republican Socialist Party
ISRP	Irish Socialist Republican Party
IT	*Irish Times*
KOD	Kirk O'Donnell Papers, Boston College
LAW	Loyalist Association of Workers
LHLPC	Linen Hall Library Political Collection
LVF	Loyalist Volunteer Force
NBC	National Broadcasting Company
NICRA	Northern Ireland Civil Rights Association
NILP	Northern Ireland Labour Party
NYUL	New York University Library
OC	Officer Commanding
OIRA	Official Irish Republican Army
ONH	Óglaigh na hÉireann
OSF	Official Sinn Féin
PD	People's Democracy
PIRA	Provisional Irish Republican Army
PRONI	Public Record Office of Northern Ireland
PSF	Provisional Sinn Féin
PUP	Progressive Unionist Party
RHC	Red Hand Commando
RIRA	Real Irish Republican Army
RPG	Rocket Propelled Grenade
RSF	Republican Sinn Féin
SAS	Special Air Service
SDLP	Social Democratic and Labour Party
SF	Sinn Féin
SFWP	Sinn Féin the Workers' Party
TIP	*The Irish People*
TNA	The National Archive, Public Record Office
TSN	*The Sovereign Nation*
UDA	Ulster Defence Association
UDP	Ulster Democratic Party
UFF	Ulster Freedom Fighters
UPRG	Ulster Political Research Group
UUP	Ulster Unionist Party
UVF	Ulster Volunteer Force
UWC	Ulster Workers Council
WP	Workers' Party

For Ian, with thanks

CHAPTER 1

The Origins of Division: The Republican Movement in the Twentieth Century, 1916–62

Dublin author Brendan Behan once quipped that the first item on the agenda of any new Irish organisation was the split.[1] From the inception of the original IRA, which fought in the Irish War of Independence between 1919 and 1921, the history of the republican movement has been plagued with division. While the focus of this study is the schismatic tendency of republicanism in the latter part of the twentieth century, it is important to contextualise this factionalism alongside what went before to facilitate consideration of later splits in the movement in a comparative perspective. This will show that although splits in republicanism have been relatively common, frequently personality driven and only occasionally violent, republican division has not necessarily created groups that have emulated their predecessors. It will also enable identification of the common themes of republican division and will trace the careers of republican actors who found themselves involved in a movement that rarely spent longer than a decade without encountering the problem of dissent and division.

The Irish Republican Army (IRA) descended from the Irish Volunteers, which itself had experienced a split in 1914. Irish Parliamentary Party leader John Redmond, hopeful of the enactment of the Home Rule Act, encouraged support of the Allied war effort on the outbreak of World War I. In the face of opposition for this move, the Irish Volunteers split from the larger National Volunteers, roughly one-fifth of whose 150,000 membership joined the 10th (Irish) and 16th (Irish) Divisions of the British Army. The remainder of the movement was intended to act as a home guard for Ireland, but the British War Office was reluctant to train a movement that was largely disorganised and could not provide

1

front-line recruits, in addition to the concern that it could have been uti-lised to enforce Home Rule on nationalist terms.[2] As the war progressed and as news of the heavy losses suffered by the Irish divisions spread, increasing the threat of conscription, support for the National Volunteers dwindled as that of the Irish Volunteers grew. This was an early example of British influence on republican division, with differences between the pragmatic and the principled significant.

Again, the issue of pragmatism arose during the build-up to Easter weekend 1916. The importance of the Easter Rising to the history of modern Ireland is evidenced by the weight of existing literature on the subject.[3] Although the Rising itself failed to achieve its objectives, the fallout from Easter week 1916 served to invigorate both the spirit of Irish republicanism and the physical force tradition inherent in the republican movement. It also represented the coming together of the nationalist and socialist tendencies of contemporary Ireland; the former represented by Patrick Pearse and the Irish Volunteers, the latter by James Connolly and his Irish Citizens Army. Both were executed in the aftermath of the Rising and joined a list of republican martyrs that would continue to grow over the course of the century. Connolly's legacy was particularly impor-tant for future republicans who would attempt to unite the national and social struggles in Ireland. Even though his socialist credentials are argua-bly overshadowed by Jim Larkin and his republican credentials pale when compared with those of Pearse, as a republican socialist his standing has remained unquestioned. Later generations of republicans would continue the quest for a credible and popular allegiance between the nationalist and socialist tendencies in Ireland. Also sentenced to death for his role in the Rising was New York-born Éamon de Valera. Saved by British con-cerns as to the reaction of the United States if an American citizen was executed, de Valera's impact on Irish history has been well documented[4] and he played an integral role in republican factionalism during the first half of the century.

The Irish Volunteers transitioned into the Irish Republican Army after the Irish Republic, proclaimed at Easter 1916, was established by the formation of Dáil Éireann in 1919, which recognised the IRA as its legitimate army. The 1918 election had seen Sinn Féin establish a majority, achieving almost half of the total votes cast. Refusing to rec-ognise the legitimacy of the parliament at Westminster, they assembled as Dáil Éireann. The Irish War of Independence broke out the following year and in the middle of the war, the Government of Ireland Act was passed which provided for two separate home rule parliaments. In 1921, elections to these parliaments effectively ratified the Anglo-Irish Treaty, which effected the end of the War of Independence. In Northern Ireland, Éamon de Valera's Sinn Féin took six seats and in Southern Ireland, the short-lived name for what became the Irish Free State in late 1922, the Second Dáil Éireann was formed by 124 Sinn Féin Teachta Dála's (TDs) and four independent unionists. No polling took place in the southern state, with the ongoing war creating an unfavourable atmosphere for an election to be held. Although Michael Collins, Éamon de Valera, Arthur Griffith, Sean McIlroy and Eoin MacNeill had won seats in both parliaments, Sinn Féin refused to recognise the separate parliaments and therefore sent all of its representatives to the Dublin parliament, establishing the lasting republican legitimacy of the Second Dáil.

Once a truce was established in July 1921, discussions could begin towards a treaty and the Anglo-Irish Treaty was signed on 6 December 1921. Following extensive debates, the treaty was ratified by Dáil Éireann on 7 January 1922 and Sinn Féin split into pro- and anti-treaty factions. Debate raged over the question of the treaty. Certainly, Sinn Féin enjoyed a considerable majority in the state that became the Irish Free State, but they were still far from the full thirty-two-county Irish republic that they had sought.[5] The Oath of Allegiance, which all TDs were required to take in order to take their seats in the Dáil, was also divisive, with profession of loyalty to King George V, although typical within the Commonwealth, particularly repugnant to Irish nationalists.

Among those in favour of the treaty were IRA Chief of Staff Richard Mulcahy, his deputy Eoin O'Duffy and Michael Collins, the Director of Intelligence. Opposed were Liam Mellows, the Director of Purchases, and Director of Munitions Sean Russell. Motivations here were complex, with issues arising of military capability and the capacity of the movement to continue the War of Independence. The favour for the treaty among the most senior IRA men indicates that the IRA campaign was nearing breaking point. Although no one wanted to see Ireland divided, let alone be responsible for it, the pragmatic view was to accept the partition of Ireland as a stepping stone from which republicans could agitate towards total independence. So much subsequent republican division has resembled the split that took place over the Treaty. With their acceptance of the Treaty and the consequential recognition of a partitioned Ireland, the Collins faction established the circumstances over which republicans would continue to disagree: the legitimacy of a parliament that did not govern the entire thirty-two counties of Ireland.

De Valera resigned the presidency in protest after walking out of the Dáil along with a significant minority of Sinn Féin TDs. With Sinn Féin now divided into pro- and anti-Treaty camps, the split that would define Irish politics began to manifest. With the 1922 Irish General Election imminent, and Sinn Féin's hegemony from 1921 no longer guaranteed thanks to the Treaty split, a pact was agreed between Collins and de Valera that pro- and anti-Treaty Sinn Féin would not compete and would form a coalition government after the election so as to minimise public expression of opinion on the Treaty itself. The pro-Treaty Sinn Féin won fifty-eight seats compared to anti-Treaty Sinn Féin's thirty-six. The drop of thirty seats when compared to the previous year indicated public opposition to the violence of the War of Independence but still provided Sinn Féin with a strong electoral mandate. In reality, however, the boycott of the Dáil on the part of the anti-Treaty Sinn Féin TDs undermined any such attempt at unison and, in light of the most significant pressure it had faced, the republican movement had irrevocably fractured.

There had been confrontations between rival IRA factions during early 1922 which halted during the election. With the electoral mandate firmly in the hands of pro-Treaty Sinn Féin following the election, civil war broke out within a week of the result. The pro-Treaty IRA was rebranded as the Irish National Army, a name that reflected the legitimacy the group was now afforded by the people of what became the Irish Free State. This legitimacy was underlined by the lack of structure that diluted the potency of the anti-Treaty IRA and the Civil War became largely a guerrilla conflict. Foreshadowing the feuding that would beset republicanism in the latter years of the century, leaders from either side were killed, including Michael Collins, Cathal Brugha and Liam Lynch. With Lynch's death in April 1923, Frank Aiken assumed control of the IRA and the group moved towards a truce.

In early December 1922, exactly a year after the signing of the Anglo-Irish Treaty, the Irish Free State was established; the north-eastern six counties of Northern Ireland quickly opted out. With the establishment of the Free State came that of the Irish Defence Forces, otherwise known as Óglaigh na hÉireann. This name has become part of republican folklore, the title of the true soldiers of Ireland self-bestowed upon each group that assumed the republican struggle during the twentieth century. The quest to be perceived as the rightful Óglaigh na hÉireann, the 'Volunteers of Ireland', or the 'real' IRA, has challenged republicans ever since.

In 1923, pro-Treaty Sinn Féin became Cumann na nGaedheal under the leadership of W. T. Cosgrave and the elections of August, although yielding forty-four seats for de Valera's Republican party, saw Cosgrave emerge victorious. This emphasised support for the Treaty among the Irish population. With anti-Treaty republicans abstaining from the Dáil, Cosgrave was able to form a minority government and set about the process of building up the Free State. The same process had begun in earnest in the northern state, which had drifted out of focus for Irish republicans during the Civil War. The IRA was damaged by its defeat in the Civil War; although it reorganised during 1925, it was still relatively weak in Northern Ireland.[6] Its continued capacity for creating political instability was evidenced by the 1927 assassination of Minister for Justice, Kevin O'Higgins.[7]

De Valera founded the Fianna Fáil party in 1926. He had been arrested and interned until 1924 following a series of arrests in the aftermath of the Civil War. With Sinn Féin unwilling to accept the Free State, even with the abolition of the Oath of Allegiance, de Valera founded Fianna Fáil along with Sean Lemass and Constance Markiewicz with the goal of republicanising the Free State. They contested the elections of 1927 and enjoyed reasonable success, only narrowly defeated by Cumann na nGaedheal in both the June and September elections. After the assassination of O'Higgins, authorities in the Free State legislated that all prospective Dáil candidates must take the Oath of Allegiance, forcing de Valera to amend his stance.[8] This shift in position, viewed across the spectrum from capitulation to pragmatism, would be a mark of republican leaders throughout the remainder of the century. More significant was the fact that state-enforced legislation, effectively implemented, had brought the dissenters towards a constitutional position. This particular lesson would only be applied inconsistently at best over the remaining years of the century, with particularly ineffective strategy implemented to the great cost of the authorities in Ireland, north and south, during the 1970s.

By the 1932 elections, Fianna Fáil's political stock had grown to the extent that the additional fifteen seats they won now placed them as the largest party in Ireland, with Cosgrave's Cumann na nGaedheal sixteen seats in arrears, falling further behind in the 1933 General Election. Cumann na nGaedheal merged with the National Centre Party and the

National Guard to form Fine Gael. Prominent members of the latter included Thomas O'Higgins, brother of Kevin, and Eoin O'Duffy.[9]

Upon his succession to the Dáil in 1932, de Valera lifted the ban on the IRA. The IRA had come under increasing left-wing influence around this time, as evidenced by the Saor Éire organisation founded in 1931 by Peadar O'Donnell which included George Gilmore, Frank Ryan and Seán MacBride. The counter movement to this shift leftward was evident from IRA General Order number four which stated that no Communist could be an IRA member, introduced in 1933.[10] Discontent at this order manifested itself in the formation of the Republican Congress in 1934, led by O'Donnell, Ryan and Gilmore. During council elections that year, Republican Congress achieved success in Westmeath and Dundalk, and became noteworthy as a result of its Shankill Road branch, present at the Wolf Tone commemorations at Bodenstown of that year.[11] The attempts of O'Donnell and his colleagues to fuse the social and republican struggles proved ultimately futile; Republican Congress unity had proven decidedly fragile and the group split at its first annual conference in September 1934. O'Donnell and others went on to fight in the Spanish Civil War against Franco's military insurgency, with former comrade Eoin O'Duffy leading the Irish Brigade which sided with the fascists. O'Duffy's departure from Fine Gael had marked the beginning of the end for the Blueshirt (National Guard) movement and it petered out well in advance of the outbreak of World War II.

Success at the 1937 and 1938 General Elections underlined support for de Valera's redrafted Bunreacht na hÉireann, the constitution of the country, adopted in 1937. The new constitution was highly republican, claiming sovereignty over the entire island of Ireland and abolishing the controversial Oath of Allegiance. While this particular obstacle could be overcome relatively easily and de Valera's constitution did go some way to appeasing republicans who had become distanced by the recognition of the partitionist southern parliament, others were less convinced of the legitimacy of de Valera's authority to govern. 1938 also saw a meeting between seven TDs of the Second Dáil and the IRA Army Council during which the TDs signed over their perceived authority over the government of Dáil Éireann to the IRA's Army Council. This heavily symbolic move has echoed throughout the history of the republican movement thanks to the longevity of Mayo South-Roscommon South TD Tom Maguire, one of those present at this meeting. De facto power may have rested with Fianna Fáil, but the de jure authority of the Second Dáil was now perceived as the IRA's.

6

World War II was to finally divide the IRA and the Fianna Fáil government, who had endured a turbulent relationship since the end of the Civil War. An underdeveloped military left the Free State at the mercy of Britain for defence, and although Ireland adopted a policy of neutrality during the war, this was 'openly benevolent',[12] particularly after America joined the war. The IRA campaign of the period, an attempt to take advantage of British preoccupation with events elsewhere through collaboration with the German Abwehr, was therefore not well received. IRA Chief of Staff Sean Russell visited Berlin and received training, but died en route back to Ireland and was buried at sea, wrapped in a swastika.[13] Frank Ryan, who had been a prominent member of the International Brigade during the Spanish Civil War but later arrested and imprisoned, was also by this stage in Germany, having been transported there by his captors. He too died without ever seeing Ireland again, perishing in Dresden in 1944. The tension of the period was best exemplified when Russell's successor Stephen Hayes stood accused of being an informer and was court-martialled under Sean McCaughey, the Northern Commander of the IRA and its Adjutant General.

While a 1939 raid at Phoenix Park storage depot had yielded the IRA a large quantity of weapons and ammunition, it also served to emphasise the finality of the division between the Fianna Fáil party and the IRA. The introduction of the 1939 Offences Against the State Act and the 1940 Amendment to the Emergency Powers Act provided the state with the legislative weaponry with which to combat the IRA. The anti-Treaty forces of the 1920s had been divided unquestionably and permanently.

Several prominent republicans emerged around this time. Cathal Goulding had joined the IRA in 1939, having graduated from Na Fianna Éireann, which he had joined with Brendan Behan eight years previously. He took part in the Phoenix Park raid but found himself in jail in 1941 for membership of an unlawful organisation, immediately reinterned upon his release the following year in the Curragh internment camp. Commentators have noted the propensity for schism among the internees at the Curragh.[14] Following the closure of the internment camps at the end of World War II, Goulding and his fellow republicans found the movement severely damaged and a return to activity was inhibited by a series of arrests during a meeting at the Ardee Bar in Dublin in March 1946,[15] but there were still republicans devoted to the cause, none more so than Sean McCaughey. Jailed for the illegal imprisonment of Hayes, he had spent five years on a blanket protest before dying on hunger and thirst strike in Portlaoise prison in May 1946. The use of hunger strike as a political weapon has been an important republican tactic, established by men such as Thomas Ashe and Terence MacSwiney. MacSwiney's 1920 death on hunger strike, after his election as Lord Mayor of Cork, established a link between elections and hunger striking that would prove powerful later in the century.

While the IRA's division with Fianna Fáil was significant to the internal dynamics of republicanism, it was also indicative of growing political discontent with the party. Although the party had been established on strong republican principles, their shift away from these principles was rapid. De Valera had, after all, not only entered the Dáil and therefore tacitly accepted the partition of Ireland, but had also legislated against the IRA, perceived by its supporters as the legitimate Óglaigh na hÉireann. Politically, the emergence of both Clann na Talmhan and Clann na Poblachta emphasised this discontent, although political dissatisfaction with a government that had ruled a country in excess of a decade does not necessarily call into question the political aptitude of a party. Nevertheless, in 1943 Clann na Talmhan had won ten seats with its core base of western farmers, an election that also saw the Labour Party achieve seventeen seats.[16]

Clann na Poblachta was formed by former IRA Chief of Staff Seán MacBride in 1946 and targeted politically motivated republicans in urban areas. It had grown out of a series of similarly named organisations, including Cumann Poblachta na hÉireann and Córas na Poblachta, which had formed from the mid-1930s onwards as republicans sought to further their struggle. Cumann Poblachta na hÉireann had begun to challenge the abstentionist principles of republicanism, promoting the idea that candidates could contest elections but would not take their seats if successful. The most significant aspect of this proposal was that the IRA was prepared to abide such a move.[17]

MacBride won a seat in the Dáil in 1947 in a by-election for Dublin County and Patrick Kinane won in the Tipperary by-election. Concern at the potential of the group forced Taoiseach de Valera to call a snap election in 1948 in an attempt to catch the party off-guard. Although Clann na Poblachta only won ten seats, they ended up in a coalition government with Fine Gael, the Labour Party, Clann na Talmhan and National Labour. Their share of the vote had been impacted by de Valera's hasty introduction of the Electoral Amendment Act of 1947 which increased the size of the Dáil from 138 to 147 seats and increased the number of three-seat constituencies from fifteen to twenty-two. The effectiveness of this tactic is obvious when comparing the fourteen seats won by Labour with their 11 per cent of first-preference votes compared to Clann na Poblachta's ten seats with over 13 per cent. With Fianna Fáil unable to form a coalition, the party quite unpopular after such a long period in government, the coalition was led by Fine Gael, although leader Richard Mulcahy stepped aside because of his prominent position in the pro-Treaty forces during the Civil War and the position of Taoiseach was filled by John A. Costello.

MacBride's party was able to capitalise on Sinn Féin's lack of organisation and seized much of the republican vote that had lost faith with Fianna Fáil.[18] The party's figurehead, MacBride brought with him impeccable republican credentials, although commentators have noted the irony in MacBride's deficiencies ultimately casting him as a political liability.[19]

There is much in the formation of Clann na Poblachta that foreshadowed future events in the republican movement. As Fianna Fáil moved towards government, certain adjustments were made in both its interpretation and application of republican ideology. With the Costello government responsible for the declaration of the Republic, the former IRA volunteers that now formed the majority of the Clann na Poblachta party had effectively recognised the existence of a non-thirty-two-county version of the Republic. The recognition of something previously considered anathema, the legitimacy of Dáil Éireann, reflects a pragmatic tendency that has been an integral part of republican ideology throughout the twentieth century. Groups have frequently found it difficult to maintain a position of principle over lengthy periods of time once it becomes apparent that the route to power lies inside government rather than outside.

The end of this period in many ways signals a new beginning for Fianna Fáil. In 1948, they were to lose power in spite of gaining the highest proportion of votes. Seán Lemass, promoted to Tánaiste, the deputy head of government, in 1945, would go on to lead the economic modernisation of Ireland during the 1960s.[20]

THE BORDER CAMPAIGN

The political change ongoing in the republican movement during the 1960s, which would create the Official–Provisional schism, owes much to Operation Harvest, otherwise known as the Border Campaign. The campaign that began in 1956 was the first northern-focused campaign of republicans since partition. While the campaign signally failed to achieve its objectives, it did stimulate a re-evaluation of the movement that created political initiatives which would fracture republicanism.

Although damaged by its campaign during World War II, the revolutionary imperative was still strong within the IRA. An Army Convention was called in 1948 to discuss the future of the movement and the 1950 reorganisation of Sinn Féin brought IRA men into positions of power in the political wing of the movement.[21] A series of raids on British army bases in the early 1950s provided arms and marked the first meeting between Cathal Goulding and young English volunteer John Stephenson when the two conspired to rob Felsted Army Training School in Essex in mid-1953. After the raid, the unit got lost and found themselves arrested, later sentenced to eight years in prison.[22]

A more successful raid on Gough barracks in Armagh, led by Sean Garland, who had signed up for the Royal Irish Fusiliers with a view to obtaining intelligence on the facility, yielded almost three hundred guns.[23] Training camps were set up in County Wicklow the following year using weapons from the raid.[24] Later that same year a less successful raid on Omagh barracks prompted the announcement at Bodenstown of IRA General Order number eight which prohibited military action against the security forces of the southern state. This provided some insight as to the IRA's plan for a northern-focused campaign. This announcement was somewhat controversial as it served to ratify, to its opponents, the legitimacy of the security forces of the Republic, itself an illegitimate state to traditional republicans. Discontent among militants was led by Joe Christle, a relative newcomer who had taken part in both the raids in Armagh and Omagh.[25]

Implicit in the decision that southern security forces should not be legitimate targets was the fact that northern security forces, namely the Royal Ulster Constabulary and B-Specials (the RUC's part-time reserve unit), predominantly Protestant organisations, were. This gave the campaign a sectarian dimension its organisers would have preferred not to have. Assaults were therefore designed to draw the Army out from their bases to minimise the number of attacks on the RUC and B-Specials.[26] The IRA stated that 'the struggle of the Resistance Movement is most certainly not against the Unionist population of the Six Counties . . . To

10

members of the RUC and B-Special Constabulary . . . We ask them to remember that they are Irishmen.'[27]

The schismatic tendency of the movement during the 1950s was particularly detrimental to the campaign. Brendan O'Boyle's unsuccessful attempts to lead a breakaway faction in the early 1950s were less of a concern to the leadership than those of Liam Kelly, who was dismissed by the IRA in 1951 for carrying out an unauthorised raid in Derry. Kelly, who had been elected to the northern parliament in 1953 for the Mid-Ulster constituency, launched Saor Uladh.[28] A political wing, Fianna Uladh, was also formed which accepted the 1937 constitution, leaving open the option of participation in the Irish parliament at Leinster House.[29] Kelly's election to the Irish Seanad in 1954, where he served on the Labour Panel, gave him an electoral mandate on either side of the Irish border, although he abstained from the Northern Irish government, housed at Stormont Castle until 1972, for the duration of his term there. Other republicans enjoyed reasonable electoral success during the mid-1950s.

In the 1955 British General Election, Sinn Féin had won two seats, in Mid-Ulster and Fermanagh/South Tyrone.[30] Pressure had been placed on mainstream nationalist parties to step aside to allow Sinn Féin to nominate IRA prisoners. It was agreed that Philip Clarke and Tom Mitchell would stand for what became Sinn Féin's first Westminster seats since 1918. Clarke and Mitchell were both imprisoned at the time for their part in the Omagh barracks raid. Both achieved a significant mandate; Clarke with 30,529 votes in Fermanagh/South Tyrone and Mitchell 30,392 in Mid-Ulster. Although they were found ineligible to sit in parliament because of their convictions and the seats ended up in Unionist hands, the political appeal of militant republicanism was boosted considerably. IRA men Tomás Mac Curtain, son of MacSwiney's predecessor as Lord Mayor of Cork, and Mannus Canning also achieved respectable votes in Armagh and Derry respectively. Politics were quickly usurped by militancy, however, as Saor Uladh launched an attack on Roslea RUC station in November 1955, raising the stakes for the IRA. A campaign was imminent.[31]

In mid-1956, the Dublin IRA split after Christle was expelled from the movement. The departure of several IRA operatives with him delayed Operation Harvest, although republican newspaper *An Phoblacht* later claimed that this was an unintentional consequence of Christle's dissent.[32] The operation was further impacted by the arrest of Commanding Officer

11

Paddy Doyle in Belfast. Although this served to undermine the campaign before its onset and suspicions were high that his arrest was a result of subterfuge on the part of an informer, the lack of a campaign in Belfast minimised potential loyalist backlash. Christle went on to lecture at the College of Commerce before leading an operation to blow up Nelson's Pillar on Dublin's O'Connell Street in March 1966. Upon his death in 1998, he was commemorated in *An Phoblacht*.[33]

There was concern that the dissident factions under Kelly and Christle might gain momentum and the IRA leadership attempted to gather intelligence on either group. A series of joint operations between the two on 11 November 1956 on border outposts pre-empted Operation Harvest by a month and it has been suggested that the IRA's hand was forced.[34] The IRA was certainly in relative disarray prior to the campaign launching; so out of touch with the Dublin leadership was Belfast that when Joe Cahill's house was raided, he was apparently unaware that the operation had even started.[35] Clearly the imperative for the campaign existed and the return of Sean Cronin from America in 1955 gave Operation Harvest its architect. Cronin's plan was to use flying columns, utilised by the IRA during the War of Independence, to attack various installations in the border regions of Northern Ireland before making a swift return to the sanctuary of the Republic. Such an idea had previously been promoted by Tom Barry and was in many ways symbolic of Cronin's admiration for Barry.[36] The guerrilla tactic of attacking the northern state before escaping to the south was deployed by the IRA post-1969 to great effect and significant diplomatic unrest.

On the night of 11 December 1956, a series of attacks were launched along the border against a variety of installations both civilian and military. The government of Northern Ireland under Basil Brooke used the Special Powers Act to intern a number of suspects, something that limited the capacity of the IRA. The northern government was supported in this instance by the Fine Gael government in the Republic. John Costello feared that the IRA activity would lead to a confrontation between Ireland and Britain and enacted the Offences Against the State Act to arrest prominent IRA members such as Sean Cronin.[37] Internment proved a successful weapon against the IRA, prompting its misguided reintroduction in the early 1970s with disastrous consequences.

Former republicans in the south were opposed to Costello's move and Seán MacBride's Clann na Poblachta withdrew its support for the government. Although the party was by this stage in decline, MacBride's influence was still significant. This withdrawal contributed to the collapse of the government, which brought de Valera back to power. He maintained his position against militant republicans, with wholesale internment for IRA members introduced after the July 1957 killing of an RUC member. In total over four hundred IRA members were interned. Also significant in the 1957 election was the reappearance of Sinn Féin, which achieved four seats on its abstentionist ticket.

In late 1956, RUC constable John Scally was killed in an attack at Derrylin RUC barracks, the first death of the campaign. On New Year's Day 1957, a misplaced attack in Brookeborough, led by Garland and Dáithí Ó Conaill, resulted in the deaths of Sean South and Fergal O'Hanlon. The two were enshrined in IRA martyrdom with the song 'Sean South of Garryowen' and Dominic Behan's 'The Patriot Game' lasting tributes. O'Hanlon's brother Eineachan stood in Monaghan in the 1957 General Election and was elected alongside Ruairí Ó Brádaigh in Longford, John Joe McGirl in Sligo-Leitrim and John Joe Rice in Kerry South. All stood on the abstentionist ticket and refused to take their seats. De Valera's Fianna Fáil were back in power in 1957. With his 1937 constitution claiming sovereignty over the entire thirty-two counties of Ireland, the constitutional imperative existed to construe action in Northern Ireland as subversion,[38] and the July killing of Constable Cecil Gregg in Belfast prompted the reintroduction of internment.

The IRA claimed that 'the campaign of resistance in Occupied Ireland which opened on Dec. 12, 1956 is now more firmly based among our people than ever before and grows stronger by the day',[39] and they backed up this determined rhetoric with over three hundred incidents during 1957. Quantity was not matched with quality and morale was low; an attack at Edentubber in November in which five volunteers died when their bomb exploded prematurely was particularly damaging.[40]

Internment was a particularly effective weapon against the IRA, with five hundred internees by mid-1958. The dissipation of the campaign permitted the closure of internment camps at the Curragh in March 1959 and in Northern Ireland in April 1961.[41] The campaign had also affected the republican movement politically. The 1959 General Election was a disaster for Sinn Féin, with the party losing 16,000 votes in Mid-Ulster and 23,000 in Fermanagh and South Tyrone when compared with 1955. While Philip Clarke did not stand, Tom Mitchell saw his vote drop and enjoyed slightly more success in defeat as an Independent Republican candidate during the 1960s. In the Republic, Sinn Féin lost all four of its seats in the 1961 election, public sympathy after the deaths of South and O'Hanlon having evaporated.[42]

The campaign had effectively been winding down for two years before the IRA finally succumbed to its own lack of success in February 1962 and declared a cessation. The movement suffered because of low popular support and the splits of the 1950s had haunted the IRA which now lacked revolutionary imperative. Equally, the lack of co-ordination with northern volunteers had perhaps undermined the campaign, although it should be considered that a hypothetical loyalist backlash could have been particularly damaging, not least because there was little chance of the IRA being capable of responding in kind. Particularly significant from a security point of view was the success that the policy of intern-ment enjoyed. With key IRA figures interned, the campaign struggled to achieve its aims under relatively inexperienced and unskilled leadership. So successful was this policy that neither government was forced into suc-cessive countermeasures against the IRA.

Another important aspect of the Border Campaign was its introduc-tion of figures who would go on to prominence in republicanism: Sean Garland and Dáithí Ó Conaill were involved in the Gough barracks raid; schoolteacher Ruairí Ó Brádaigh joined the Fermanagh column when school holidays allowed, and was arrested for possession of ammunition; a teenage Seamus Costello cut his teeth commanding the Magherafelt column; and Proinsias De Rossa was arrested along with Garland in a May 1957 raid in the Wicklow mountains.

Although not relevant to the IRA's military campaign at the time, but hugely significant to the future path of republicanism, was the fact that, in the words of C. Desmond Greaves, 'in the politically dramatic decade of the 1930s, with fascism advancing on the continent, some of the best of Britain's young intelligentsia moved to the left'.[43] Similar politicisation was going on in Ireland, Roy Johnston being part of a 'sort of Marxist underground group'[44] as early as 1944. This group was to go on to form the core of the student Left at Trinity College Dublin, which practised a form of Marxism influenced by James Connolly. For Johnston, the 1950s left-wing movement in Dublin failed to attract popular support, allowing the IRA to claim the revolutionary momentum.[45] He notes the:

> lack of understanding on the part of the mainstream British Marxists of the com-plexities of the Irish national question . . . the left in Ireland had on the whole got off to a bad start; dominated by bookishness, by respect for Stalin and the

Cominform . . . it provided meagre raw material for intelligent Marxist analysis of the Irish situation.[46]

Ireland generally lacked a coherent communist group, a fact that forced politically motivated young people towards republicanism.[47] With the failure of the Border Campaign indicating that militant republicanism could not succeed in achieving unification, Irish socialists saw an opportunity, driven by their inability to really press their agenda on politically motivated factions of the republican movement during the 1950s.

The scene was therefore set for the infusion of the republican movement with socialist principles, established by figures such as James Connolly and Peadar O'Donnell. Prominent republicans who emerged from the Border Campaign were shaken but resolute in their belief that the correct application of socialist politics to the revolutionary imperative in the movement could provide a route towards freedom. The relative electoral successes were therefore considered evidence that republican politics alone could further the movement's cause. The early 1960s provided ample evidence that, in the absence of an event to unify republicanism and draw moderate nationalists into the fold, the movement was still some distance from providing a credible political force. The movement was ultimately revitalised by such a unifying force, in the form of the Northern Ireland Civil Rights Association (NICRA) and its campaigning over the latter years of the 1960s.

During the 1950s, the republican movement suffered from factionalism that ultimately helped to undermine the campaign of the IRA during the latter years of the decade. Although not every split resulted in the formation of a legitimate republican group, schism had been an integral aspect of republican history throughout the first part of the twentieth century. Equally, splits had occurred over a variety of issues, but militarism and socialism had remained constant and would be persistently divisive issues over the remaining years of the century.

NOTES

1. *Irish Times* 2/2/2005.
2. Townshend, C., *1916: The Irish Rebellion* (London: Allen Lane, 2005), p. 62; Reid, C., 'The Irish Party and the Volunteers: Politics and the Home Rule Army, 1913–1916,' pp. 33–55, in Nic Dháibhéid, C. and Reid, C. (eds), *From Parnell to Paisley: Constitutional and Revolutionary Politics in Modern Ireland* (Dublin: Irish Academic Press, 2010).
3. Townshend, *1916*; McGarry, F., *The Rising Ireland: Easter 1916* (Oxford: Oxford

15

University Press, 2010); Foy, M. and Barton, B., *The Easter Rising* (Stroud: Sutton, 1999); Dudley Edwards, O. and Pyle, F. (eds), *1916 – The Easter Rising* (London: MacGibbon and Kee, 1968).

4. Lee, J. J. and Ó Tuathaigh, G., *The Age of de Valera* (Dublin: Ward River Press, 1982); Coogan, T. P., *De Valera: Long Fellow, Long Shadow* (London: Hutchinson, 1993); Dudley Edwards, O., *Eamon de Valera* (Cardiff: GPC, 1987) among others.

5. English, R., *Armed Struggle: The History of the IRA* (London: Macmillan, 2003), pp. 32–5.

6. Ibid., pp. 42–3; Hanley, B., *The IRA 1926–1936* (Dublin: Four Courts Press, 2002) p. 11.

7. McGarry, F., *Irish Politics and the Spanish Civil War* (Cork: Cork University Press, 1999), p. 5.

8. English, *Armed Struggle*, pp. 44–5.

9. Manning. M., *The Blueshirts* (Dublin: Gill and Macmillan, 2006); Cronin, M., *The Blueshirts and Irish Politics* (Dublin: Four Courts Press, 1997); McGarry, F., *Eoin O'Duffy: A Self-Made Hero* (Oxford: Oxford University Press, 2005).

10. Hanley, B. and Millar, S., *The Lost Revolution: The Story of the Official IRA and the Workers' Party* (Dublin: Penguin, 2009), p. 6.

11. Garland, R., *Gusty Spence* (Belfast: The Blackstaff Press, 2001), p. 10; see also Gilmore, G., *The Irish Republican Congress* (Cork: Cork Workers' Club, 1978; 1st edn 1935).

12. Foster, R. F., *Modern Ireland 1600–1972* (London: Penguin, 1988) p. 561.

13. English, *Armed Struggle*, p. 63.

14. Hanley and Millar, *Lost Revolution*, p. 2.

15. Flynn, B., *Soldiers of Folly: The IRA Border Campaign 1956–1962* (Cork: The Collins Press, 2009), p. 14.

16. Dunphy, R., *The Making of Fianna Fáil Power in Ireland 1923–1948* (Oxford: Clarendon Press, 1995), pp. 284–307; MacDermott, E., *Clann na Poblachta* (Cork: Cork University Press, 1998) pp. 27–8; Flynn, *Soldiers*, p. 3.

17. MacDermott, *Clann na Poblachta*, p. 10.

18. Flynn, *Soldiers*, pp. 14–15.

19. MacDermott, *Clann na Poblachta*, p. 23.

20. Bew, P. and Patterson, H., *Sean Lemass and the Making of Modern Ireland* (Dublin: Gill and Macmillan, 1982).

21. Hanley and Millar, *Lost Revolution*, p. 4.

22. Flynn, *Soldiers*, pp. 21–2.

23. Hanley and Millar, *Lost Revolution*, pp. 8–9.

24. Flynn, *Soldiers*, p. 27.

25. English, *Armed Struggle*, p. 72; Hanley and Millar, *Lost Revolution*, pp. 11–12.

26. Flynn, *Soldiers*, p. 66.

27. IRA Manifesto August 1957, New York University Library, Archives of Irish America, AIA 9: The Papers of George Harrison, Box 1, Series A, Personal Papers.

28. Hanley and Millar, *Lost Revolution*, p. 11.

29. Flynn, *Soldiers*, pp. 33–5.

30. Elections Ireland: The 1955 Northern Ireland General Election http://www.electionsireland.org/results/general/ni/1955.cfm 01/05/2006.

31. Flynn, *Soldiers*, pp. 43–7.

32. 'A Legend Dies', *An Phoblacht* 20/8/1998.
33. Ibid.
34. Hanley and Millar, *Lost Revolution*, p. 13.
35. Flynn, *Soldiers*, p. 75.
36. English, *Armed Struggle*, pp. 72–3; Flynn, *Soldiers*, pp. 48–50.
37. Flynn, *Soldiers*, p. 83.
38. Ibid., pp. 148–9.
39. IRA Manifesto August 1957, NYUL, AIA 9: The Papers of George Harrison, Box 1, Series A, Personal Papers.
40. Flynn, *Soldiers*, pp. 152, 155.
41. Hanley and Millar, *Lost Revolution*, p. 18.
42. Flynn, *Soldiers*, p. 192.
43. Coughlan, A., *C. Desmond Greaves 1913–1988: An Obituary Essay* (Dublin: Irish Labour Society, 1990), p. 3.
44. Johnston, R. H. W., *Century of Endeavour: A Biographical and Autobiographical view of the Twentieth Century in Ireland* (Dublin: The Lilliput Press, 2006) (USA: Academica/Manusel, 2003), p. 80.
45. Johnston, *Century of Endeavour*, p. 99.
46. Ibid., pp. 115, 118.
47. Milotte, M., *Communism in Modern Ireland: The Pursuit of the Workers' Republic since 1916* (Dublin: Gill and Macmillan, 1984), p. 229.

CHAPTER 2

The Movement Divides: The 1960s

Beginning the decade in the midst of the ultimately futile Border Campaign, the Irish republican movement would find itself irrevocably divided before the 1960s were finished. The pragmatic and the principled of republicanism would diverge during this decade as a new direction was imposed on the movement by the leadership. Externally, the 1960s were marked by the rise of the protest movement, and the establishment of a Northern Irish civil rights movement mirrored international developments. Also important, and certainly more sinister, was the rise of loyalist violence as a series of key anniversaries over the early years of the decade heightened inter-communal tension. Politically, the republican movement found itself on the outside looking in, as it was unable to capitalise on political successes enjoyed in the previous decade. A series of strategic misjudgements proved very costly as the movement was led further away from armed struggle just as the need to defend the northern nationalist communities arose.

AN END TO MILITARISM? THE FAILURE OF THE BORDER CAMPAIGN

The Border Campaign indicated that the movement was in need of revitalisation. It had been unable to capitalise on the notable political gains of 1955; for many, the ending of the campaign had led to unrealistic expectations being placed on the ability of republican politics to succeed where armed struggle had failed.[1] The idea that electoral success had paved the way for an armed campaign had dominated the movement and the failure of the military campaign cemented the superiority of political

18

agitation in the minds of those who rose to positions of leadership and militarists began to drift away from the movement, in many cases exiling themselves until the call to arms was reissued at the end of the decade.

Cathal Goulding was appointed IRA Chief of Staff in September 1962.[2] John Lowry notes that he 'had instigated a whole reappraisal of the role of the republican movement and amongst the issues that began to emerge then was (a) a rejection of militarism . . . and (b) redefining the notion of freedom as being more than simply British withdrawal'.[3] Allied to Goulding was Dessie O'Hagan, who observed the 'promotion of radical democratic politics in Northern Ireland and the Republic'.[4] The concept of British withdrawal from Ireland proved a conundrum beyond the capabilities of the republican movement; while it was a central tenet of republican policy, effective strategy to realise this aim became increasingly elusive. Recent reflective accounts from republican figures have noted that the achievement of this aim became increasingly distant as the IRA campaign developed.[5]

The local history of Ireland tells of a decline of militarism among republicans, but the international history of the time highlights the increased popularity of the political left and the international dimension proved as tantalising for Irish thinkers as it did for many others. Revolutionaries in Ireland have traditionally gravitated towards the republican movement, and with the influx of politically radical members the republican movement gradually fell under the influence of the political left. The militarist tendency in the movement had not died with the Border Campaign; the Cork-based Irish Revolutionary Forces argued that 'we have always held that revolutionary politics and military action are indivisible . . . the criterion of a good revolutionary: a man who is competent both politically and militarily'.[6] They also aimed to fight 'all forms of revisionism parading under the banner of Irish Republicanism'.[7] The idea of combining the political and the military struggles in the fight for a united socialist Republic did attract notable support. Future Irish Republican Socialist Party (IRSP) member Thomas 'Ta' Power highlighted that although his movement didn't form until late 1974, 'it didn't spring up fully formed out of the blue; it, like everything else, had its roots in history, going back to the 1960s and the leftward direction which the Republican Movement was embarking on.'[8]

Many republicans saw little merit in the political struggle other than to serve as a companion to the armed struggle. The misjudgement of the 1955 election indicated a lack of understanding among republican leaders of the Irish situation during the 1950s. In retrospect, Roy Johnston observes a great deal of confusion as to what even constituted the republican movement at this time; such was the lack of coherence among the membership.[9] The military campaign had proven highly costly to political aspirations, which in turn had ramifications for the popular appeal of republicanism. Gerry Adams, at this point a young republican in Belfast, stated that the 1965 version of Republican Clubs, as proscribed Sinn Féin was then known, lacked 'political acumen'.[10] Johnston highlights a lack of leadership from the Labour Party which caused low levels of recruitment among young people with leftist persuasions, leaving them open to advances from the IRA.[11]

Gerry Adams claimed that the path of the movement was now defined by those involved in politicising the movement. The last time, he notes, that this was attempted was in the era of James Connolly, Patrick Pearse, Liam Mellows and the Republican Congress of the 1930s.[12] Efforts made towards this redefinition were hindered by a lack of understanding within the movement as to the concept of republicanism.[13] For Dessie O'Hagan, too many sought their way out of this by simply paying 'lip service to the changes' that were ongoing in the republican movement without actively engaging with them in any meaningful way.[14]

Apathy existed across the movement. The politically minded were losing confidence in the movement as an appropriate vehicle for their aspirations; they were unable, even, to organise a convention, because of the scrutiny the wider movement had brought upon itself as a result of the military campaign.[15] Although the root of their frustration lay in their subordination to the militarists in the movement, the militarists themselves were becoming perturbed by their inability to impose revolution on Ireland, an inability partially attributed to politicos within the movement. On one side, young pragmatists who had recently joined the movement; on the other older, longer-serving members, married to the image of the revolutionary republican fighting for Irish freedom with strong republican pedigree and little appreciation for republican political struggle, only the armed struggle that their fathers and grandfathers had given their lives to and, in many cases, given their lives for. The *Irish News* discussed a 'war of ideas' between the two groups.[16] As the older members began to drift away from the movement, the political tendency took hold and a renewed pragmatism quickly asserted itself. The leadership and leading members began considering issues that were perceived as more identifiable to contemporary republicans and began to look beyond historic tendencies that were considered irrelevant.[17]

Goulding's reappraisal took the form of what has been termed the 'stages theory', the first of which was the destruction of sectarian barriers in the north, combined with agitation in the south to allow for an all-Ireland alignment. There was no room for violence in either of these initial stages. While the political party had been weakened by its waning fortunes since the 1955 elections, increasing apathy had claimed the impetus essential for IRA activity. The military failures of the Border Campaign and World War II had provided no inspiration for new recruits and created indifference among existing members, which resulted in a vacuum that the movement seemed unable to repel itself from. Understandably, the focus of many was towards the political party, the wing of the movement that had most recently provided a platform from which republicanism could be advanced. For John Lowry:

> there would have been a greater awareness then of social and economic education particularly in the south and the need for Sinn Féin as an organisation in the south not to act merely as a propaganda support unit as it were for the IRA in the north or for a campaign of British withdrawal but in fact to become heavily involved itself in political agitation in the south of Ireland and then, leading on from that, over a period of time, there is no doubt that there was a growing left wing socialist tendency within the movement and I think all of those things created tensions which were there over a period of years.[18]

The media continued to cover the division, although the *News Letter* report that 'the extremists are breaking loose from the control of the moderates'[19] is not particularly revealing as to which group was which.

THE KEY PERSONALITIES

While the republican movement had traditionally utilised force to achieve its aims and the Goulding leadership was intent on subordinating this tendency, it would not be accurate to say that the leadership was disposing of republican tradition altogether. The importance of republican tradition is obvious to any scholar of Irish republicanism with historical figures held in high esteem, particularly the leader of the United Irishmen, Theobald Wolfe Tone, and the 1916 leaders such as Patrick Pearse and James Connolly, or more recent figures such as the hunger strikers of the 1980s. Significantly, although Pearse and Connolly were able to look beyond their ideological differences, their successors failed to balance the two traditions: Pearse's romanticism and justification of violence with

Connolly's Marxism and harsh realism. Pearse's Irish Volunteers constituted the majority of the 1916 insurrectionists, with Connolly's Irish
Citizens Army the minority stakeholder. Connolly toiled to reconcile his
own socialist tendencies with the overwhelming nationalist atmosphere
of the early twentieth century, and Irish socialists would face a similar
struggle during the late 1960s. Commentators have suggested that the
re-evaluation of republican and socialist traditions within the movement
during this period led to significant ideological weight being placed on
leaders such as Lalor and Connolly.[20]

Connollyite socialism, like the man himself, was very much a product
of a specific time and place. The Ireland of Connolly's time was considerably different from the divided island that came into existence after his
death. What Connolly might have made, therefore, of the divided island
and politically divided working class in Ireland cannot be anything other
than a matter of speculation. The value of Connollyism in the context
of a divided Ireland is certainly questionable and the attempt to apply
what quickly became an outdated political model to a modern political
structure is fraught with difficulties. Everything Connolly had presumed
to be true of the Irish working class had been formulated in the context
of a united Ireland. Post-partition, Irish socialists now had to develop
theoretical frameworks within which to consider the partitioned workers
of Ireland. Over the course of the twentieth century, the workers of
Ireland, north and south, struggled for unity on many issues and the strict
adherence of many on the Irish left to Connolly must be considered as a
significant factor in this.

While many Irish thinkers looked to Connolly for the foundation of
their socialist reasoning, there was also a strong international dimension;
Dessie O'Hagan noted the importance of 'the emergence, via Wolfe Tone
and the United Irishmen, of the principles of the French Revolution
Liberty, Equality and Fraternity as the new, revolutionary dynamic in
Irish political life.'[21] Cynics, such as Derry Kelleher, dispute the relevance
of the international to Ireland at the time, arguing that 'Ireland did not
need to learn Republicanism from the French Revolution'.[22]

It was not just an historic influence that France had over republicans
during the 1960s; comparisons with contemporary French issues were also
important, namely their struggles in Algeria, captured so dramatically in
Gillo Pontecorvo's *The Battle of Algiers*. The influence of the Algerian
experience on Irish thinkers at this time should not be overlooked: 'That
was the sort of thing that we were watching at the time . . . it made us

22

think', notes Shaun McKeown, a prominent figure in The Workers' Party in central Belfast.[23] Others note the influence of Frantz Fanon on left-leaning republicans.[24] Certainly there is much about Algeria that demonstrated potential problems for the British in Northern Ireland. Of particular coincidence, but perhaps not offering a great deal of comparative worth immediately, was the ending of hostilities in 1962, with the six-year republican struggle proving considerably less potent than events in Algeria. The internecine violence that was so costly to Algerians during this period offers particularly interesting comparison with the series of Irish republican feuds that would occur over the course of the remainder of the twentieth century. Robert Fisk so expertly discusses the gravity of the situation that France was dealing with in its crumbling colonial empire in *The Great War for Civilisation*.[25] While the bloodshed in Algeria was considerably greater than Northern Ireland, with some estimates placing the number of dead at over a million,[26] the danger of failing to adequately deal with a violent nationalist uprising was made all too obvious. As it learned lessons in post-colonial small wars such as Kenya and Aden, the British state saw the Algerian struggle bring the collapse of the French Fourth Republic in 1958. Principles of guerrilla warfare that would later be adopted by physical force republicans were applied successfully in Algeria. The international context was again important on the outbreak of violence in Northern Ireland as republicans offered and sought ideological alignment.

Among those socialists attempting to consider the contemporary Irish situation was Roy Johnston. In his prominent role among those attempting to politicise the republican movement, Johnston assumed the role of scapegoat when these plans went awry during 1969. Following the split, Provisional republicans named the Irish Workers' Party as the leaders of the conspiracy to assume control of republicanism, with Johnston and his colleague Anthony Coughlan alleged to have been under direction from the IWP or the Connolly Association of Desmond Greaves.[27]

Johnston returned to Ireland in 1963, on taking up a job with national airline Aer Lingus, and arrived with impressive republican pedigree as a distant relative of the founder of the 1913 Irish Volunteers, Bulmer Hobson,[28] the man who had sworn Pearse in as an Irish Volunteer. His politics were influenced by Desmond Greaves and the republican socialists of the 1930s such as Peadar O'Donnell and George Gilmore.[29] Greaves was also an important ideological influence on Anthony Coughlan.

Coughlan was a lecturer at Trinity College Dublin and first arrived on the republican scene in October 1964, when he attended his first Wolfe Tone Society meeting. With his influence over both Coughlan and Johnston, Desmond Greaves cast an imposing shadow over much republican thinking at this time. Johnston himself observes the role of Greaves in shifting the Connolly Association towards the civil rights strategy from the mid-1950s.[30]

On his arrival, only a year after the Border Campaign had ended, Johnston noted that moves towards politics were already well underway: 'Prior to my return to Ireland in September 1963, the republican movement had been feeling its way under the influence of Cathal Goulding and others, towards politicising its approach to national unification.'[31] It is important to note that external figures such as Johnston and Coughlan merely acted as accelerators and facilitators to the political process, rather than actively directing it, particularly considering the vitriol directed towards Johnston in the aftermath of the split. Johnston travelled around Ireland in order to acquaint himself with Officers Commanding (OCs) of the IRA in an attempt to establish a network for political education.[32] It is significant that Johnston should have targeted the IRA leaders for his political education programme as he attempted to impose a very unmilitary version of republicanism on the movement.

Although the 'Connolly Association was slow to adapt to the post-war circumstances and the advent of the Cold War',[33] the emergence of the Northern Ireland Civil Rights Association provided a platform for Johnston and Coughlan to push the politicisation of republicans. Coughlan recalls 'trying to encourage an interest in the civil rights issue in the north of Ireland and that did have the effect of inducing Goulding and Garland and company to throw their weight behind the civil rights movement'.[34]

By involving himself in the civil rights movement, Goulding actually helped create circumstances in the movement that would ultimately facilitate the split that cost him control of the movement. Although Goulding-led republicanism was politically inclined and the IRA was weak, its military capabilities should not be totally dismissed; the military imperative within the movement was still strong, albeit dormant.[35] Goulding's relationship with Seán MácStíofain is particularly interesting, MácStíofain being dismissive of Goulding's support for the radical left: 'the idea of abolishing the parliamentary abstention policy was to enable Republicans to take their seats if they won elections. But in Ireland the "radical left" had never had a cat's chance in elections. In fact, it hardly existed.'[36]

Goulding had risen to the top of the republican movement with impressive republican credentials; 'his whole family background was one of involvement in the Irish revolutionary struggle stretching back to the middle of the 19th century'.[37] Tomás Mac Giolla:

> The Gouldings were one of a small number of Dublin republican working class families who had a great influence on political developments in the capital for the past 150 years. They were involved in the Fenian Movement, backed the Invincibles, supported Connolly and Larkin in 1913, took part in the Easter Rising of 1916 and the subsequent War of Independence, struggled against reaction and counter-revolution in the 1920s and '30s.[38]

Goulding's background helped mark him as a target for internment during Operation Harvest and his absence from the theatre of war meant that upon its failure, he emerged unscathed in the eyes of the support base. He rose to the role of IRA Chief of Staff with little competition, such was demoralisation within the movement.[39] Strong ties to historical republicanism were integral to Goulding's attempts to revolutionise the politics of the movement.[40] Indeed, Seán MácStíofáin admitted:

> I was pleased by Goulding's appointment. I was confident that he would make a really militant leader and that we would get things done. By 1964, however, it was apparent that some of the new leadership were heading off in a very different direction. They were becoming obsessed with the idea of parliamentary politics and wished to confine the movement almost entirely to social and economic agitation. It went without saying that agitation on social and economic issues was part of the struggle for justice. But I believed that we should not allow ourselves to get so committed to it that we would lose sight of the main objective, to free Ireland from British domination.[41]

MácStíofáin's position as a physical force republican was therefore established. Quite why it took him two years to establish that Goulding was not going to be the militant leader that he expected him to be is less obvious. Although Goulding's strategy had room for the IRA, it was in a considerably reduced role designed to placate militant republicans. He appointed Seán MácStíofáin to a key role within the northern IRA, for Roy Johnston 'an almost incredible error of judgement', as it provided him 'carte blanche to undermine the politicisation process which was going on via the Republican Clubs, and lay the basis for the subsequent rapid emergence of the Provisionals'.[42] Such counterproductive decisions highlight how problematic control of republicanism was at this time, particularly in terms of balancing the political and military tendencies that were becoming increasingly irreconcilable. MácStíofaín's republicanism was that of Patrick Pearse; a romanticist who believed strongly in the armed struggle. Unlike Goulding, he had a very atypical republican back-story.

Born in London in 1928 to a mother of Protestant Irish descent, John Stephenson was educated at a Catholic school in London where he came into contact with Irish nationalists. After completing his national service with the Royal Air Force, he became increasingly active in Irish organisations in London and became an active republican during the 1950s, at which time he learned the Irish language. He moved to Ireland in the latter years of that decade, at which point he gaelicised his name to Seán MácStíofaín. A devout Catholic, MácStíofaín was strongly opposed to the socialism that Goulding was promoting within the movement, one of the many points of contention between the two. MácStíofaín emphasises that Goulding 'was a great prison comrade',[43] that comradeship factoring into Goulding's decision to promote MácStíofaín. However, as the embodiments of their respective schools of thought, the differences between the two manifested themselves when 'Goulding began to lead the movement away from Fenian traditions of violence and towards a more subtle Marxist strategy . . . MácStíofaín, a puritanical practising Catholic, a non-smoker and a non-drinker, clung to the old doctrine of re-uniting Ireland by the use of the gun.'[44]

Roy Johnston believes that, as a former trade unionist, MácStíofaín was repelled from the politicisation process because of his specific distrust of Stalinism rather than leftism in general.[45] The distinction between Stalinism and socialism would have been easily overlooked during the 1960s, the era of the Berlin Crisis, the Cuban Missile Crisis and the Vietnam War. Pejorative accusations of Stalinism would later plague the Workers' Party, emphasising the unpopularity of that particular ideology in the Irish context.

MácStíofaín and Johnston became involved in a dispute over commemoration speeches, Johnston in favour of these being used to promote the new direction of the movement and removing the rosary from all commemorations on the grounds that it served to define them as distinctly Catholic and in some way therefore sectarian.[46] John Lowry recalls 'sometimes . . . it had to be in Irish as well, that's a small thing, but it's important. It's very indicative of the time.'[47] Johnston's argument centred on the principles of Tone, that republicanism should be for all Irish men, irrespective of religious persuasion. In removing the rosary from commemorations, republican commemorations would appear increasingly secular, important in attempts to gain support outside of Irish Catholics. A distinctly socialist aspiration, the involvement of Protestants in the republican movement would remain a major concern of left-leaning republicans throughout the latter half of the twentieth century.

MácStíofáin, who left the movement in 1981, 'never got too deeply involved in Sinn Féin politics, preferring, as he puts it himself, "the other side of the House"'.[48] He was not shy of declaring his militarism, stating that 'I was convinced that the situation in Ireland morally justified an armed uprising', joining the IRA because it was obviously the only organization that was going to organize an armed uprising.[49] Maria McGuire, later a Conservative councillor in Croydon,[50] recalled that 'many members of the movement seemed to go in dread of MácStíofáin'.[51] Cathal Goulding described him as:

> a very rigid kind of person, he is not a person who thinks a lot . . . he is a very narrow man and he is a man who won't accept or examine new ideas and in his rigidity he is convinced that there is only one solution to this problem and that is by physical force. He has no time for politics of any kind and a revolutionary who has no time for politics is in my opinion a madman.[52]

MácStíofáin claims that he 'got on better personally with some of the revisionist leaders than with some of those who went the same way as myself',[53] and a strong sense of respect persisted,[54] but the ideological differences served as evidence that the organisation could not continue in its unified state.[55]

The IRA was deeply divided even prior to the onset of the civil rights campaign. MácStíofáin recalls that 'in the autumn of 1966 . . . at the top level of the organisation . . . three of us were against the new proposals to divert the IRA into the never-never land of theoretical Marxism and parliamentary politics'.[56] In appointing MácStíofáin to an intelligence role, Goulding had attempted to persuade the militarists of the good nature of his intentions, but had actually given the militarists a more prominent platform from which to oppose his proposals. He did, however, retain the support of the Army Executive: changes 'could not be carried through without the support of the executive'.[57]

While MácStíofáin opposed the changes from within, other republicans, notably Joe Cahill, simply left the movement. Born in Belfast in 1920, Cahill joined the IRA during World War II and served again during the Border Campaign, when he was among those republicans interned. During the former campaign, he was sentenced to death for killing a police officer and only avoided execution following pressure from the southern government on the British, who were keen to retain the 'openly benevolent'[58] neutrality of the Irish Free State at this time. After being interned during Operation Harvest, he recalled that 'when I came out of internment, I felt that there were moves afoot to run down the military wing, to run down the IRA'.[59] He became one of a number of 'people who had abandoned the whole concept of republicanism even in their terms',[60] after what he saw as 'a deliberate attempt to gain control of the Republican movement. There were outside elements some of whom had close affiliations with the Communist Party.'[61] This disillusionment manifested itself in the widespread drift away from republicanism during the 1960s, coinciding with the rise of Goulding and the increased prominence of the new brand of republican politics.

MácStíofain's continued influence provided a rudder by which militarist republicans could maintain their struggle and was therefore absolutely crucial to the split that took place at the end of the decade. In the south, Kerry republicans began to distance themselves from the leadership, refusing to distribute the *United Irishman* newspaper because of 'stories about housing conditions in Dublin . . . stories of that type beginning to appear in the *United Irishman* which some people interpreted as a growing communist influence'.[62]

Concerns as to the intentions of those politicising the movement grew when moves were made to end the long-standing republican policy of abstention. In the aftermath of the Anglo-Irish Treaty of 1921, Sinn Féin and the wider republican movement refused to recognise any institution that did not govern over the entire thirty-two counties of Ireland. The 1921 elections, which came after the passing of the Government of Ireland Act that effectively partitioned Ireland, were designed to create the House of Commons of Northern Ireland as well as the House of Commons of Southern Ireland. Sinn Féin participated but refused to recognise the separate nature of the two parliaments, therefore the Second Dáil was inclusive, theoretically, of members from the entirety of Ireland and thereafter became the focal point for perceptions of republican legitimacy. The central tenet of any claim for the title of the true inheritors of the republican struggle was the means and the willingness to fight for the principles of the Second Dáil; the reunification of Ireland so that the Second Dáil could reconvene and preside over the thirty-two counties. Inherent in this, however, was the refusal to recognise the legitimacy of the existing parliaments in Dublin and Belfast. The decision to abstain from the houses of parliament on the island of Ireland caused considerable political damage to the movement; unwilling to represent areas where they did enjoy political credibility and unable to increase their political support base on issues outside the national question. Although ideologically strong, abstentionism ran against the pragmatic tendency that was emerging throughout the movement. A controversial debate emerged within republicanism as to the ending of abstention during the late 1960s.

Ruairí Ó Brádaigh, a man whose career would be closely allied to the principle of abstentionism in his later roles as President of Sinn Féin and subsequently Republican Sinn Féin, believes that 'it was very clear, from about 1965, that a group within the republican movement wanted to remove abstentionism and were determined to do so, majority or no majority'.[63]

Ó Brádaigh was nothing if not loyal to the principles of traditional republicanism. His father, Matt Brady, was a former member of the IRA and had stood as an independent republican candidate in local government elections in June 1924. Brady was shot in 1919 during the Anglo-Irish War and never properly recovered from his wounds. His mother, Mary Caffrey, was a former member of the IRA's female wing, Cumann na mBan. The early influence of his parents helped shape his own personal brand of republicanism. Ó Brádaigh was born Peter Roger Casement Brady in Longford on 2 October 1932, adopting the Irish version of his name. Ó Brádaigh joined the movement in the 1950s and was prominent throughout his republican career, interned during the Border Campaign before becoming the first President of Sinn Féin.

Political pragmatism effectively forced the revision of abstentionism. During the self-imposed exile of republicans such as Joe Cahill, the momentum of politically inclined republicans was strong. It was therefore realistic to push through the significant policy changes necessary to abandon abstentionism. The controversy surrounding these moves was crucial in undermining the authority of the leadership among the more military inclined republicans. In retrospect, Roy Johnston lamented 'the failure to reform Sinn Féin in the direction of acceptance of political participation in the Dáil and Westminster, at the 1968 Ard Fheis . . . The incoming Ard Comhairle had a substantial majority of politicisers.'[64] Both Johnston, a supporter of political participation, and Ruairí Ó Brádaigh, its most intransigent opponent, suggest that so low was the movement's political acumen, in the event of achieving election

29

republicans would not have known what to do.[65] Associated to this was 'the clear belief amongst the leadership that abstentionism was a dead policy and it needed to be jettisoned'.[66]

Significantly, the issue of abstention was brought up a year previously; on 18 November 1967, Seamus Costello, who would lead another split in the movement seven years later, proposed the abandonment of abstentionism as a principle. A nine-point proposal had been drafted by Sean Garland in the aftermath of the Border Campaign and was announced by Goulding in April 1964.[67] The proposal recommended the ending of abstention from Dáil Éireann and the formation of a National Liberation Front with the Irish Communist Party. Association with communists would have done little to quell concerns over this further dramatic turn to the left, although, as Gerry Adams notes, during this period it was not uncommon for republicans to be associating with groups such as the communists.[68] The political momentum of the period facilitated such links, even though associations with communists would later prove damaging to republicans. Costello's proposal failed, much to the chagrin of Roy Johnston:

> If Costello had got his way, the Provisional split would have taken place at this 1967 Ard Fheis. It could be argued plausibly that the split, had it occurred in 1967 or 1968, would not have given the Provisionals the initial momentum generated subsequently by the 1969 events in Belfast & [if] the core Provisional movement had walked out in December 1968, they would not have had the August 1969 events initially to fuel their renascent militarism. With a unified political-republican leadership, the NICRA would have held the middle ground, and perhaps August 1969 would have passed off without an armed Orange pogrom.[69]

Based on this logic, it can be reasonably argued that the recent history of Northern Ireland could have been dramatically different. Despite the Ulster Volunteer Force killings of 1966, the Catholic-defender mentality did not really permeate republicanism until 1969 and Johnston believes that 'we might have been able to activate the Northern Clubs better in support of the NICRA'.[70] With the republican split occurring prior to August 1969, the ability of the Provisional IRA to recruit would likely have been reduced. With increased influence over the civil rights movement, the radical elements may have been contained and the inflammatory events of 1968 and 1969 may never have occurred. However, such speculation is largely futile. The civil rights marches would certainly still have occurred and met with loyalist opposition. Equally, in the event of

August 1969 occurring as it did, the Provisional IRA would have had eighteen months to train and equip.

THE PROBLEMS OF LEFTIST POLITICS

When Seán MácStíofain spoke of the 'never-never land of theoretical Marxism',[71] he spoke for those in republicanism who grew to oppose the political direction the movement was being taken in during the 1960s. The lack of popularity that the political left has enjoyed in Ireland has been partially explained by high levels of migration that Ireland has experienced historically, leaving the working class as an ideological group in disarray.[72] Allied to the religious and national division within the working class, Ireland has proven problematic for socialists, who have blamed those responsible for the partition of the island for conspiring to divide the working class in order to undermine socialist aspirations.

Another problem for Irish socialism has been the lack of a strong ideological figurehead. James Connolly has been considered to have effectively abandoned his socialist principles to further the nationalist cause, undermining his claim to such a position. As leader of the Irish Citizens Army he became ideologically dominated by Patrick Pearse and the Irish Volunteers. The superior numerical strength of the Volunteers provided Connolly with a platform for revolution, influencing his decision to subordinate his own revolutionary socialist tendencies to join with Pearse, which has been lamented by Irish socialists ever since. It has been asserted that James Connolly allowed the Irish left wing to become caught up in events leading up to the Easter Rising of 1916 because there was no possible outcome to the rising that would have left a socialist legacy.[73] Others argue that it was a lack of conceptual tools for evaluation, in this case the lack of a coherent concept of the state, that led to the failure of Irish Marxists,[74] or that Irish socialists have a simplified class perspective because they have had to develop their theories in the absence of a bourgeois revolution.[75] It has also been suggested that it was not so much that Marxism had failed the Irish left wing, but because the Irish left wing had failed to use Marxism correctly, arguing that their use of Marxism went only as far as to use Marxist rhetoric to legitimise their own subordination of socialism to nationalism;[76] the implication being that Marxism was in fact too complicated for Irish socialists to utilise properly, effectively rendering the ideology impracticable.

The potential for a Marxist group to emerge clearly existed, but was fraught with difficulty. The inability of a left-wing organisation to properly position itself so as to capitalise on this potential would leave the movement in danger of becoming isolated, from both its nationalist and socialist tendencies. An attempt to reconcile the two would lead a movement into complicated theoretical territory, many commentators arguing that the two cannot coexist; Walker Connor argues that 'Nationalism and Marxism are philosophically incompatible', also talking of 'the classical Marxist projection of no role for nations under socialism'.[77] This is at odds with Connolly, who argued that 'Nationalism without Socialism . . . is only national recreancy . . .'[78]

With the national issue a crucial aspect of politics in Ireland, it was important that a socialist group offer a reasonable programme that had the potential to appeal to the Protestant working class on class-based issues. Stretching back to the Battle of the Diamond in 1795, tension between Catholics and Protestants in Ireland has frequently taken the form of violence. Although admirable, attempts to unite across the sectarian divide at a time when violence was so clearly in the air seems rather naïve. The sectarian campaign of the 1966 Ulster Volunteer Force had already suggested that the loyalist working class was unlikely to welcome such attempts. The threat of loyalist sectarian violence also helped to increase the support base of the Provisional IRA in the aftermath of the split.

Many among the republican movement had not forgotten perceived crimes against their community perpetrated by the unionist government at Stormont. The decidedly anti-Catholic nature of the Stormont government, with nationalist representatives rarely reaching double-figure representation in contrast to the thirty-plus elected officials from the Unionist Party, a result of deliberately gerrymandered electoral boundaries, had created the disenfranchisement of the Catholics of Northern Ireland. This created anger among Catholics and fear among Protestants, who saw the organisation of Catholics into protest movements as a challenge to their way of life.

In the revolutionary spirit of the 1960s, with independence spreading across Africa, the election of President John F. Kennedy in the United States, the left-of-centre Italian coalition government and the success of Labour in the 1964 United Kingdom General Election, Irish thinkers absorbed the international leftward shift. It has been argued that in this climate, Marxism had become somewhat fashionable and as a result was enjoying a spell of falsely inflated popularity, causing an overemphasis to be placed on its relevance to the political context in Ireland generally and Northern Ireland specifically;[79] the desire to be part of the revolution creating ideological realignment which posed problems for those less inclined towards the politics of the left. Those who went on to lead the Provisional republican movement were careful to simultaneously position themselves on the left of the political spectrum while also guarding against positioning themselves too far to the left, a move which would have been detrimental to their political ambitions.[80] It was later claimed that such was the hostility felt by Provisional republicans towards socialism that they organised a book-burning, where books from the political left were collected and burned en masse, mirroring actions that had taken place in Nazi Germany.[81]

Seán MacStíofain, a strong proponent of the merits of armed struggle to achieve the much sought-after revolution, recalls that while imprisoned, 'I tackled *Mein Kampf* and *Das Kapital* as well. Parts of Hitler's book made me laugh and other parts depressed me. I made several fresh attempts to get through Marx, but I never succeeded all the way.'[82]

His contemporaries in the Provisional republican movement had to be careful to keep themselves on the green side of socialism. Roy Johnston recalls a special Sinn Féin Ard Fheis on 12 and 13 June 1965 during which attempts were made to turn Sinn Féin into a radical political force and notes that at that time a great deal of the opposition to such moves was based on a perception that moves to the left would lead Irish republicanism towards Stalinism rather than 'Connollyism'.[83] During the early 1960s, the Cork-based Irish Revolutionary Forces had argued that 'the failure of Irish Communists lies not in that the Irish people were, or are, priest-ridden; but, in the fact that they themselves are Moscow-ridden.'[84] Concerns that green socialism would become subordinated by red socialism proved problematic as left-leaning republicans sought ideological alliances with both Americans and Russians during the Cold War.

Roy Johnston was at the heart of attempts to redefine Marxism in the Irish context that was both closer to the socialism of James Connolly and as distant as possible from Soviet socialism. These moves sought to increase the popularity of the brand of socialism promoted by the Irish republican movement, nationally and internationally. Within Ireland, the republican leadership had encountered hostility as a result of its declared socialist policy. Allegations of a Fianna Fáil-led conspiracy to undermine the Goulding leadership have proven persistent. It was suggested that such was the opposition of the Fianna Fáil government in the Republic of Ireland to socialism that they actively supported anti-communists; some Official republicans arguing that their expressed intent of marginalising leftist republicans went so far as to offer material aid to anti-communists if they split the republican movement.[85] Particularly embittered by this period, Roy Johnston argues that historical evidence of Fianna Fáil supporting or at least encouraging alternatives to the left highlights their hostility towards left-wing politics.[86] Brendan Clifford believes that the ruling class in the Republic was responsible for arming the militant republicans in favour over those 'whose Republican instincts were inhibited by a petty bourgeois socialist ideological confusion'.[87] Roy Foster has remarked that such allegations are 'unproven',[88] rather than completely ruling out such an occurrence.

External factors were also important in creating the circumstances that led to the split in the movement. Associated with the international shift to the left was the rise of a civil rights culture that became influential across Ireland during the latter years of the decade.

CIVIL RIGHTS TO ARMALITES?

The international revolutionary spirit of the 1960s took hold in Northern Ireland in a variety of forms, but none more powerful than the Northern Ireland Civil Rights Association (NICRA) which was formed in early 1967, with prominent issues including fair housing allocation, the amendment of historically abhorrent electoral boundaries that helped to maintain the perceived Protestant supremacy, and the reviled B-Specials, the reserve unit of the Royal Ulster Constabulary, itself very unpopular. Political reform was swift, indicating the success of the movement during 1968, and the Derry Citizens Action Committee called a halt to all marches in December.

Defiant, the radical People's Democracy organised a four-day march from Belfast to Londonderry beginning on New Year's Day 1969, echoing the Selma to Montgomery march in the USA. For Anthony Coughlan, 'there's no sense in which the Burntollet march was agreed on, there were groups holding meeting after meeting until they got a majority'.[89] This march clashed with a large Protestant crowd at Burntollet Bridge, near Londonderry. It has been alleged that police did not act against the violence and that many of the crowd were themselves members of the B-Specials, perhaps aggrieved at the civil rights movement's opposition to their organisation, perhaps acting out of naked sectarianism.

Associated with the violence were claims that the marches had been somehow created by the IRA in order to provoke social disturbances; claims that do not sit comfortably with the apparently dwindling IRA of the 1960s. Nonetheless, 'the general perception among Protestants was that, even from the start, civil rights was a front for the Provos'.[90] Significantly, however, while their politics were viewed with increasing hostility by unionist communities and violence against civil rights marches did occur, loyalists chose not to use their guns against the marchers and did not do so until it became clear that an actual IRA campaign was underway.[91] Protestant fear of the IRA was evidenced by the UVF killings of 1966, associated with the fiftieth anniversary of the 1916 Easter Rising.

Anthony Coughlan notes the coincidence of a series of important republican anniversaries during the mid-1960s: the 1963 bicentenary of Wolfe Tone's birth, the fiftieth anniversary of the 1913 lockout and the 1968 centenary of James Connolly's birth all factoring in the minds of those on the republican left.[92] It was 1966 that provoked violence from loyalists, their murderous activities ostensibly arising from fear of a republican uprising that never appeared. The presence of noted republicans at early civil rights meetings certainly played into the hands of those who perceived the movement as a front for the IRA. Republicans were present from the earliest meetings and commentators have noted that the civil rights strategy was similar to an initiative of the old IRA, with the expressed intention of bringing down the Northern Irish state.[93] Others have claimed that members of various left-wing groups and republicans 'worked together because they had developed a personal commitment to the association, and not because they were directed by any outside influence'.[94]

Interaction between persons of a revolutionary persuasion does not necessarily mean that the civil rights movement was directed by republicans, nor does this mean that republicans could not seize the initiative of the movement at a later date. Anthony Coughlan:

> I think it's fair to say that Desmond Greaves was the source of the idea of a civil rights movement as the way to break unionist hegemony in the north. The idea that the two communities should have the same civil liberties had huge potential for dividing unionism. You'd argue that the rational basis of unionists wanting to be unionists was to be top dog over nationalists and Catholics rule out 'top doggery' and you remove the rational basis of unionists wanting to be unionists, particularly the working class.[95]

In undermining unionism, the hope was that the civil rights association could aim to reform it, but the persistent accusations of IRA involvement, fuelled in part by 'the far left development of the People's Democracy (PD); there were those in the civil rights who weren't too happy with that',[96] undermined NICRA, even though most civil rights members possessed less radical views than those in republicanism.[97] Brendan Clifford, of the British and Irish Communist Organisation, argued that 'the Civil Rights movement rapidly developed into the Republican terrorist campaign because the Unionist leaders pretended that the Civil Rights movement was Republican',[98] but there was no need to pretend; the IRA link with NICRA was very visible, with IRA members serving as stewards on marches and IRA leaders present at meetings.[99] Recent accounts of the civil rights movement have noted the confrontational actions of those with apparently unintentionally subversive motives.[100]

The revolutionary spirit of the times was embodied within NICRA in the form of the radical People's Democracy, whose founders included Bernadette Devlin and Michael Farrell. They argued that civil rights could only be achieved through the establishment of an all-Ireland socialist republic and sought reforms of the Northern Ireland government that went beyond those demanded by NICRA. Johnston and Coughlan both rued the intervention of this 'adventurous and inexperienced ultra-leftist trend',[101] which facilitated the drift of the civil rights momentum towards republicans. Coughlan believes that trade unionists were better equipped to resist the pressure from the ultra left, allowing the civil rights strategy to develop more effectively.[102]

The PD did more closely represent the revolutionary interests of young Catholics. While they could not relate with the older generation of intellectuals that seemed to be directing the political protest movement, Devlin was a personality with whom they could identify. Although the PD became associated with the drift towards militancy, the subsequent career paths of its membership suggest that this was unintentional. Devlin's brief alliance with the Irish Republican Socialist Party ended because of her opposition to the Irish National Liberation Army campaign; Farrell maintained involvement in civil liberties issues; Eamonn McCann remained a prominent political commentator and activist.[103]

Clifford argues that the IRA usurped NICRA 'just when the moment was ripe for spectacular political advances to be made through the CRA breaches in the Unionist establishment',[104] but for Coughlan:

If the republicans and the left-wing members of the civil rights executive, who co-operated together and were committed to the civil rights programme one person, one vote, leave the constitutional issue aside if they had been able to hold hegemony, things might have been different. They were undermined by the far left activities of the PDs; one person, one vote wasn't enough, they wanted one man, one job which was a totally different programme . . . then O'Neill in turn was undermined by his own. The temperature rose and it led to August 1969 and the rampaging in Belfast which in turn gave rise to the IRA.[105]

August 1969: The Issue of Defence

While the political disagreements within the republican movement during the 1960s were important, these disputes took place in the absence of serious violence. It was not until the summer of 1969 that a lasting split developed in the movement. The inability of the republican leadership to provide adequate defence for the nationalist community, particularly in urban areas of Northern Ireland, was for many the final straw. Individuals in the movement, perturbed by the emphasis that was being placed on the political side of the movement, finally had evidence that these moves were acting to the detriment of the wider republican community and took this opportunity to create the decisive division. The importance of the role of the IRA as the defenders of the Catholic community in the North is central to understanding just how serious their failure to carry out this act was. Tomás Mac Giolla argued that 'the riots provided the ideal opportunity for encouraging the militarist and every advantage was taken of it. Those who fell for this were mainly older traditionalists who had lost all perspective of the meaning of the struggle for freedom in their determination to get another "campaign" started', which meant that 'by 1971 the revolutionary impetus was lost. By 1972 the back of the people's struggle was broken North and South and it was subsequently beaten into the ground.'[106]

This assertion is given credence by the interpretation of Joe Cahill, one of the modern republican movement's most prominent members, who argues that 'the real reason [for the split] was the lack of defence for nationalists in the North. It was the desertion of the people of the North.'[107] This is echoed by Danny Morrison: 'They left the community defenceless which left a huge impetus for those who came to inherit the physical force tradition.'[108] Although the IRA had clearly declined to the point of inaction during August 1969, Goulding noted that 'there were training camps during the mid-1960s. That was because there was so

37

much opposition to what I was doing, it was very difficult to please every-body.'[109] Maria McGuire observes that 'so sure were the IRA leadership that it would take many years for the political phase to develop to the stage where arms would be needed, that in 1968 they actually sold some of their "precious" weapons to the Free Wales Army.'[110]

One republican source stated that 'there was a break long before the '69 split. In fact, there was lots of little breaks . . . people became disillu-sioned and I think that the Kerry Ard Chomhairle pulled away from Sinn Féin altogether.'[111] The south-west of Ireland had strong revolutionary traditions, evidenced by the schism that occurred there during the early 1960s.[112] Gerry Adams had argued frequently with Liam McMillen as he felt that neither the leadership in Belfast nor Dublin recognised exactly what was likely to arise out of the tense political climate in Northern Ireland during the late sixties and notes that he recognised the potential for violence well before trouble broke out; a rather obvious statement in light of the 1966 murders and a series of loyalist bombs in April 1969. For Adams, 'the primary problem was lack of politics, a shortcoming which was to remain even after guns had become plentiful . . . the leadership was clearly lacking in political understanding and this led to their failure to prepare properly on all fronts'.[113]

Seán MácStíofain argued that although 'it was not the fault of the vol-unteers there that the movement had been unable to provide maximum defence for nationalist areas', northern commanders had failed to exert sufficient pressure on the leadership and 'simply had not stood up to the political theorists at HQ and hammered home their case'.[114] However, Cathal Goulding claimed that:

> It was not a tactical mistake. It was a complete impossibility. We didn't have any arms. The border campaign had left us with very little arms. Officially we only had enough weapons for one active service unit in the North. If we had sent all them to Belfast and the pogroms started in, say Derry, we would have been criticised for that instead.[115]

The southern-based leadership saw no reason to equip the northern IRA. Anthony Coughlan recalls that 'in spring '69 it wasn't very obvious that the north was going to blow up in August, I can assure you'.[116] For Roy Johnston, even as late as the 12 July parade of 1969, there was no sense of the escalation of violence that would occur the following month. The loyalist parades led to violence and two days later Francis McCloskey was fatally injured after a police baton charge in Dungiven, County Derry. Although a pensioner, McCloskey was buried with republican honours.

Two days later, Samuel Devenney from Londonderry was beaten and fatally injured by police.[117] Their deaths show that deadly violence was a reality prior to August 1969. Significantly, both had been killed by the RUC.

August 1969 saw the deaths of eight people: six Catholics, including one soldier who was on leave and home in West Belfast when killed by the police, and two Protestants. The deaths of fifteen-year-old Gerald McAuley and Herbert Roy were significant; the former a member of the IRA's youth wing and the latter killed by republicans.[118] These deaths suggest that the IRA was operational prior to the split and fuel allegations that August 1969 'only became the excuse'[119] for the split. Seán MácStíofain had assumed de jure control of the northern IRA during the 1960s, Roy Johnston recalling that 'I was indeed uneasy about the way the republican movement was going ... I had no inkling of the impending Provisional threat. MácStíofain was playing his cards close.'[120] Anthony Coughlan notes that 'Roy Johnston holds the view that MácStíofain was consciously walking towards this for a long time. I don't know; I'd be more sceptical that MácStíofain had any long-term intentions.'[121]

With the IRA seemingly in disarray but still with a functional youth wing and with active volunteers, the allegations that it had provoked the civil disturbances of 1969 that led to the violence of August are complicated. It was noted that 'republican leaders ... haven't a clue as to how such a war is to be waged, and they show no desire to find out'.[122] Along with the lack of capability that the IRA had in 1969, the lack of arms and lack of direction, the only rationale that republicans could have had for provoking violence would have been to create the circumstances to facilitate a split. In creating a situation that the republican leadership neither wanted nor was capable of responding to, but one that also demanded some sort of response, the radicals could legitimately claim they were being misguided by their leaders, break away from them and then move to seize the initiative.

Roy Johnston cites the provocative intervention of the People's Democracy, who 'helped reduce Civil Rights to a Catholic ghetto movement and made it difficult for Protestant trade-unionists to rally in support of local government electoral rights. After Burntollet, Civil Rights became a crypto-Nationalist issue.'[123] As noted previously, the likelihood of this being a deliberate attempt to pave the way for the IRA is small, given the subsequent actions of the PD leadership. This is also to discount the equally provocative actions of the loyalist crowd which attacked the march at Burntollet Bridge.

Fuelling traditional republican hostilities was the arrival of the British Army on 14 August 1969, following violence after an Apprentice Boys march in Londonderry. Although their initial duty appeared to be the defence of Catholic communities, their presence merely emphasised the fundamental problem republicans had with the Northern Irish state. Recent deployments in former colonial territories had not prepared the Army well for its deployment in Northern Ireland and inappropriate strategy served to drive a wedge between the Army and the nationalist communities. While ideology and historical precedent made the targeting of domestic security forces problematic, republicans had no such problems embarking on a violent campaign against the British Army.

August 1969 was integral to the split that occurred at the end of the year. The IRA had failed to act when its community came under attack, but it should not be forgotten that, although many have claimed the IRA's basic raison d'être was the defence of the nationalist communities, throughout the mid-twentieth century it had been preoccupied with offensive action against the British presence in Ireland. It had clearly not prepared itself for a loyalist reaction to such action. When this occurred in response to the civil rights campaign, perceived within loyalism as a vehicle for the IRA, it was found wanting. Goulding found himself caught in a dilemma:

> He had these people coming down from the Falls Road saying 'we're being attacked we want some guns to defend ourselves', republicans came out of the woodwork from the 1940s who hadn't been involved in civil rights and who might have been encouraged by MácStíofáin. On the other hand . . . the production of guns is a shift of gear from the civil rights movement which he had been support- ing and urging republicans to support until now and going back to shooting at the British Army or policemen, that's a complete change of policy . . . a tragic position in many ways.[124]

These 'disgruntled elements from the twenties and forties . . . rose to the fore in the leadership of the Provisionals',[125] ultimately wresting control of republicanism from Goulding.

The IRA Splits

The republican movement at the end of 1969 was full of regret. Some lamented their inability to head off the drift towards militarism that had seemed consigned to the past. Anthony Coughlan recalls 'republicans had set aside physical force . . . but they hadn't dissolved the IRA and in retrospect it is a pity they hadn't'.[126] Others maligned the fact that the republican movement had been taken down the path of politics and the nationalist community had found itself in need of defence during the sectarian violence of the late-1960s.

Although republican politics had been closely aligned with the civil rights strategy, the momentum had been seized by the more radical elements of NICRA, notably the People's Democracy, which had prompted loyalist retaliation. When this loyalist reaction itself demanded a response, the IRA was unable to do so and instead the nationalist communities had to be protected by the British Army. The IRA had been disgraced and a split was inevitable. Politically, the meeting of the Army Council in October 1969 supported the ending of abstentionism and was backed by the Army Convention in December, but dissent over abstentionism was merely symptomatic of wider grievances that existed within the movement. MácStíofáin and Ó Brádaigh's Provisional IRA held their first meeting on 18 December.

Notes

1. Purdie, B., 'Reconsiderations on Republicanism and Socialism', pp. 74–95, in Morgan, A. and Purdie, B. (eds), *Ireland: Divided Nation Divided Class* (London: Ink Links, 1980), pp. 74–5.
2. Hanley and Miller, *Lost Revolution*, p. 1.
3. John Lowry, interview with author, Belfast, 9/8/2007.
4. O'Hagan, D., 'The Concept of Republicanism', pp. 85–112, in Porter, N. (ed.), *The Republican Ideal: Current Perspectives* (Belfast: The Blackstaff Press, 1998), pp. 86–7.
5. McDonald, H., *Gunsmoke and Mirrors: How Sinn Fein Dressed up Defeat as Victory* (Dublin: Gill and Macmillan, 2008).
6. *An Phoblacht* (Cork) Vol. 1 No. 1 September 1965.
7. Ibid.; Hanley and Millar, *Lost Revolution*, p. 45.
8. Power, T., *The Ta Power Document* http://irsm.org/history/tapowerdoc.html 27/7/2004.
9. Johnston, *Century*, p. 122.
10. Adams, G., *The Politics of Irish Freedom* (Dingle: Brandon, 1986), p. 6.
11. Johnston, *Century*, p. 152; Purdie, B., 'Reconsiderations on Republicanism and Socialism', pp. 74–95, in Morgan and Purdie (eds), *Ireland*, p. 92.
12. Adams, *The Politics*, p. 8.
13. Johnston, *Century*, p. 122.
14. Dessie O'Hagan, interview with author, Belfast, 9/8/2007.
15. White, *Ruairí Ó Brádaigh*, pp. 110, 113.
16. *IN* 30/12/1969.

17. Bowyer Bell, *The Secret Army*, p. 340.
18. John Lowry, interview with author, Belfast, 9/8/2007.
19. *News Letter* 20/12/1969.
20. Smith, *Fighting For Ireland*, p. 74.
21. O'Hagan, D., *The Concept of Republicanism* (Dublin: The Workers' Party, undated), p. 5. Linen Hall Library Political Collection.
22. Kelleher, D., *Irish Republicanism: The Authentic Perspective* (Greystones: Justice Books, 2001), p. 93.
23. Shaun McKeown, interview with author, Belfast, 10/7/2007.
24. Hanley and Miller, *Lost Revolution*, p. 221.
25. Fisk, R., *The Great War for Civilisation: The Conquest of the Middle East* (London: Harper Perennial, 2006; 1st edn 2005), pp. 631–719.
26. Ibid., p. 640.
27. Milotte, *Communism*, p. 277.
28. English, *Armed Struggle*, p. 85.
29. Ibid., pp. 86–7.
30. Johnston, *Century*, pp. 177, 180.
31. Ibid., p. 174.
32. Johnston, *Century*, p. 202.
33. Coughlan, C., *Desmond Greaves 1913–1988*, p. 6.
34. Anthony Coughlan, interview with author, Dublin, 15/6/2010.
35. English, *Armed Struggle*, pp. 84, 91.
36. MácStíofain, S., *Memoirs of a Revolutionary* (Edinburgh: Gordon Cremonesi, 1975), pp. 134–5.
37. The Workers' Party, *Cathal Goulding: Thinker, Socialist, Republican, Revolutionary 1923–1998* (Dublin: The Workers' Party of Ireland, 1999), p. 30.
38. The Workers' Party, *Cathal Goulding*, p. 30.
39. Patterson, *The Politics of Illusion*, p. 96.
40. The Workers' Party, *Cathal Goulding*, pp. 9, 22.
41. MácStíofain, *Memoirs*, p. 92; White, *Ruairí Ó Brádaigh*, p. 178.
42. Johnston, *Century*, p. 411.
43. MácStíofain, *Memoirs*, p. 83.
44. *Sunday Times* 12/9/1971.
45. Johnston, *Century*, p. 170.
46. White, *Ruairí Ó Brádaigh*, p. 131.
47. John Lowry, interview with author, Belfast, 9/8/2007.
48. *Guardian* 26/1/1989.
49. White, *Provisional Irish Republicans*, p. 46.
50. *Daily Telegraph* 3/12/2008; *Guardian* 7/12/2008.
51. McGuire, M., *To Take Arms: A Year in the Provisional IRA* (London: Macmillan, 1973), p. 72.
52. *Sunday Times* 12/9/1971.
53. MácStíofain, *Memoirs*, p. 136.
54. Kelleher, *Irish Republicanism*, p. 223.
55. White, *Ruairí Ó Brádaigh*, p. 178.
56. MácStíofain, *Memoirs*, p. 99. The Army Council contains seven members.
57. Dessie O'Hagan, interview with author, Belfast, 9/8/2007.

58. Foster, *Modern Ireland*, p. 561.
59. White, *Provisional Irish Republicans*, pp. 49–50.
60. Dessie O'Hagan, interview with author, Belfast, 9/8/2007.
61. Interview with Joe Cahill, *IN* 30/1/1990.
62. John Lowry, interview with author, Belfast, 9/8/2007; Conclusions of a meeting of the Cabinet. Friday, 18 April 1969. PRONI ref CAB/4/1446.
63. Ruairí Ó Brádaigh interview, *IN* 29/1/1990.
64. Johnston, *Century*, p. 242.
65. White, *Ruairí Ó Brádaigh*, p. 121.
66. John Lowry, interview with author, Belfast, 9/8/2007.
67. Ryan, P., *The Birth of the Provisionals – A Clash between Politics and Tradition* CAIN web service http://cain.ulst.ac.uk/othelem/organ/docs/ryan01.htm (last update 2001) 7/9/2006.
68. Adams, *The Politics*, p. 9.
69. Johnston, *Century*, pp. 222, 251.
70. Roy Johnston, Personal Correspondence with author, 4/3/2008.
71. MácStíofain, *Memoirs*, p. 99.
72. Bowyer Bell, *The Secret Army*, p. 340.
73. Howell, D., *A Lost Left: Three Studies in Socialism and Nationalism* (Manchester: Manchester University Press, 1986), p. 140.
74. Bew, P., Gibbon, P. and Patterson, H., 'Some Aspects of Nationalism and Socialism in Ireland 1968–78', pp. 152–71, in Morgan and Purdie (eds), *Ireland*, p. 157.
75. Morgan, A., 'Socialism in Ireland – Red, Green and Orange', pp. 172–225, in Morgan and Purdie (eds), *Ireland*, p. 175.
76. Walsh, P., *Irish Republicanism and Socialism: The Politics of the Republican Movement 1905–1994* (Belfast: Athol Books, 1994), p. 133.
77. Connor, W., *The National Question in Marxist-Leninist Theory and Strategy* (Princeton: Princeton University Press, 1984), p. 5.
78. Quoted in Davis, H. B., *Nationalism and Socialism* (London: Monthly Review Press, 1967), p. 121.
79. Patterson, *The Politics of Illusion*, p. 171.
80. Purdie, 'Reconsiderations on Republicanism and Socialism', pp. 74–95, in Morgan and Purdie (eds), *Ireland*, p. 84.
81. Woods, A., *Ireland: Republicanism and Revolution* (London: Wellred Books, 2005), p. 15.
82. MácStíofain, *Memoirs*, p. 59.
83. Johnston, *Century*, pp. 188, 190.
84. *An Phoblacht* (Cork) Vol. 1 No. 2 November 1965, LHLPC.
85. Martin, R., 'Ireland: The Split in the Workers' Party' in *Workers' Press* 23/1/1993.
86. Johnston, *Century*, p. 154.
87. Clifford, *Against Ulster Nationalism*, p. 21.
88. Foster, R. F., *Luck and the Irish: A Brief History of Change, 1970–2000* (London: Penguin, 2007), p. 70.
89. Anthony Coughlan, interview with author, Dublin, 15/6/2010.
90. Sammy Duddy, interview with author, Belfast 10/11/2006.
91. Wood, I. S., *Crimes of Loyalty: A History of the UDA* (Edinburgh: Edinburgh University Press, 2006), p. 6.

92. Anthony Coughlan, interview with author, Dublin, 15/6/2010.
93. English, *Armed Struggle*, pp. 82, 88.
94. Purdie, *Politics in the Streets*, p. 155.
95. Anthony Coughlan, interview with author, Dublin, 15/6/2010.
96. Ibid.
97. English, *Armed Struggle*, pp. 81–2, 98.
98. Clifford, B., *Against Ulster Nationalism* (Belfast: Athol Books, 1992), pp. 20–1.
99. Anthony Coughlan, interview with author, Dublin, 15/6/2010.
100. Prince, S., *Northern Ireland's '68: Civil Rights, Global Revolt and the Origins of the Troubles* (Dublin: Irish Academic Press, 2007); Prince, S., '"A Third Road": Constitutional Nationalism, Militant Republicanism, and Non-Violence in the Civil Rights Era', pp. 159–81, in Nic Dháibhéid and Reid, *From Parnell to Paisley*, pp. 175–7; Anthony Coughlan, interview with author, Dublin, 15/6/2010.
101. Johnston, *Century*, p. 242; Prince, *Northern Ireland's '68*, pp. 194–211; Arthur, P., *The People's Democracy 1968–1973* (Belfast: The Blackstaff Press, 1974), especially p. 75.
102. Coughlan, C. *Desmond Greaves*, p. 10.
103. Arthur, *The People's Democracy*.
104. Clifford, *Against Ulster Nationalism*, p. 51.
105. Anthony Coughlan, interview with author, Dublin, 15/6/2010.
106. Text of an address given by Tomás Mac Giolla, president of Sinn Féin, to the Boston Irish Forum, 31/8/1975.
107. Interview with Joe Cahill, *IN* 30/1/1990.
108. Danny Morrison, interview with author, Belfast, 24/1/2005.
109. Cited in Sharrock and Devenport, *Man of War, Man of Peace? The Unauthorised Biography of Gerry Adams* (London: Macmillan, 1997), p. 42.
110. McGuire, *To Take Arms*, p. 38; Johnston, *Century*, p. 286.
111. White, *Provisional Irish Republicans*, p. 50; John Lowry, interview with author, Belfast, 9/8/2007.
112. Hanley and Millar, *Lost Revolution*, p. 45.
113. Adams, *The Politics*, pp. 31, 35.
114. MácStíofain, *Memoirs*, p. 124.
115. Interview with Cathal Goulding, *IN* 31/1/1990.
116. Anthony Coughlan, interview with author, Dublin, 15/6/2010.
117. McKittrick et al., *Lost Lives*, pp. 32–3.
118. Ibid., pp. 33–41; English, *Armed Struggle*, p. 102.
119. John Lowry, interview with author, Belfast, 9/8/2007.
120. Ibid., p. 238.
121. Anthony Coughlan, interview with author, Dublin, 15/6/2010.
122. *An Phoblacht* (Cork) No. 4 March 1966, LHLPC.
123. Johnston, *Century*, p. 242.
124. Anthony Coughlan, interview with author, Dublin, 15/6/2010.
125. John Lowry, interview with author, Belfast, 9/8/2007.
126. Anthony Coughlan, interview with author, Dublin, 15/6/2010.

CHAPTER 3

The Split and its Aftermath: The 1970s

The 1970s was the most violent decade in the history of Northern Ireland. By the end of the decade, over two thousand people had died as a result of 'the troubles', roughly half at the hands of the Provisional IRA. The impotence of the IRA in August 1969 contrasted with its rapid transition to a movement capable of deadly insurgency. The split in the movement had been finalised during the Sinn Féin Ard Fheis of 10 and 11 January 1970, and the purpose of this chapter is to consider the development of either faction in the aftermath of this division. Approaches to post-split republicanism would prove crucial as the possibility of reunification as well as the threat of further division remained constant for both the Provisional and Official republicans.

The split was cast as one between the political and the military tendencies of republicanism, the *Irish Press* defining five reasons for the split: the recognition of the parliaments at Stormont, Leinster House and Westminster; the growth of extreme socialism which was felt to be leading towards a dictatorship; a dispute over internal methods used within the movement; the failure of the armed wing to defend Belfast Catholics; and the campaign to retain rather than abolish Stormont.[1] This is not to say that the republican leadership necessarily supported the Stormont parliament, rather they sought to embrace it and challenge it from within. They felt that the goal of achieving political mandate from the electorate across Ireland required the movement to work within existing structures. Their opponents felt otherwise. The loyalist community also viewed events in republicanism with concern, former Ulster Defence Association man Sammy Duddy noting that 'we were very aware and indeed concerned because we saw a split . . . as a bigger threat than ever before. It could have meant that we'd have been attacked on both fronts.'[2]

Although the split proved durable, and it has been suggested that the division was inevitable,[3] at the time it was speculated that the rifts may have been temporary: 'there are real possibilities; immediately of ad hoc co-operation and gradually of re-unification, as the situation develops.'[4] The British Army noted that 'if the Provisionals and Officials combined to form an active alliance not only would they pose a far more powerful threat but they would also probably attract more tangible support from international terrorist organisations'.[5] Collaboration between the Official and Provisional IRA also supported this,[6] but the differences between the two factions proved irreconcilable. Seán MácStíofain later admitted that:

> Some of the people on our side couldn't be contained from promoting their own conspiracy, to push through these proposals. This was wrong. There should have been open honest discussion, on an intelligent and logical basis . . . We won the debate at the Army Convention, but some of the people on our side melted like snow when the work had to be done for the Ard Fheis. They became very arrogant with party members.[7]

Official republicans continued to cite southern interference, with Cathal Goulding claiming that several delegates present at the 1970 Ard Fheis had been planted by Fianna Fáil.[8] Although MácStíofain claimed that 'the Provisional Army Council was not financed by Fianna Fáil',[9] he did not go so far as to refute Goulding's claim. Communists claimed those in Fianna Fáil were motivated by suspicions of socialism.[10] The Arms Trial of 1970, described by Roy Foster as an astonishing series of behind-the-scenes 'skulduggeries',[11] justified much of the suspicion of those within Official republicanism.

Charles Haughey, whose father had fought the Irish War of Independence for the IRA, was at the centre of the scandal. He had supported internment without trial in his role as Minister for Justice during the last few months of the Border Campaign. Also involved was Neil Blaney, then the Minister for Agriculture and Fisheries. Haughey was part of a cabinet sub-committee that was established to organise emergency assistance and relief to northern nationalists who had been forced from their homes, in sole charge of £100,000 worth of government money. In 1969, before the split, Haughey met with Goulding, but it was Blaney, through his connection with Irish army Captain James Kelly, who sought out arms which Haughey attempted to arrange customs clearance for. Taoiseach Jack Lynch sacked Haughey and Blaney in May 1970 and Minister for Defence Kevin Boland resigned in protest. By

October the case against all concerned had collapsed. Haughey returned to lead Fianna Fáil in 1979 and went on to serve as Taoiseach on three occasions. The involvement of prominent Fianna Fáil members and the reticence of Jack Lynch to take action provoked Official republican suspicions.

Similarly, the seemingly discretionary application of the Special Powers Act during 1969, with prominent Official republican Malachy McGurran in jail while Seán MácStíofain remained at large, fostered further distrust among Official republicans. Roy Johnston argued that the northern government approved of the reinvention of the IRA and so instructed the security forces to ease their transition.[12] Tomás Mac Giolla argued that the British deliberately provoked militarism in order to hinder the forces of revolution.[13] This does rather ignore the presence of divisive issues within the movement. Notable was a religious dimension to the split. While republicanism has never been an exclusively Catholic ideology, it is fair to say that the majority of republicans have been at least notionally Catholic. During the split, the brand of Catholicism practised by either faction was important; with both groups having a Catholic nationalist perspective, the Vatican II brand of Catholicism practised by the Officials, complete with links to Marxism, separated them from the Provisionals, more traditional Catholics of the Vatican I variety.[14]

On an individual basis, Catholicism has shaped the character of republicans for generations.[15] Post-split the Provisional movement played the religion card in an attempt to undermine the Official republicans: 'We urge you to think very carefully before committing your votes to this socialist party. It is a known fact that the members of this godless party are all godless Marxists who's [sic] sole aim is to destroy the Irish Catholic Church.'[16] Lenin had argued that 'religion must be of no concern to the state and religious societies must have no connection with governmental authority . . . discrimination among citizens on account of their religious convictions is wholly intolerable . . . we demand complete disestablishment of the Church', also adding that 'that does not mean in the least that the religious question ought to be advanced to first place, where it does not belong at all'.[17] Later, the Workers' Party noted an 'unhealthy development', namely the 'renewed political role of elements of the Roman Catholic Church. A shift to the Right has taken place within the Church and this found expression in the Church's role in the so-called "pro-life" constitutional amendment.'[18]

47

Although the majority of religious leaders opposed the men of violence, certain figures became associated with republicanism, notably Father Edward Daly, who was described by the British Foreign and Commonwealth Office as an 'extremist',[19] as well as Father Raymond Murray and Father Denis Faul. Their involvement proved problematic for the British state, their accounts of security force brutality difficult to deny; Murray and Faul publishing material with a distinctly anti-British perspective. Faul would later be particularly visible during the 1981 hunger strikes.

These differences would influence the respective brands of republicanism that supporters of either faction would practise. Goulding's plans for his faction were indicated during a speech at Glasnevin cemetery in April 1970 which highlighted the importance of both the ideas of James Connolly and the role of the IRA to his movement, despite Roy Johnston's concerns at the latter.[20] Clearly some attempt had been made to maintain a role for the militarists in the movement, as the Official IRA continued to kill in significant, if not large, numbers until its ceasefire of 1972. The struggle between the nationalist and socialist tendencies in the republican movement has been at the core of much division and the 1970s would emphasise this.

The Growth of the Provisional Republicans

During the 1970s, the paths that either republican group would take diverged drastically. The Official republicans went through a series of important transformations as they attempted to create the politicised movement with a broad base of support that they had so desired since the early 1960s and yet found themselves further and further away from the levels of popular support that they desired. Although the split was by no means a political–military divide, the sequence of events that contributed to the dominance of the Provisional IRA during the early 1970s certainly helped give that impression.

The summer of 1970 was a pivotal time for republicans, particularly as the loyalist marching season got underway. The B-Specials had been disbanded at the end of April and with the Arms Trial due to begin in Dublin roughly a month later, both events contributed to tension across loyalist communities. Equally, the memory of August 1969 was still fresh for republicans and hostility towards those who now formed the Official IRA leadership was still widespread. On 26 June, five people, including two children, were killed when a bomb exploded prematurely at the home of IRA bomb maker Thomas McCool, increasing tensions and setting the scene for violence to erupt, which it duly did the following day during an Orange Order march.

Loyalist incursions on the small nationalist enclave of Short Strand in East Belfast demanded a response from the IRA. Unlike the previous summer, this was forthcoming as IRA gunmen took up sniping positions in St Matthew's Church and defended the area, killing two Protestants and a Catholic. Three more Protestants were killed in clashes north of the city. It was initially claimed that Henry McIlhone, the sole Catholic victim, had been killed by loyalists, but the revelation that it had been an IRA volunteer who had accidentally shot McIlhone in crossfire would have serious ramifications for the movement. It has been suggested that McIlhone's inadvertent assassin was Denis Donaldson, who was recruited as a British agent in the months and weeks following. At the time, it was highly significant that the Provisional IRA had succeeded where its predecessors had failed and defended the Short Strand: it could legitimately claim that it 'could and would defend the oppressed nationalist people'.[21] There were more immediate consequences in the form of an Army weapons search as the security forces attempted to confiscate the IRA's arsenal.

The Army received a tip-off about an IRA arms dump in Balkan Street in the lower Falls area of West Belfast, an area where support for the Official IRA was strong. At this early stage of the conflict, weaponry was a sensitive issue. Keen to retain its arms, the OIRA chose not to attack the troops, but stone throwers attacked the Army, who deployed CS gas before a curfew was imposed on the area.[22] This provoked rioting across Northern Ireland with three civilians killed during this period.[23] These deaths again demanded a response from the IRA.

The initial deployment of the Army had been as a peace-keeping force, hence relatively cordial relations had existed between the troops and the nationalist communities but the curfew had suggested to republicans that the Army was prepared to utilise deadly force against their communities. The perception that the Army was targeting republicans, rather than the loyalist aggressors who had attacked the Short Strand, was widespread and soldiers from the time recall rumours that the troops were 'under orders to go and do another operation in the Shankill area and they were ready and marching out of the barracks to do it when they were ordered to stop'.[24] Many republicans, however, had long opposed the presence of the British Army on the streets of Ireland. Early tactical mistakes were welcomed: 'I thought they handled it very badly and I think from a republican perspective that was good.'[25]

The republican movement benefited from increasing recruitment, but the perception that the Provisional IRA was more competent to deal with the issue of the British Army saw the momentum slip away from the Official movement.[26] Over the course of 1970, the Official IRA did not kill anyone, an indication of the non-violent strategy that was being pursued behind the scenes, relative to the fifteen killed by the Provisional IRA, who were killing security force personnel from as early as August.[27] The PIRA campaign against the security forces stepped up in early 1971, as the first soldier to die in Northern Ireland, Gunner Robert Curtis, was killed on 6 February in the New Lodge area of North Belfast. The Ardoyne IRA was especially active and ruthless in its campaign against the security forces, never more so than in March.

Three young soldiers from the Royal Highland Fusiliers, John and Joseph McCaig, aged 17 and 18, and their friend and colleague Dougald McCaughey, 23, were drinking in a city centre bar and were lured by female IRA volunteers to a party. Their bodies were found at the side of a road on the north-western outskirts of the city, each shot in the back of the head. This operation disturbed some volunteers: 'I think as republicans we should have certain standards, we're supposed to be revolutionary soldiers.'[28] In their struggle, the Ardoyne IRA also lost key members: 'Paddy McAdorney and Gerry McDaid, shot dead: "Dutch" Doherty and Martin Meehan in sanctuary in the south.'[29]

McAdorney was killed on 9 August as the Army enforced the introduction of internment without trial. The success of internment as a countermeasure to the IRA's Border Campaign influenced British and Northern Irish government policy in the 1970s.[30] Operation Demetrius was launched with a series of early morning raids which were designed to detain all known IRA volunteers as a means of halting IRA activity. The operation was highly successful in arresting and interning suspected IRA volunteers, with over three hundred detained.[31] Unfortunately, and rather remarkably, Operation Demetrius failed to arrest the right people, one soldier commenting that 'at the time of internment the list of those I was ordered to "lift" had little resemblance to the list of IRA wanted men we had previously been searching for.'[32] Inadequate intelligence reports meant that the vast majority of those interned during the initial round of arrests were inactive or entirely innocent. Several leading Provisional IRA men were based in the Republic, with many others seeking refuge there after advance warnings.[33] Both sides were able to act upon the counterproductive operation. Reflections on the internment raids inevitably drew criticism to those in charge of operations. Although militarily the Parachute Regiment claimed that 'Internment as a weapon of attrition against the IRA has proved so successful',[34] ideologically it was disastrous. Particularly controversial were allegations of brutality on the part of security force personnel, the 'five techniques' of interrogation later bringing the United Kingdom to trial at the European Court of Human Rights, although the British government rejected 'any suggestion that the methods currently authorised for interrogation contain any element of cruelty or brutality. The report of the Committee confirms this view.'[35]

Reaction was widespread, with both IRA factions engaging the British Army. However, the Official IRA suffered as a result of internment; although British intelligence was outdated, the intelligence they had had led them to OIRA volunteers and the organisation saw many key figures interned.[36] The ability of Provisional IRA figures to evade capture at this time allowed that organisation to capitalise on the momentum provided by internment, escalating their campaign with a series of bomb and gun attacks. Although Official republicans cried conspiracy – Roy Johnston citing the similarity with a series of arrests prior to the 1969 IRA split in that 'the only leading republicans to be imprisoned where [sic] those who were in the lead of the politicisation process'[37] – the internment of key members effectively undermined the organisational capabilities of the Official republicans, who were already in the process of shifting towards their ultimate ceasefire. As with the Falls curfew, both sides recruited in light of internment but the control of the republican struggle was moving towards the Provisional republican movement with an increasingly irresistible thrust.

Alongside the increasingly experienced Provisional IRA volunteers who remained at large were fresh recruits, angry and disillusioned young people from nationalist areas across Northern Ireland. Although the majority of the nationalist population in Northern Ireland have never been supportive of the IRA, there is no doubt that portions of this population were propelled towards the republican armed struggle as a reaction to internment. For Richard O'Rawe:

> The campaign was really starting to kick off in 1971, prior to internment coming in . . . the bombing campaign . . . was gathering pace . . . but it was really internment that was the catalyst for a huge upsurge in activity and gave the IRA a sort of political cover . . . I'm not so sure it had the widespread support that it needed

51

to endure for any sustained period but internment gave it that. Internment was so obnoxious to the psyche of nationalists that they sort of rallied against the state not necessarily into the arms of the IRA, more of a broad republican support base . . . it galvanised nationalists in the working class as well as middle class support, which had been dormant.[38]

Father Edward Daly said that 'the army isn't the problem. The IRA is not the problem . . . The thing that has alienated Catholic people more than anything else is the issue of internment.'[39] Eoin Ó Broin considers that the increase in support for the Provisional IRA at this time was because:

the organisation which was seen as bringing the fight to the enemy with the greatest degree of strength and commitment clearly would have garnered much more public support and that would have put the emerging Workers' Party political organisation, I think, at a loss, irrespective of your view of whether it was doing the right or wrong thing.[40]

For Seán MácStíofain, 'sympathy and support for the people of the North rose to a new peak after the imposition of internment . . . Everywhere men and women of Irish birth and descent rallied to the cause of national freedom.'[41] This is not to say that the quality of recruit was as high as some would have wished. Marian Price reflects 'there were people coming into the republican movement who I would not have termed republicans. They would have been more the Catholic defender type . . . they wanted to join the IRA to defend Catholic communities. I don't think that did the movement any favours.' For Price, this set the movement up for the series of dramatic revelations that would occur thirty years hence.[42]

The period demanded responses. In response to internment, the republican armed struggle grew. Equally, the protest movement was reinvigorated as NICRA re-emerged to champion the anti-internment movement. On the unionist side, much was expected of the security forces in response to the increase in republican violence. Loyalist paramilitaries took action into their own hands, the UVF bombing of McGurk's bar in North Belfast particularly gruesome.

In early 1972, all of these tendencies collided to deadly effect. Anti-internment marches took place in late 1971. Eamonn McCann cites ten illegal marches (all parades had been banned in August 1971) between the introduction of internment and 30 January 1972,[43] emphasising the momentum that the campaign was able to achieve relatively quickly. One protest at Magilligan internment camp outside Derry had prompted the

Parachute Regiment to deploy CS gas to disperse the protesters. Their Commanding Officer Derek Wilford defended these actions, saying that 'the Paras are tough men ... never brutal'.[44] The following weekend, another march in Derry city took place, again with the Parachute Regiment present. The deaths of thirteen people, with another fatally wounded, on what became known as Bloody Sunday, was both a product of preceding events and itself decisive in producing the violence that beset Northern Ireland during 1972. The Army themselves reflected that 'an isolated incident, such as "Bloody Sunday", can radically alter support for violence',[45] and the mass outbreak of violence in Northern Ireland during 1972 would support this assertion. Although majority support for violence was still absent, many were motivated to join the two factions of the IRA, particularly in light of the innocence of the victims of Bloody Sunday, only Gerald Donaghy having been proven to have been an active republican, a member of the Provisional IRA's Fianna Éireann youth organisation.[46] 1972 also saw Libyan arms arriving in Ireland for the Provisional IRA courtesy of Colonel Gaddafi.[47]

After Bloody Sunday, both wings of the IRA managed to recruit, with many deciding to join the Official IRA thanks to the subtle difference in tactics between the two; the Official IRA was seen to exist for the purposes of defence, the Provisional IRA for purposes of attack.[48] The desire for offensive action indicated by the defection of members from the Official IRA during this period,[49] the inability of the OIRA to adequately respond indicated by their murder of ex-Para David Seaman, a former psychiatric patient, and their bombing of Aldershot barracks. The Official IRA ceasefire left the Provisional IRA as the only active republican paramilitary group and its deadly capabilities were in evidence throughout the summer of 1972.

On 21 July, the PIRA planted a series of bombs in central Belfast, with nine killed and hundreds injured in 'Bloody Friday'. This proved counterproductive as the attacks provided the security forces with the excuse they needed to abolish the republican no-go areas, which had been established the previous year in nationalist areas of Northern Ireland to provide sanctuary for republicans. Ten days after Bloody Friday, Operation Motorman brought down nationalist barricades and reasserted the authority of the security forces. The flood of members seeking involvement in the northern struggle required structural reorganisation of the movement. Gerry Adams was part of a republican delegation that had visited London for secret talks two weeks before Bloody Friday and from this point on, the man considered by fellow republicans to be 'just another member of the brigade staff . . . I never thought that Gerry was any kind of genius, he was just another guy',[50] enjoyed a rapid rise through the republican movement. Adams would lead the establishment of a Northern Command which would control military operations in the northern counties of the Republic and all of Northern Ireland. This gave Belfast significant autonomy and allowed the Adams faction to assume control of the IRA by the end of 1976.[51] They were aided in this by a disastrous ceasefire:

> The driving forces behind the ceasefire were Billy McKee, Ruairí Ó Brádaigh, Seamus Twomey, Dáithí Ó Conaill, all on the Army Council at that time . . . the ceasefire came about and Sinn Féin came out of the doldrums. It started to set up incident centres to monitor the ceasefire . . . on the day that the '75 ceasefire came into being a lot of IRA volunteers were of the opinion that the movement was stagnant, that the army was coming apart at the seams. That may not have been the case, I didn't realise it because I had been in Ballymurphy and we'd been very positive, full companies of brilliant volunteers up there, many of whom like myself had got out of internment again and there was a surge.[52]

The Provisional IRA spent much of 1975 on ceasefire, having declared a cessation over Christmas in 1974 which ended on 17 January 1975. The movement re-established its ceasefire on 10 February, which lasted officially until 23 January 1976. This surge took the form of the seventy-nine deaths which were attributed to the Provisional IRA during 1975. The publication of a document entitled 'Terms for a bi-lateral truce' suggests that the republican movement was, even at this early stage of the conflict, thinking about an end to armed struggle.[53] This document was produced because 'we were being told that the Brits were disengaging, that the Brits were trying to come up with a methodology by which they could disengage from Ireland and as it went on the evidence of this became very threadbare and people asked, "Where's the statement of intent? We don't see it."'[54] The Adams takeover of the movement was carefully co-ordinated, Adams being able to capitalise on perceived errors on the part of the old leadership:

> Adams and Bell were educating at leadership level, even though they were in jail they were engaging people's minds and they were saying 'this ceasefire is a disaster and it will destroy the army'. Ivor Bell got out of jail first, he became a force against those who had been responsible for the ceasefire . . . Adams then got out and there was a purge – McKee was pushed out, Dáithí Ó Conaill wasn't pushed out but his role in a military sense was diminished . . . you had this young vibrant leadership, not totally Belfast based, you still had . . . people like Ruairí Ó Brádaigh . . . Ó Conaill was still on, but there was a feeling that the Adams leadership, the guys

that criticised the ceasefire [and] the feud . . . wanted to restore the army, they told the volunteers that there would never be another ceasefire . . . short of a British withdrawal from Ireland or an internationally recognised statement of intent so we, in the IRA, felt very good about this, it didn't ever cross my mind at that stage that we would lose this war or could possibly come anywhere close to losing it.[55]

Martin McGuinness later reflected on 'the disgraceful attitude' of the then leadership 'during the disastrous 18 months ceasefire in the mid-1970s'.[56] In many ways the 1975 ceasefire represents the split that never was for the Provisional IRA. A new leadership emerged, but rather than heading a new republican movement, it usurped the existing leadership that was perceived to be out of touch with the realities of the northern campaign. With the movement seemingly beginning to stagnate, promi-nent Belfast volunteer Brendan Hughes cited the increasing sophistica-tion of the security forces as a reason for this.[57] It was important that the IRA reorganise at a time when the loyalist paramilitaries were proving a deadly foe: the UVF killing seventy-eight, including forty-eight Catholics. Although the IRA ceasefire had been motivated by persuasive political reasoning, it handed the initiative to the sectarian murder cam-paign led by the UVF.

Particularly controversial among the UVF killings of 1975 was the 31 July slaughter of members of the Miami Showband. The band were returning south after playing a gig in Banbridge, County Down, when they were stopped at what appeared to be a UDR checkpoint near Newry. The checkpoint was actually manned by ten UVF members, at least four of whom were also in the UDR. The band was ordered out of their vehicles as a bomb was planted in their van; the intention was that the bomb would explode as they returned to the Irish Republic, framing the band as bomb couriers. The bomb exploded prematurely, killing two UVF men, at which point the others launched a vicious attack on the band; singer Fran O'Toole was shot twenty-two times in the face. The killings put considerable strain on Anglo-Irish relations, with the Irish government demanding that more be done to stop the sectarian assas-sinations.[58] Subsequent allegations that, in addition to members of the UDR, Captain Robert Nairac of the British Army was also involved served to further heighten aggravation towards the Army.[59] Nairac was particularly active in operations against the IRA, his ill-advised attempts to gather intelligence including appearing in bars in South Armagh pre-tending to be a Belfast Official IRA member, costing him his life in May 1977.[60]

In response to the Miami Showband killings, the IRA launched an attack on the Bayardo Bar, located in the UVF's West Belfast heartland of the mid-Shankill Road. The gun and bomb attack only succeeded in killing four civilians, the counterproductive sectarian violence of the period[61] emphasised by the death of four-year-old Siobhan McCabe, who died when she was hit by a stray bullet during a gun battle. Brendan 'Bik' McFarlane was later jailed for the Bayardo attack, going on to command the IRA in the Maze prison and becoming involved in peace process discussions during the 1990s.

Few PIRA operations during early 1975 spoke of the armed revolutionary movement that many volunteers had believed they were joining during the early 1970s. A series of attacks in London in August 1975 seemed to suggest a new commitment to the campaign; bombs in Ulster had achieved little and the London government, the only agent able to effect British withdrawal from Ireland, now appeared to be a more appropriate target.[62] However, on 1 September, under the cover name South Armagh Republican Action Force, IRA volunteers shot dead five Protestants in an attack at an Orange Hall in Newtownhamilton. The UVF responded with the killing of twelve people on 2 October. Tit-for-tat sectarian killing continued into the New Year, Northern Ireland seemed on the brink of an all-out sectarian war and the Provisional IRA were very much an integral part of the problem. The UVF killed five in attacks either side of the border in late December, before the IRA responded with the murder of ten Protestant workmen at Kingsmills in early January. What had become a mockery of a ceasefire was ended on 23 January. The spiral of sectarian violence took on a new dimension during this period with the emergence of the Shankill Butchers, a renegade UVF faction led by Lennie Murphy who roamed the streets of Belfast, targeting suspected Catholics on the basis of their location before brutally murdering them.

Also damaging was PIRA involvement in a feud with the Official IRA which began in late October. From the perspective of the Provisional IRA, the feud was 'very damaging [and] served no tactical purpose . . . Billy McKee was seen to be the driving force behind that feud and that was a major criticism against him.'[63] These circumstances provided the Adams faction with the opportunity it needed to oust the Provisional leadership, which was both older and largely southern-based and perceived as incompetent to direct what had become a northern-focused movement. Adams was appointed the joint Vice-President of Sinn Féin in 1978 and the highly symbolic merger of the organisation's newspapers,

Republican News in the North and *An Phoblacht* in the South, suggested a unity of purpose, focusing on the Northern campaign. It was during this period that a series of articles, penned by a writer known as 'Brownie', appeared in *Republican News* which pointed at new political initiatives in the movement.[64]

The Adams programme would lead the republican movement away from its armed struggle and into the field of politics. External circumstances conspired to aid Adams in this as the deeply political issue of republican prisoners rose to the fore. Internment without trial had ended in late 1975, replaced by a programme of criminalisation and normalisation. Those convicted of terrorist offences would now be treated as ordinary criminals, as political status for prisoners was abolished on 1 March 1976. The most symbolic requirement of prisoners convicted after this date was the wearing of prison-issued uniform. The blanket protest began when Kieran Nugent refused his prison-issue uniform in September 1976, famously announcing that the authorities would 'have to nail it to my back',[65] instead covering himself with a blanket. Provisional republicans contended that the policy represented the decision 'that republican prisoners were to be broken as a means of breaking the republican community'.[66] Tom Hartley argued that 'when they thought themselves all powerful, the British government in Ireland had already lost their attempt to criminalise the republican people and their struggle',[67] with Danny Morrison describing the prison campaign as 'our 1916'.[68] The campaign matured gradually and did not completely capture the republican movement despite the publicity it generated:

> It took a few months of people being processed through the courts before numbers built up to the stage where it was no longer productive for the prison regime to put us in blocks where there were guys who were wearing the uniform so they put us in the one block. From then on it was the blanket protest for the next five years. The numbers built up to about 350 I think was the highest it ever was at one time. It fluctuated, some guys put the gear on, some guys don't join. There were more who didn't join the protest than did.[69]

The Official republicans had long distanced themselves from the campaign, arguing that 'such killers are not entitled to any special POW status when captured', arguing instead for a broad-based campaign.[70] Official republican opposition to the prison campaign had solid ideological foundations. By the late 1970s, few Official IRA volunteers remained imprisoned.[71] The ceasefire and relatively low levels of violence perpetrated by the movement since had reduced security force concerns over the

OIRA, with remaining militarists largely departing to the INLA in 1975. Problematic, however, was the widespread support for the prisoners that developed rapidly, the support developing into the type of broad-based campaign that the Official republicans themselves sought.[72] The group published a position paper, *H-Block – The Socialist Perspective*, which was widely supported in the movement.[73]

It has been suggested that Official republicans allowed their hostility towards their former colleagues to cloud their judgement of the prison campaign.[74] The broad-based nature of the prison campaign placed it close to Official republican social policy, but deep personal and ideological differences made it very difficult for them to support prisoners who had been jailed for crimes associated with the armed struggle. To support the demands of the prisoners would have undermined the non-violent campaign of Official republicanism and would have exposed the organisation to accusations of opportunism.

Significant was the involvement of loyalist prisoners in the early stages of the blanket protest, who were taken off the protest because of its associations with republicanism.[75] Loyalists could not actively associate with republicans in light of continued PIRA operations, including the La Mon Hotel bomb in early 1978 which killed twelve Protestants. The PIRA campaign had been invigorated under new leadership and a new cell structure, implemented in 1977, had redefined operational strategy, streamlining the movement to increase its efficiency. The British Army observed that 'PIRA's organisation is now such that a small number of activists can maintain a disproportionate level of violence. There is a substantial pool of young Fianna aspirants, nurtured in a climate of violence, eagerly seeking promotion to full gun-carrying terrorist status and there is a steady release from the prisons of embittered and dedicated terrorists.'[76] Evidence of this new-found efficiency was provided in August 1979.

On Monday 27 August 1979, the PIRA launched a two-pronged attack that hit at the heart of the British presence in Ireland. From their hiding place on the opposite side of Carlingford Lough, two IRA operatives watched a convoy of Parachute Regiment soldiers travelling towards Newry. As the convoy passed the gates to Narrow Water Castle, a bomb hidden in the bed of a truck exploded, killing six soldiers. At the sound of gunfire, the soldiers took refuge behind the gates to the castle, where a second bomb was hidden. Once reinforcements had arrived, the second bomb detonated, killing a further twelve, including Lieutenant Colonel David Blair, the most senior Army officer to die in the troubles. On the same day in County Sligo, the IRA killed Lord Louis Mountbatten along with three of his companions with a bomb hidden on his pleasure craft. The attacks emphasised the potent threat that the IRA posed, the sophistication of their engineering department being particularly advanced. Certainly, the British Army noted that 'we expect the Provisionals to remain the dominant terrorist organisation throughout the next five years . . . our evidence of the calibre of rank and file terrorists does not support the view that they are merely mindless hooligans drawn from the unemployed and unemployable'.[77]

The increasing potential for propaganda with the developing prison campaign and the considerable military success of 27 August suggested to volunteers that the movement was now in a position to enhance its campaign against the British. This proved not to be the case:

> In 1979 you had Narrow Water, where 18 Paras were killed, and on the same day you had Mountbatten being killed, so there was a great feeling of 'The boys are back in town. The IRA's back in business, we're going to drive forward.' But . . . Narrow Water was a peak and it was never reached again and things started to go back to the usual one being shot here, or if you were really lucky, four being blown up in a landmine down in South Armagh . . . that was very par for the course and that's the way it stayed. Then, of course, the most important event of the whole struggle occurred – the 81 hunger strike.[78]

Balancing the Political and Military

Although Goulding's 1970 Glasnevin speech suggested the continuation of the Official IRA, key figures in the movement were discussing 'the futility of "military campaigns"'.[79] Particularly important was the retention of an armed wing for the purposes of defence, even though it was noted that 'there is an increasing tendency among some members of both groups to give their main emphasis to the specialist activities of their own group and to ignore the effects of their activities'.[80] Among those who still saw merit in the armed struggle was Seamus Costello, a car salesman from Bray in County Wicklow who had been prominent during the Border Campaign while still a teenager.

Goulding's IRA had drawn some concern from the Northern Ireland government,[81] and plans had been made during the late 1960s for a renewed military campaign. This drew concern from the politicos in the movement who believed that such a move would cause destabilisation.[82] Historically republicans had faced considerable difficulties when the interests of the political and armed wings of the movement came into conflict.[83] In their quest for political credibility, the Official republicans began to use code names for the party (Group A) and army (Group B), because 'the legality and ability of Group A to operate openly is to a large degree protected by its separate structure and leadership. It is felt by the vast majority of both groups that this position should be protected at all costs.'[84]

It was recognised that the activities of the Army would serve to undermine the credibility of the political wing. The ending of abstentionism, itself a move aimed at enhancing the political credibility of the movement, had clearly indicated that politics, rather than armed struggle, was the priority within Goulding's Official republican movement. Goulding argued that 'whether concerning housing or civil rights or issues like that, our job is to defend these people. Our philosophy is that physical force has its greatest justification when it is used in defence of the people. It should be the last phase of revolution.'[85] The perceived lack of militancy cost the Official republicans the support of Na Fianna Éireann, one volunteer noting that 'there was a really militant crowd in the Fianna . . . Fianna units reported having heavy machine guns, explosives, rifles and handguns.'[86] For Des O'Hagan, 'in terms of republican ideology . . . the vicious Provisional sectarian campaign to supersede the civil-rights-inspired democratic struggle was objectively counter revolutionary'.[87] This was a common view from the Irish left, the Communist Party arguing that Marxist-Leninist revolutionary theory dictated that:

> armed struggle which does not have popular support amongst the majority of our oppressed people cannot defeat imperialism and oppression . . . What the Communist Party is saying is not that armed struggle is morally wrong, but that the present campaign is politically premature . . . Further it reinforces the sense of commitment of the Protestant population to the British union, because the victims are increasingly members of their community.[88]

The mutual distaste that developed between the Communist Party and the Provisional IRA was underlined in IRA General Order number four, republican policy forbidding membership of a communist organisation.[89] Na Fianna Éireann cited their motivation for siding with the Provisionals following the split:

> It was not difficult for Na Fianna Éireann to make a choice. The doctrine of Karl Marx is contrary to the Fianna teaching. It is contrary to the Fianna declaration which states – I pledge my allegiance to God and the Irish Republic. Marx also stated that the working man has no country. We of the Fianna for the most part

are the sons of workers but we have a country and we love it very dearly. We can in no way be associated with International Socialism.[90]

There is evidence of socialism within the Provisional movement at this time, a letter appearing in the *Irish News* declaring that 'the Republican Movement (Provisional) is a socialist movement dedicated to the establishment of a democratic socialist Republic in Ireland . . . we wish to see the working class in Ireland regardless of religion, unite and destroy the corrupt and evil system of capitalism which holds this island in a vice like grip.'[91] Gerry Adams has also declared that because I am a socialist I continue to be a republican . . . you cannot be a socialist and not be a republican . . . If you say you are a republican socialist you are implying that there is such a thing as a "non-republican" socialist; but of course there is not and cannot be.'[92] Official republicans dismissed 'the sordid and obscene terrorism of those pseudo Republicans, who by word and deed, daily make a mockery of the entire meaning of the 1916 Proclamation, a message whose essential humanity is its vibrant strength and continuing relevance'.[93] Cathal Goulding declared the Provisionals to be blackshirts in balaclavas,[94] despite compelling evidence of left-wing literature on Provisional republican wings of the Maze prison.[95]

REPUBLICANS AND PROTESTANTS

The overtly politicised nature of the religious divide in Northern Ireland, the persistence of which was emphasised in the 2003 Life and Times Survey,[96] has undoubtedly stood in the way of class unity. Danny Morrison notes that 'if they [Ulster Protestants] look into history, look into their own history, they will find that there were very many extremely progressive people from within their own ranks, who gave us our Republicanism. It was the Protestants who gave us our Republicanism.'[97] Morrison is referring to the United Irishmen of the 1790s, prominent leaders Theobald Wolfe Tone and Robert Emmet both being born into Presbyterian families. Despite being a stated non-sectarian organisation, they were by no means bloodless revolutionaries. Provoked by the formation of the Orange Order in 1795 following the bloody Battle of the Diamond near Loughgall, County Armagh, United Irishmen members were involved in sectarian acts during their 1798 rebellion. Tone remained an ideological figurehead for republicans, Cathal Goulding speaking of 'a full-blooded revolutionary . . . the first and the greatest Irish Republican'.[98]

Just as the civil rights movement had attempted to 'remove the rational basis of unionists wanting to be unionists',[99] Official republicans continued to reach out to the Protestant working class, declaring that 'we guarantee you . . . full freedom of conscience and civil and religious liberty in a united and independent Ireland . . . Orange and republican, Catholic and Protestant toil side by side in factory and mill, all equally victims.'[100] The ideal of Wolfe Tone – the unification of Protestant, Catholic and Dissenter in the common name of Irishman – had proved durable; radical republicans from the 1930s had placed hope in the potential for class union to overcome sectarian division.[101] Seamus Costello argued that 'the support of the Loyalist working class is essential, if we are to have a socialist republic, however their support in the struggle must be sought on the basis of a principled explanation of the correct relationship between the national question and the class question'.[102] Costello's Irish Republican Socialist Party (IRSP), formed out of a 1974 split in Official republicanism, admitted that community divisions 'will not be combated by appeasing loyalism or attempting to find a socialist consciousness within the loyalist organisations that most definitely is not there',[103] while simultaneously arguing that 'there can be no doubt that a socialist revolution cannot succeed without winning at least a section of the Protestant working class to a revolutionary perspective. This can only be achieved by confronting Loyalism with principled socialist politics.'[104] John Lowry notes:

> At various points from even as far back as 1970 . . . with varying degrees of success there were attempts to open up channels if you like or some sort of co-operation or dialogue . . . between ourselves and representatives from various Protestant groups . . . in a broader political sense you were publicly highlighting the sort of commonality of problems which the working-class people had whether they lived on the Shankill or the Falls Road and to try and draw this to their attention.[105]

Official republican opposition to armed struggle was based on both its negative impact on working-class unity and the fear of sectarian retaliation from Protestants.[106] Billy McMillen argued that armed struggle left republicanism 'not on the brink of victory but on the brink of sectarian disaster',[107] echoing Tomás Mac Giolla's comment that 'the greatest immediate danger facing us is massive sectarian conflict . . . If the bombing campaign is not halted within the next couple of weeks July could bring catastrophe to Ireland.'[108] Des O'Hagan recalled, 'we pointed out at that stage . . . what was going to happen here: A sectarian civil war; not on a total scale, but it was going to escalate into something like that.'[109]

During the Border Campaign, operations against the security forces were designed to minimise local casualties, and the instruction for Official IRA volunteers to act only in self-defence contrasted sharply with the Provisional IRA campaign against the security forces that gathered momentum over the early years of the 1970s. With the majority of security force members from the Protestant communities of Northern Ireland, the Communist Party of Ireland (CPI) asked: 'Can it be honestly stated that your activities and practice, as distinct from words, contribute to an effort to win over the maximum support of the Protestant section of the people in the North?'[110] Cathal Goulding also claimed that the Provisional IRA's 'campaign has extended hatred amongst more Protestant families in the North. The ideal of Irish unity is now further away as a result of their campaign of sectarian murder.'[111] Maria McGuire alleged that Seán MácStíofáin said, 'What does it matter if Protestants get killed? They're all bigots, aren't they?'[112] Although MácStíofáin disputes this, arguing that she 'invented that "comment" expressly to discredit me, and through me the movement',[113] as the UDA themselves note, 'it is not always that which is true which is important, but that which is believed to be true'.[114] Official republicans argued:

> Nothing could be more contrary to the revolutionary strategy of the Republican Movement than the indiscriminate bombing and burning campaign of certain elements. It is completely sectarian in that all targets are Protestant owned and seems designed specifically to alienate the Protestant people from the struggle for justice of their Catholic fellow-citizens.[115]

Loyalists were also conscious of this, Sammy Duddy recalling that 'the very idea of class politics didn't last because of the fear and suspicion being generated . . . This was a great recruiting agent, of course, because people flocked to join the UDA and UVF.'[116] The Ulster Political Research Group explained that:

> Ulster 'Protestants' do not fear nor mistrust Ulster 'Catholics' because they are Catholics but because they believe them to be Irish Nationalists . . . intent on the destruction of Northern Ireland . . . the more loyalists suspect 'Catholics' of being Irish Nationalists, the more defensive they become and close ranks. The more defensive 'Protestants' become, the more 'Catholics' believe themselves to be excluded and display disaffection and agitation usually through the medium of Irish Nationalism.[117]

This simply underlines the basic premise of the UDA: to defend Protestants from the perceived threat of republicanism. The UDA itself claimed that its transition from community activities to vigilantism did not take place until 1973,[118] implying that the movement was not established solely for the purposes of violence. Hostility towards republicans was not confined to paramilitary groups, Desmond Greaves blaming Ian Paisley and Terrence O'Neill, along with the lack of organisation on the Irish left, for ruining hopes of Protestant radicalism.[119]

Greaves believed that deliberate attempts to divide the Irish working class had taken place at a governmental level. He argued that 'religious sectarianism had practically died a natural death when in 1920 Edward Carson, a Tory die-hard, deliberately inflamed it in his speeches'.[120] However, during the 1960s the Communist Party of Northern Ireland (CPNI) had managed to draw support from Protestants,[121] and there were Protestants who continued to support communist organisations during the 1970s. Protestant trade unionists had been active during the 1960s,[122] and Protestant working-class support for the Northern Ireland Labour Party also suggested the potential for working-class politics prior to the outbreak of the troubles.[123] Afterwards, these relationships became rather less conventional. Dave Fogel of the UDA spoke of the British and Irish Communist Organisation (BICO) as being 'the only Marxist group that recognises Ulster. It wants the Catholics to come out categorically for the recognition of the border. It's this which keeps the Catholic and Protestant working class apart. Once the Prods lose their fear of Dublin then the way is open to a united working class.'[124] BICO was the self-professed 'only body which has consistently made sense of Northern Ireland affairs since 1969',[125] but there was some distance between its position and the republican stance that the border had helped divide the working class and had to be abolished in order to achieve working-class unity.

There is evidence of class consciousness existing within loyalism at this time. The Official IRA and UVF co-operated on prison issues during the early 1970s,[126] with the UVF's Billy Hutchinson admitting that 'we learned quite a lot from republicans . . . We learned politics.'[127] Gusty Spence met with Provisional republicans during the 1970s,[128] and in 1981 acknowledged his commitment to socialism, an event that coincided with the arrest of his nephew for Official IRA membership.[129] There were strong family ties to the politics of the left; his brother Eddie, or Ned, Spence was a prominent neo-Maoist within the Communist Party in Belfast, and had been active in the civil rights movement.[130]

This was also true within the UDA. Ernie Elliott, second in command in Woodvale, was convinced that the UDA should embark on a political programme and sought talks with Dessie O'Hagan.[131] Elliott, nicknamed 'Che Guevara'[132] by his UDA colleagues, was murdered in December 1972 and his deputy, Dave Fogel, another with an interest in socialism, had to flee Ulster. Although Elliott's murder appears to have been over an internal dispute, Fogel's exile has been attributed to his close relationship with Elliott, a friendship borne of kindred political spirits.[133] Also significant around this time was the appearance in UVF magazine *Combat* of 'quite a number of articles which were very seriously left-wing' for republican socialists, a very brief window of opportunity that closed when 'the editor was ousted and in some of the following issues they sort of put in apologies for the previous editions which contained all this "communistic" stuff, as they called it'.[134]

Nothing better represented the collective power of the Protestant working class than 1974's Ulster Workers' Council strike, organised in protest at the establishment of a power-sharing executive provided for in December 1973's Sunningdale Agreement. Most objectionable to loyalists was the provision for cross-border involvement in Northern Irish governance, something that would be integral to later political agreements. A general strike was announced on 14 May 1974, to commence the following day. Workers who showed up for work on the fifteenth were persuaded by a series of meetings to leave – the extent of this persuasion being highly controversial because of the central role of loyalist paramilitaries, better known for intimidation than negotiation skills, particularly when taken in the context of the Dublin and Monaghan bombings of 17 May which killed thirty-three. The UDA were also prominent, although they later declared opposition to direct rule, stating it to be both an undemocratic and unaccountable form of government.[135] The prominence of the loyalist paramilitaries and the Protestant domination of skilled work aided perception of the strike as a Protestant class action.[136] While the loyalist paramilitaries flexed their muscles throughout the strike, the UWC also exerted influence, particularly on the UDA; Andy Tyrie pressed the case for the UDA to launch discussions with Catholics over power sharing, even if this meant talking to IRA men.[137]

Post-UWC, the UDA created a lecture briefing form which stressed their view that 'the Provisionals intend to drive forcefully from Ulster any Protestants who survive their terrorist campaign',[138] emphasising the raison d'être of the Ulster *Defence* Association. Equally important was the fact that loyalists either struggled, or were unwilling, to differentiate between republicans, Sammy Duddy noting that 'in those days loyalists tended to lump them together under one label – Provos'.[139] For Dessie O'Hagan:

> It took a long time for many Protestants to distinguish between what they would have seen as the competing arms of the Official IRA and the Provisionals. It took a long time for us to get across that we were campaigning on a different set of issues . . . we actually had the UDA come to us . . . we had formal meetings . . . we had the UVF . . . down to Dublin around '73 or '74 and then we went to representatives of the Provos to try and talk them into it . . . and we did go to see the UDA.[140]

Responses from the political left to the UWC strike were overwhelmingly positive. A conference in Amherst, Massachusetts was organised in the summer of 1975 to which the UDA was invited. The Provisional republicans found themselves unable to acquire entry visas for the United States, but the then-legal UDA suffered no such difficulties, nor did Seamus Costello. Dr Noel Browne, at the time a member of Seanad Éireann for the Socialist Labour Party, noted that Costello 'gave a scintillating display of good humour, history, politics and hard facts'.[141] The National Council of the Churches of Christ (NCCC) in the USA were not as convinced as to the merits of Costello, his organisation, or their politics: 'The presentation of the Irish Republican Socialist Party and their approach to the situation are frightening and must be condemned as dangerous to any constructive solution.'[142]

Reports suggest that Costello and the loyalist representatives enjoyed amicable interaction at the conference, particularly with Andy Tyrie.[143] The NCCC supported this, stating that 'there was good humour and respect present almost all the time'. They also noted that 'the Ulster Defence Association presentation by Glen Barr . . . took courage as well as conviction'.[144] Indeed, the IRSP had, quite stunningly, claimed that 'anybody who refuses to accept the UVF and UDA as progressive working class organisations is a sectarian bigot',[145] a statement quite distant from later claims that 'we regard the Orange Order as a sectarian anti-Catholic organisation that uses the false arguments of a British culture to justify its hate-filled creed'.[146] At the conference, Glen Barr explained that:

> Protestants in the North fear the prospect of an army from the Republic moving in to fight them; they fear the domination of the Catholic Church in the Republic. Catholics in the North fear that the Protestant section would try to wipe them out . . . if we fight, it will be to the death for thousands of our people in Ulster . . . and after that, what? I hope that those here who differ from my view will go home and

say that Glen Barr does not have horns, as I have seen that Seamus Costello . . . does not have horns.[147]

There was much to suggest a common agenda, UDA leader Andy Tyrie noting that 'it's not always been the case of simply the Roman Catholic population wanting to remove the British from Ireland. You find quite a lot of Protestants wanting to remove them because they victimise us as well.'[148] However, the Official republican movement was:

> less successful in the wider Protestant community because most of the Protestant community associated republicans . . . as just being one group of people who were . . . engaged in a campaign of violence against them so therefore there was little chance of any sort of appreciation of saying 'look, we're really socialists, we're different type of people'. Some elements of the UDA and UVF at different times did grow to appreciate that . . . but . . . some of the leaders of the UVF were actually shot dead because of their contacts with us . . . some of the wilder military elements within the UVF and UDA saw themselves engaged more with the Provos, just as the Provos weren't interested in political activity or social-economic activity, neither were they and they weren't willing to listen to any talk of common agitation.[149]

The politics of left-wing republicans meant nothing to a loyalist working class who were literally afraid for their lives, but the division went a little deeper than that, as noted by Eoin Ó Broin: 'simply because people are working class doesn't mean they have the same sets of interests . . . you can't deny the existence of those different political aspirations and political identities'.[150] Anthony McIntyre highlighted that 'socialism's inextricably linked to Irish nationalism'.[151] It is also important that the Official republicans were considered a nationalist group that preached socialism, rather than a socialist group that happened to be nationalist.[152] This was a significant problem, for Gusty Spence: 'we in Northern Ireland are plagued with super-loyalists . . . If one does not agree with their bigoted and fascist views then one is a "taig-lover" or a "communist".'[153] He also noted that 'on the Shankill there was a tendency to label thinkers . . . communists'.[154] Sammy Duddy considered that Protestant working-class education 'hasn't improved over the years, yet on the republican front, it's come on leaps and bounds . . . they're putting people through colleges, universities, while the Protestant people seem to have stood still'.[155]

There was therefore a need for those on the republican left to adequately put across their case to the Protestant working classes. Maria McGuire recalls that the Official republicans were 'very good at talking, explaining, arguing and justifying, but strangely hesitant when it came to actually doing anything'.[156] Also problematic, Sammy Duddy recalled that 'it was nearly forbidden to read any of their literature. It was frowned on. If you were caught with a copy of any of their publications, you kidded on it was for intelligence purposes, not for educational content.'[157] John McMichael, 'although no intellectual ... more articulate than many UDA commanders',[158] recalled difficulties during attempts at political education: 'We tried to educate them. We did night classes on history but they weren't fuckin' interested. Outward bound and arms training, no bother at all, but getting them to read anything or think, you just couldn't do it.'[159]

Those within loyalism have found the transition from political violence to politics difficult: Tommy Herron was unable to translate his paramilitary standing into political votes and John McMichael achieved only 576 votes in the 1982 South Belfast by-election. McMichael stood little chance of achieving Catholic or middle-class Protestant votes with a UDA background, with the latter voting in numbers for the Ulster Unionist candidate Martin Smyth.[160] Roy Johnston argued that 'the accumulated military experience of activists in an armed movement makes adaptation to subsequent democratic politics extremely difficult'.[161]

To this end, the UDA produced two publications: *Beyond the Religious Divide* appeared in March 1979 and *Common Sense* in January 1987. These asserted the movement's position on the future of the Protestant working class and the political state of Northern Ireland generally. Workers' Party member Seamus Lynch spoke favourably of both and launched discussions with the UDA based on the latter.[162] *Common Sense* particularly suggested a willingness to move beyond violence, promoting discussion of Ulster independence on the logic that the negotiated independence of Ulster could allow both sides to claim victory and enjoy a new shared identity as equal citizens in the new Ulster state. This bore similarity to the Provisional republicans' 'Éire Nua' policy, implemented under Ruairí Ó Brádaigh, who made it a matter of strategy that Protestants should not be dominated in a Catholic state.[163]

Although highly desirable in terms of building a credible socialist movement in Northern Ireland, attempts to reach across the sectarian divide proved unsuccessful. It was impossible for individuals on either side to look beyond the rising violence. When the Official republicans suggested joint OIRA and UDA patrols in an attempt to end sectarian assassinations,[164] a UDA bomb killed two Catholic children in North Belfast. In the aftermath of the Amherst conference, a nakedly sectarian

IRA attack at Kingsmills that killed ten Protestant workmen undermined any trust that had built up. With the ideological weight given to a social-ist programme integral to Goulding's strategy for republicanism during the 1960s, associations with militarism were destructive. From a political perspective, the continued activity of the Official IRA was deeply prob-lematic.

THE OFFICIAL CEASEFIRE AND THE OIRA–INLA SPLIT

Issues of militarism plagued the Goulding leadership both before and after the 1969–70 split in the movement. They could hardly expect to increase their support base as long as they remained part of an armed organisation. The cessation of military activity in 1972 was therefore a logical move from the perspective of the political wing of the movement. The momen-tum of the armed struggle had been quickly assumed by the Provisional IRA, a fact borne out by the death toll at the end of 1972: Provisional IRA 335, Official IRA 29. Goulding had been conscious of maintaining a role for the IRA within his plans for the movement and had claimed that he was actively seeking to re-arm the movement,[165] even though 'between the end of the last IRA campaign in 1962 and the beginning of the Ulster troubles in 1968 the IRA has become more politically than militarily orientated and knowledge of how to obtain military supplies has not been kept up to date'.[166] How serious his attempts to maintain the IRA as a credible army were is therefore unclear.

Although it was claimed that 'the Marxist Officials, not the Provisionals . . . coldly set out to break up the confidence that threatened to develop between the British Army and the Ulster Catholic community in the winter of 1969',[167] the reality was that Official IRA weapons were for defensive purposes and appeals for arms were made on this basis.[168] To this end, the Official IRA did confront the British Army in July 1970 with the imposition of the Falls curfew, action that boosted recruitment but also saw several volunteers arrested.[169] Statistics prove that the Provisional IRA assumed the armed struggle almost immediately, killing significantly more than the Official IRA during each of the early years of the troubles.[170]

The need for weaponry for defensive purposes became all-too obvious as feuding broke out between the two factions in early 1971. Although the split had no clear geographical basis, the Official republicans found themselves strongest in the Lower Falls area of West Belfast, with the

Provisionals strongest in Ardoyne, in North Belfast.[171] The feuding was overtaken by clashes with troops as the PIRA killed their first soldiers, effectively heeding the call of Tomás Mac Giolla for the groups to face their common enemy rather than each other.[172] The Official IRA continued to recruit, particularly after the introduction of internment without trial in August 1971.[173] Late that same year, they killed unionist senator Jack Barnhill in Strabane, a killing that prompted the resignation of Roy Johnston from the movement.[174]

Those military operations that the Official IRA did embark on during 1972 were largely counterproductive. The Official IRA fired at soldiers on Bloody Sunday, undoubtedly contributing to the violence of the day.[175] They then retaliated against the Parachute Regiment by bombing the Aldershot barracks of the regiment in February; a bombing that failed to kill a single soldier, rather claiming the lives of five female civilians and an Army chaplain. On 16 April, they killed three soldiers in Derry, but then lost talismanic volunteer Joe McCann that month, killed by the Parachute Regiment. The comparative efficiency of the Derry wing of the OIRA was undermined by mass protests against the movement following their murder of Ranger William Best in May. Goulding's attempts to retain the support of militarists was now acting to the detriment of organisational aims, and although Des O'Hagan could argue that the ceasefire 'showed the political understanding and the capacity to grasp what was actually happening in Northern Ireland which no one else had',[176] the truth was that the Official IRA campaign had damaged the political credibility of the movement, which the leadership could not abide. The Official IRA declared a ceasefire on 30 May 1972. For John Lowry:

> It would be wrong to suggest that in May 1972 the decision to declare the ceasefire was greeted . . . with 100 per cent approval . . . in Belfast . . . there would have been a large influx of members whose motivation was largely coming from '69 . . . when the ceasefire was announced in May 1972 and when it dawned on them within weeks that this was actually for real – this wasn't some sort of PR stunt – they became disgruntled. The vast majority of them walked away and left . . . there could have been as many as 250 members in Andersonstown, by 1973 and 1974 that had been reduced to maybe 50 and it was because of . . . a rejection of the ceasefire.[177]

While contrary to the political ambitions of the leadership, militarism persisted within the movement, led by Seamus Costello:

> Costello himself never really accepted it . . . Costello believed that you could have socialist politics in one hand and armed struggle in the other. He first got

into trouble in the 1973 Ard Fheis . . . he had been at that ever since 1972 . . . it was very much the case that he still very much believed in armed struggle in the North and that's why he did maintain contacts with the likes of Brian Keenan [and] Dáithí Ó Conaill . . . he had this attitude . . . there were young Provisionals who we should seek an alliance with . . . by 1974 he had been suspended from the organisation.[178]

Continued militarism is evidenced by the fact that the OIRA continued to kill through to 1977.[179] It is important to note that a series of OIRA operations from this period bore all the hallmarks of an efficient guerrilla movement, notably the killings of RUC Sergeant Thomas Morrow of Newry and UDR captain and Catholic Ulster Unionist Party member Marcus McCausland of Derry.[180] In the midst of these attacks, the death of Bernadette Hyndman during an OIRA attack on soldiers reminded those in the organisation that it could not reasonably claim to be a movement of the people while it was killing innocent civilians.

Official IRA operations declined noticeably from 1972 to 1973 and remained at a low level the following year. During 1974 Michael Gaughan died while on hunger strike in Parkhurst prison on the Isle of Wight. He had been sentenced for his part in a bank robbery in London where £530 was stolen.[181] Gaughan had joined the English wing of the Official IRA, Clann na hÉireann, in 1971 while in London seeking employment. He joined the hunger strike in support of the Price sisters, Dolours and Marian, in their quest for political status and the right to be transferred to an Irish prison. Marian recalls, 'he died in the week that our hunger strike ended. His death pushed forward any moves to bring our hunger strike to a conclusion from the British government.'[182] The treatment of Gaughan and his fellow hunger strikers, notably the British policy of force feeding, drew considerable attention. He died after sixty-four days and his coffin was draped in the same tricolour that had been used for Terence MacSwiney's funeral in 1920.

During 1974, the Official IRA was active, killing former members and involving itself in gun battles with the Army.[183] The militants within the organisation were becoming agitated: 'the Provos in 1974 were bombing bars in the Shankill and getting involved in blatant sectarian actions on the border. There was an element within the army that wanted action on this front.'[184] The press noted that 'militant members of the Official IRA who have been held in restraint with increasing difficulty since the movement declared a ceasefire on May 30th, 1972, are becoming increasingly restive and it is thought that some significant defections to the Provisionals cannot for long be delayed'.[185] The physical force tradition remained strong and the PIRA campaign in England, notably the Guildford bomb of 5 October and the Birmingham bomb of 21 November 1974, underlined the new dimension of their campaign and served as evidence of the lengths that Provisional republicans could and would go to in order to bring the struggle for Irish freedom to the door of the British.[186]

These problems had cost the movement support in the aftermath of the split. Martin McGuinness recalled, 'the Officials wouldn't give us any action . . . Occasionally [they] gave out Molotov cocktails which couldn't even go off.'[187] While some have argued that the Officials remained the more numerous and effective of the two republican factions and the militancy of OIRA men in Derry helped to stymie the growth of the PIRA there until 1972,[188] the physical force tradition was powerful. However, the political struggle of the movement had begun in earnest; Official Sinn Féin had contested its first Dáil election in late February 1973, achieving a mere 15,000 votes. It was considered that military activity had undermined the political agenda of the movement. Division was, once again, imminent. On 8 December 1974, Seamus Costello founded the Irish Republican Socialist Party. Also prominent was Bernadette McAliskey, née Devlin, who argued, 'the Provos are concentrating on getting rid of the British in a military campaign without any policy on the class war, and the Officials now have no policy on the national question . . . We will agitate on both the national and class issues.'[189]

ENDING ABSTENTION

The political programme of the Official republicans inevitably challenged the policy of abstentionism. It had been an issue for Cathal Goulding from the point he assumed control of the movement.[190] The move away from abstentionism was justified on the grounds that it 'did not imply recognition of these bodies but was intended to subvert their authority from within'.[191] An OIRA-published pamphlet claimed that the decision removed 'restrictions on the leadership in regard to electoral policy so that they could use the tactics best suited to the occasion to smash the power of the establishment', adding there was 'no question of ever giving recognition to the legitimacy of the authority of these parliaments'.[192]

Historical precedent suggested that, as controversial as the abandonment of abstentionism was throughout republican history, groups entering electoral politics quickly reaped the benefits of the move. Roy Johnston argued that Sinn Féin could have won the 1966 Mid-Ulster election, where Independent Republican Tom Mitchell lost to Unionist George Forrest by 2560 votes, if they had not been abstaining at this time, even though some felt that the republican movement was unready for parliament.[193] This was a seat Mitchell had previously won in 1955, only to be unseated because his conviction as a felon made him ineligible. The 1969 election of Bernadette Devlin to this seat emphasised that the radicalism the Official republicans perceived within their own movement could be attractive to constituents there. In the immediate aftermath of the split in Sinn Féin, Tomás Mac Giolla stated quite confidently that support was mounting in the party for a change in their abstentionist policy.[194] This was corroborated by the fact that the majority of delegates at the fateful 1970 Ard Fheis actually supported the motion, although the necessary two-thirds majority was not achieved.[195]

Allied to the decreased military activity on the part of the OIRA, many recognised the opportunity for the movement to embrace and integrate into working-class politics.[196] The perception of the movement as becoming increasingly politicised was indicated by the fact that as early as 1972 Northern Ireland Secretary of State, William Whitelaw, spoke of removing the ban on the Republican Clubs. Soon after, the Officials became registered with the Registrar of Political Parties under the Electoral Act,[197] which meant they were now free to contest elections, a privilege they quickly took advantage of. It is interesting to note that although Republican Clubs were legalised in the North, Sinn Féin (Gardiner Place)[198] remained a proscribed organisation. It was noted that 'Republican Clubs leaders in the North have been at pains to emphasise that Sinn Féin (Gardiner Place) is exactly the same organisation as the Six County Republican Clubs.'[199] This served to fuel further allegations of conspiracy, with Ulster Vanguard Unionist leader William Craig declaring the OIRA to be just as dangerous as the PIRA[200] and stating that 'it would not only be unwise but illegal for any club, however constitutional in character, to call itself Republican'.[201] Social Democratic and Labour Party (SDLP) leader Gerry Fitt, on the other hand, 'had always regarded Republican Clubs as a legitimate political movement, and while there might be areas with which he might disagree, he would fight tenaciously to ensure that they had the opportunity to put their politics and programme before the electorate'.[202]

Declared legal in April, Republican Clubs contested the May 1973 local government elections, entering eighty-three candidates. Although they had abandoned their stated policy of abstention, they declared that in the event that they achieved success at these elections, they were planning to maintain abstentionism in protest at the continuation of internment without trial, a stance they maintained in the 1974 Westminster election campaign.[203] Republican Clubs polled a total of 20,680 votes, 3 per cent of the valid poll in 1973, gaining two seats in Belfast, one in Armagh, one in Cookstown, one in Derry, one in Magherafelt and two in Newry and Mourne for a total of eight seats; those standing as Official Republicans won in Dungannon and Omagh, giving the movement ten seats in total. Although they were some distance from the eighty-three seats of the SDLP and the group had hoped for greater representation, the signs were encouraging for the movement. The geographic spread of their vote was particularly encouraging, with their ability to attract support across Northern Ireland providing a solid foundation.[204]

In the February 1974 General Election, they achieved 15,152 total votes, fewer than Bernadette McAliskey achieved on her own. Republican Clubs were 16,000 votes short of success in West Belfast, 28,000 votes short in South Down and 29,000 votes short in Londonderry. When Harold Wilson called a second General Election in October in an attempt to achieve a Labour majority at Westminster, Republican Clubs increased both their total vote and share of the vote, but they only achieved six seats during the 1977 local elections and their vote fell again in the 1979 General Election. The change of name to Sinn Féin The Workers' Party in 1977, part of an attempt to reach out to the working class and to distance themselves from PIRA violence, had proven unsuccessful.[205] There was evidence of potential within the party, but this potential was contingent on the expansion of their support base. At a relatively early stage in their post-abstention era, they were in a considerably stronger position from which to make political advances than they had been a decade previously, but still toiled for legitimacy within the Northern nationalist communities. The Official republicans found themselves squeezed politically by a variety of non-sectarian groups that had a far more stable foundation than Republican Clubs, and were certainly not tarred by links to paramilitary groups. Militarily, the Official IRA ceasefire told its own tale. Official republicans no longer saw merit in the armed struggle, and its abandonment effectively cut the group off from the support of those who did. The military initiative was therefore seized by the Provisional republicans, and other important reasons for this can be found in a series of events from the 1970s that polarised the British security forces and the nationalist communities of Northern Ireland.

SEAMUS COSTELLO, THE IRSP AND THE INLA

Efforts on the part of Official leaders had failed to marginalise the militarists within the movement. The military struggle had largely been abandoned, but the militaristic tendency persisted. The desire for action manifested itself in a split. With the Provisional IRA ceasefire of late 1974, there was no republican paramilitary group involved in offensive action against the state. Into this void appeared the Irish Republican Socialist Party and Irish National Liberation Army.[206] They argued that their split 'represented divisions of a deeper nature concerning the Officials' analysis that the movement had to integrate its commitment to Ireland's national liberation with a revolutionary orientation towards the economic and social interests of the working class'.[207] Seamus Costello, who had given up his career as a car salesman in his quest for revolution in Ireland, had been keen to open up a new way forward, balancing the national and social questions. For him, this meant fighting elections in the Republic and entering the Dáil, the refusal to do so he viewed as self-defeating, and developing a radical social policy.

Some considered the OIRA ceasefire as the beginning of the IRSP,[208] although Costello had believed the ceasefire to be tactical, designed to free volunteers from internment. Thomas 'Ta' Power declared that 'the 4th December 1974 is the date when the IRSP publicly and formally announced its formation, but it didn't spring up fully formed out of the blue; it, like everything else, had its roots in history, going back to the 1960s and the leftward direction which the Republican Movement was embarking on.'[209] The leadership had 'used bureaucratic manipulation and subterfuge to cripple internal democracy, thereby permitting them to push through a ceasefire in mid-1972 and to steer a course towards political reformism'.[210] The Costello faction disagreed strongly with the politics of reformism, assuming a stance that was completely at odds with the leadership of the movement. The leadership began to move against Costello during 1974. Many future members of the IRSP had already left the movement either by expulsion or resignation. Official republicans in Dun Laoghaire claimed that 65 per cent of its membership had departed because of opposition to the leadership.[211] Towards the end of the year, a motion to reinstate Costello was defeated by an overwhelming majority and the split became inevitable.

For Danny Morrison, the IRSP split was 'welcomed as a recognition that they [Official Republicans] had got it wrong on a number of fronts including

75

reformism, their ceasefire, the fact that they had actually feuded with our organisation'.[212] The Spa Hotel Lucan in the outskirts of Dublin was the location for the first IRSP meeting on 8 December. Eighty like-minded republicans joined Costello with the aim of finding a means to 'end imperialist rule in Ireland and establish a 32-county democratic socialist republic with the working class in control of the means of production, distribution and exchange'.[213] The Official leadership in Dublin denied the split at the time, in spite of the resignation of one hundred members in the North Munster region,[214] although they have been accused of being 'totally out of step with the mass struggle that was going on'.[215]

As had been common during the early 1970s, the IRSP reached out to Protestants, stating that 'if the British presence in the country were ended, and if the loyalist working class in the North were convinced that it was ended . . . we feel that the natural tendency on their part would be to think in terms of class politics within this island'.[216] Their position was that republicanism had never appealed to Protestants because of internal republican tensions, but maintained that 'it is only those on the left of republicanism who have anything relevant to say to the protestant working class in the North'.[217] Their claims were legitimised thanks to the presence of Ronnie Bunting, the son of Paisley-ally Major Ronald Bunting, and one of the few Protestants interned in 1971.

In the main, the IRSP attracted former Official republicans who were aggrieved at the refusal of the Ard Chomhairle to implement democratically decided policies on the national question, a lack of internal democracy regarding their reformist policies and the contesting of Assembly elections, a divisive issue in the split five years previously. Roy Johnston claimed that best attempts had been made to 'transform the Fenian conspiratorial tradition into an open principled democratic one, using the best aspects of the Marxist democratic-revolutionary tradition, and trying to avoid top-down Stalinism, though this kept surfacing via Costello and those for whom the military tradition was dominant'.[218]

It was argued that Costello sought a campaign of '"tit-for-tat" sectarian killings in the North',[219] and defections from the PIRA did occur. Dessie O'Hagan believes that Costello 'was envious of the whiff of sulphur that the Provos were generating in the north and he wanted to be part of that . . . Dáithí Ó Conaill he . . . maintained close links with'.[220] The culture of personality that permeated the IRSP and INLA throughout their history can be traced back to Costello. For Marian Price, 'you will find that some people are really good with the theory of things and the politics but when it comes to the military side of things, they're not so good . . . Seamus Costello was someone who had both.'[221] The IRSP speak reverentially of him:

> he was a one-off character, the likes of whom I doubt we'll ever see again, Connolly's daughter said it was the closest thing to her dad she'd ever seen. Dr Noel Browne said that he went to watch Costello in action . . . He kept this audience for three hours . . . Another 200 people came back that night at 7 o'clock to listen to him again and he went through it all over again. He seemed to have a boundless energy. His wife told us that he would have slept a total of 3 or 4 hours . . . He was Chief of Staff of the INLA, he was national chairperson of the IRSP, he was on 26 different committees at the time of his assassination . . . Some would say he was a very intelligent but arrogant man, very impatient. Seamus knew what had to be done, wanted it done now and expected everyone to be as energetic as him. Those round him were 110% committed . . . but there might have been other things going on – health . . . family . . . work that they just couldn't give 23 hours a day to it like Seamus seemed to be doing.[222]

Although Costello's brand of republican socialism drove the party, much of its political credibility rested with Bernadette McAliskey, who had served as Member of Parliament for Mid-Ulster from 1969 until 1974 and was a highly visible figure in the civil rights movement. She stood out among the IRSP for her lack of republican background, although her husband Martin had been an Official IRA member.[223] One cynic remarked that 'Mrs McAliskey's interest in the new party stemmed from two needs which she keenly felt – the need for membership of a party to end her isolated individualist position and the need for funds for the convention elections.'[224] The party quickly established itself, with thirty-five branches by January 1975 and a membership of around six hundred.

The recruitment of McAliskey and the politically charged rhetoric could not mask the militarism that existed in the movement. The Irish National Liberation Army, as it would come to be known, was founded a matter of minutes after the political party:

> Costello formed the IRSP first and as everybody left to go about their business, Costello and five or ten others remained and decided to form an organisation that through time would be known as the INLA. They were busy then procuring weapons and money to procure weapons, a lot of this, believe it or not, without people like Bernadette McAliskey and Terry Robson even knowing . . . they were away doing their political work and it was only when people made it known to Costello that the Officials, certainly in Belfast, weren't going to take this lying down, the centre of the organisation switched to the INLA.[225]

The armed wing was to be 'the cutting edge of the party',[226] and recruitment across the organisation was a priority. Drawing support from Official republican areas, notably the Markets and Divis Flats areas of central Belfast, the IRSP recruited heavily from Fianna Éireann, the youth wing of the OIRA which at the time was run by Billy McMillen. One source estimated that approximately 60 per cent of Fianna Éireann left to join the new group.[227] One such youth was Gerard Steenson, who became one of the most notorious republican gunmen of the troubles. Official republicans in Belfast were fearful of the loss of territory and the Divis Flats quickly became known as the 'Planet of the Irps', although the group was also strong in Derry, already noted as being an area of OIRA militancy.[228] The initial lack of recruitment from PIRA changed as the IRSP became a refuge for nomadic republicans. Rather than attracting motivated republicans, Eamonn McCann argues the group aimed to 'recruit the hooligans into a socialist organisation . . . But what the hooligans wanted now more than anything else was action . . . At every meeting someone would ask sooner or later when the guns were going to be handed out.'[229] Jim Cantwell of Republican Clubs argued that 'the whole logic of the IRSP drift is to engage in sectarian warfare'.[230]

Predictably, the descent into internecine feuding was rapid. After announcing its formation on 4 December, the IRSP became involved in a feud with the Official IRA eight days later, for the IRSP, a 'policy decision made by the Army Council of the Officials to smash the IRSP at any cost'.[231] Seamus Costello contended the feud indicated the 'total irrelevance and political bankruptcy'[232] of the OIRA and argued that 'the IRSP is undermining the Officials organisationally'.[233] The irony in the latter comment would not have been lost on Official republican leaders; the fact that Costello and his militarist tendencies had been undermining Official republican attempts to move away from violence was precisely the reason that he was forced out of the movement.

If the first item on the agenda for any new republican group was the split, the early 1970s suggested that the second item may well have been the feud. Billy McQuiston, a former UDA volunteer, recalled that 'the general feeling among working-class loyalist people was "great, go ahead, kill each other"'.[234] The OIRA–IRSP feud stunted the political development of the latter, with Bernadette McAliskey commenting that the IRSP's fastest-growing branch was located in Belfast's Royal Victoria Hospital.[235] For Eoin Ó Broin:

> The IRSP and the INLA were in trouble from the very beginning in real terms . . . [while] the project might have had, from their point of view, some credibility at an early stage, the rapid onset of in-fighting, of feuding and criminality by an

element of people within that organisation made its existence hugely untenable and hugely volatile.[236]

Rather bizarrely, while embroiled in the feud, the IRSP leaders were busy promoting their theoretical anti-imperialist broad front. Costello had promoted this idea within the Official republican movement in 1972, but it met with suspicions that it would merely be a vehicle for swinging the party's support behind Provisional republicanism. At the IRSP's first Bodenstown commemoration in 1975, he stated that 'the most important and immediate task now confronting us, is the creation of a broad front in the struggle for national liberation . . . we believe unity is essential, if we are to succeed'.[237] The irony of calling for unity in the aftermath of a split may have been lost on Costello, and commentators noted that 'instead of a broad front, however, the republican movement was about to witness the worst factional blood letting in many years'.[238] The Official IRA claimed that 'these people were stealing our weapons, raiding our dumps and beating up our members . . . Personally I couldn't care less if they left the organisation. But there was no way they were going to use our weapons to wage sectarian war.'[239]

Goulding himself admitted that the 'confrontation between OIRA and IRSP was inevitable. The main reason for this was the theft of arms . . .'[240] A second, more serious, feud began in late February 1975. The first member of the INLA to die was nineteen-year-old Hugh Ferguson, shot dead by Official IRA gunmen. The feud centred on the Divis Flats complex at the foot of the Falls Road, with a series of deaths occurring nearby. From the IRSP perspective:

> [There were] a couple of shootings, five or six people were kneecapped and Costello was told 'they're going to kill, we need to protect the IRSP, they're putting posters up and they're being shot', so the People's Liberation Army was formed by people in Belfast who had a few weapons and Hugh Ferguson was shot dead, the first to be killed. Even at 18 years of age he was holding meetings in community centres with two or three hundred people. Provisionals have told me listening to him speak was unbelievable, he was sort of like a Costello-type figure. He was shot dead and his comrades in Belfast went buck mad to be honest and that grudge was always held against Billy McMillen.[241]

While the IRSP claimed to be acting in self-defence, and certainly evidence suggests that Official republicans had been the initial aggressors,[242] the rapid escalation of the INLA campaign rather undermined this claim. The IRSP claimed that the INLA was merely a group of individuals sympathetic to their cause, claims that were important to retain the political legitimacy of the IRSP, particularly McAliskey. The People's Liberation Army, a title commonly used by socialist forces, and the National Liberation Army initially claimed responsibility for operations before the army decided to call itself the INLA. As late as 1982 the group continued to claim that 'the INLA and the IRSP are two independent entities, with no relationship between them, although some of us may belong to both. In order to increase popular support for the armed struggle it is essential that we have a party that can work openly.'[243] For their part, the IRSP claimed that 'we support the Irish National Liberation Army . . . it shares our belief that the social and national struggles are inseparable and recognises . . . that their arms should not be laid down until the final victory of the working class'.[244] Certainly, political posters from the time clearly link the two groups.[245]

The feud damaged both participants. Perhaps the most prominent victim of the feud was Official IRA leader Billy McMillen. After two months of feuding, on 28 April a meeting took place during which McMillen called for a cessation of violence so peace talks could begin with the IRSP.[246] Shortly after he gave this order, he was shot dead by sixteen-year-old Gerard Steenson in the lower Falls area of West Belfast. This act would become symbolic of the INLA; the contrast between what is politically beneficial to the group (in this case not killing a prominent leader of a rival faction) and what is desirable militarily in terms of a trophy killing. Steenson was later dubbed 'Dr Death' by the media, such were his abilities as 'one of Northern Ireland's most case-hardened terrorists'.[247] Journalist Kevin Myers recalls the sight of Steenson firing on an Army patrol even prior to the McMillen killing, describing an 'infant Rommel'.[248] A judge, sentencing him in the 1980s, called him 'undoubtedly the most dangerous and sinister terrorist – a ruthless and highly dedicated, resourceful and indefatigable planner of criminal exploits who did not hesitate to take a leading part in assassinations and other crimes . . . society needs protection from him',[249] yet a former comrade described him as 'in the same class as Michael Collins. Like Collins, he was a military genius.'[250] To others, 'he looked like an altar boy but he was a psychopath',[251] 'he just looked like a . . . fresh-faced, conservatively dressed businessman. His father, who didn't drink or smoke, a strict Catholic, was totally shocked when he found some of the things Gerard had carried out.'[252]

McMillen's murder deeply angered Seamus Costello; not only was he on good terms with McMillen, the death undermined hopes of political settlement between the warring factions and brought unwanted attention on the movement:

> Costello hadn't sanctioned that. Costello swore and cursed and smashed the phone to pieces because he knew what was going to happen, he wasn't a stupid man. He was more angry because the name INLA was used to claim the killing and that angered him more because he had Airey Neave in his sights, these plans were being made and here were a couple of boys in Belfast who'd bucked it up.[253]

The IRSP condemned 'without reservation the shooting of Billy McMillen and the IRSP was in no way involved'.[254] In response to the killing, the Official IRA Army Council sentenced Seamus Costello to death.[255] The plan to kill Airey Neave was postponed and took a further four years.

The man labelled 'the authentic voice of working-class Belfast'[256] by Cathal Goulding was a significant loss to the Official republicans. Danny Morrison recalls that 'Billy McMillen was actually fairly well "got" amongst republicans and Gerry Adams would have still been on speaking terms with him, they'd gone back to the sixties together . . .'[257] Indeed, Adams was invited to join the movement by McMillen, who had expected Adams to join the Officials following the split.[258] Adams acknowledges McMillen's influence on him at a young age,[259] and Roy Johnston notes the efforts that McMillen had made to learn politics during the 1960s.[260] McMillen had been important in pushing for political activity as a means of educating the younger members of the organisation, in addition to maintaining military training for new recruits.[261] It was noted that 'a lot of volunteers stayed loyal to the Officials because of Billy McMillen. He was respected within the organisation.'[262] McMillen had been able to expand the Belfast battalion to such an extent that the IRA had to divide it into three companies.[263]

At his funeral, Goulding spoke emotively about McMillen, but the implicit siege mentality within Official republicanism was also noteworthy:

> An Orange Junta sent Liam McMillen to prison because he fought for separation. The Provisional Alliance attempted to assassinate him because he held his socialist principles and fought for civil rights. The RUC and the British Army of occupation harassed and hounded him because he was a socialist republican. A small, mad band of fanatical malcontents, the sewer rats of Costello and McAliskey who finally laid him low.[264]

The Provisional IRA's 1975 ceasefire saw members depart to join the INLA.[265] The increase in membership prompted a rise in INLA activity and increased the profile of the organisation. This, in turn, prompted Costello and McAliskey to hold a series of public meetings in May 1975 to raise the profile of the party.[266] Around the same time, the issue of abstention was raised when McAliskey called for the party to contest elections, the party never having declared its stance towards the policy. Although she was supported by Costello, the motion was defeated on the grounds that the party rejected the existence of Stormont and considered it unrevolutionary and reactionary that the Official republicans had decided to contest elections; they argued that 'there is no parliamentary route to socialism',[267] and therefore would only contest elections for self-promotion. Although McAliskey's popularity was on the wane by 1974, she still achieved 16,000 votes, 21,000 fewer than four years previously, but still a credible return for the IRSP.

McAliskey ally Eamonn McCann applied to join the IRSP in the summer of 1975. Keen to avoid links with the 'politically irrelevant far left',[268] Costello asked that first he resign from the International Socialists. McCann withdrew his application and the episode tarnished the Costello–McAliskey relationship. Towards the end of 1975, McAliskey refused Costello's invitation to join the Army Council and, fearful of further splits, led her supporters out of the party. McAliskey described the IRSP as 'being objectively indistinguishable from either wing of the republican movement and possibly combining the worst elements of both',[269] later icily commenting that the INLA's philosophy was just 'an armalite in one hand and a blast bomb in the other'.[270]

During its first two years of operation, the INLA killed five and six. This was considerably lower than the PIRA totals of seventy-nine and 112 and hardly spoke of a movement that was effectively conducting its military campaign. With sectarian murder rising during 1976, the PIRA Kingsmills massacre and the Shankill butcher killings notable, along with further OIRA–PIRA feuding,[271] INLA operations became increasingly sophisticated.

The shooting of Private Alan Watkins in Derry on 3 August 1976 appeared fairly typical until the military support squad found that the INLA had booby-trapped the building from which Watkins was shot in anticipation of a search-and-arrest operation, the Army describing this as 'particularly macabre ingenuity'.[272] The organisation's improved bomb-making capacity troubled the security forces. A former E4A officer[273] noted that because of the small size of and lack of structure in the INLA, especially in the Derry area, operations were typically planned and carried out within a matter of hours, decided upon by a few individuals.[274] To conceive and almost execute such a deadly attack on the Army in a relatively short space of time highlighted the potency of the INLA at this early stage of their war. The relative efficiency of the OIRA in Derry prior to the ceasefire should also be recalled, suggesting OIRA defections had been high in the North-west.

Events of 1977 altered the path of republican socialism permanently. The murder of pensioner Hester McMullan, the mother of an RUC reservist, was an historic case for Ireland and involved the INLA. Provisional IRA volunteer Dominic McGlinchey, considered by Special Branch to be a 'psycho killer',[275] was the first person to be extradited from the Republic to Northern Ireland for the killing. By the time his extradition passed, he had switched allegiance to the INLA, a symbol of the renegade military ethos that pervaded the movement:

> They say that when he was in Portlaoise that he left the Provos and went to the INLA. The Provos say that he couldn't take orders, he wanted to be the big guy, so they threw him out, court-martialled him . . . some would say there was other stuff involved.[276]

The INLA killed only two that year; one victim was seventy-three-year-old Robert Whitten, the brother of Unionist Party Convention member Herbert Whitten,[277] but it was the losses that they suffered that caused the most damage. Since the murder of Billy McMillen, Seamus Costello had remained quite 'fatalistic'[278] and on 5 October his fears were realised. The death sentence passed down to Costello by the Official IRA had never been revoked but Costello continued to carry out his business as normal: 'it was so easy for the Officials to kill him that day because he didn't tell people where he was going, he didn't want bodyguards with him'.[279] He had set up a series of meetings in Dublin to discuss the importation of arms, making the mistake of developing a routine, which was spotted by OIRA volunteers. 'He was just sitting reading the paper when Jimmy Flynn shot him dead.'[281] The 'murderous actions of counter-revolutionaries'[281] was the first assassination of a party leader in the history of the Republic,[282] and a hammer blow from which the IRSP would never fully recover. For Thomas 'Ta' Power:

> With no disrespect to those around at the time of Seamus Costello's assassination, there wasn't simply any individual person there to match his intellectual and political maturity, nor his ability as chief of staff . . . Without Costello [acting as a] buffer zone the balance tilted in favour of 'physical force' men . . . [283]

Even in 2010, the IRSP still reflects ruefully upon the loss of Costello:

The blow with Seamus being assassinated was unbelievable. Basically everything Seamus kept in his head. Militarily, the INLA suffered because all the routes to bring weapons in, the contacts, some very large dumps that people to this day say are lying in the Wicklow mountains, that was all in Seamus's head . . . A lot went with Seamus and a lot of people then went and left . . . There was turmoil and those behind it, which was certainly establishment as well, knew that by killing Costello what would happen. Noel Browne said, 'You weren't going to stop him, you'd have to kill him.'[284]

The organisation was now forced to completely restructure and university lecturer Miriam Daly took over the leadership of the political party. The group took on an increasingly criminal element, one robbery of a Brinks-Mat security van near Limerick yielding almost half a million pounds, facilitating the purchase of their head office. Costello House still operates on the junction of Donegal Road and the Falls Road in West Belfast. Further tribute was paid to Costello when the INLA carried out the murder of Airey Neave, an operation that had apparently been five years in the making.

Neave was one of the key personnel behind Margaret Thatcher's rise to the position of leader of the Conservative Party, which at the end of the seventies found itself in opposition to James Callaghan's Labour government. Callaghan's Secretary of State for Northern Ireland, Roy Mason, had masterminded the introduction of the deeply unpopular Ulsterisation/criminalisation policy which targeted paramilitary prisoners in particular. Miriam Daly, involved in IRSP prisoner welfare, had accused Mason of attempting to smash the IRSP.[285] A plan to kill Mason's political agent before targeting Mason at his funeral was formulated,[286] strikingly sociopathic even for a Northern Irish paramilitary group. When this proved unworkable and the Labour government began to look electorally vulnerable for the 1979 General Election,[287] Neave re-emerged as their target. The INLA targeted Neave because 'he was well known for his rabid militarist calls for more repression against the Irish people and for the strengthening of the SAS murder squads'.[288] So unpopular among republicans was Neave, it was reported that the IRA had been targeting him, only to be beaten to the killing by the INLA.[289]

Surprisingly weak security at the House of Commons allowed the INLA operatives to enter the car park below on 30 March disguised as workmen. They used a mercury tilt-switch bomb, rather complicated in design; the circuit remained incomplete until the car drove up an incline, at which point the mercury would slide into place, completing the circuit and detonating the bomb. As Neave drove up the exit ramp on his way out of the car park, the bomb detonated, Neave dying in hospital shortly afterwards. It was estimated that the bomb that claimed his life cost £5.12.[290] Neave was the first Member of Parliament to be assassinated since the 1812 killing of Prime Minister Spencer Perceval.[291] When compared to almost any other INLA operation, the killing of Neave was so complicated and professional that some commented that the INLA had merely been 'lucky'.[292] The tilt-switch bomb was uncommon and somewhat ahead of its time, another aspect that makes this a rather atypical INLA operation. Afterwards, the INLA claimed 'that in terms of firepower it is now the most formidably equipped paramilitary group in the country'.[293] History suggests that this claim was slightly premature, the group only killing six people in 1979, another six in 1980 and nine in 1981, although they did, in 1982, kill thirty-one, making them the second most deadly paramilitary group in the country behind the Provisional IRA.

Politically, it is easy to dismiss the IRSP. The INLA quickly assumed control of the movement and, with the loss of Costello, the only personality who could remedy this imbalance, the party was unable to reassert itself on the movement. Once McAliskey departed, again thanks to the actions of the INLA, the IRSP was doomed to life in the shadows of its paramilitary wing. The INLA ended the decade in an uncertain position. They were still suffering from the loss of Costello, but had proven their abilities as deadly insurgents. The integrity of the group throughout the 1970s was crucial to their campaign but cracks began to appear just as the movement placed itself alongside the Provisional IRA during the prison protests that culminated with the 1980 and 1981 hunger strikes.

Austen Morgan argued that the IRSP represented the party that the Officials could have become; as republicans searched for new revolutionaries, the desire to attain such status has become counterproductive and has marginalised working-class politics. The Officials reoriented their enemy from the British to the Irish bourgeoisie, which Morgan attributes to the group taking themselves too seriously.[294] Those organisations on the left of Irish republicanism had paid a particularly high price for the incessant feuding that led to the deaths of two charismatic leaders in Seamus Costello and Billy McMillen. The feuds themselves were bitterly ironic given the aspirations of those involved to create some form of broad-based movement to support the cause of Irish unity. Although the republican socialist political tendency and its ideological broad front

edged closer to oblivion over the course of the 1970s, the Official republicans moved ever closer to their stated aim of political participation as a
means to create their own broad front.

THE 1970S: CONCLUSIONS

The republican movement's proclivity for schism was in evidence throughout the 1970s. What was significant about the splits that took place over
the course of the 1970s was the durability of the newly formed organisations. The onset of the troubles provided a different context in which the
new organisations had to develop, with the period defined by militarism,
support for which, although never all-encompassing, increased through
rising communal tension associated with the civil rights campaign and
boosted by loyalist and security force action during the late 1960s and
early 1970s. Strategically, organisations could focus on the very visible
presence of the British Army, in addition to the local security forces, as
both a grievance and an outlet for militarism. Socialist aspirations were
badly affected by the targeting of the RUC and UDR as Protestants began
to perceive a sectarian element to the republican armed struggle.

The ability to take the republican struggle to the enemy was integral to
the ability of republicans, post-split, to attract support. The political programme had proven relatively unpopular and the inability to defend the
Catholic communities of Northern Ireland had cost the republican movement dearly. The lack of awareness of the northern struggle was evident
throughout the 1970s as matters increasingly focused on the North. The
Provisional republican movement assumed the momentum thanks to the
Northern takeover by a younger leadership, more acutely aware of the
needs of republicans in Northern Ireland.

The success of the Provisional republicans was supported by the international network that the movement looked to. While Official republicans were often found looking towards the Soviet Union, the Provisional
IRA enjoyed much more success by tapping into the strong republican
imperative that existed in the United States of America.

By the end of the decade, the politicisation process that Official
republicans had gone through during the 1960s was beginning to seep
into Provisional strategy, most noticeably through the H-Block/Armagh
campaign in support of the demands of paramilitary prisoners. The
cyclical nature of the republican struggle was therefore established and
Cathal Goulding argued that 'we were right too soon, Gerry Adams is

right too late and Ruairí Ó Brádaigh will never be fucking right'.[295] For ex-Provisional Anthony McIntyre, however, 'It's a fair enough point. The problem is Goulding wasn't right.'[296] In the process of being 'right', Goulding had ended the struggle of his IRA and placed the political wing of the movement in charge of the republican movement and set in motion events that would radically alter the history of Ireland.

NOTES

1. *Irish Press* 5/11/1970; Hanley and Millar, *Lost Revolution*, pp. 146–7.
2. Sammy Duddy, interview with author, Belfast, 21/1/2005.
3. Smith, *Fighting For Ireland*, p. 84.
4. *This Week* 17/7/1970.
5. Northern Ireland Future Terrorist Trends – Secret British Army report c. October 1979. BCBL.
6. Hanley and Millar, *Lost Revolution*, p. 166.
7. *IN* 31/1/1990.
8. Milotte, *Communism*, p. 279; English, *Armed Struggle*, p. 119.
9. MácStíofain, *Memoirs*, p. 140.
10. Clifford, *Against Ulster Nationalism*, p. 54.
11. Foster, *Luck and the Irish*, p. 70.
12. Johnston, *Century*, p. 246.
13. Text of an address given by Tomás Mac Giolla, President of Sinn Féin, to the Boston Irish Forum, 31/8/1975.
14. Walsh, *Irish Republicanism*, pp. 103–4.
15. Marian Price, interview with author, Belfast, 1/7/2010; English, *Armed Struggle*, pp. 25–6, 130–2; O'Doherty, *The Trouble with Guns*, p. 20.
16. *An Important Message to the Voters of Waterford*, undated, LHLPC.
17. Lenin, V. I., *Lenin Collected Works* (Moscow: Progress Publishers, 1965), pp. 83–7.
18. *The Politics of The Workers' Party*, undated, LHLPC.
19. Policy Department Internal Memo, 14/2/1972, TNA, FCO 87/101.
20. See Johnston, *Century*, p. 285.
21. *An Phoblacht/Republican News* 28/6/1980.
22. Hanley and Millar, *Lost Revolution*, pp. 157–9.
23. McKittrick et al., *Lost Lives*, pp. 52–4.
24. Lieutenant General Sir Alistair Irwin, former General Officer Commanding, Northern Ireland, interview with author, Aberlour, 16/2/2009.
25. Marian Price, interview with author, Belfast, 1/7/2010.
26. Hanley and Millar, *Lost Revolution*, p. 159.
27. McKittrick et al., *Lost Lives*, pp. 56–7.
28. Marian Price, interview with author, Belfast, 1/7/2010.
29. *Hibernia* 21/1/1972.
30. This operation was justified in the Northern Irish government because there were 'known IRA agitators present in Northern Ireland'. See Conclusions of a meeting of the Cabinet, Thursday, 14 August 1969 at 4.15pm. PRONI ref CAB/4/1460. The

Secretary of State for Foreign and Commonwealth Affairs Sir Alec Douglas-Home stated that the army should respond aggressively to propaganda over internment, indicating the resoluteness of British confidence in the tactic. See Notes of a Meeting at Chequers, Thursday, 19 August 1971. PRONI ref CAB/4/1607.

31. Her Majesty's Stationery Office, The Compton Report: Report of the enquiry into allegations against the Security Forces of physical brutality in Northern Ireland arising out of events on the 9th August, 1971, paragraph 9. Available at http://www.cain.ulst.ac.uk/hmso/compton.htm

32. Smith, D. G., Lt Col. J. D. Watson RE and Harrison, E. P. J., Defence Operational Analysis Establishment Memorandum 7221, 'A Survey of Military Opinion on Current Internal Security Doctrine and Methods based on Experience in Northern Ireland', October 1972. DEFE 48/256, National Archives, p. 27.

33. English, Armed Struggle, p. 140.

34. Pegasus: The Journal of Airborne Forces, Vol. XXVII No. 2 April 1972, p. 8.

35. Her Majesty's Stationery Office, The Compton Report: Report of the enquiry into allegations against the Security Forces of physical brutality in Northern Ireland arising out of events on the 9th August, 1971, paragraph 17. Available at http://www.cain.ulst.ac.uk/hmso/compton.htm

36. Hanley and Millar, Lost Revolution, pp. 170–1.

37. Johnston, Century, p. 278.

38. Richard O'Rawe, interview with author, Belfast, 15/2/2010.

39. Transcript of National Public Radio Programme interview with Father Daly, 25/2/1972; TNA, FCO 87/102.

40. Eoin Ó Broin, interview with author, Belfast, 20/5/2005.

41. MácStíofain, Memoirs, p. 190.

42. Marian Price, interview with author, Belfast, 1/7/2010.

43. Socialist Review, February 1998.

44. News Letter 26/1/1972.

45. Northern Ireland Future Terrorist Trends – Secret British Army report c. October 1979. BCBL.

46. McKittrick et al., Lost Lives, pp. 148–9.

47. Oppenheimer, A. R., IRA The Bombs and Bullets: A History of Deadly Ingenuity (Dublin: Irish Academic Press, 2009), p. 163.

48. Hanley and Millar, Lost Revolution, pp. 174–5.

49. MácStíofain, S., Memoirs, p. 193.

50. Marian Price, interview with author, Belfast, 1/7/2010.

51. See English, Armed Struggle, p. 212.

52. Richard O'Rawe, interview with author, Belfast, 15/2/2010.

53. 'Terms for a bi-lateral truce', TNA, PREM 16/521/2.

54. Richard O'Rawe, interview with author, Belfast, 15/2/2010.

55. Ibid.

56. Speech by Martin McGuinness, then Vice-President of Sinn Féin, on the issue of abstentionism (Resolution 162), Sinn Féin Ard Fheis, Dublin (2 November 1986) http://cain.ulst.ac.uk/issues/politics/docs/sf/mmcg021186.htm

57. Moloney, E., Voices from the Grave, pp. 167–71.

58. McKittrick et al., Lost Lives, pp. 555–8.

59. News Letter 1/8/2005.

60. Parker, J., *Death of a Hero: Captain Robert Nairac, GC and the undercover war in Northern Ireland* (London: Metro, 1999).
61. McKittrick et al., *Lost Lives*, pp. 560–2.
62. English, *Armed Struggle*, p. 163.
63. Richard O'Rawe, interview with author, Belfast, 15/2/2010; Hanley and Millar, *Lost Revolution*, pp. 316–17, 322.
64. *Republican News* 18/10/1975, 29/10/1975 and 1/5/1976.
65. *An Phoblacht* 11/5/2000.
66. Ibid.
67. Ibid.
68. Ibid.
69. Gerard Hodgins, interview with author, Belfast, 25/3/2010.
70. *United Irishman* November 1978.
71. Hanley and Millar, *Lost Revolution*, p. 382.
72. Ross, F. S., *Smashing H-Block: The rise and fall of the popular campaign against criminalisation, 1976–1982* (unpublished PhD Thesis, Queen's University, Belfast 2008).
73. Hanley and Millar, *Lost Revolution*, p. 397.
74. Walsh, *Irish Republicanism and Socialism*, pp. 204–5.
75. Cusack, J. and McDonald, H., *UVF* (Dublin: Poolbeg, 2000), p. 188.
76. Northern Ireland Future Terrorist Trends – Secret British Army report c. October 1979. BCBL.
77. Ibid.
78. Richard O'Rawe, interview with author, Belfast, 15/2/2010.
79. O'Hagan, *The Concept of Republicanism*, p. 6, LHLPC.
80. *Internal Official Republican Movement document relating to Structure of Movement* August 1973, LHLPC.
81. English, *Armed Struggle*, p. 83.
82. Johnston, *Century*, p. 142.
83. Maillot, A., *New Sinn Fein* (London: Routledge, 2005), p. 13; Garvin, T., *The Evolution of Irish Nationalist Politics* (Dublin: Gill and Macmillan, 2005), p. 142.
84. *Internal Official Republican Movement document relating to Structure of Movement* August 1973, LHLPC.
85. Quoted in Berresford Ellis, P., *A History of the Irish Working Class* (London: Pluto Press, 1985), p. 321.
86. Notes from an interview by unnamed source with OIRA volunteer, 20/6/1992, LHLPC.
87. O'Hagan, *The Concept of Republicanism*, p. 11, LHLPC.
88. Communist Party, *Open Letter from the Communist Party of Ireland to the Provisional IRA*, June 1987, in *Armed Struggle* (Dublin: A Communist Party Pamphlet, 1988), pp. 2, 8.
89. See White, *Ruairí Ó Brádaigh*, p. 120.
90. Quoted in *IN* 24/12/1970.
91. *IN* 6/5/1976.
92. Adams, *The Politics*, pp. 131–2.
93. Republican Clubs Craigavon Councillor Malachy McGurran, quoted in *News Letter* 27/3/1978.

94. Cathal Goulding oration from Workers' Party *Wolfe Tone Commemoration Bodenstown 1987*, p. 20.
95. Coombes, A. E., *History after apartheid: Visual Culture and Public Memory in a Democratic South Africa* (Durham, NC: Duke University Press, 2003), p. 82.
96. The poll indicated that only 1 per cent of Catholics had voted UUP and 1 per cent DUP, while 1 per cent of Protestants had voted SDLP with 0 per cent voting Sinn Féin. Source: NI Life and Times Survey *2003 Vote NI* http://www.ark.ac.uk/nilt/2003/Political_Attitudes/VOTENI.html 19/9/2006, last updated 31/5/2004.
97. *Marxism Today* December 1981, p. 31.
98. Cathal Goulding oration from Workers' Party *Wolfe Tone Commemoration Bodenstown 1987*, p. 14.
99. Anthony Coughlan, interview with author, Dublin, 16/6/2010.
100. *IT* 12/4/1971.
101. English, *Armed Struggle*, p. 91.
102. Costello, S., Oration at the First Annual Wolfe Tone Commemoration, Bodenstown, 8/6/1975, LHLPC.
103. IRSP Pamphlet Reprint http://irsm.org/history/loyalism.html 16/6/2004.
104. Ibid.
105. John Lowry, interview with author, Belfast, 9/8/2007.
106. Greaves, C. D., *Northern Ireland: Civil Rights and Political Wrongs* (Dublin: Communist Party Pamphlet, 1969), p. 46.
107. Billy McMillen, Bodenstown 1973, quoted on Clondara Street mural, West Belfast and in Hanley and Millar, *Lost Revolution*, p. 200.
108. Speech by Tomás Mac Giolla, Lurgan County Armagh, 11/6/1972, LHLPC.
109. Dessie O'Hagan, interview with author, Belfast, 9/8/2007.
110. Communist Party, *Open Letter from the Communist Party of Ireland to the Provisional IRA*, June 1987, in *Armed Struggle*, p. 3.
111. Interview with Cathal Goulding, *IN* 31/1/1990.
112. McGuire, *To Take Arms*, p. 116.
113. MácStíofáin, *Memoirs*, p. ix.
114. Ulster Political Research Group, *Common Sense: Northern Ireland – An Agreed Process* (Belfast: Ulster Political Research Group, 1987), p. 1.
115. *In the 70s The IRA Speaks* A Repsol Pamphlet No. 3, undated.
116. Sammy Duddy, interview with author, Belfast, 21/1/2005.
117. Ulster Political Research Group, *Common Sense*, p. 1.
118. *A Brief History of the UDA/UFF in Contemporary Conflict Northern Ireland 1969–1995* (Belfast: UDA, undated), p. 23, LHLPC.
119. Greaves, C. D., *Northern Ireland*, p. 9; Milotte, *Communism*, p. 262.
120. Greaves, *Northern Ireland*, p. 4.
121. Milotte, *Communism*, p. 253.
122. Johnston, *Century*, p. 187, discusses a meeting at the Association of Transport and General Workers Union hall in Belfast in 1965 with both Protestant and Catholics present.
123. Edwards, A., *A History of the Northern Ireland Labour Party: Democratic Socialism and Sectarianism* (Manchester: Manchester University Press, 2009).
124. *Sunday Times* 4/2/1973.
125. Clifford, *Against Ulster Nationalism*, p. 5.

126. *Marxism Today* December 1981, pp. 28–9.
127. Bruce, *The Red Hand*, p. 63.
128. Berresford Ellis, *A History of the Irish Working Class*, pp. 326–7, 331.
129. Garland, *Gusty Spence*, pp. 243–5.
130. Milotte, *Communism*, p. 240.
131. Wood, *Crimes*, pp. 15–16, 19.
132. Sammy Duddy, interview with author, Belfast, 10/11/2006.
133. Dillon, M. and Lehane, D., *Political Murder in Northern Ireland* (Harmondsworth: Penguin, 1973), pp. 147–8; Wood, *Crimes*, pp. 15, 19. See also Berresford Ellis, *A History of the Irish Working Class*, p. 327, and McKittrick et al., *Lost Lives*, pp. 300–1.
134. John Lowry, interview with author, Belfast, 9/8/2007.
135. Ulster Defence Association, *Devolution: The Road to Progressive Democracy* (Belfast: UDA, 1987).
136. *Tribune* 7/6/1974; Wood, *Crimes*, p. 48.
137. Wood, *Crimes*, p. 48.
138. UDA lecture briefing form, LHLPC.
139. Sammy Duddy, interview with author, Belfast, 21/1/2005.
140. Dessie O'Hagan, interview with author, Belfast, 9/8/2007; see also Dillon, M. and Lehane, D., *Political Murder in Northern Ireland*, p. 250.
141. Seamus Costello: Political Biography (The Seamus Costello Memorial Committee, 1979) http://www.irsm.org/irsp/costello/bio/
142. National Council of the Churches of Christ in the USA September 1975 Info Bulletin, NYUL, AIA 22: Irish Republicanism Collection, Box 1 Series A Organizations.
143. Wood, *Crimes*, p. 62.
144. National Council of the Churches of Christ in the USA September 1975 Info Bulletin, NYUL, AIA 22: Irish Republicanism Collection, Box 1 Series A Organizations.
145. Statement from IRSP National Executive, 9/3/1975, LHLPC.
146. *The Plough* Vol. 2 No. 43 14/7/2005.
147. National Council of the Churches of Christ in the USA September 1975 Info Bulletin, NYUL, AIA 22: Irish Republicanism Collection, Box 1 Series A Organizations.
148. *Marxism Today* December 1981, p. 27.
149. John Lowry, interview with author, Belfast, 9/8/2007.
150. Eoin Ó Broin, interview with author, Belfast, 20/5/2005.
151. Anthony McIntyre, interview with author, Belfast, 7/9/2005.
152. Walsh, *Irish Republicanism and Socialism*, p. 135; also Morgan, A., 'Socialism in Ireland – Red, Green and Orange', pp. 172–225, in Morgan and Purdie (eds), *Ireland*, p. 214.
153. Quoted in Sinnerton, *David Ervine*, p. 89; Garland, *Gusty Spence*, p. 55.
154. Garland, *Gusty Spence*, p. 55
155. Sammy Duddy, interview with author, Belfast, 21/1/2005.
156. McGuire, M., *To Take Arms*, pp. 18, 31.
157. Sammy Duddy, interview with author, Belfast, 21/1/2005.
158. Bruce, *The Red Hand*, p. 232.
159. Ibid., p. 235.
160. Wood, *Crimes*, pp. 29, 75. Figures from Northern Ireland Elections 'South Belfast 1973–1984' http://www.ark.ac.uk/elections/csb.htm
161. Johnston, *Century*, p. 413. This is also noted by Crawford, C., *Inside the UDA*, p. 32.

162. Ibid., pp. 72–5.
163. White, *Ruairí Ó Brádaigh*, pp. 168–9.
164. *Irish Independent* 4/11/1972.
165. Cathal Goulding, quoted in *Daily Telegraph* 13/1/1970.
166. Ibid.
167. *Observer* 17/10/1971.
168. Hanley and Millar, *Lost Revolution*, p. 151.
169. Ibid., pp. 157–8.
170. See Malcolm Sutton, An Index of Deaths from the Conflict in Ireland http://www. cain.ulst.ac.uk
171. *Sunday Times* 15/8/1971.
172. *Sunday Press* 14/2/1971.
173. Hanley and Millar, *Lost Revolution*, p. 175.
174. Ibid., p. 246.
175. Bloody Sunday Enquiry Report, 'The Events of the Day' Chapter 3, Vol. 1, 3.11.
176. Dessie O'Hagan, interview with author, Belfast, 9/8/2007.
177. John Lowry, interview with author, Belfast, 9/8/2007.
178. Ibid.
179. See Malcolm Sutton, An Index of Deaths from the Conflict in Ireland http://www. cain.ulst.ac.uk
180. McKittrick, D. et al., *Lost Lives*, pp. 159–60, 164–5.
181. McKittrick, D. et al., *Lost Lives*, pp. 457–8.
182. Marian Price, interview with author, Belfast, 1/7/2010.
183. McKittrick, D. et al., *Lost Lives*, pp. 456–7, 470.
184. Notes from an interview by unnamed source with OIRA volunteer, 20/6/1992, LHLPC.
185. *IT* 19/7/1974.
186. McGladdery, *The Provisional IRA in England*, p. 88.
187. Martin McGuinness quoted in Toolis, K., *Rebel Hearts*, p. 303.
188. Bishop and Mallie, *The Provisional IRA*, p. 120; Patterson, *The Politics of Illusion*, p. 155.
189. *IT* 14/12/1974.
190. Bowyer Bell, J., *The Secret Army*, p. 344.
191. *IN* 28/3/1970.
192. *In the 70s The IRA Speaks* A Repsol Pamphlet No. 3 undated, IRA Box 3, LHLPC.
193. Johnston, *Century*, pp. 202, 226.
194. *IN* 20/12/1969.
195. English, *Armed Struggle*, p. 107.
196. Purdie, B., *Ireland Unfree* (London: International Marxist Group Publications, 1972), p. 37.
197. *Financial Times* 5/8/1971; *IN* 3/4/1973.
198. In the Republic, the two Sinn Féins were distinguished by reference to their head office location. The Officials were based at Gardiner Street and the Provisionals at Upper Kevin Street in Dublin. Gardiner Street had been the Sinn Féin offices prior to the split, a fact that lent legitimacy to Official republicans.
199. *Sunday Press* 8/4/1973.
200. *Irish Independent* 12/4/1973.

201. *Sunday Press* 8/4/1973.
202. *IN* 15/5/1973.
203. *Irish Press* 3/4/1973; *IT* 20/2/1974.
204. Hanley and Millar, *Lost Revolution*, p. 224.
205. Ibid., pp. 336–7.
206. Walsh, *Irish Republicanism and Socialism*, p. 147.
207. Irish Republican Socialist Movement Twenty Years of Struggle http://irsm.org/history/irsm20yr.html 15/06/2004.
208. Sean Flynn, interview with Jack Holland and Henry McDonald, 10/4/1993, available in IRSP box, LHLPC.
209. Thomas Power, *The Ta Power Document* http://irsm.org/history/tapowerdoc.html 27/7/2004; also Holland, J. and McDonald, H., *INLA: Deadly Divisions* (Dublin: Torc, 1994), p. 31.
210. Irish Republican Socialist Movement Twenty Years of Struggle http://irsm.org/history/irsm20yr.html 15/6/2004.
211. *Daily Telegraph* 7/12/1994.
212. Danny Morrison, interview with author, Belfast, 24/1/2005.
213. Press Statement from the IRSP 13/12/1974, LHLPC, IRSP Box.
214. *IN* 7/12/1974.
215. Liam O'Ruairc, 'The Legacy of Seamus Costello', in *The Blanket: A Journal of Protest and Dissent* October/November 2002 http://lark.phoblacht.net/scostello1.html 7/3/2004.
216. *Aims, Principles, and Politics* http://www.irsm.org/history/costello/seamus03.html 30/6/2004.
217. *Republicans and the Protestant Working Class: A Discussion Document* Starry Plough 2/5/2003 http://www.irsm.org/statements/irsp/current/030502.html 30/6/2004.
218. Johnston, *Century*, p. 322.
219. Notes from Confidential Republican Source, IRSP box, LHLPC.
220. Dessie O'Hagan, interview with author, Belfast, 9/8/2007.
221. Marian Price, interview with author, Belfast, 1/7/2010.
222. Fra Halligan, IRSP, interview with author, Belfast, 25/2/2010.
223. Hanley and Millar, *Lost Revolution*, p. 225.
224. Notes from Confidential Republican Source, IRSP box, LHLPC.
225. Fra Halligan, IRSP, interview with author, Belfast, 25/2/2010.
226. Holland and McDonald, *INLA*, p. 32.
227. Journalist, interview with author, Belfast, 15/11/2004.
228. Hanley and Millar, *Lost Revolution*, pp. 284, 290.
229. McCann, E., *War and an Irish Town* (Harmondsworth: Penguin, 1974) p. 84.
230. *BT* 8/3/1975.
231. Statement from the IRSP Ard Chomhairle 12/12/1974, LHLPC, IRSP Box.
232. Costello, S., Address to first Ard Fheis of the IRSP 5, 6/7/1975, LHLPC, IRSP Box.
233. Interview with Seamus Costello http://www.irsm.org/history/costello/seamus08.html 30/6/2004.
234. Billy McQuiston, interview with author, Belfast, 1/7/2010.
235. *Scotsman* 27/3/1987.
236. Eoin Ó Broin, interview with author, Belfast 20/5/2005.

237. Seamus Costello, Oration at the first annual Wolfe Tone commemoration Bodenstown, 8/6/1975, LHLPC, IRSP Box.
238. Holland and McDonald, *INLA*, p. 45.
239. Notes from an interview by unnamed source with OIRA volunteer, 20/6/1992, LHLPC.
240. Notes from an interview by unnamed source with Cathal Goulding, 25/5/1993, LHLPC.
241. Fra Halligan, IRSP, interview with author, Belfast, 25/2/2010.
242. Hanley and Millar, *Lost Revolution*, p. 287.
243. *IT* 12/7/1982.
244. IRSP Pamphlet Reprint *National Liberation Struggle* undated http://irsm.org/history/liberation.html 16/6/2004.
245. Yvonne Murphy et al. (eds), *Troubled Images* (Belfast: Linen Hall Library, 2001), p. 109.
246. Hanley and Millar, *Lost Revolution*, p. 296.
247. *Guardian* 19/3/1987.
248. Myers, K., *Watching the Door: Cheating Death in 1970s Belfast* (London: Atlantic Books, 2006), pp. 77, 204–5.
249. McKittrick et al., *Lost Lives*, p. 1066.
250. Holland and McDonald, *INLA*, p. 299.
251. Marian Price, interview with author, Belfast, 1/7/2010.
252. Fra Halligan, IRSP, interview with author, Belfast, 25/2/2010.
253. Ibid.
254. Press Statement on behalf of the Ard Chomhairle of the IRSP, 28/4/1975, copy in LHLPC, IRSP Box.
255. Confidential Internal IRSP document, c. April 1975, LHLPC.
256. Cathal Goulding oration at funeral of Liam McMillen, LHLPC.
257. Danny Morrison, interview with author, Belfast, 24/1/2005.
258. Sharrock and Devenport, *Man of War, Man of Peace?*, pp. 37, 69, 83; English, *Armed Struggle*, p. 110.
259. Adams, G., *The Politics*, p. 2.
260. Johnston, *Century*, p. 215.
261. Patterson, *The Politics of Illusion*, p. 108.
262. Notes from an interview by unnamed source with OIRA volunteer, 20/6/1992, LHLPC.
263. Patterson, *The Politics of Illusion*, p. 108.
264. Cathal Goulding oration at the funeral of Liam McMillen, LHLPC.
265. Danny Morrison, interview with author, Belfast, 24/1/2005.
266. *IT* 14/2/1975.
267. Power, 'The Ta Power Document' http://irsm.org/history/tapowerdoc.html 27/7/2004.
268. Holland and McDonald, *INLA*, p. 87.
269. Ibid., p. 88.
270. Kevin Toolis, 'An Anatomy of the INLA's Bloody Feuds', *Observer* Report, undated, copy in LHLPC, IRSP Box.
271. Hanley and Millar, *Lost Revolution*, pp. 312–13.
272. Cited in McKittrick et al., *Lost Lives*, p. 668.
273. The RUC's anti-terrorist unit.

274. Ex-E4A Officer, interview with author, Scotland, 18/7/2009.
275. Ex-Special Branch Officer, interview with author, Scotland, 30/7/2009.
276. Fra Halligan, IRSP, interview with author, Belfast, 25/2/2010.
277. See McKittrick et al., *Lost Lives*, p. 728.
278. Journalist, interview with author, Belfast, 15/11/2004.
279. Fra Halligan, IRSP, interview with author, Belfast, 25/2/2010.
280. Ibid.
281. IRSCNA: Seamus Costello Commemoration 21/9/2001http://www.irsm.org/statements/firsca.010921.html 30/6/2004.
282. Flackes, W. D. and Elliott, S., *Northern Ireland: A Political Directory 1968–88* (Belfast: The Blackstaff Press, 1989), p. 105; Hanley and Millar, *Lost Revolution*, pp. 402–3.
283. Thomas Power, *The Ta Power Document* http://irsm.org/history/tapowerdoc.html 27/7/2004.
284. Fra Halligan, IRSP, interview with author, Belfast, 25/2/2010.
285. *Sunday Press* 21/1/1979.
286. Holland and McDonald, *INLA*, p. 131.
287. *Scotsman* 28/3/1979.
288. *Sunday News* 1/4/1979.
289. *Irish Press* 5/4/1979.
290. Holland and McDonald, *INLA*, p. 139.
291. *IN* 20/3/1999.
292. Kevin Toolis, 'An Anatomy of the INLA's Bloody Feuds', *Observer* Report, undated, copy in LHLPC, IRSP Box.
293. *Sunday World* 1/4/1979.
294. Morgan, A., 'Socialism in Ireland – Red, Green and Orange', pp. 172–225, in Morgan and Purdie (eds), *Ireland*, p. 212.
295. Cathal Goulding, speaking in 1990, quoted in *Observer* 3/1/1999.
296. Anthony McIntyre, interview with author, Belfast, 7/9/2005.

CHAPTER 4

The American Dimension: How Support from America Directed the Path of Irish Republicanism

As the republican campaign developed over the course of the late twentieth century, the United States of America and its considerable Irish population became an important actor.[1] The influence of Irish-America helped to direct the path of republicanism, both politically and militarily, particularly during the 1970s and 1980s, as US-based organisations and individuals sent large sums of money to Ireland, much of which supported and enhanced the military campaign of the IRA. When considered alongside the powerful Irish-American lobby that exerted influence over elected representatives, there is little doubt as to the importance of the American dimension to the Northern Irish troubles. In addition to the finance that supported the republican struggle, the legitimacy afforded to Irish republican groups by international support prompted groups to seek to form alliances both east and west. It was therefore of great consequence for republican groups to place themselves in a position from which they could successfully exploit connections with groups in the United States. The tactics deployed by republicans in the United States would establish a platform from which funds could be raised to enhance the republican struggle in Ireland. This chapter considers the establishment of Irish-American support for Irish republicans during the early 1970s and how this aspect of the republican struggle impacted on the recent split in the movement.

Almost thirty-five million Americans claim Irish ancestry, making Irish-America the second-largest diaspora population in the United States after German-Americans.[2] Because most Irish migrants to the United States were Protestant and enjoyed smoother assimilation into American culture than their Catholic counterparts, the majority of the

96

Irish in the United States largely lost interest in Irish affairs over time.[3] The fact that the United States should then become an influential actor in the violence that beset Northern Ireland from the 1970s is a matter of historical importance.

Continued resentment, over the potato famine and the harsh conditions that many faced in their new homeland, was maintained towards the British state as Irish migrants began to settle in the United States during the nineteenth century. The defeated rebels of 1867 strengthened the republican imperative in the United States, with John Devoy, later a key figure in Clan na Gael, among their number.[4] The importance of the United States for the republican cause was again evident after the 1916 Easter Rising when the life of New York-born Éamon de Valera was spared. The executions of the other leaders was publicised across the United States through the Friends of Irish Freedom, a group partially established by Clan na Gael. The threat of American support for republicans has also been cited as motivating David Lloyd George in the negotiations that led to the Anglo-Irish Treaty.[5] With the treaty signed, the United States lost much of its interest in Ireland, with partition considered to be much less important than the eradication of British rule in the majority of Ireland. The internecine blood letting of the Irish Civil War also disillusioned many across the Atlantic.[6]

As World War II broke out, the neutrality of Ireland was an issue for the United States, particularly as de Valera complained about the presence of American GIs in Northern Ireland. Strengthened British American relations from the period, along with Irish links with the Nazis and the hostility towards American soldiers, served to undermine the republican cause in the United States.[7]

Lack of interest in Ireland was emphasised by the *Irish Republican Observer* in 1951, which complained that a raid on Ebrington barracks was not given 'sufficient publicity',[8] but Clan na Gael member Michael McGinn emphasised that 'Clan na Gael stands today where it always stood and will always stand: behind the Irish Republican Movement's struggle for a free Ireland ... we shall give whatever aid we can to the guerrilla fighters of the Republican Movement.'[9] Although the support of the century-old Clan na Gael, with roots back to 1858 and the foundation of the Fenian Brotherhood in New York, provided a solid foundation on which Irish republicans in the United States could organise, support for republicanism during the middle part of the twentieth century was very much a minority view. This is represented by the disengagement with Irish republicanism that Michael Flannery went through after his migration to the United States. Having fought in the Irish War of Independence and with anti-Treaty forces in the Civil War, he migrated to the United States in 1927 and took up employment as an insurance salesman, a position he only relinquished when he established the Irish Northern Aid Committee, or Noraid.

Politically, the ascension of John F. Kennedy to the American presidency raised hopes that Irish causes would now enjoy greater prominence, the new president possessing both an impeccable Irish bloodline and strong Irish-American credentials. The Kennedy family had a complicated relationship with Ireland: Joe Kennedy, Sr served as United States Ambassador to the United Kingdom between 1938 and 1940, and the perception that the family were Anglophiles was supported by the marriage of Kathleen Kennedy to the Marquess of Hartington in 1944 and the close relationship between John and British Prime Minister Harold Macmillan throughout his presidency.[10] As became a consistent position of US presidents on Northern Ireland, Kennedy refused to be drawn on the issue of partition, even during his visit to Ireland during 1963.[11] The development of African-American civil rights around this time did have important ramifications for Northern Ireland.

Early activists in the Northern Ireland Civil Rights Association openly sought analogy with the African-American example, conducting sit-down protests and singing the same protest songs.[12] Gerry Adams also wrote of the inspiration of the African-American struggle.[13] Although the Irish analysis of the civil rights movement in the United States was simplistic, the analogy was easily made, particularly in the media. Media coverage brought the Irish struggle back into the consciousness of the American public and made good use of the civil rights analogy: National Broadcasting Company (NBC) *Nightly News* in August 1969 contended 'the Catholics in Ulster are the same as the Blacks in the United States', Newsweek earlier having told of 'the White Negroes'.[14] An American Broadcasting Company report in early 1969 related the two civil rights struggles and predicted the imminence of violence.[15] The comparison facilitated ideological links between the political situation in Northern Ireland and that in the United States, regardless of the analogical issues inherent in such a comparison. It also created problems; conservative Irish-Americans were unable to equate the struggle of northern Catholics with that of African-Americans, the mindset of 'Niggers out of Boston, Brits out of Belfast' being common.[16]

Irish-American influence on the republican struggle was widely rec-ognised during the 1970s. *Time* magazine noted in 1974 that the United States was the 'second largest source of IRA funds after Ireland itself',[17] with other sources claiming that three-quarters of paramilitary funding came from private United States sources, and that by the mid-1980s total remittances exceeded $3 million.[18] In mid-1974, the British Foreign and Commonwealth Office (FCO) stated: 'It is an established fact that the US is one of the principal sources of foreign funding for the IRA. Since August 1969 Irish-Americans are thought to have donated between one and two million dollars to Irish "relief" funds',[19] with the Irish Northern Aid Committee, who were of the philosophy that 'the more coffins sent back to Britain, the sooner this will be over',[20] responsible for roughly one million dollars.[21]

IRISH NORTHERN AID COMMITTEE

Michael Flannery visited Ireland in December 1969, where he met with leaders of the fledgling Provisional IRA. Joe Cahill and Dáithí Ó Conaill visited the United States soon afterwards, in the aftermath of the repub-lican split, and the Irish Northern Aid Committee was duly established in April 1970, with its foreign principal registered as the 'Northern Aid Committee Belfast' representative Joe Cahill; Cahill would later have his US visa cancelled because of his prior convictions.[22] Its purpose was declared to be the rather vague 'humanitarian relief',[23] an indication that even though it was not illegal to raise money for armed Irish republicans, it was important that Noraid be established with popular legitimacy from the outset. The FCO noted that it was impossible to tell how much money had been spent on arms, although a representative 'admitted that his organisation had no control over the funds when transferred to Ireland and at least some of them were almost certainly spent on arms'.[24]

Much of the money it raised is suspected to have been spent on guns supplied by Flannery's colleague George Harrison. Harrison, a County Mayo native, was central in the supply of armaments to the IRA and was once described as 'the IRA's Master Gunrunner'.[25]

Noraid was an active participant in what developed into a publicity war with the British state apparatus in the United States. Flannery featured in a *New York Times* article on Irish-America alongside supporters of repub-lican groups justifying their position. One claimed that 'like the Jews, I have a moral responsibility to help my own'; another that '[it] feels any indifference here is in large part caused by . . . the failure of the American press, until recently, to present the issues fully. Everyone quickly heard in the media about the tarring and terrorism . . . but the more widespread civil-rights grievances of the northern minority do not command equal attention.' Individual motivation for donating to the cause altered over the early years of the troubles, as noted by Noraid member Thomas Enright: 'a year ago they'd say "Here's some money for the cause, but not for guns", but now what a turnaround! We don't have to collect outside the churches. They're coming to us.'[26] It was not until 1979 that the Justice Department attempted to force Noraid to register itself as an agent of the Provisional Irish Republican Army, even though fundraising for the group was not in itself an illegal act.[27] Some explanation of the Irish situation was provided by an extensive article in *Time* magazine in early 1972 that offered historical context to the reader and partial explanation as to how the IRA campaign had become 'the strategy of determined, desperate men'.[28]

Understanding how Noraid developed over the course of the first decade of the troubles is therefore integral to attempts to understand the increasing dominance of the Provisional republicans in the aftermath of the split. Most important here would be the justification of armed struggle, which came to be the popular tool by which to differentiate between the two factions. How the Provisional republicans were able to convince ordinary Americans that their campaign against a country that had only twenty-five years previously fought alongside American troops in World War II was not only justified but merited their moral and financial support, and how the Official republicans sought to keep pace with their former comrades in the United States while their organisation was increasingly looking to Moscow for ideological inspiration, together tell the most important international tale of the 1969–70 split in the republican movement.

THE TROUBLES AND THE IRISH PEOPLE

After the IRA split was finalised, the quick establishment of Noraid emphasised the magnitude of international support for the Provisional republicans. The Official republicans were also quick to exploit US connections made by Cathal Goulding on prior visits; supply routes for weapons were created and Irish Republican Clubs of the US and Canada was launched in 1971.[29] The tactics adopted by republicans were unashamedly exploitative. Maria McGuire noted that 'we were quite ready to play for all they were worth the new Republican myths that were being created out of the current campaign . . . There should be copious references to the martyrs of 1916 and 1920–1922 – the period most of the audience would be living in.'[30] A Noraid circular also pressed historical grievances: 'Dear Friend: Congratulations! You have been selected to help end 800 years of British misrule in Ireland.'[31] These appeals would have the dual purpose of reaching older generations of Irish-Americans with relative financial security as well as the younger, politically motivated generations whose political activism could be exploited for political gains. As noted by Ulster Unionists:

> a traditional anti-British attitude is kept alive in Irish American Associations. The United Ireland theme is cynically canvassed and the Provisional IRA marketed as the 20th century heirs of the Irish Volunteers, the Fenians and the IRA 1916 vintage. Those Irish Americans who would genuinely support a United Ireland but who do not subscribe to violence or to the purchase of arms are persuaded that donations are for social or welfare work.[32]

In addition to spreading the republican view of Irish history, it was also important to create the perception that the mass media was conveying information that was inaccurate, one-sided, or heavily influenced by British sources. Tom Boyle of the Irish American Heritage Center in Chicago argues that 'loyalist violence was never fully reported here, the press were strongly biased towards the British position'.[33] Monsignor John V. Sheridan complained that:

> They are being told the civil order of the 'English' province is being disturbed by 'IRA terrorists', 'rampaging mobs of Catholic guerrillas', 'crazed snipers and bombers of the IRA,' and 'wild-eyed ideologues who want to force the Protestant-dominated British province into the Catholic-dominated southern Irish Republic.' The British Army meanwhile, is depicted as a 'peace-keeping force' trying to save Her Majesty's subjects from terrorist attacks often 'emanating from the Republic to the South.'[34]

Dealing with comments made by members of the clergy on the situation in Northern Ireland was a tricky task for officials across the UK and Ireland; while statements made by men of violence could be easily refuted, it was not so easy to deal with claims made by men of God. The guidance department of the FCO suggested that 'if there is clear evidence available that any Roman Catholic Bishop is lending his good name to IRA fund raising . . . then I think that if we wished to do so steps to stop this might be possible in Rome'.[35] While the British could easily work towards countering Irish republican efforts in the mainstream press, the creation of Irish-American media sources, created and distributed within the community and much less accessible to the British, made the publicity war considerably trickier. Although it could be considered that those exposed to reports in the Irish-American media would more than likely be members of that community, the radicalisation of Irish-America could create a more loyal, reliable support network within the United States. As 'the voice of Irish republicanism in America',[36] the Noraid newspaper, *The Irish People*, assumed a leading role. First published on 12 July 1972, the newspaper's purpose was 'to provide the truth to concerned Americans about what was going on in Ireland'.[37] It then quickly established its support for the republican armed campaign, stating that 'any student of Irish history realizes you cannot bargain with the British, they only understand force'.[38] It was described as 'the organ of the Provisional IRA in the United States'.[39] With interest in the Northern Irish situation growing rapidly over the early 1970s, the publication of this newspaper represented a further boost for the republican movement in the United States and an additional challenge for the British state, attempting to minimise the impact of pro-republican views.

Bloody Sunday and the American View

While the Foreign and Commonwealth Office Annual Review for the United States of America in 1970 noted that 'Anglo-American relations are extremely good',[40] the rising civil rights movement in Northern Ireland was highlighting the relevance of the struggle to many Americans. In a letter to Sir Denis Greenhill,[41] the British Embassy in Washington, DC said that 'the Civil Rights Movement and the rise of the negro as well as the Vietnam war have encouraged different groups in America to distinguish themselves from one another in ideological terms',[42] with Irish-America part of this.

The election of Bernadette Devlin to Westminster in 1969 and her prominent role in the civil rights campaign captured the imagination of the American audience. She visited the United States shortly after her election, but her trip served to create disunity within conservative Irish-America as she sought analogy with the African-American civil rights struggle. Among her controversial acts was her labelling of prominent Irish-American and Mayor of Chicago Richard Daley as a 'racist pig'.[43] As an Independent Socialist, Devlin had hoped to raise $1 million but met with hostility, the FCO noting that 'her tour fetched $200,000, of which half was taken by the Provisionals to buy guns'.[44]

The issue of internment was also important; prominent in anti-internment protests in the United States was attorney Luis Kutner, the chairman of the Commission of International Due Process of Law. Kutner claimed Northern Ireland is 'like one big concentration camp . . . I saw a little girl who has done nothing wrong but sit and stare at walls since her mother was killed by soldiers . . . I went to one of the internee camps and saw an 80-year-old man who is blind and crippled.'[45] Kutner's radicalism on the Irish question was emphasised by his involvement in a lawsuit against the British on behalf of the Irish people during the 1980s.[46]

In October 1971, Senator Edward Kennedy, who had noted that 'Americans of all religious and political persuasions are becoming increasingly concerned about the violence and bloodshed in Northern Ireland',[47] offered a resolution to the House of Representatives along with Connecticut Senator Abraham Ribicoff and Representative Hugh Carey of New York proposing support for British withdrawal from Northern Ireland. Kennedy, a strong opponent of United States involvement in Vietnam,[48] stated that 'Ulster is becoming Britain's Vietnam',[49] a statement that provoked outrage from the United Kingdom and one that he later came to regret.[50] The Vietnam analogy was popularised in the media, Ken Ward observing that in Northern Ireland, 'symbolism of Vietnam was in virtually every film story from 1971',[51] and although he noted that the relation of Northern Ireland 'to US domestic concerns . . . was created by reporters and news presenters',[52] the association between the prisoner-of-war camps and the internment camps was easily made.

As the issue of internment revitalised American interest in Northern Ireland, further television documentaries raised FCO concerns as to the portrayal of the situation in Northern Ireland. *Terror in Northern Ireland*[53] aired on ABC in December 1971, followed by NBC's *Suffer the Little Children* in mid-January 1972. The two programmes aired during 'prime time' early in the week, and with roughly 95 per cent of all homes (sixty-five million housing units) in possession of a television set in 1970,[54] an unfavourable portrayal of the United Kingdom could have played into the hands of US-based Irish republicans seeking to broaden their support base. With only three major television networks in the United States in 1972, it is significant that two should devote a prime-time slot to programmes on Northern Ireland in such quick succession. The concern of the FCO was partially justified: although the former programme was considered 'not too bad',[55] the latter was seen as 'much more hostile' and yielded 'a number of telephone calls . . . protesting about the way in which it portrayed the work and behaviour of the British Troops'.[56] Certainly there was much to trouble the FCO, the show suggesting that 'since July, 1970, the British Army has been at war with the Roman Catholic Community . . . the Protestants have the jobs, the money, the government, the control, and at least 110,000 licensed guns', although it balanced such rhetoric with one statement blaming 'the IRA . . . they're doing all the damage that can be done'.[57] The latter programme also prompted a US citizen to write to the British Embassy highlighting the fact that 'I am uninformed . . . if I were to believe half of the content of the aforementioned television program I would be forced to the conclusion that the British role in Northern Ireland is to subjugate all of the Irish population by Gestapo methods'.[58] Such methods were discussed by journalist Joe Duffey in *The Village Voice*, who claimed that the Catholic community in Derry 'found themselves "driven into the arms of the IRA" . . . Led on by the placid reasoning of Kitson-like minds, the British insist "no talks until the violence stops," while they themselves escalate the terror.'[59]

Although dealing with the American dimension during 1970 and 1971 was tricky for the British, in the aftermath of Bloody Sunday it became considerably more difficult. In a confidential memo to the US Ambassador, Foreign Secretary Alec Douglas-Home stated that 'it is now important to be careful about what is said in public on the actual events of last Sunday. In the Prime Minister's view there is a risk that if you get into detailed discussion about the shootings, your remarks might be distorted',[60] the official line being that 'it is best to let sleeping dogs lie and not gratuitously to provoke controversy on Irish issues'.[61]

Bloody Sunday made front-page news across the United States, with the *St Louis Globe Democrat* commenting that 'the British government must stand before the court of world opinion as guilty of massacre in Northern Ireland . . . when will the British learn that Ireland should be one country?'[62] The *New York Times* described 30 January as 'an awful slaughter' in its editorial of 1 February, although it did note that 'the brief clips of the Catholic demonstration shown on American television prove beyond doubt that the provocation for the troops was deliberate and great', opining that the dissolution of Stormont would be a drastic but perhaps necessary response.[63] The *Los Angeles Times* highlighted what it perceived as British intransigence on issues of discrimination and suggested the implementation of an international inquiry, although it did also note the confrontational nature of the IRA.[64] Mayor Daley of Chicago compared the Parachute Regiment to Nazi storm troopers.[65]

The British position was made more difficult when Patrick Hillery, the Irish Minister for Foreign Affairs and later the sixth President of Ireland, travelled to the United Nations in New York to demand UN intervention in Northern Ireland. Although it was later claimed that Hillery recognised that the UN would not intervene and the Jack Lynch government was merely attempting to reach out to powerful figures, the trip created considerable problems for the British in the post-Bloody Sunday diplomatic landscape.[66] The fact that intervention was never likely was indicated by Hillery's statement that 'we do not regard it as internal to Britain because the territory is disputed. But we accept that in UN terms it is internal . . . The British have repeatedly tried to bring it into our territory, with border crossings, incursions across the frontier, shooting across the frontier and the construction of an internment camp in full view of the Irish Republic as a provocation to Irish opinion.'[67] Hillery asked, 'Has the society which evolved in Northern Ireland vindicated the forceful resistance of the Northern Unionists to the democratic wishes of the mass of the Irish people?' He justified this on the basis of 'the threat of violent reaction from Orange extremists and armed militia'.[68]

Secretary of State William Rogers noted that 'I don't myself see that there is anything that we could do to be useful',[69] and although he expressed 'the deep concern that President Nixon has concerning the recent tragic events in Northern Ireland . . . I told the Foreign Minister of Ireland that we were not in a position to intervene in the area.'[70] While the American government adopted a position sympathetic to the United Kingdom, the Kennedy-led resolution brought about a series of hearings on the issue of Northern Ireland. Kennedy, who would argue at the hearings that 'there could be no more gross intervention in the affairs of Ireland than the presence of British troops in Ulster',[71] was in a particularly tricky position politically during the early 1970s. As part of the Kennedy-Fitzgerald political dynasty, he was widely expected to run for President in 1972 until the Chappaquiddick incident in July 1969, when he was involved in a fatal car accident before leaving the scene without reporting to the police. Incumbent president Richard Nixon considered Kennedy a real threat to his re-election, and over three-quarters of voters expected Kennedy to gain the Democratic nomination.[72]

Some politicians of note attended the hearings; Congressmen Leo Ryan and Herman Badillo were early speakers at the hearings, along with Congresswoman Bella Abzug. Although the three represented communities with Irish populations – northern California, upstate New York and New York State respectively – the fact that none maintained their interest or support for Irish issues beyond 1972 indicates the utility of a prominent platform offered to them during an election year.

Easily the dominant participant at the hearings, Kennedy hypothesised about America's options for intervention, implying that a Naval Communications Station near Londonderry offered justification for such recourse, and also noting that 'Ulster cannot fairly be called the internal affair of Britain. Not a day goes by without new evidence of the deep involvement of the Republic of Ireland in the crisis.' He claimed that 'were I neither Catholic nor of Irish heritage, I would feel compelled to protest against the killing and violence in Northern Ireland'.[73] He again criticised the 'repressive policy of internment . . . the soaring daily toll of bloodshed, bullets, and bombing in Ulster is a continuing awful reminder of how wrong that policy was . . . the launching of internment has brought British justice to her knees'.[74] While some republicans have noted 'prior to internment there was an IRA campaign going on, I'm not so sure it had the widespread support that it needed to endure for any sustained period but internment gave it that',[75] the fact that Kennedy appeared to attribute all the violence in Northern Ireland to internment suggested that his understanding of the Irish situation was somewhat underdeveloped. Kennedy advanced the Vietnam analogy he had previously made, calling Bloody Sunday 'Britain's My Lai'.[76]

The hearings were notable for the lack of erudition among the participants. Representative James O'Hara also pointed to internment, describing it as 'reminiscent of the worst features of totalitarianism', and also calling for the 'dissolution of the Parliament of Northern Ireland, which is simply an instrument of colonial suppression'.[77] Congressman Jonathan Bingham argued that 'in judging the significance of [Bloody Sunday], it is worth recalling that in the famous – or infamous – Boston massacre of 1770 only five citizens were killed by British troops . . . two centuries after the American revolution, the British seem to be following the same kind of bull-headed policy in reacting brutally to demonstrations of protest'. He also compared Bloody Sunday to the Sharpeville killings in South Africa, where sixty-seven were killed in 1961, and the Algerian civil war, before stating that 'the British must recognize that it is their policies which lead to such acts'.[78]

It is significant that he chose not to analogise Bloody Sunday with violence that met African-American civil rights protests. The Selma to Montgomery marches inspired NICRA marches and offered easy and relevant comparison; there was also a 'Bloody Sunday' on 7 March 1965 when marchers were attacked by police in Alabama. This omission is particularly conspicuous with the Sharpeville comparison included and points to a politician ill at ease in dealing with domestic racial politics. Bingham, like many other representatives who took an interest in Northern Ireland during the early 1970s, could ill afford to closely identify the Northern Irish situation with that in the United States for fear of delegitimising it in the eyes of conservative Irish-Americans who did not support the African-American civil rights campaign. The British noted that Bingham 'used to be friendly disposed towards British policy but the influence of his Zionist wife (as well as his Irish constituents) seems to have affected his outlook'.[79]

Kennedy's testimony spoke of the 'terrible death and destruction brought by Britain's inability to deal fairly and justly with the people of Ireland . . . a new chapter of violence and terror is being written in this history of Ireland . . . written in the blood of a new generation of Irish men and women and children',[80] and firmly placed the blame for the problems in Northern Ireland at the door of the British. In 1972, with 'the cruel and repressive policy of internment'[81] still fresh in the minds of the international audience and the bombing of the Abercorn restaurant in Belfast, which really marked the escalation of the IRA campaign, still to take place, it was easy to do so and the November presidential election meant that the Irish-American lobby was difficult to overlook.[82] Indeed, the fortuitous timing of many incidents in Northern Ireland played into the hands of Kennedy seeking to rehabilitate his political image after his involvement in Chappaquiddick. Kennedy was also challenged at this time by anti-desegregation organisations such as Restore Our Alienated Rights. The group divided the races, with blacks claiming it had a racist core and whites arguing that it was merely opposing the seemingly intractable loss of white rights during the civil rights period.

The FCO noted that many of the participants 'were making statements for their own political purposes in total ignorance of the facts',[83] emphasising the self-promotion that was ongoing and that although Kennedy's 'demagogic statement . . . was televised and will no doubt be extensively reported',[84] O'Hara 'went on so long as to bore the few members of the sub-committee present'.[85] Equally, there was relief expressed that Kennedy's 'suggestion that the US should intervene in some way in

Ireland attracted a good deal of adverse editorial comment and was highly unpopular with the press and general public opinion'.[86] The response of other US politicians would also have been welcomed by British figures, with Martin Hillenbrand, the assistant Secretary of State for European Affairs, speaking in favour of the principle of consent.[87]

While 1972 had seen the entrenchment of Irish-American opposition to British policy in Northern Ireland, it also marked the peak of main-stream Irish-American antagonism to the United Kingdom. It was during this year that Kennedy met John Hume and his 'understanding of the situation in Northern Ireland really began to evolve . . . in late 1972 . . . John began the great education of Edward Kennedy about Northern Ireland and established the seeds that grew into a wonderful relationship.'[88] Kennedy began to speak out against IRA violence and he became increasingly opposed to the armed struggle when Gordon Hamilton-Fairley was killed by a bomb planted under the car of his neighbour Sir Hugh Fraser, with whom Kennedy's niece Caroline was staying during a visit to the United Kingdom. The possibility of a Kennedy dying at the hands of the IRA was described by the *New York Times* as 'a narrow escape', and the *Boston Globe* considered that 'this brings the tragedy much closer to most Americans than have most other terrorist acts'.[89] The British government sought to capitalise on this, approaching Kennedy to publicly speak out against IRA fundraising in the USA, although the FCO noted that 'we have to recognise that it is most unlikely that he will speak out during an election year'.[90] As the *Boston Globe* noted, 'having lost two brothers to assassination, Kennedy became outspoken against IRA violence, even as he criticized British policies he said drove young Catholics to join the IRA',[91] a statement that suggests that the concept of constitutional nationalism was not fully grasped in the United States, even as late as 2009. The lack of understanding, noted by Conor Cruise O'Brien in a 1979 letter to Kennedy's colleague Daniel Moynihan, who wrote that 'for a highly competent, interested politician and social scientist, you knew *remarkably* little about Ireland',[92] permeated Irish-American views on Northern Ireland and facilitated unnecessarily radical viewpoints, assumed with the purpose of self-promotion.

It was only once Hume began to exert influence over constitutional figures like Kennedy that Irish republicans were forced to rethink their American strategy. This influence was emphasised by a claim on the part of *The Irish People* which spoke of 'those in America who lose their credibility in Ireland to linkage with the SDLP'.[93] There could hardly be more telling praise than condemnation from this newspaper. British Prime Minister Heath noted that:

> there is much misunderstanding of the situation there [Northern Ireland] even in some of the highest quarters in the United States, though not I hasten to add, the President. It seems not to be understood that the great majority of people in Northern Ireland are Protestants, that Northern Ireland is part of the United Kingdom and that the majority wish to stay in the United Kingdom.[94]

The second longest-serving Speaker of the House of Representatives, Thomas P. O'Neill, Jr, better known as 'Tip', was also prominent in Irish issues. Upon his election in 1977, he gave a declaration marking St Patrick's Day which both denounced violence and criticised both the IRA and Americans who had funded them.[95] O'Neill would become a prominent member of the Congressional Friends of Ireland along with Kennedy, Governor Hugh Carey and Senator Daniel Moynihan.

O'Neill was born in 1912 in North Cambridge, Massachusetts, and recalled that 'I knew I was Irish before I knew I was American', also observing that 'we had a tremendous hatred of the English' when he was growing up. He attended Gaelic school and was taught by a relative of Terence MacSwiney.[96] The Irish nationalist influence on his early years was strong, but it is significant that in his memoirs he speaks little of Ireland other than the Irish-America that he grew up in. Although he 'once admitted to supporting the border campaign during the 1950s',[97] he then maintained a consistent position on the Irish question; pro-unity but anti-violence, often highlighting the low popularity of the IRA.[98] His private research papers also reveal his nationalist leanings, arguing that 'the principal obstacle to a political solution in Northern Ireland is the intransigence of Unionist/Protestant opinion'.[99]

He had a complicated ancestral relationship with Ireland, his great-great grandparents having left County Cork in advance of the great famine, although their subsequent return meant that his grandfather did depart Ireland in 1846 at the height of the famine era. He tended to defer to the White House or the State Department on issues of foreign policy, although he did once write to Secretary of State Rogers to complain that 'the policy of the government of Ulster is one of absolute discrimination and deprivation of the rights of the Catholic minority', having gathered 102 signatures seeking President Nixon's intervention.[100] He was also influenced by John Hume, his St Patrick's Day statement of 1977 renouncing 'any action that promotes the current violence or provides support or encouragement for organisations engaged in violence'.[101]

While Irish officials were appreciative of O'Neill's efforts to undermine armed republicans,[102] the British were more guarded in their appreciation, Northern Ireland Secretary of State Humphrey Atkins noting that 'I welcome their interest when it is used constructively',[103] the implicit hostility a result of much interference from earlier years.

Atkins' statement suggested that, although most American politicians had by then adopted a far more constitutional position than was evident during the early 1970s, some politicians were still conducting themselves in a manner considered confrontational by the British. The statement marked the year that O'Neill visited Great Britain and Ireland as part of a fact-finding mission. Prior to his visit, the Department of State carried out a threat assessment which noted the increased 'terrorist activity by Irish terrorists in London . . . even though the Speaker has made numerous speeches in the US against Irish-American support (an important financial source) for the IRA, any actions by Irish terrorists against the Speaker would only alienate this Irish-American support base'.[104] There would be little for Irish republican groups to achieve in targeting O'Neill but the recent murders of Sir Richard Sykes and Airey Neave had raised concern as to the safety of elected officials.

Most politicians who involved themselves in Irish affairs did so either because of ancestral ties or because they represented communities which had a strong Irish population. Prominent within the latter group was Mario Biaggi, a Democratic Congressman for the Bronx district of New York City, home to thousands of Irish migrants even as recently as 2000.[105] Biaggi, considered a 'Bronx Rabble Rouser',[106] would lead a campaign to provide $50 million in foreign aid to Northern Ireland on the condition that Britain announced its intention to pull out.[107] It has been considered by economists that British withdrawal from Northern Ireland would leave the province economically unviable. As reported by The Sunday Times in early 1974 following a conference at the University of Ulster in Coleraine, 'In a Free Ulster, the inevitable loss of those £300m-odd of British help would mean cruel hardship; it would be worsened by the raising of extra money for diplomacy and defence; and fleecing local capitalists, the remedy beloved of local revolutionaries, would actually diminish the local wealth by discouraging investment.'[108] With an average 1970s exchange rate between the American dollar and the British pound of 0.46 dollars,[109] Biaggi's proposed aid would have fallen around £275 million short. This proposal highlights both Biaggi's desire for self-promotion and his total lack of understanding of the Northern Irish situation. Biaggi's confrontational style attracted similarly radical views to his Ad Hoc Committee on Northern Ireland, which was still reticent to condemn IRA violence.[110] It was this reticence that saw Biaggi overshadowed by the constitutional figures of Kennedy and O'Neill, which drew criticism from *The Irish People*.[111] Biaggi also drew criticism from The National Association for Irish Freedom, which argued that he acted 'with headlines every step of the way . . . style and no substance'.[112] Irish Taoiseach Jack Lynch ordered his cabinet ministers not to speak to Biaggi,[113] with other figures describing him as being 'too militant'.[114] By the late 1970s, Biaggi's cynical radicalism was overshadowed by the increasingly constitutional position of figures such as Edward Kennedy. A 1977 statement by President Carter, declaring that 'violence cannot resolve Northern Ireland's problems; it only increases them and solves nothing',[115] emphasised the changed circumstances and, for Kennedy, this was the 'most important and constructive initiative ever taken by an American President on the Irish issue'.[116] With opposition to violence becoming a pillar of mainstream Irish-American opinion, radical Irish-Americans were becoming increasingly pressured into justifying their continued support for armed republicanism.

REPUBLICAN VIOLENCE AND IRISH-AMERICA

Bloody Sunday had presented a reasonable opportunity for Irish-Americans who supported the republican armed struggle. The American Committee for Irish Independence wrote to the British government in New York, declaring 'WE WILL KILL YOU WITHOUT WASTING WORDS . . . Withdraw your troops from Northern Ireland, and give our people the right of self-determination! Remember we have warned you! INDEPENDENCE FOR IRELAND – OR DEATH TO YOU!'[117] The name had been used by a group from the 1920s and was likely a cover for disgruntled factions within Irish-America.[118]

The considerably more popular[119] American Congress for Irish Freedom also appealed to the UN, alleging that 'While English soldiers fired the guns, Prime Minister Edward Heath gave the orders to fire . . . Mr Heath has adopted an apartheid system of government which is racist in nature . . . Yet Mr Heath still dreams of Empire. His dream has meant massacred civilians and concentration camps to the Irish.'[120] They were later to claim that Heath had authorised shoot on suspicion orders to security forces, and although their sources are unclear, such a policy was discussed within the Ministry of Defence during the early 1970s:[121] the propaganda value of such reports is clear.[122] Britain clearly still had to make some headway in the publicity war, with one proposed solution being particularly controversial:

> We have come to the conclusion that we should also look around for friends of Britain whose services we could enlist in a similar way . . . This exercise, which can be quite informal, will have to be conducted with great discretion . . . It would be appropriate to give such trustees unclassified material . . . particular care should be exercised over the lobbying of Congressmen. Occasions might arise when a trustee would be willing to take this on. But if this were in any way linked with us it could be interpreted as an interference in US domestic affairs so we should be careful to put nothing in writing to members of the public about this.[123]

While there is much to suggest that the British were always in receipt of sufficient support from United States politicians, the fact that this radical suggestion was made intimates the doomsday mindset brought on by the rising violence in Northern Ireland and the increasingly acute awareness that a significant amount of support was being raised for an armed anti-state group from the territory of an historic ally.

Noraid declared remittances of $312,700 for the six months following Bloody Sunday, significantly higher than the $121,722 it raised the following year. Noraid had in excess of seventy chapters and a membership of over 80,000 during this period, but it should also be noted that the Ancient Order of Hibernians sent $35,000 to the PIRA around the same time.[124] By the mid-1970s, the Irish-American dimension to the Northern Irish troubles was a prominent issue, with fundraising complemented by gun-running. One such case occurred in the port city of Baltimore, an area where Noraid raised over $20,000 in 1975.[125] The five arrested included an Irishman and a Northern Irishman. During their trial, 'IRA supporters packed the court in an obvious attempt at intimidation'.[126] Prime Minister Harold Wilson launched an attack on misguided Irish-American supporters of the IRA, stating that:

> those who subscribe to the Irish Northern Aid Committee are not financing the welfare of the Irish people, as they might delude themselves. They are financing murder. When they contribute their dollars for the old country, they are not helping their much-loved shamrock to flower. They are splashing blood on it.[127]

These sentiments were echoed by Irish Minister for Foreign Affairs Garret Fitzgerald, who stated that 'every dollar bill contributed to agencies such as the Irish Northern Aid Committee contributes to the killing of Irish people'[128] during a visit to the United States.

Sean Walsh of the Irish National Caucus defended the activities of his organisation, arguing that 'there is no evidence that our money goes to buy arms. There is evidence to the contrary.'[129] Their support for violence was clear; Walsh: 'I think it's proper to kill British soldiers', and Fred Burns: 'Americans have no problem with the IRA killing British soldiers.'[130] Other members of the organisation claimed that 'The money goes for . . . the wee ones of some mightily brave men. I wouldn't give if I didn't believe that'; and, 'As far as we know, if goes for shelter, food and clothing for the widows of the struggle, and the dependents of those men locked up in internment camps. We check up on it occasionally, when our people go over for vacation, but we can't be certain where every dime goes.' But 1916 veteran Matthew Higgins made the salient point that 'If I was involved in gun-running would I admit it? Of course not, I would either deny it or keep it quiet.'[131]

The INC boasted that it was 'the only organization which has succeeded in embracing so many groups for a single, clearly defined political purpose: To establish Irish Freedom, Independence, and sovereignty as an American political-moral issue, through every legal and political means possible.'[132] This was a shared philosophy across Irish-America, with the challenge not only to promote the Provisional Irish republican movement as the vessel for Irish nationalism in the United States, but to adequately explain IRA violence that was being targeted by United States politicians. By carefully utilising Irish-American media sources, notably *The Irish People*, Provisional republican supporters could maintain levels of support for the cause, helping to ensure the continued dominance of the Provisional republicans in the wider field of Irish republicanism as well as justifying the use of violence by the Provisional IRA.

In *The Irish People* violence was often portrayed as a necessary evil for the purposes of the republican struggle and yet unacceptable when it came from security forces or loyalists. Perception of the Northern Irish conflict as a war was crucial here; if the conflict could be established as being a war situation, acts of violence were more easily justified. *The Irish People* claimed that 'killing is justified in a just war and this is agreed upon by both Catholics and Protestants.[133] It was also claimed that there were 'tortures and brutalities being inflicted on the naked, defenceless Prisoners-of-war' in Long Kesh prison.[134] It was important that the troubles be portrayed as a war to cast the British security forces as the enemy of the people. After the IRA bomb attacks on central Belfast of 21 July 1972, known as 'Bloody Friday', *The Irish People* carried the headline '13 Killed

as British Army Refused to Warn Citizens',[135] rather unconvincingly dis-
placing the blame for the deaths. Brendan Hughes, who helped organise
the attacks, admitted that 'even if there wasn't any collusion or deceit
on the part of the British, I don't believe they were capable of handling
so many bombs at one time'.[136] Of course, with the 'over-reaction by the
military forces in Northern Ireland to civil disturbances [serving] to spur
the growth of the IRA',[137] it would not be surprising that the Army should
be blamed for one of the IRA's earliest atrocities.

When the British Ambassador to Ireland, Christopher Ewart-Biggs,
was killed by a landmine attack on his official car in Sandyford, Dublin,
The Irish People argued that 'it must be considered, the theory that a
Loyalist group was responsible'.[138] This change of tack suggests that if
the perception was allowed to grow that the IRA was prepared to target
elected officials, the hypothetical targeting of American politicians was
not a huge ideological leap.

As the IRA campaign was escalated in 1979, the newspaper celebrated with a story that led, 'British-occupied Ireland reeled under a
massive wave of IRA bombings last week in one of the biggest, most
concentrated bomb blitzes ever mounted by the Provisionals',[139] which
supported their previous assertions that 'every day the people's armed
Republican vanguard proves in action that Britain cannot rule her six-
county colony',[140] and that 'British Army morale is falling to pieces in
the Six British-occupied counties in Ireland. They cannot withstand the
expert fighting tactics of the Provisional Irish Republican Army guerrilla
fighters.'[141] On 27 August 1979, the IRA enjoyed one of its most successful days against the British state, killing eighteen soldiers during a bomb
attack at Warrenpoint, County Down, as well as Lord Louis Mountbatten
in Sligo in the Irish Republic. *The Irish People* spoke of the attack as
a battle of considerable magnitude: 'the Provisional Irish Republican
Army engaged a British Army convoy today at Warrenpoint . . . the
battle occurred . . . the largest engagement between British troops and
the Provisional IRA in the current ten year struggle'.[142] Although hardly
an engagement,[143] the success of the attack was noteworthy and the
newspaper also noted how 'the Provisionals caused the death of British
military figure Louis Mountbatten, thereby focusing the attention of the
British people upon the continuing war and occupation in Ireland, and
the inhuman conditions in which Britain confines the "blanket men"
of Long Kesh'.[144] It reflected on August 1979 as 'a Republican month
. . . as the summer days came, and quickly went, so did Mountbatten

and 18 Brits',[145] and its argument that 'the British response'[146] was the UDA murder of a Catholic man, an unspecific attack given that three Catholics were killed by loyalists in the subsequent few days,[147] was rather misleading.

While there was shock at the death of Mountbatten, much revulsion at the attack was centred on the deaths of fourteen-year-old Nicholas Knatchbull, fifteen-year-old Paul Maxwell and eighty-three-year-old Lady Doreen Bradbourne, as well as the serious injury of Timothy Knatchbull, twin brother of Nicholas.[148] That these deaths were overlooked by *The Irish People* suggests they could not be justified even to the radical Irish-American audience. It was therefore better to ignore them. Gerry Adams justified the operation, declaring, 'what the IRA did to him was what Mountbatten had been doing all his life to other people; and with his war record I don't think he could have objected to dying in what was clearly a war situation.'[149] Mainstream newspapers in the United States condemned the attacks: the *Boston Globe* said that 'The IRA would have the world believe that the British presence is the only thing standing between them and peace in Ulster. Nothing could be further from the truth . . . the Provisional army's action against Mountbatten and others engenders no sympathy for their cause';[150] and the *New York Times* suggested a London–Dublin partnership as a means of 'how to punish the IRA'[151] following the attacks, having earlier condemned IRA violence, particularly the reports that 'most of the guns used by the Irish Republican Army are coming from America'.[152]

BRITISH SECURITY FORCES AND IRISH-AMERICA

With the British Army portrayed as active on colonial duty in Northern Ireland during the 1970s, memory of American revolutionary history was easily invoked by Irish-American organisations. The British Army noted the significance of the American dimension to their own role in Northern Ireland, a secret report observing that 'although by no means all expatriate Irish are sympathetic to the Provisionals, powerful lobbies have been built up to give political encouragement to Republicans in Northern Ireland and to criticise British policy', although this analysis was somewhat undermined by the suggestion that 'there is little chance of the Provisionals receiving increased financial aid from overseas'.[153]

The Irish People enjoyed guest contributions that helped press home the case against the British security forces. American Pearse Kerr explained, upon his release from custody, that 'were I not an American citizen, I could have been locked up for twenty years on a false charge'.[154] Another article spoke of Bronx youth Billy Reid being arrested and undergoing 'the most sadistic torture imaginable'.[155] It was also claimed that the RUC shot a seven-year-old girl in the back and 'to cover up this dastardly murder, the RUC then pretended . . . that she was killed in crossfire'.[156] An analysis of Lost Lives suggests that no such death even occurred.[157] The brutalisation of children was a recurring theme, with it claimed that on 22 October 1978 two British soldiers in Andersonstown had 'held a 15-year-old boy and cut him up leaving 18 deep knife wounds – 14 which were across his throat'.[158] While this allegation was difficult to prove, with an audience that sought little substantiation, what was perceived to have occurred was considerably more important than what actually had.

Political figures were outspoken in their opposition to the activities of the security forces in Northern Ireland. Tip O'Neill stated that he was 'deeply distressed . . . by the accounts of police brutality in Northern Ireland',[159] in correspondence with Patrick MacAuley, who had suggested he push for Catholic recruitment to the RUC by noting that 'Catholics are not willing to join the force for a number of reasons. Fear of retaliation by the IRA is one of the most prominent.'[160] Although O'Neill's understanding of the situation in Northern Ireland was clearly developing, his opposition to a proposed arms sale from the US State Department to Britain for use by the Royal Ulster Constabulary was deeply problematic for the British.[161] O'Neill's argument was that the sale would 'draw extensive media coverage and result in dramatically increased contributions to the IRA by Irish-Americans', explaining to Secretary of State Lord Carrington that 'it would have been better if you had secured the guns elsewhere, but since you sought them in this manner it would be on my conscience when hostilities increased as a result of the added contributions to the IRA'.[162]

Although O'Neill's statement was carefully worded, his hostility towards the RUC was scarcely concealed by genuine concern as to potential increases in IRA support. The New York Times observed that 'IRA gunmen seem to have less trouble stocking up in the United States . . . there is no basis in law or logic for denying a license for the export of guns to combat political murder in Northern Ireland'.[163] The veto placed on this purchase of arms created difficulties for the British government, who had assumed the challenge of promoting the role of the Northern Irish police force in domestic security in 1976. O'Neill claimed that 'The

[State] Department's action in this matter undermines efforts by US political leaders to reduce support by US citizens that seek to unify Ireland through violence', before contending that the RUC was partisan and that 'the sale will therefore be viewed by many here as US Government support for a particular faction in Northern Ireland'.[164]

O'Neill received a letter from future Sinn Féin MLA Francis Brolly which argued that 'the RUC are probably the most dangerous of the Loyalist factions because of the fact that they have a cloak of respectability which is not worn by the UDA, UDR or UVF . . . the decent young men of the RUC are decent young Loyalists'.[165] It is interesting that Brolly should have sent this letter from St Patrick's High School given the fact that in 1979, when the letter was written, he was twenty-two years old. Another letter contended that 'the Protestants of Northern Ireland will use these guns for the sole purpose of depriving Catholics of their civil rights and ultimately to kill some of them'.[166]

The British Ambassador in Washington, Peter Jay, expressed 'surprise and regret' over O'Neill's position,[167] and Humphrey Atkins stated, 'I very much regret that a body of men and women who have borne so much of the brunt of the terrorist campaign during the past ten years . . . should be made the subject of controversy over the provision of modern weapons to defend the community and themselves from attack by mindless assassins',[168] indicating the frustration felt by British politicians over the issue. Daniel Byman has discussed the 'informal backing that states can provide by looking the other way as a terrorist group raises money, recruits, or otherwise sustains its organization from the state's territory',[169] highlighting the controversy of the United States position at this time.

The issue was further complicated by the fact that while obstructing the RUC gun sale, the United States was pressing Britain to coalesce on the issue of perceived Iranian terror, which would climax in the Iranian Embassy siege of 1980. O'Neill welcomed new Prime Minister Margaret Thatcher to the United States in 1979, thanking her for her 'staunch support for our efforts to end the illegal occupation of our embassy in Tehran . . . I also wish to take note today of your government's early effort in pursuing a political initiative in Northern Ireland.'[170] Thatcher recalled her good relationship with President Jimmy Carter, but also noted that he was quite unprepared for the Iranian problems and, on the blocked gun sale, stated that 'the Americans must be brought to face the consequences of their actions'.[171] Kirk O'Donnell, aide to O'Neill, warned that 'Thatcher is going to criticize American involvement in UK matters . . . any sale of arms to the RUC would be seen as victory for the British and the Irish American communities would be very angry', also noting the decreasing amount of financial support sent to the IRA by American organisations.[172]

The sale of arms was further delayed by the intervention of President Carter, in one of his final acts as president. Carter's decision was guided by Edward Kennedy, who noted that the RUC was 'a force that many Catholics viewed as oppressive and dangerous'.[173] The RUC was eventually forced to purchase arms from West Germany. Such interventions ultimately served to boost the IRA, who saw the legitimacy of the security forces undermined by elected officials in the United States.

IRISH-AMERICA AND LOYALISM

While the war between Britain and Irish republicans was relatively easy to explain and frame for an Irish-American audience, the concept of loyalism was a little harder to quantify, indicated by a series of often bizarre claims about loyalist groups. The fact was that a significant proportion of Irish in the United States that were of Protestant Irish origin gave Irish-American organisations problems when it came to defining loyalism; the risk of either rousing Protestant Irish support for anti-Irish republican causes or depicting the Northern Ireland conflict as a religious war forced Irish-America to handle the issue with due care and attention. Loyalists in Northern Ireland noted the 'huge influence of America for republicans,'[174] and the Ulster Unionist Council wrote to then-President Jimmy Carter in 1979 to voice their concern that Provisional republicans sought 'American money but not American Democracy'.[175]

A notable story early in the publication history of *The Irish People* was after the Abercorn bomb in March 1972, 'when the explosion was attributed to the Provos who denied responsibility. The UDA exultantly claimed credit but this was not reported in the American Press.'[176] The UDA was described as the 'largest and best organized of the Loyalist paramilitary groups [and backed by the British Army]',[177] although the newspaper did also suggest that loyalists were set to bomb London, claiming that the Ulster Constitution had provided for such an attack.[178]

The Irish People declared that loyalism 'is a philosophy best understood by Americans by analogy to Ku Klux Klan thinking in the southern United States',[179] the geographical concentration of Irish-Americans in the northeast being important to this claim, playing up to the historic rivalry between these regions of the United States. The newspaper was careful to distinguish between Protestantism and loyalism, the possibility of defining the Irish conflict as a religious war being too risky: 'The Irish Republican Army has no quarrel with Protestants per se . . . There are today Protestant members of the IRA.'[180] The newspaper also argued that 'the majority of Ulstermen, Loyalist or Nationalist, have suggested and in fact demanded a British withdrawal'.[181]

Although this was declared to be so, *The Irish People* still framed loyalist organisations as very much an enemy of republicanism, reporting that, as Bobby Sands neared death on hunger strike, 'Andy Tyrie, the self-styled supreme commander of the Ulster Defence Association, maintained yesterday that Loyalist paramilitary groups were preparing only for defence. But well-placed sources reported that death squads, which have claimed responsibility for killing six Republican activists in recent months, were ready to "wipe out the agitators".'[182] By Sands' death on 5 May, the IRA had killed fifteen since the turn of the year and the INLA four, compared to one each by the UDA and UVF. The portrayal of Tyrie as a 'self-styled' leader, rather than the legitimate head of the organisation, also serves to mislead the reader as to the true structure of the largest loyalist paramilitary group. Speaker O'Neill was advised of 'their cavalier attitude in choosing victims. PIRA generally selects its targets; Loyalists sometimes just went looking for a Catholic',[183] the implication being that PIRA also 'sometimes' just went looking for a Protestant.

The UWC strike was also important in Irish-America; *The Irish People* argued that 'while Loyalist politicians engaged vainly in parliamentary sabotage, the UWC recruited workers in key industries to its campaign and succeeded in cementing a common front with Protestant paramilitary groups – the UDA, UVF, Red Hand Commandoes, etc',[184] although they did note that the 'Loyalist rebellion . . . has brought the North to the brink of total anarchy, [and] has probably inflicted more damage to the economy of the area than all the bombs unleashed by the Provisional IRA'. It was claimed that the strike was costing the economy £3 million a day.[185] When Congressman Hamilton Fish, Jr called for the UDA to be proscribed, the British responded that 'these are decisions that can only be taken by the elected government responsible to the people directly concerned'.[186] Edward Kennedy was also critical of the failure to proscribe the organisation: 'the political activities of the UDA cannot be used to sanitize or justify the close association between the UDA as an organization and the violent activities of its members'.[187]

Given the lack of real political action on the part of the KKK, the UWC strike prompted Noraid to redefine loyalism for its readership, with it declared that 'The Loyalist is true to the state or Province of Ulster. This would have the overtones of an Irish connection rather than the strict British implication. The loyalty to Ulster is based on a tradition rooted in Ireland by Irish Ulstermen, taking its rightful place with other Irish traditions in full equality.'[188] This increasingly sophisticated understanding reflects that of elected officials in the United States. A 1978 delegation of the Ulster Political Research Group was received by Speaker O'Neill in Washington, DC and Glen Barr wrote to O'Neill's aide, Kirk O'Donnell, saying that he thought the trip had been very successful.[189]

REPUBLICANISM, SOCIALISM AND THE UNITED STATES

With the concept of loyalism so problematic for Irish-American supporters of the Irish republican cause, they would have been particularly confused by attempts on the part of republicans to reach out to the Protestant working class on class-based issues. The socialist nature of the republican movement was particularly challenging in the United States given the tense Cold War climate of the 1970s. Commentators on Irish-America have noted that supporters of the republican cause were far more likely to support a group that appeared less socialist in nature, with socialist views of the Irish struggle rejected angrily.[190]

The instinctively socialist rhetoric of Gerry Adams was toned down in order to keep the Americans on-side.[191] Adams was quoted in *Time* magazine as saying 'the Republican movement has always been socialist in the Irish tradition of radical thinkers. It has never been a Marxist movement.'[192] Support groups in the United States also made efforts to distance Irish republicans from allegations of Marxism: 'Governor Hugh Carey's claim that the Nationalist groups are "killers" and "Marxists" completely misinterprets the political and economic situation there.'[193] Comments from INC Director Sean Walsh had a distinctly socialist tone: 'Britain – 1776 and Britain – 1974 hasn't changed significantly. She remains the colonizer, guilty of perpetrating economic and social abuses. Two-hundred years ago, Americans were victims of her atrocities, today it is Ireland.'[194]

Clearly the difference between Irish socialism and Marxism would perhaps not be obvious to many Irish-Americans, but Adams was careful to make the distinction in this instance. This allowed readers the freedom with which to conclude that radicalism in Ireland was but a natural offshoot of Irish nationalism, rather than the considerably more controversial Soviet brand of socialism. For Adams, 'to be a Republican in the true sense . . . you have to base it on the 1916 declaration which in itself is a radical document'.[195] Again, Adams' language was careful, using subjective terms like 'radical', leaving his audience free to interpret it in almost any way they wished. Mitchell McLaughlin later argued that the proclamation was indeed socialist: 'the signatories understood what they were about. They had declared a revolution and that revolution was socialist'.[196] It also made note of Ireland's 'exiled children in America',[197] a fact that indicates the importance of the Irish in America during the early twentieth century. James Connolly himself spent much time touring North America around the end of the nineteenth century and, in the early years of the twentieth century, in 1903 moved his family across to the United States until 1910.[198]

The Irish People described 'attempts to portray the Irish Republican Movement as Marxist' as 'British propaganda'.[199] A further statement read that 'the IRA is in fact neither Soviet inspired not Soviet funded nor Marxist nor terrorist'.[200] Understandably it was the Soviet dimension that was the most sinister to Irish-Americans and therefore associations with the Soviet Union that had to be checked in the Irish-American media. By the end of the 1970s, the Official republican movement was considerably smaller than the Provisionals and offered little threat, politically or militarily, to Provisional hegemony. The purpose, therefore, of these anti-Marxist claims was to clarify the position of Provisional republicanism rather than to undermine Official republicans. Links between the Official IRA and the Soviet Union had been established by the middle of 1970, immediately creating difficulties for the organisation in the United States. Although the Official republicans did achieve some success in gathering support in America, this was on a considerably smaller scale than the Provisional republicans.[201]

IRISH-AMERICA: CONCLUSIONS

As the republican movement developed, the international dimension became increasingly important and the ability to exploit the largest foreign-based Irish community for support, both moral and financial, significantly increased the capacity of the Provisional movement to further their cause and further subordinated the Official republican movement to their erstwhile comrades. The role that *The Irish People* played here is crucial. The propaganda effect of their presentation of Irish news to the Irish-American community considerably boosted international awareness of their cause and helped shift scores of Americans towards a position of republican sympathy. Retaining existing support and broadening their North American support base clearly impacted on Provisional republican thinking during the 1970s, a time when the major strategic concern of republicanism was the continuation and advancement of the struggle against the British. The ability to fulfil this aim was directly related to the popularity and therefore support of the movement internationally. The FCO noted that 'the IRA has also looked to Irish communities elsewhere to obtain cash for its terror campaign of the past four years', also noting the presence of fundraising organisations in Canada and Australia, and an attempt to establish connections in New Zealand.[202]

Radical Irish-America's establishment as a support base for Irish republicanism was a result of the efforts of republicans on either side of the Atlantic. Reasons for this support fell into three categories: people were either misled as to how their contributions would be used; they simply misunderstood the Irish situation at this time, in many cases aided in this misunderstanding by often mischievous reports from Irish-American media sources; or they were active supporters of the IRA. These patterns of republican support suggest that only a fraction of those who supported the IRA's campaign could actually be counted upon for consistent support over a longer period of time, a fact that made it important for the republican movement to consolidate its support base in the United States going into the second decade of conflict. As interest in Northern Ireland dwindled over the late 1970s, the developing prison campaign provided an opportunity for the reinvigoration of Irish-America.

NOTES

1. English, *Armed Struggle*, p. 117; Byron, R., *Irish America* (Oxford: Oxford University Press, 1999), pp. 257–8; Wilson, A., *Irish America and the Ulster Conflict 1968–1995* (Belfast: The Blackstaff Press, 1995); McCafferty, L., *The Irish Diaspora in America* (London: Indiana University Press, 1976); Doorley, M., *Irish-American Diaspora Nationalism: The Friends of Irish Freedom* (Dublin: Four Courts Press, 2005) or Guelke, A., 'The American Connection to the Northern Ireland Conflict', in *Irish Studies in International Affairs* Vol. 1 No. 4, 1984, pp. 27–39.

2. United States – Selected Characteristics in the United States: 2005 http://factfinder.census.gov/servlet/ADPTable?_bm=y&-geo_id=01000US&-qr_name=ACS_2005_EST_G00_DP2&-ds_name=&-_lang=en&-redoLog=false&-format= 26/6/2007.

3. Wilson, *Irish America*, pp. 14, 73; McCafferty, *Irish Diaspora*, pp. 59, 156–7, 176; Doorley, *Irish-American*, p. 159; Akenson, D. H., 'The Historiography of the Irish in the United States of America', pp. 99–127, in O'Sullivan, P., *The Irish World Wide: History, Heritage, Identity Vol. 2: The Irish in New Communities* (Leicester: Leicester University Press, 1996), pp. 99–100; McAuley, J. M., 'Under an Orange Banner: Reflections on the Northern Protestant Experiences of Emigration', pp. 43–69, in O'Sullivan, P., *The Irish World Wide: History, Heritage, Identity Vol. 5: Religion and Identity* (Leicester: Leicester University Press, 1996), p. 45; *Boston Herald American* 3/8/1980.

4. Wilson, *Irish America*, pp. 3–8.

5. Carroll, F. M., *American Opinion and the Irish Question, 1910–1923* (New York, 1978).

6. Wilson, *Irish America*, p. 14; Carroll, *American Opinion*, pp. 179–80.

7. Carroll, *American Opinion*, p. 174; English, *Armed Struggle*, p. 63; *Irish Independent* 7/1/2007.

8. *Irish Republican Observer* Vol. 1 No. 1 July–August 1951.

9. *The United Irishman* Vol. 10 No. 7 July 1958.

10. 'Kennedy-Macmillan Telephone Conversation', 26/10/1962 http://www.jfklibrary.org/jfkl/cmc/pr_jfk_macmillan_phone_call.html

11. Ellis, S., 'The historical significance of President Kennedy's visit to Ireland in June 1963', *Irish Studies Review* Vol. 16, Issue 2, May 2000, pp. 115–17; Fair, J. D., 'The Intellectual JFK: Lessons in Statesmanship from British History', *Diplomatic History* 30, January 2006, pp. 119–42, cited in Ibid.; 'Kennedy's Irish roots, understanding grew with the passage of time', *Boston Globe* 28/8/2009.

12. Purdie, B., *Politics in the streets: the origins of the civil rights movement in Northern Ireland* (Belfast: The Blackstaff Press, 1990); Prince, S., *Northern Ireland's '68: Civil Rights, Global Revolt and the Origins of the Troubles* (Dublin: Irish Academic Press, 2007).

13. Adams, G., *The Politics*, p. 10.

14. NBC *Nightly News* 15/8/1969; Robert Korengald 'The White Negroes', *Newsweek* 2/12/1968.

15. Ward, K., 'Ulster Terrorism: The US Network News Coverage of Northern Ireland, 1968–1979', in Alexander, Y. and O'Day, A. (eds), *Terrorism in Ireland* (London, 1984), p. 204.

16. Dooley, B., *Black and Green: The fight for civil rights in Northern Ireland and black America* (London: Pluto Press), p. 76.

17. *Time* 23/12/1974.

18. *Scotsman* 5/2/1983; Guelke, A., 'The United States, Irish Americans and the Northern Ireland Peace Process', pp. 521–36, in *International Affairs* Vol. 2 No. 3 July 1996, p. 524.

19. Confidential Draft from JPB Simeon FCO Republic of Ireland Department 4/7/1974, The National Archive, Public Record Office, FCO 87/366.

20. *New York Times* 2/12/1971.

21. Statement on International Peace Keeping Forces in Northern Ireland, in North America and the Northern Ireland Problem, undated, TNA, FCO 82/487.

22. *Time* 13/9/1971.
23. Wilson, *Irish America*, p. 43.
24. Statement on International Peace Keeping Forces in Northern Ireland, in North America and the Northern Ireland Problem, undated, TNA, FCO 82/487. See also Hanley, B., 'The Politics of Noraid', *Irish Political Studies* Vol. 19 No. 1 (Summer 2004), pp. 1–17.
25. *Sunday World* 14/5/1989.
26. *New York Times* 2/12/1971.
27. *Time* 26/11/1979.
28. *Time* 10/1/1972.
29. Hanley and Millar, *Lost Revolution*, pp. 150, 215–16.
30. McGuire, *To Take Arms*, p. 108.
31. Irish Northern Aid, fundraising appeal letter, New York University Library, Archives of Irish America, AIA 9, Box 1, Series A, Organisations.
32. Letter from Ulster Unionist Council to President Carter, 29/5/1979. Boston College Burns Library.
33. Tom Boyle, interview with the author, Chicago, 10/4/07.
34. *The Irish People*, Vol. I No. 1 12/7/1972.
35. Confidential Memo from AGL Turner, Guidance and Information, Policy Department to Mr Simeon, FCO Republic of Ireland Department 15/5/1974, TNA, FCO 87/366.
36. Irish Northern Aid website http://irishnorthernaid.com/ 9/7/2009.
37. *TIP* 04/09/2004 http://www.inac.org/irishpeople/headlines/2004-09-04/index.html 26/6/2007.
38. *TIP* Vol. III No. 24 15/6/1974.
39. National Association for Irish Freedom, Fact Sheet July/August 1975, NYUL, AIA 9, Box 1, Series A, Organisations.
40. The Foreign and Commonwealth Office Annual Review for the United States of America in 1970, 8/1/1971, TNA, FCO 82/43.
41. The British Permanent Under-Secretary of State for Foreign Affairs from 1969 to 1973.
42. Letter from UK Embassy to Sir Denis Greenhill, KCMG OBE, undated, TNA, FCO 82/43.
43. *Chicago Daily News* 28/8/1969.
44. *Observer* 17/10/1971.
45. *Chicago Sun-Times* 6/1/1972.
46. *Chicago Sun-Times* 9/4/1988.
47. Notes on Kennedy letter to Cork Corporation, 11/1/1972, TNA, FCO 87/100.
48. Adam Clymer, *Edward M. Kennedy: A Biography* (New York, 2009), 99–103.
49. *Time* 1/11/1971.
50. *Boston Globe* 28/8/2009.
51. Ward, *Ulster Terrorism*, 207.
52. Ward, *Ulster Terrorism*, 202.
53. *Terror in Northern Ireland* aired American Broadcasting Company 20/12/1971 8pm to 8.30pm Eastern Standard Time.
54. United States Census 'Housing Characteristics for States, Cities and Counties', 1970 http://www2.census.gov/prod2/decennial/documents/13276827v1p1ch01.pdf 6/5/2010.

55. Letter to British Embassy Washington, TNA, FCO 87/100.
56. Letter to British Embassy Washington, TNA, FCO 87/100.
57. *Suffer the Little Children*, 11/1/1972 8.30 to 9.30pm, National Broadcasting Company. Produced and reported by Robert Northshield, directed by Eric Flamenhaft, transcript, TNA, FCO 87/102.
58. Letter from N. Britton to Embassy re. NBC show, 13/1/1972, TNA, FCO 87/100.
59. Joe Duffey, 'Ulster and Vietnam: the "Peacekeeping" to end all Peacekeeping', *Village Voice* 27/1/1972.
60. Confidential Memo to US Ambassador from Douglas Home, 4/2/1972, TNA, FCO 87/100.
61. Internal memo, 31/1/1972, TNA, FCO 87/100.
62. Wilson, *Irish America*, pp. 62–3.
63. *New York Times* 1/2/1972.
64. *Los Angeles Times* 1/2/1972.
65. *Chicago Tribune* 1/2/1972.
66. 'Patrick Hillery, President of Ireland from 1976 to 1990' Obituary, *Guardian* online http://www.guardian.co.uk/world/2008/apr/14/ireland 10/2/2009.
67. Dr Hillery press conference response, 3/2/1972, TNA, FCO 87/100.
68. Delegation of Ireland Statement by Dr Patrick S. Hillery TD, Minister for Foreign Affairs of Ireland, during the General Debate at the Twenty-Sixth Session of the General Assembly of the United Nations 7/10/1971, NYUL, AIA 9, Box 5 Series B: Prisoners.
69. Internal Memo, 6/2/1972, TNA, FCO 87/101.
70. Text of Secretary of State Rogers' press conference transcript, 4/2/1972, TNA, FCO 87/101.
71. Hearings on Northern Ireland, Testimony of Senator Edward Kennedy, House of Representatives Committee on Foreign Affairs, Subcommittee on Europe, 28/2/1972, TNA, FCO 87/102.
72. Jenna Russell, 'Conflicted ambitions, then, Chappaquiddick', *Boston Globe*, 17/2/2009.
73. Hearings on Northern Ireland, Testimony of Senator Edward Kennedy, House of Representatives Committee on Foreign Affairs, Subcommittee on Europe, 28/2/1972, TNA, FCO 87/102.
74. Ibid.
75. Richard O'Rawe, interview with author, Belfast, 15/2/2010.
76. Wilson, *Irish America*, p. 64.
77. Testimony of Representative James G. O'Hara before the Subcommittee on Europe, House Committee on Foreign Affairs on H Res. 745 – Calling for Peace in Northern Ireland, undated, TNA, FCO 87/102.
78. Remarks of Congressman Jonathan B. Bingham before the Subcommittee on Europe, Committee on Foreign Affairs, House of Representatives, Washington, DC, 29/2/1972, TNA, FCO 87/102.
79. Memo on Bingham, 10/4/1972, TNA, FCO 87/102.
80. Hearings on Northern Ireland, Testimony of Senator Edward Kennedy, House of Representatives Committee on Foreign Affairs, Subcommittee on Europe, 28/2/1972, TNA, FCO 87/102.
81. Ibid.

82. Confidential Memo to US Ambassador from Douglas Home, 4/2/1972, TNA, FCO 87/100.
83. Memo on Sub-Committee Hearings, 6/3/1972, TNA, FCO 87/102.
84. Telegram on Congressional Hearings on Northern Ireland, 1/3/1972, TNA, FCO 87/102.
85. Ibid.
86. Unclassified Memo, 17/3/1972, TNA, FCO 87/102.
87. Statement on the Northern Ireland Situation by Martin J. Hillenbrand, Assistant Secretary of State for European Affairs, 29/2/1972, TNA, FCO 87/102.
88. Kennedy, E. M., *True Compass* (New York: Twelve Books, 2009), p. 355.
89. *New York Times* 24/10/1975, *Boston Globe* 27/10/1975, McKittrick, *Lost Lives*, p. 588.
90. Letter from J. Hartland-Swann FCO Republic of Ireland Dept to Sykes, 8 March 1976, TNA, FCO 87/577.
91. *Boston Globe* 28/8/2009.
92. Open Letter to Senator Daniel Patrick Moynihan from Conor Cruise O'Brien, 10/6/1979. KOD, BCBL.
93. *TIP* Vol. X No. 15 18/4/1981.
94. *New York Times* 6/3/1972.
95. See McManus, Father S., *Towards Justice* 2005 lecture reproduced by *The Blanket: A Journal of Protest and Dissent* http://www.phoblacht.net/smcmn1008054g.html 11/7/2007.
96. O'Neill, T. and Novak, W., *Man of the House: The Life and Political Memoirs of Speaker Tip O'Neill* (London: The Bodley Head, 1987), pp. 7–8.
97. *Irish Echo* 12–18/1/1994.
98. Undated quote from O'Neill in 'Report on the fact-finding mission to the United Kingdom, Belgium, Hungary and Ireland April 12–23, 1979. Submitted by Thomas, p. O'Neill, Jr. – Speaker United States House of Representatives.' O'Neill Biographical Information BCBL.
99. T. P. O'Neill Research Papers 16/6/1977. BCBL.
100. Farrell, J. A., *Tip O'Neill and the Democratic Century* (Boston: Little, Brown, 2001) pp. 29–32, 510–11.
101. Ibid., p. 512.
102. Letter from Richard J. Dennis, Fine Gael, Dublin SE to T. P. O'Neill, 25/5/1977. BCBL.
103. British Information Services Policy and Reference Division Policy Statements. 21/79. Northern Ireland: Talks with political leaders. Mr Humphrey Atkins, Secretary of State for Northern Ireland, in the House of Commons on May 24, 1979, 25/5/1979. BCBL.
104. Department of State Memorandum, Threat Assessment for Congressional Visit of Speaker O'Neill to the United Kingdom, Belgium, Hungary and Ireland April 12–23, 1979. BCBL.
105. See US Census Bureau, Census 2000, Bronx County, New York http://factfinder. census.gov/servlet/QTTable?_bm=y&-geo_id=05000US36005&-qr_name=DEC_ 2000_SF3_U_QTP13&-ds_name=DEC_2000_SF3_U&-redoLog=false
106. *News Letter* 19/4/1979.
107. *TIP* Vol. X No. 49 19/12/1981.
108. *Sunday Times* 10/1/1974.

109. 'Foreign Currency Units per 1 U.S. Dollar 1948–2007' http://fx.sauder.ubc.ca/etc/USDpages.pdf.
110. Overview Document of Press Coverage of 'Friends of Ireland' in Britain and Northern Ireland. T. P. O'Neill papers, BCBL.
111. *TIP* Vol. VIII No. 24 24/6/1979.
112. National Association for Irish Freedom, Fact Sheet July/August 1975, NYUL, AIA 9, Box 1, Series A, Organisations.
113. *TIP* Vol. VII No. 45 25/11/1978.
114. Letter from Rev. James P. Downey, Newtonards to O'Neill, 15/3/1979. BCBL.
115. Jimmy Carter, 'Northern Ireland: Statement on US Policy', 20 August 1977 http://www.presidency.ucsb.edu/ws/index.php?pid=8014 5/12/2009.
116. Ted Kennedy Providing a Leading Voice for Human Rights and Democracy around the Globe http://tedkennedy.org/service/item/foreign_policy 5/12/2009.
117. Letter from British Government Offices NY to FCO London re: Series of Letters Addressed to members of the mission on 1/3/1972, TNA, FCO 87/102.
118. *New York Times* 8/6/1920.
119. Kenny, K., 'American-Irish Nationalism', pp. 289–302, in Lee, J. J. and Casey, M. R. (eds), *Making the Irish American: History and Heritage of the Irish in the United States* (New York: New York University Press, 2006), p. 297.
120. Letter from James Heaney, American Congress for Irish Freedom to all UN Delegations, 16/2/1972, TNA, FCO 87/102.
121. Northern Ireland: Contingency Planning (GEN 79(72) 28) c. 13/12/1972, TNA, DEFE 25/282.
122. American Congress for Irish Freedom Report on Northern Ireland, undated, TNA, FCO 87/102.
123. Letter from British Embassy Washington to all Consulate-General, 8/3/1972, TNA, FCO 87/102.
124. Ibid.
125. *Baltimore Sun* 24/1/1976.
126. Letter from D. C. Walker British Embassy Washington to J. B. Donnelly FCO Republic of Ireland Department, 10/7/1974, TNA, FCO 87/366.
127. *New York Times* 18/12/1975.
128. *Washington Post* 1/1/1976.
129. Ibid.
130. *Washington Star* 19/11/1975.
131. *Washington Post* 25/1/1976.
132. Irish National Caucus Position Paper 3/2/1975, NYUL, AIA 9, Box 1, Series A, Organisations.
133. *TIP* Vol. I No. 5 12/8/1972.
134. *TIP* Vol. VII No. 15 15/4/1978.
135. See *TIP* Vol. I No. 3 29/7/1972.
136. Cited in Moloney, *Voices*, p. 105.
137. *TIP* Vol. I No. 4 5/8/1972.
138. *TIP* Vol. 5 No. 10 31/7/1976.
139. *TIP* Vol. VIII No. 13 31/3/1979.
140. *TIP* Vol. VII No. 16 22/4/1978.
141. *TIP* Vol. VIII No. 9 3/3/1979.

142. *TIP* Vol. VIII No. 32 1/9/1979.
143. Dupuy, T. N., *Understanding War: History and Theory of Combat* (London: Leo Cooper, 1992), p. 65.
144. *TIP* Vol. VIII No. 33 8/9/1979.
145. *TIP* Vol. IX No. 2 12/1/1980.
146. *TIP* Vol. VIII No. 33 8/9/1979.
147. McKittrick et al., *Lost Lives*, pp. 799–800.
148. Ibid., pp. 795–6, 799.
149. *Time* 19/11/1979.
150. *Boston Globe* 29/8/1979.
151. *New York Times* 29/8/1979.
152. *New York Times* 21/5/1978.
153. Northern Ireland Future Terrorist Trends – Secret British Army report c. October 1979. BCBL.
154. *TIP* Vol. VI No. 48 3/12/1977.
155. *TIP* Vol. VIII No. 17/2/1979.
156. *TIP* Vol. VII No. 29 29/7/1978.
157. See McKittrick et al., *Lost Lives*, pp. 758–64.
158. *TIP* Vol. VII No. 43 11/11/1978.
159. Statement by O'Neill 19/6/1978. BCBL.
160. Letter from Patrick MacAuley to O'Neill 4/9/1979; letter from O'Neill to Patrick MacAuley, 24/9/1979. BCBL.
161. Further information in Thompson, J. E., *American Policy and Northern Ireland: A Saga of Peacebuilding* (London: Praeger, 2001), p. 86.
162. Minutes of Meeting between T. P. O'Neill and Lord Carrington regarding the purchase of guns for the RUC, 5/5/1980. KOD, BCBL.
163. See *New York Times* 28/5/1980.
164. Statement by Speaker Thomas, p. O'Neill, Jr. on State Department Authorization of Shipment of US manufactured arms to Northern Ireland Police 18/5/1979, KOD, BCBL.
165. Letter from Francie Brolly, St Patrick's High School, Dungiven, Co. Derry to O'Neill, 6/6/1979, KOD, BCBL.
166. Letter from A. R. West to O'Neill, 18/12/1979, KOD, BCBL.
167. *Boston Globe* 6/6/1979.
168. Statement by Humphrey Atkins, undated (c. June 1979), KOD, BCBL.
169. Byman, D., *Deadly Connections: States that Sponsor Terrorism* (Cambridge: Cambridge University Press, 2005), p. 3.
170. Remarks by Speaker Thomas, p. O'Neill Jr. Welcoming Prime Minister Margaret Thatcher December 17, 1979, KOD, BCBL.
171. Thatcher, M., *The Downing Street Years* (London: HarperCollins, 1993), pp. 68–9; *Daily Mail* 30/12/2009.
172. Thompson, J. E., *American Policy and Northern Ireland: A Saga of Peacebuilding* (Westport: Praeger, 2001), p. 91.
173. Kennedy, *True Compass*, p. 356.
174. Sammy Duddy, interview with author, Belfast, 10/11/2006.
175. Letter from Ulster Unionist Council to President Carter, 29/5/1979, KOD, BCBL.
176. *TIP* Vol. I No. 9 9/9/1972; McKittrick et al., *Lost Lives*, p. 161; Centre for Defence

and International Security Studies http://www.cdiss.org/Documents/Uploaded/
CDISS%20Programme%20-%20Database%20of%20Terrorist%20Incidents%20
-%201970-1979.pdf 26/06/2007.

177. *TIP* Vol. VI No. 30 23/7/1977.
178. *TIP* Vol. II No. 34 1/9/1973.
179. *TIP* Vol. XII No. 30 30/7/1983.
180. *TIP* Vol. X No. 45 21/11/1981. The NI government did note that among the internment arrests, 'one or two Protestants' were among those arrested for suspected IRA activities. Conclusions of a meeting of the Cabinet, Friday, 20 August 1971 at 2.15pm. PRONI ref CAB/4/1610.
181. *TIP* Vol. III No. 25 22/6/1974.
182. *TIP* Vol. X No. 17 2/5/1981.
183. Airgram from American Consulate Belfast to Department of State 2/11/1978, KOD, BCBL.
184. *TIP* Vol. III No. 24 15/6/1974.
185. *TIP* Vol. III No. 22 1/6/1974.
186. Letter from Nicholas Henderson, British Embassy, Washington, DC, to Congressman Hamilton Fish, Jr, 24/5/1982. KOD, BCBL.
187. Statement of Senator Edward M. Kennedy Opposing the use of Plastic Bullets in Northern Ireland and calling for a ban on the Ulster Defence Association, 15/7/1982. KOD, BCBL.
188. *TIP* Vol. III No. 9 2/3/1974. For detailed accounts of the durably and profoundly unionist quality of loyalism, see, among others, Wood, *Crimes of Loyalty*, McAuley, J., *The Politics of Identity: A Loyalist Community in Belfast* (Aldershot: Avebury, 1994) or Bruce, S., *The Edge of the Union: The Ulster Loyalist Political Vision* (Oxford: Oxford University Press, 1994).
189. Letter from Glen Barr to Kirk O'Donnell, 31/1/1979. BCBL
190. Wilson, *Irish America*, p. 42; Holland, J., *The American Connection: US Guns, Money and Influence in Northern Ireland* (New York: Penguin, 1987), pp. 54–5.
191. Maillot, *New Sinn Fein*, p. 144.
192. *Time* 19/11/1979.
193. Human Rights for Ireland Conference, Statement 14/5/1977, NYUL, AIA 9.
194. Statement of Sean W. Walsh, Executive Director, Irish National Caucus, NYUL, AIA 9.
195. *TIP* Vol. VIII No. 42 10/11/1979.
196. See *An Phoblacht* 31/1/2002.
197. Declaration of Independence 1916 http://www.failteromhat.com/declare.htm 19/7/2009.
198. Reeve, C. and Reeve, A. B., *James Connolly and the United States: The Road to the 1916 Irish Rebellion* (Atlantic Highlands, NJ: Humanities Press, 1978).
199. *TIP* Vol. VIII No. 42 10/11/1979.
200. *TIP* Vol. X No. 10 14/3/1981.
201. Hanley and Millar, *Lost Revolution*, pp. 150, 215–16.
202. 'Fundraising and the IRA', May 1974, TNA, FCO 87/366.

CHAPTER 5

Prison, Politics and Violence: The 1980s

The 1980s was a transitional decade for Irish republicanism and the Northern Ireland conflict. Overall violence was considerably reduced, with 1200 fewer deaths occurring compared to the previous decade, as the Provisional republican movement shifted the focus of its struggle towards the political arena, reconceptualising its military struggle. It was ironic that the armed struggle effectively created the transition away from militarism, but through the prison struggle the militarists became increasingly sidelined as Provisional politics became dominant. The huge ideological journey taken by the Provisional republicans was integral to the 1986 split in the movement. Elsewhere, the Official republicans further distanced themselves from their erstwhile colleagues and the INLA continued to underline its propensity for violence.

Irish republicanism during the 1980s is inextricably linked to the hunger strikes of 1981, the culmination of five years of protest inside Northern Irish prisons as a result of the 1976 normalisation policies that the British government introduced as a means to de-legitimise the republican struggle. The prison campaign had massive ramifications domestically and internationally, as republicans in the United States enjoyed something of a renaissance during the early 1980s. With the strategic focus of the movement now firmly on the political arena, the American dimension evolved similarly as prominent political figures exerted increasing influence on the Northern Irish situation. Republican splits spilled into Irish-America during the decade, with the Sinn Féin split mirrored by a division in Noraid. The impact on Irish-America is also important to understanding the changing role of Irish-America for Irish republicanism.

The significance of the hunger strikes of 1980 and 1981 has meant that the topic has been historically well covered by commentators.[1] However, with recent revelations about the hunger strike period radically redefining existing perceptions of republican political development, it is important to re-evaluate the period in light of the considerable dissent that has fermented against the Provisional republican leadership.

THE HUNGER STRIKES AND THE PATH OF IRISH REPUBLICANISM

The 1980 and 1981 hunger strikes are considered by some to be 'the most important event of the whole struggle'.[2] The struggle that had begun in 1976 over the right to wear their own clothes, to refuse prison work, to enjoy freedom of association, extra recreational facilities, more letters and visits, and the return of remission lost on protest quickly outgrew the confines of Northern Ireland's prison system and became symbolic of the battle against British rule in Ireland. Hunger striker Gerard Hodgins recalls, 'We'd question among ourselves "Is it easier for an intelligent man or a stupid man to do this?" It was more about the commitment and the bond that built up. That comradeship I've never felt it or experienced it since. It was just shared adversity.'[3]

In addition to the increased political profile of republicanism, republican violence was intensified after the ending of the first hunger strike. Of the 113 killed in 1981, over half were victims of the IRA, with thirty-nine of their victims from the security forces, although the murder of census worker Joanne Mathers in April was a stark reminder how counterproductive a lack of discipline could be. This year the INLA killed nine, its highest total to date.

Irish republicans had died on hunger strikes during the 1970s but the deaths of Michael Gaughan and Frank Stagg, who died in 1974 and 1976 respectively, had not succeeded in generating the same publicity despite the harsh treatment Gaughan endured during attempts to force-feed him.[4] The individual nature of these protests and the relative geographical isolation the men suffered, in the Isle of Wight and Yorkshire, differentiated these protests from the mass campaign in close proximity to Belfast, and the republican publicity machine had developed considerably over the duration of the prison protest. The 1980 hunger strike, led by prominent Belfast republican Brendan 'The Dark' Hughes, was ended on 18 December after Sean McKenna became critically ill. Although it has been suggested that a British offer was imminent, Hughes had promised McKenna that he would not let him die, so the strike was ended for humanitarian reasons.[5] Gerard Hodgins recalls:

> They went back on to the normal wings whenever it was called off. There was a big dark cloud over them . . . Whenever the first hunger strike ended, I remember the morning the governor came around about half seven with a statement from the Northern Ireland Office: 'the hunger strike is over.' No one gave a shite about his statement. The confusion there was then was amazing. You'd just had five solid years of blanket protest and 100 per cent unity and everything fell apart. A lot of bad things said about the Dark, people saying they should have let people die. I think the Dark lived with that for the rest of his days.[6]

The impetus to resume the hunger strike came from Bobby Sands, although this met with opposition from Hughes, who felt that the movement would be better working within the existing system rather than forcing change themselves.[7] 'Bobby had declared, right away, that he was going on hunger strike. He said that on 1 January he was going to try and recapture the momentum . . . Then it got dragged out until 1 March.'[8] Between Sands beginning his strike and 3 October when the strike was called off, seventy-nine people were killed, including thirty-four civilians. Each death further entrenched the communal division, providing a list of martyrs with which support or opposition for republican strategy could be associated. The IRA was responsible for the vast majority of deaths during this period, which, combined with the political success the movement enjoyed, presented the Provisional republicans as a formidable organisation.

On 5 March, the Independent MP for Fermanagh and South Tyrone, Frank Maguire, died of natural causes. Maguire had supported the prison campaign and it was decided that a prisoner would stand in the by-election to provide the prison struggle with unprecedented legitimacy; could the British government really argue that a man elected as an MP had no political mandate? Noel Maguire, Frank's brother, was persuaded not to stand in opposition to the most prominent prisoner at the IRA's disposal, Bobby Sands. Prominent southern republican Dáithí Ó Conaill's role was integral.[9] Ó Conaill could scarcely have been aware what changes he was helping to bring about. On 9 April, Sands was duly elected, defeating Unionist candidate Harry West by 1,447 votes. Inside the prisons, the reaction was jubilant:

> I thought it was brilliant. I wasn't looking at it as a political theorist or anything, I was looking at it from the point of view that if we could take this seat, then he might live. We all know what Margaret Thatcher's mettle was, there was an

acceptance that someone was going to have to die before she would move but actually getting elected as an MP . . . on one hand the government is saying Bobby Sands you are a criminal, you are not a political prisoner, on the other hand he's getting 30,000 votes that say you are political, you're an MP. You don't get any more political than that.[10]

The prisoners were tragically mistaken; Sands perished less than a month after his election. Sands entered popular culture, with streets named for him internationally, several films depicting the hunger strikes, most recently *Hunger* from 2008,[11] and he was cited as an inspiration by Los Angeles rock band Rage Against The Machine in their eponymous debut album.[12] Domestically he continues to be referenced by republicans, but it is the Provisional republican movement he is most closely identified with, thanks largely to the iconic mural of Sands on the side of Sinn Féin's Falls Road office.

The constituency of Fermanagh and South Tyrone was an appropriate location from which to launch the Provisional republican political programme: IRA prisoner Philip Clarke won the seat for Sinn Féin May 1955 by a narrow margin and Frank Maguire was a former IRA internee. There was enough to suggest that a significant republican support base existed in the area, providing sufficient mobilisation occurred. Sands' election agent Owen Carron was nominated in the subsequent by-election at a time when the campaign for June's Dáil elections was well underway; republicans again capitalised on the groundswell of popular opinion with Kieran Doherty winning the Cavan-Monaghan seat, Paddy Agnew elected in Louth and Joe McDonnell only narrowly defeated in the Sligo-Leitrim constituency.

Beginning with Maguire's death, the organic growth of republican politics had assumed a clear path away from armed struggle through the ending of abstentionism to ultimate participation in the political institutions of a partitioned Ireland. Small pockets of dissent manifested themselves in the form of a series of relatively small splits, but no major rupture occurred in the republican movement as the political agenda, led by Gerry Adams, grew with its solid foundation of the election of Bobby Sands in 1981. This all changed in 2005 when former IRA prisoner Richard O'Rawe published his memoir *Blanketmen*. Therein, he alleged that the hunger strike, ostensibly the climax of the campaign for the restoration of political status, had been cynically manipulated by the republican leadership who allowed prisoners to die in order to promote their political agenda. Gerard Hodgins observes, 'there's sufficient evidence to suggest there was something going on. The accounts coming from Danny Morrison and Bik [McFarlane] have shifted that much since Richard first wrote his book that they should put themselves up for scrutiny just to clear the whole thing up and let people know the truth.'[13]

O'Rawe's book claimed that the Provisional leadership had manipulated the hunger strikers for the purposes of enhancing the political wing of the movement: he claimed that prior to the death of Joe McDonnell on 8 July, an offer had been made by the British government through Michael Oatley, their intermediary known as the 'Mountain Climber', that would have restored almost full political status but was rejected by the leadership, without consultation with the prisoners, to increase Owen Carron's chances of retaining Sands' seat amid the backdrop of dying hunger strikers.[14] O'Rawe argues that:

> The offer came in, the offer was accepted, the offer was rejected by Adams and his committee on the outside . . . Adams and McGuinness had been on the Army Council at the time of the hunger strike and they made sure the other five Army Council members were kept in the dark about the fact that the Mountain Climber had been involved in the second hunger strike and had made an offer. So that was all kept secret . . . Adams . . . did not tell the hunger strikers the details of the Mountain Climber offer, and you have to ask: why not? It is my opinion that cold-heartedly hiding the contents of the offer from the hunger strikers, that Adams put the hunger strikers in an impossible position, leaving them with little option but to continue on with their fast – and die accordingly. And remember: before Adams set foot in the prison hospital, Bik McFarlane censored the one man who knew the 'nitty gritty' of the offer, Pat 'Beag' McGeown . . . if Pat Beag had been permitted to speak freely about the offer, then hunger strikers might have said 'there's enough there' and ended the hunger strike and if the hunger strike had ended . . . on 29 July, if Adams had gone in there and said, 'Lads, here's an offer, make your own minds up: you can have your own clothes, you'll have segregation, work will be educationally based, there will be a portion of remission. You're not going to get free association, can you live with that? He didn't do that . . . he told them lies for one reason, because he wanted Carron elected . . . if they had ended the hunger strike on 29 July, Owen Carron . . . would not have been elected.[15]

Carron retained the seat with an increased majority on 20 August, the day that Michael Devine, the tenth and final hunger striker, died. Almost a month previously, the family of Paddy Quinn had intervened to save his life, an early indication that the resolve of those associated with the strike was becoming increasingly less firm. There was also constitutional imperative for the election to take place; parliamentary convention was that a member of the party holding a vacated seat moves a parliamentary motion to begin the by-election process. From the perspective of the republican movement, it was also crucial that the election take place with the hunger strike ongoing. With no other H-Block/Armagh MPs, Sinn Féin approached Plaid Cymru MP for Meirionnydd, Dafydd Elis-Thomas, asking him to start the process. Thomas's decision was unpopular both within the party and without, but he felt it his duty to ensure the democratic rights of the Northern Irish people.[16] Little mention had been made in parliament of the possibility of a by-election taking place, and the implication behind this silence was that no other MP was overly concerned if the by-election waited until the hunger strike had passed. Resolve was still strong in the camp, as noted by Gerard Hodgins, who joined the hunger strike on 14 September: 'You didn't want to back down because so many of the lads were dead [but] you couldn't criticise anybody's family for [taking men off] . . . you just had to understand that it's a hard thing to watch your son or husband day by day [but it is] a major impediment to the effectiveness of hunger striking.'[17] For Marian Price:

I think the whole thing was an absolute tragedy. I always believed, even at the time, that once Bobby Sands had died, they had proved they weren't criminals and I think the hunger strike should have been called off then because after that it just became a long march to the grave and I think at that stage that's when the republican leadership should have stepped in. Now people will say that the men make the decision themselves and you can't be ordered on hunger strike and that's absolutely true, but you can be ordered off, the movement does have that power. If the movement had have taken a strong stand . . . I believed at the time that they should have ordered them off and that was without any of the knowledge that I have today. With the knowledge that I have since gained, I absolutely think that it was criminal.[18]

The elections provided republicanism with a platform for its politicisation under the Adams leadership. In the 1970s, Adams had sent volunteers to the United States to obtain weapons to escalate the armed campaign, but a decade later he was leading the movement towards politics.[19] Adams admitted that because the prisoners' electoral campaign was solely based on support for the five demands, 'anyone voting for them would have to be content with the notion of not being represented in Leinster House – a consideration of particular significance in a state where politics is so dominated by clientilist concerns and approaches'.[20]

Brendan Hughes 'saw the situation in the blocks as a tool to help the leadership on the outside – specifically Gerry – to build up a propaganda machine',[21] and while Adams could claim that he had initially opposed the hunger strike on moral grounds,[22] with 'the focus of republicans so intensely towards the armed struggle at that point that, really, republicans weren't even thinking politically beyond the politics of armed struggle',[23] Adams' agenda for political republicanism needed invigoration. As disenfranchised as nationalists may have felt, it would be naïve to assume that electoral support for republican prisoners was solely motivated by ideological support for prison conditions, even though all stood as H-Block/ Armagh or independent candidates. Indeed, to support the campaign for the five demands was to oppose Britain's criminalisation policy and, by extension, British rule in Northern Ireland. Adams' statement highlights the inherent weakness in the abstentionist policy, to which Provisional republicans had loyally adhered since the late 1960s.

Over the next few years, the political base of the Provisional republican movement was consolidated. Sinn Féin participated in the 1982 Assembly elections, achieving 10 per cent of the vote and five seats. In the General Election of 1983, Sinn Féin stood fourteen candidates, with leader Gerry Adams successful in West Belfast. In Mid-Ulster, Danny Morrison finished seventy-eight votes behind Democratic Unionist William McCrea, while Carron was defeated by 8000 votes. These results established the strength of republicanism as a political force, even without the emotive H-Block campaign, with significant implications for the IRA. For Adams, the hunger strike had provided Sinn Féin with the political credibility to challenge the IRA for dominance within the republican movement.[24] Crucial to improving the circumstances under which the political party could prosper, however, was the re-examination of abstentionism. Adams was reasonably able to claim that the nationalist political initiative had effectively been handed to the SDLP thanks to 'conspiratorial methods and approaches'.[25] The Local Government Elections of 1981 confirmed the SDLP's position as the dominant nationalist party, the press noting that the Provisional movement was 'badly demoralised, believing that the electoral successes of their political wing actually helped their rivals for Catholic support, the Social Democratic Labour Party, by encouraging a spate of political initiatives, including the New Ireland Forum, in which the SDLP have played a prominent part'.[26] The cost of politicising the republican people without offering them a true republican party to vote for was considerable gains for the SDLP.

In 1983, Adams succeeded Ruairí Ó Brádaigh as President of Sinn Féin. The Northern takeover of the movement was now complete, with the role of IRA Chief of Staff filled by Ivor Bell and Kevin McKenna.[27] The foundations for a challenge to abstentionism were laid and Adams began with his first presidential address, speaking of a 'conscious reorientation of Sinn Féin towards an electoral strategy and the orientation of our policies towards the radical roots of our republican ideology'.[28] This reorientation was allied to a shift towards political participation and, perhaps more significantly, away from armed struggle.

Those opposed to the ending of abstentionism were led by Ruairí Ó Brádaigh, but Ó Brádaigh's credibility had been badly damaged by the 1975 ceasefire and he was becoming increasingly viewed as a republican dinosaur. The shift away from militarism therefore presented more of a challenge for Adams. That the IRA's struggle would have to be reconceptualised was inevitable; there was still a strong imperative towards violence and the IRA had killed over a thousand people, including nearly six hundred security force members, during the 1970s. They continued to average over fifty murders a year throughout the 1980s, striking at the British establishment to deadly effect: an October 1981 bomb at Chelsea barracks killed two and injured 40; on 20 July 1982, bombs at Hyde Park and Regent's Park in London killed nine soldiers as well as seven Army horses; Unionist MLA Edgar Graham was shot dead outside Queen's University on 7 December 1983; and most significantly, on 12 October 1984, they very nearly killed Prime Minister Margaret Thatcher, blowing up the Grand Hotel in Brighton during the Conservative Party Conference. Five died in an attack that struck at the heart of the British government. They also killed renegade loyalist and Shankill Butcher leader Lenny Murphy on 16 November 1982.

During the mid-1980s, Colonel Gaddafi responded to perceived British support for the American bombing of Libya in April 1986 by renewing arms shipments to the IRA. The scale of these shipments was indicated by the interception of the *Eksund* vessel in November 1987 by French and Irish authorities. The coup of intercepting the huge arms shipment aboard the *Eksund* was tempered by the knowledge that this was only a portion of the weaponry that Gaddafi had sent.

For the Adams strategy to succeed, it was essential that the IRA remain on board with his programme for the movement. For former Northern Ireland Office member, Ian Pearson MP, 'it's quite clear to me that the major critical decisions being taken by Sinn Féin have the approval of the privy council of the IRA'.[29] Unable to secure the support of Tom Maguire, who was resolutely opposed to the ending of abstentionism,[30] Adams had to create the perception across the IRA that the armed campaign was set for escalation.[31] Adams claimed that comparisons with 1970

137

were inaccurate: 'at that time the IRA leadership had decided to abandon armed struggle and then decided to drop abstentionism . . . we are not engaged in any new departure'.[32] Increased IRA violence during 1987, utilising the 136 tonnes of weaponry that successfully arrived in Ireland from Libya,[33] did much to allay the militarists' fears.

LONG WAR OR LONG PEACE?

Given the pattern of republican splits had established the convention of the formation of a new political party along with a new military group, in the aftermath of the Sinn Féin split, 1987 was a crucial year for the Provisional IRA. Retaining the support of politically inclined republicans for the new political programme was considerably less challenging than convincing the IRA rank-and-file that participation in Dáil Éireann did not mean the ending of the armed struggle. In the aftermath of the hunger strikes, it could reasonably be argued that contesting elections was merely a case of riding the momentum, but it was becoming increasingly apparent that politics was becoming a matter of policy rather than a short-term tactic to promote the republican struggle.

In the autumn of 1986, the IRA had held its first Army Convention since 1970. Given the requirement for attendance of all senior IRA figures, the organisation of such a meeting required complex choreography. Republicans were vague about when or where this had taken place and it was considered an embarrassment to security forces across Ireland that it had occurred. The meeting also fuelled conspiracy theories that alleged tacit state support for the change,[34] particularly after the Army Convention voted to support the ending of abstentionism. This was ill-received by older volunteers; former Chief of Staff Seán MácStíofain stated, 'I challenge the right and authority of the IRA to take such compromising decisions',[35] and Geraldine Taylor opined that 'all those men who were present at that Army Convention were guilty of treason'.[36]

The new acquisition of semtex, the Czech-made plastic explosive, as part of the Libyan arms shipments boosted the IRA's bomb-making capacity and it was important that with the means to escalate the IRA campaign, an increase in activity took place. The escalation was inevitably misdirected. Compared to 1986, an additional ten civilians were killed relative to only four extra security force personnel. Still, *An Phoblacht* boasted of 'devastating attacks' that 'demonstrated the IRA's flexibility and determination',[37] 'the increased impact of IRA operations',[38] and 'a week of intensive IRA actions [rattling] the crown force's confidence and morale to its core'.[39] The death of Lord Justice Gibson and his wife in April also indicated that public figures were still susceptible to attack. This killing has since been reviewed as part of the Cory inquiry into alleged collusion between state and paramilitary groups.[40] Troubling for volunteers were increased security force successes against the IRA; among the arrests, eight volunteers were killed in 1987 and seven the following year. The only years in which the IRA suffered greater losses to the security forces were 1971, 1972 and 1973. Whereas the IRA could target large numbers of security force personnel by planting bombs, the Army, RUC and UDR dealt primarily in arrest operations, with the shooting of suspected paramilitaries a last resort. With the deployment of sophisticated observation, surveillance, patrolling and counter-improvised explosive device (IED) tactics and the firm establishment of a command structure to control security operations,[41] the IRA were less able to strike at the Army and adapted their tactics accordingly, with greater success in 1988 and 1989.

Along with improved security force capability, the deployment of the Special Air Service (SAS) to Northern Ireland gave the security operation a cutting edge which the IRA struggled to contend with. The SAS was first deployed as part of the Military Reaction Force in the early 1970s before their first official deployment in 1976. Co-operation between the various intelligence agencies involved in security operations meant that the SAS were deployed with ruthless efficiency throughout the 1980s, but during the middle years of the decade their operations were alleged to be on a shoot-to-kill basis. Two engagements in particular fuelled these allegations.

In May 1987, an eight-man unit from the Provisional IRA East Tyrone Brigade was wiped out in an SAS ambush as they attempted to destroy Loughgall RUC station, an operation geared at increasing the republican zone of liberation in the region.[42] Inherent in this strategy was the declaration that construction workers repairing security force buildings would be targeted, the threat leaving multiple barracks in a poor state of repair.[43] The execution-style killings indicated that the British forces were now targeting the destruction of the IRA. In attempting to escalate the armed campaign, the IRA had encountered their most formidable foe in the SAS, Brendan Hughes recalling, 'the IRA was in a very bad state; it was in disarray. I argued on many occasions that operations should not take place, especially in places like South Armagh, Tyrone and Donegal.'[44] An

Phoblacht detailed how the volunteers were 'brutally slain', and how 'it is clear that the RUC and British troops taking part in the ambush had, under instructions from their political masters, established a killing zone within which no-one was to be left alive'.[45]

Suspicion was rife after the loss of one of the IRA's deadliest fighting units, with it suspected across the movement that an informer had surrendered crucial information about the operation.[46] The IRA had planned to use a stolen digger to breach the exterior of the base, before exploding a bomb inside to destroy it, a tactic they had already used in the area.[47] Given the improvements in British security, and particularly intelligence, policy since the 1970s, the theft of vehicles that were to be used at Loughgall undoubtedly helped trap the IRA volunteers. After a strategic rethink,[48] the IRA resumed operations but the demand for reaction only brought tragedy with the Remembrance Day bombing of Enniskillen. A bomb that was supposed to have targeted soldiers on patrol before or after the service exploded, killing ten civilians and an RUC reservist, and injuring sixty-three. A republican said 'politically and internationally it is a major setback', with Adams admitting that 'our plans for expansion will have been dealt a body blow'.[49]

The SAS struck again in 1988, killing three volunteers during Operation Flavius in Gibraltar. Intelligence sources suggested that the IRA was planning an attack on a parade of British military bands, a tactic they had used with deadly efficiency in 1982 in Hyde Park and Regent's Park. On 6 March the suspected IRA volunteers were spotted acting suspiciously near a parked car that had been associated with the operation and followed. After the IRA volunteers identified their pursuers, they were shot dead. Although it transpired that Mairéad Farrell, Seán Savage and Dan McCann were unarmed and the suspect car was clean, another car was later found, primed with 140 lb of semtex. Although the European Court of Human Rights declared that Britain had acted in contravention of its regulations at Loughgall and Gibraltar, no action was taken and the Stalker Inquiry, which, under Deputy Chief Constable John Stalker of the Greater Manchester Police, had been established in 1984 after a series of controversial shootings in late 1982, was closed down before its findings could be published.

Although drawing huge controversy, not least in the European Court of Human Rights, the new offensive strategy employed by the British Army is integral to understanding why the IRA campaign was allowed to be scaled back at a time when it had ample resources at its disposal after the

Libyan arms shipments. The fact that, in 2010, Gaddafi felt compelled to compensate victims of IRA attacks emphasises how wide the violence of the 1980s was felt.[50] However, rather than increased IRA activity defining this period, it was the British Army who turned IRA policy back on republicans: rather than demoralising British public opinion by sending soldiers home in coffins, the focus was on the large-scale and heavily policed republican funerals.[51] Although the republicans would argue that 'Loughgall proved . . . that the sectarian six-county state cannot be held without the British Army . . . the highly-trained and elite SAS terrorists of the British Army were needed to carry out the Loughgall ambush',[52] the SAS were forcing the point across that the British Army might not only be unbeatable militarily, but had the means to wage an aggressive offensive campaign that could actually push the IRA towards defeat.

Heavy security force presence at republican funerals merely reinforced the point, intentionally or otherwise. Trouble frequently occurred at republican funerals between mourners and security force personnel, and by the time the Gibraltar volunteers were buried it was standard policy for the RUC and Army to keep well back from Milltown cemetery. This distance enabled renegade loyalist Michael Stone to carry out an attack on the funeral, killing three. At the funeral for Kevin Brady, an IRA volunteer who happened to fall victim to Stone's attack, plain-clothes soldiers corporals David Howes and Derek Wood were brutally murdered by mourners. The two had been observing the funeral procession in their unmarked car when, inexplicably, they drove at speed towards the procession before becoming trapped among the cortège. The two were dragged from their car, driven to nearby waste ground and killed. The brutal slaying of the corporals emphasised the climate of fear within the republican community but, as noted by Marian Price, 'Gerry Adams was there and all Gerry Adams would have had to do was to say "get that stopped" and it would have stopped.'[53]

From the British perspective, the deployment of the SAS and their controversial means effectively tightened their grip on Northern Irish security. Richard O'Rawe opines that 'the SAS had an impact in terms of ensuring that the leadership knew to lay down their arms . . . "This is the future – we're not going to take you prisoner, we're going to kill you."'[54] The fact that, had it so desired, the SAS could easily have struck at the IRA on a larger scale has troubled republicans since; those killed, notably at Loughgall 'were people who would have opposed Adams' attempts to wind down the IRA'.[55] Marian Price adds:

141

key figures in the republican movement were taken out. Key people who would not have gone down the road that Mr Adams had embarked on and who would have posed a major threat. People who could have been placed in leadership roles, who people would have followed and who would have caused serious problems for Mr Adams . . . Mairéad [Farrell] would not have been someone who disagreed with the path that they were embarking on without being very vocal in her opposition to it and I do believe she would have been opposed to it. I think that it's very telling that in Gibraltar, there was a four-man team and the only one who came home was Siobhan O'Hanlon who was Mr Adams' secretary, I think that tells a lot.[56]

The allegation that the republican leadership had deliberately esca-lated the IRA campaign in the knowledge that such disasters would occur has contributed to the revision of republican history that has gathered in momentum since 2005. Loughgall and Gibraltar served to undermine the armed struggle and, by extension, legitimise political republicanism, erad-icating those likely to oppose the shift towards politics at the same time.[57] Jim Lynagh and his East Tyrone brigade of the IRA had been identified as one which could head the new 'Tet' offensive based on the Viet Cong campaign of 1968, particularly with the newly acquired arms.[58] Even with substantial stores of semtex, 'one of the most powerful non-nuclear explosives',[59] the large-scale bombing capacity this gave the IRA was only partially realised,[60] deployed at Enniskillen and in an attack on an Army bus at Ballygawley as a booster rather than a primary explosive. A former volunteer noted that 'we were having plenty of success without semtex . . . at Ballygawley we "only" got eight, but it was a bus of about fifty-six. If we'd used a fertiliser bomb, the whole bus would have been destroyed.'[61]

The IRA continued to strike at the Army for the remainder of the decade, with ten marines killed in a bomb at Deal barracks in Kent in 1989 and two soldiers killed at Derryard vehicle checkpoint in Fermanagh later that year in a 'very rare example of them actually . . . having a go at a place'.[62] The latter attack was the first major domestic operation for the IRA since Loughgall.

The Libyan arms had provided the IRA with the capacity for destruc-tion on an unprecedented scale. Although the *Eksund* had been inter-cepted along with the bulk of the shipment, substantial weaponry did arrive between August 1985 and October 1986. The loss of the *Eksund* was not a significant blow to the republican movement; they had no financial investment in the shipments and the increasing perception is that they had no strategic investment in them either: 'it was the one that nobody wanted to come into Ireland'.[63] What they did provide was an opportunity for the leadership to prove that it was at least attempting to escalate the armed campaign: 'It proves that you're out there trying to procure arms . . . nobody's doing any damage with them but you can still turn round to your grass roots and say "listen lads, we're out there trying to get weapons".'[64]

Events during the 1980s, deliberately or unintentionally, began to highlight the limitations of the armed struggle. At a time when increasing Sinn Féin political successes pointed to the benefits of that avenue, the Provisional republican machine seemed able to adapt to whatever circumstances it faced. In the aftermath of a potentially tricky split, the Adams leadership's ability to offer a progressive strategy was crucial.

REPUBLICAN SINN FÉIN

I have opposed the republican policy since 1981 . . . I am against the way republicanism has been moving since 1986, and before that, to the 1921 partitionists who created the problem. (Ruairí Ó Brádaigh)[65]

Despite the considerable political successes of 1981, it was forbidden to even discuss the ending of abstentionism until 1984. A motion was passed at the Ard Fheis which facilitated a debate the following year and, ultimately, the ending of abstentionism through a motion at the 1986 Ard Fheis which permitted successful Sinn Féin candidates to take their seats in the Dáil.[66] The 1986 Ard Fheis took place in Dublin on 1 and 2 November and centred on the issue of resolution 162: 'this Ard-Fheis drops its abstentionist attitude to Leinster House. Successful Sinn Féin parliamentary candidates in 26-County elections: a. Shall attend Leinster House as directed by the Ard Chomhairle; b. Shall not draw their salaries for personal use.'[67] Gerry Adams argued:

We are a political organisation and political organisations must, by their very nature, discuss and debate issues which they consider pertinent. We cannot do so properly unless all sides of the argument are articulated, unless all sides are accorded equal respect and consideration and unless all are bound by the democratic wishes of their comrades.[68]

Inevitably there was dissent to such a move and even though Adams could declare that 'there is going to be no split in Sinn Féin', he almost immediately contradicted himself by adding 'some comrades may decide to leave us . . . To leave Sinn Féin is to leave the struggle.'[69] These sentiments were echoed by Martin McGuinness: 'there isn't going to be any split in Sinn Féin . . . If you allow yourself to be led out of this hall today, the only place you're going – is home. You will be walking away from the struggle.'[70] One such comrade was Ruairí Ó Brádaigh:

> The discussion is totally out of order if this constitution of Sinn Féin means anything . . . it says there that no person who approves or supports candidates going into Leinster House, Stormont or Westminster shall be admitted to membership or allowed to retain membership, and yet on this floor we have plenty of resolutions proposing to go into Leinster House . . . because they want abstentionism ended altogether . . . how do you expect to build a democratic socialist republic out of Leinster House? How can serious social change come out of Leinster House? . . . we have not been wrong for 65 years . . . we have been right and we should continue to be right.[71]

Ó Brádaigh's impassioned appeal failed to convince delegates, with 429 of the 628 voting in favour of Resolution 162, just over the necessary two-thirds majority. As a particularly well-attended Ard Fheis, accusations of conspiracy were quickly forthcoming.[72] For those in Republican Sinn Féin, the conspiracy was obvious from an early stage:

> Adams picked new delegates so he could get the vote he wanted. All the ones up here were all Adams and that's why they shifted, he organised it and orchestrated it and the men on the run in the Free State all set up cumanns deliberately to get the vote through in the '86 Ard Fheis, soon as that Ard Fheis was over, all those new cumanns were defunct, they were there for one reason only: to carry that vote through.[73]

Ruairí Ó Brádaigh noted the similarities with the 1969 split in the party:

> on both occasions . . . the conspiracy to push for an end to abstentionism was hatched long before the vote took place . . . the people who formed the Workers' Party were more open about it. They wanted to go down the constitutional road and said so. In 1985, at our Ard Fheis, the whole platform party left the stage when abstentionism was debated. To me, that was dishonest.[74]

Ahead of the Ard Fheis, clearly seeing the writing on the wall, Ó Brádaigh had made reservations at a nearby hotel and led his supporters out of the Ard Fheis and into Republican Sinn Féin. Journalist Kevin Toolis recalled 'a motley collection of aged southern Republicans' meeting:

> There was a mad theatrical air to the proceedings. I was expecting Dáithí Ó Conaill, the archetypal fifties IRA gunman, to produce a Webley revolver from each pocket of his voluminous trench-coat, call the meeting to order and urge his followers to attack a border post that night.[75]

This was hardly the portrayal of credible Irish revolutionaries. This group claimed to 'stand by the Republic of 1916 and the First All-Ireland

Dáil of 1919',[76] a claim authenticated by the blessing given to them by Tom Maguire, 'the last general officer of the Irish Republican Army of 1921 ... also the last faithful survivor of the Second [All-Ireland] Dáil elected in the same year'.[77] With his use of the word 'faithful', Ó Brádaigh covers himself for what otherwise would have been an erroneous statement: Maguire was the only surviving *anti-Treaty* member of the Dáil; pro-Treaty TD Gearoid O'Sullivan was also still alive at this time. Maguire, who in 1986 was now 97 years of age, stated that 'I hereby declare that the Continuity Executive and the Continuity Army Council are the lawful Executive and Army Council respectively of the Irish Republican Army, and that the governmental authority, delegated in the Proclamation of 1938, now resides in the Continuity Army Council, and its lawful successors.'[78] Maguire explained his change of allegiance: 'I do not recognise the legitimacy of any Army Council styling itself the council of the Irish Republican Army which lends support to any person or organisation styling itself Sinn Féin and prepared to enter the partition parliament of Leinster House.'[79] His position was consistent with that of 1970, when he had supported the Provisional republican movement.[80] Ó Brádaigh later wrote a reverential book about Maguire entitled *Dílseacht*, or loyalty. Few militarists in the movement had forgiven Ó Brádaigh for presiding over the ill-fated 1975 ceasefire. He was increasingly isolated in the movement to the point when his family were involved in a car crash and only Martin McGuinness visited them in hospital; Gerry Adams and Danny Morrison, pointedly, stayed away.[81]

He was joined at the helm of Republican Sinn Féin by Dáithí Ó Conaill. Ó Conaill was born into a republican family in Cork in 1938 and joined Sinn Féin in 1955. Some compared him with Michael Collins because of 'his six foot-plus thin figure, whispering Cork accent and preoccupation with intelligence activity'.[82] He had been a central figure in the embryonic Provisional IRA as well as during the foundation of Irish Northern Aid in New York. He remained at the helm of the party until his sudden death at the age of 52 on New Year's Day 1991.

Both had experience in republican politics: Ó Conaill had helped convince Noel Maguire not to stand against Bobby Sands in 1981 and Ó Brádaigh had been elected to the Dáil in 1957, as one of four Sinn Féin TDs, representing Longford. He also stood for election to Westminster in 1966 as the Independent Republican candidate for Fermanagh/South Tyrone, finishing third but achieving a credible 10,370 votes. Both rejected Gerry Adams' plea for 'republicans to grasp the centrality, the primacy and the fundamental need for republican politics'.[83]

Although Ruairí Ó Brádaigh felt that 'the 1986 split was more painful because of the sacrifices in the intervening years. Our people felt . . . the soul of the movement was at stake',[84] the truth was that the republican movement had travelled a great distance down the road towards political participation since the start of the decade. The death toll was rising towards three thousand and Ó Brádaigh questioned, 'What was it all about since 1922? Why not accept the bloody Treaty in the beginning and be done with it?'[85] Cathal Goulding was also 'very very bitter about . . . the 1986 Ard Fheis when they voted to accept seats in the 26 Counties. People in the past have been killed on both sides because of that question. Many of the best people in the movement murdered and now they finally accept that abstentionism was a mistake.'[86] Ó Brádaigh commented that, 'If I found out that, after nearly twenty years in the movement, I suddenly discovered that the Workers' Party had been right, and people had died because of that question on every side, I would be very unhappy with myself.'[87] Although much of the IRA's old guard had opposed the move, Joe Cahill claimed that he considered participation in the Dáil to be acceptable, but he 'would have a real problem about Westminster or Stormont'.[88] Marian Price recalls, 'I couldn't for the life of me understand . . . why people were forcing a split in the movement over entering Leinster House . . . of course since it's become quite clear, it's because they had plans to enter everywhere else, Leinster House was just the start of a long line of concessions.'[89]

Adams had carefully shifted the republican movement to a position where the ending of abstentionism seemed like the most reasonable course of action.[90] It was relatively obvious from the 1985 Ard Fheis that it was only a matter of time before abstentionism would be jettisoned. While he claimed that prior to his 1983 General Election success, 'I would never have considered standing for election',[91] as his takeover of the movement was in full flow during the mid-70s, the Adams-penned 'Brownie' articles, which discussed the concept of 'active abstentionism', appeared, calling for republican policy to be used in a more constructive manner.[92] That Ruairí Ó Brádaigh did not know the true identity of 'Brownie' underlines Ó Brádaigh's marginalisation.[93]

There were pragmatic reasons for this shift; most voters in the Republic of Ireland now accepted and supported the institutions of the 26-county state. Voter turnout in the late 1970s was over 70 per cent and only dipped slightly in the 1980s.[94] Adams commented in 1983 that 'to ignore this reality is to blinker republican politics, to undermine the development of our struggle and is to have a basic flaw in our analysis'.[95] For Provisional republicans, electoral success 'vindicates the dropping of abstentionism',[96] and that 'our electoral intervention has exploded the myth that the republican movement enjoyed no support'.[97]

There was some sorrow at the departures of Ó Brádaigh and Ó Conaill, alluded to in the speech by Martin McGuinness at the Ard Fheis and also noted by Joe Cahill, who recalled that 'they should have fought their corner. It was a mistake, which I made myself, leaving the Republican movement in the 1960s . . . I regretted them going. Those people had given a life's service . . . But they have gone nowhere since.'[98] This view was echoed in Irish-America: 'It seems inevitable given the patriotism and honorable motives of those who walked out of the Ard Fheis last Sunday, that they will soon return and be welcomed with respect.'[99] The ego-massaging abruptly ended when it became apparent that there was no possibility that the pair could be persuaded back into the mainstream republican fold. For Mitchel McLaughlin, 'in political terms they never went anywhere . . . Their analysis of what was happening in 1970 I think was justified . . . But their analysis of what was happening in 1986 was, I think, flawed by virtue of the fact that their politics hadn't developed in the intervening years.'[100]

Although loyal to the principle of abstentionism, there was little evidence that their loyalty extended to militarism; Ó Brádaigh denied that a military wing had been formed.[101] It would not be until the following decade that the Continuity IRA would emerge, with a firing party present at Maguire's graveside in early 1994.[102] The CIRA had clearly existed prior to Maguire's funeral and Geraldine Taylor suggests that 'I would assume that they were building it up.'[103] Others recall rumours that 'Ó Conaill was going to be shot dead. That's the story that done the rounds, so the Continuity IRA were secretive for an amount of years in case Ó Conaill was shot dead. Whether that's true or not, I'm not sure.'[104] The sense of disappointment felt in the 1986 split also played a part: 'Dave O'Connell was a very bright man and a very good thinker and I think he just felt totally betrayed and I think he was a bit disgusted because he realised he'd been outmanoeuvred.'[105] Certainly, republicans who had been marginalised during the 1970s along with those expelled during the 1980s as dissent fermented within the movement were present and capable of waging a military campaign.[106]

147

In the absence of a military campaign, Republican Sinn Féin adopted Ruairí Ó Brádaigh's 'Éire Nua', federal policy, first created in the 1970s and jettisoned early in the 1980s because it was considered outdated by the Adams leadership. 'Éire Nua' was indicative of the geographical divide between the Ó Brádaigh and Adams factions. Ó Brádaigh still felt that his theoretical Dáil Uladh could offer northern unionists political autonomy within the Republic, even though it has been claimed as little more than a reworking of a Roy Johnston policy from the 1960s.[107] The federal Irish state had been envisioned by Marx as early as 1867, who wrote to Engels stating that 'previously, I thought Ireland's separation from England impossible. Now I think it inevitable, although after separation there may come federation.'[108]

OFFICIAL REPUBLICANISM IN THE 1980S: ELECTORAL SUCCESS, STALINISM AND THE OIRA

The gulf between Provisional and Official republicanism widened considerably during the 1980s. Having adopted the title 'Sinn Féin The Workers' Party' in 1977, their electoral breakthrough took place in the midst of the hunger strike as Joe Sherlock won the Dáil seat for Cork East.[109] Their meteoric political rise continued the following year as a further two seats were won and the party ended up in a coalition government with Fianna Fáil. These political successes were tempered by continuing issues over the Official IRA as members gradually shifted towards criminality as a means to attract new members.[110] The group further distanced itself from Provisional republicanism by altering its name to The Workers' Party, described by the Provisional movement as a 'long overdue decision . . . the stickies are recognizing that they long ago abandoned any connection with Irish Republicanism'.[111] The movement was also troubled by issues associated with international communism.

Although the group opposed the hunger strike, they did enjoy notable political success in its midst. Opposition was a logical position for the Official republicans, particularly given the close association between the hunger strike and their former comrades of the PIRA and INLA. Initial suspicions that the strike would be crushed by the Thatcher government turned to bitterness as Officials saw the intransigence of the British government play into the hands of the Provisionals.[112] The movement did lose out on potential support as it was noted that 'nationalist Ireland identified with the tide of sentiment released during this period'.[113] This did not appear to have impacted on the movement too severely, with Joe Sherlock becoming the party's first TD in 1981. The February 1982 election saw further success as Proinsias De Rossa and Patrick Gallagher won seats in Dublin North West and Waterford respectively. Although the Workers' Party gave their support to the Haughey government, the twenty-third Dáil was insufficiently stable to hold government for even a full year and the country faced its third general election in eighteen months. The finances of the Workers' Party had been stretched by the almost continual electioneering that had gone on since early 1981 and the party took a bank loan to finance their campaign for the November election.[114] This election was less successful for the movement, Sherlock losing his Cork East seat and Gallagher losing Waterford, losses that were tempered by the victory of Tomás Mac Giolla in Dublin West. The party did also achieve a slight increase in first-preference votes.

As the decade progressed, so did the Workers' Party in the Republic, achieving four TDs in the 1987 election as Sherlock regained his old seat and Pat McCartan gave the party its third Dublin TD. They went on to achieve seven TDs in 1989, adding Eric Byrne in Dublin South Central, Pat Rabbitte in Dublin South West, and Eamon Gilmore in Dun Laoghaire, while Sinn Féin struggled, achieving less than 2 per cent of first-preference votes. With the significant figure of six TDs in Ireland's capital, the Workers' Party could reasonably claim to enjoy the support of working-class Dublin. Their seven deputies allowed them access to secretarial and debating facilities in the Dáil and significant state funding.[115]

While the movement's opposition to the hunger strikes had not proven overly costly, the party was becoming increasingly dominated north of the border by Sinn Féin: falling 80,000 votes behind in the 1984 European elections and fifty-four councillors behind in the 1985 local council elections. The Workers' Party's 20,000 votes in the 1987 General Election was 60,000 less than Sinn Féin. Several candidates failed even to have electoral deposits returned. Standing in West Belfast, Mary McMahon was 15,000 votes behind Gerry Adams in both the 1983 and 1987 Westminster elections. Neither Tommy Owens nor Paddy Joe McLaren in Mid-Ulster, David Kettyles in Fermanagh/South Tyrone, Eamonn Melaugh in Foyle nor Dessie O'Hagan in South Down achieved the requisite 5 per cent of the vote. They enjoyed more success in local elections; three councillors in 1981 and five in 1985. The party also reported increasing numbers of votes coming from Protestant areas. John Lowry

notes the party achieving considerable votes in East Belfast in addition
to the 'clear evidence . . . that Protestant working-class people were
quite prepared to come to The Workers' Party for advice . . . in practice
we were the only political party that was able to canvass in Protestant
and Catholic areas and we did'.[116] In the Oldpark area of North Belfast,
Seamus Lynch was one notable success. The constituency had previously
elected a Northern Ireland Labour Party MP to the Northern Ireland
Parliament as recently as 1969. While this may have suggested that the
Workers' Party could now hope to reach out to Protestants, the group
was still troubled by persistent allegations as to the continued existence
of the Official IRA. In mid-1982, the party recognised how costly links to
militarism were. The murder of Jim Flynn, the alleged assassin of Seamus
Costello, and an exposé in April's *Magill* magazine pressured the movement on the issue of the influence of the Official IRA.[117]

The Workers' Party claimed that it 'has consistently opposed terrorism in Northern Ireland', declaring it to be 'a substitute for political
struggle, and a denial of the political process. Counter-revolutionary in
character, terrorism is contemptuous of the popular will in that it asserts
the primacy of the individual act of terror over mass political action.'[118]
The continued existence of their own military wing was therefore problematic. Flynn was given an Official republican funeral, although not an
Official *IRA* funeral,[119] the movement deciding that the symbolism of
an Official IRA funeral ten years after the ceasefire was potentially too
damaging.

The OIRA had indeed persisted since the ceasefire and the 1974 INLA
split. What purpose an individual may have seen in maintaining membership in an armed organisation that was on ceasefire is unclear and suggests
a decidedly subversive element; certainly the OIRA had barely contributed to the overall armed struggle. A series of robberies were attributed to
the OIRA,[120] creating discontent in the movement that manifested itself
in a further split during the early 1990s. John Lowry explained:

> members of the party in the North were always under attack from the
> Provisionals . . . it erupted in its most serious forms in killing, particularly in the
> seventies, but in the eighties . . . there would have been incidents of members
> being assaulted and defending themselves and this was blown up out of all pro-
> portion [with] sections of the media saying that this was evidence of the Official
> IRA re-emerging. It was nonsense . . . it's totally illogical and a nonsense to
> suggest that in the 1980s someone would want to resurrect some form of military
> organisation.[121]

The association proved politically damaging and the increasing shadow of the Official IRA precipitated further division. The credibility of the party was further damaged during this period by links to international communism. Dominated by the Provisionals in the United States, the Official republicans had looked east for aid from the early 1970s onwards and leading members visited Moscow and North Korea during the early 1980s,[122] and indeed, appealed to Moscow for support later in the decade.[123] The deep recession which Ireland was stuck in during the mid-1980s had convinced the movement that it was only a matter of time before the masses looked to the political left for their salvation.

The 1980s were difficult years for socialists internationally. The rise of conservative neoliberal governments, notably the Margaret Thatcher and Ronald Reagan governments in the United Kingdom and United States, attacked the welfare state as an impediment to private entrepreneurship. European socialists were forced to reconfigure their agendas within the framework of the free market. In Soviet countries, shortages of consumer goods and the lack of individual rights began to disillusion communists as some looked to institute forms of market socialism. Such associations were hardly likely to ever really benefit the Workers' Party. Whether or not the Soviet links were accurate became largely irrelevant, rather the perception of continued Soviet links continued to hinder the domestic credibility of the Workers' Party.

THE REPUBLICAN SOCIALISTS IN THE 1980S: BLOOD AND SOCIALISM

Considerably less affected by the difficulties of international socialism during the 1980s were the Irish Republican Socialist Party. So dominated had the party become by the INLA since the inception of the movement, party members were forced to operate in the shadows for fear of assassination as the movement lurched between internecine feuds. 1979 had seen the assassination of Airey Neave and this operation suggested that the INLA may have shaken off the imprecision that marked most of their early activity. Unsurprisingly, the INLA enjoyed an increased presence in the prison wings of Northern Ireland.

As early as the summer of 1975, a group of fifteen IRSP men had appeared naked in court in protest at their alleged mistreatment in the Crumlin Road prison.[124] Kieran Nugent began the blanket protest in September 1976 and the first INLA member, the rather appropriately named James Connolly Brady from Derry, joined soon after. Seamus Costello had been cautious about joining the blanket protest, 'because it had started spontaneously. It was only once it became a national issue that he began to pay it some attention.'[125] Clearly some form of mass action was inevitable as soon as the decision to scrap political status had been made. It was not like Costello to act so opportunistically.

Not content with simply paying attention, the INLA ensured that once the prison protest began to gather momentum, it was at the forefront of the campaign. IRA Officer Commanding Brendan Hughes led the first hunger strike on 27 October 1980 and, after some disagreement, INLA OC John Nixon became the seventh hunger striker.[126] They assumed an even more prominent role during the second hunger strike, Nixon's replacement, 'Patsy O'Hara . . . insisted that the INLA were going to have a presence on the hunger strike and he was going to be one of the first ones to be on it.'[127] The three INLA volunteers who died on hunger strike – O'Hara, Kevin Lynch and Michael Devine, all from County Derry – represented a far higher proportion of INLA prisoners than the seven PIRA men who died. The commitment to the hunger strike was evident to current IRSP members because of the relatively short sentences that the three men were serving: 'Patsy O'Hara . . . Kevin Lynch, Mickey Devine they were walking out of jail . . . If Mickey Devine had put a pair of boots on and walked out of the wing, he'd have been out within three months. For the IRSP and the INLA, per capita, three men dying on hunger strike was a massive figure, I think the Provisionals had 625 men and the INLA had 40 or 50.'[128] Despite their significant sacrifice, the Republican Socialist movement noted that the 'main beneficiaries [from the hunger strikes] were the Provisional Republican Movement, who both revitalised and increased their membership, had a vast increase in their financial base, and gained a political experience they would have never got'.[129]

O'Hara in particular became hugely symbolic for the entire movement. Only thirteen years old when he went on his first civil rights march, one year later he joined Fianna Éireann in Derry. He was shot and injured while manning a barricade in Derry in 1971 and was interned during 1974. He joined the IRSM on his release in April 1975, provoked by the Official IRA ceasefire.[130] In prison he conducted bomb-making classes, including instruction on mercury tilt-switch bombs similar to that used to assassinate Airey Neave.[131] He was arrested in 1979 for possession of a hand grenade and joined his brother Tony on the blanket protest.[132] For O'Hara, 'if the prisoners are criminalised, then the struggle for Irish freedom is criminalised'.[133] After his death, having gone sixty-one days without food, on 21 May, Bernadette McAliskey, long since estranged from the IRSP, spoke at his funeral, paying tribute to the courage of the hunger strikers.[134] The IRSM claim that his funeral turnout exceeded that of the victims of Bloody Sunday,[135] and a Patsy O'Hara Youth Movement formed in the Markets area of central Belfast, a youth movement that attracted future IRSP leaders such as Thomas Power and John O'Reilly.[136]

Kevin Lynch took part in the 1981 Dáil election and achieved a respectable 7.5 per cent of first-preference votes, only 126 votes behind Sinn Féin candidate Paddy Gallagher in Waterford.[137] He was the seventh man to die, on 1 August. Devine, the tenth and final hunger striker, passed away on 20 August. Subsequent allegations about Sinn Féin manipulation of the hunger strike are consistent with the fact that one-third of the remaining hunger strikers to die were INLA.[138] Although they had intended to replace each of their men, by the time Devine died 'the Irish Republican Socialist Party was split over the question of continuing the hunger strike since there was no sign that Thatcher was going to give in and because all the INLA volunteers in the Blocks would be dead within six months if the current ratio of seven IRA to three INLA fasters were maintained'.[139] Of those participants in the hunger strike who did not die, only one was in the INLA compared to twelve IRA men; it should be noted that the 22:4 ratio was a little closer to being representative of the republican prison population.

The INLA reflected that 'the lack of a political strategy from the beginning to win the 5 demands' led to the 'failure of the campaign'.[140] The IRSP noted that 'the negative consequences of the hunger strikes were we became marginalized. The Provos . . . hijacked the campaign',[141] and that the movement was 'unable to have any control over a mass movement that the Provos so clearly and so successfully set out to dominate'.[142] When the families of hunger strikers visited the United States on a Noraid-organised fundraising trip, Sean Sands and Malachy McCreesh had to insist that Liz O'Hara was allowed to join them and the IRSP received little or no finance from the trip.[143]

For Eoin Ó Broin, this is not 'a credible suggestion . . . the IRSP . . . and the Workers' Party are probably the only organisations who would even allege that at this point',[144] and Danny Morrison believes that 'in critical situations like this . . . you can only be involved in such a strategy and in such an operation if there's one command, so to speak'.[145] Anthony McIntyre notes that 'the endless feuding [of the INLA] enabled the Provos to dissociate from . . . the behaviour of the INLA volunteers. It was easy to sell to people: "Do you think these three guys who died on hunger strike would be associated with this crowd today?" I think the INLA only have themselves to blame.'[146]

The unity of purpose evident in the H-Block/Armagh campaign had, for Republican Socialists, shades of the 'broad front', an idea promoted by IRSP member Terry Robson. Robson argued that the 1916 Easter Rising was the first example of a broad front, that its purpose was more than simply a uniting of forces against a common enemy. He suggested that this would only advance the interests of the dominant group in the alliance.[147] For Liam O'Ruairc, 'the IRSP put too much emphasis upon the strategy of the Broad Front . . . the Broad Front is not the decisive catalyst for struggle . . . the development of the Broad Front should be subordinated to the necessity of building the revolutionary vanguard party based on scientific socialism as the decisive vehicle to bring about national liberation and socialism.'[148]

The IRSP considered that 'any broad anti-imperialist front without the Provos will be overshadowed by their non-involvement . . . to a certain extent the IRSP is the Broad Front', and that the Provisional republicans would only become involved in such a movement if they could dominate it. They also criticised the People's Democracy for 'latching onto mass movements and achieving a certain amount of publicity for themselves is about as much as they can hope for'.[149] That the Provisional republicans dominated the H-Block/Armagh campaign was, for members of the movement, perfectly logical. Danny Morrison: 'most of the resources that were being supplied in the campaign were resources that the Republican Movement provided . . . paying for posters, paying for leaflets . . . organising buses';[150] Eoin Ó Broin notes that 'the overwhelming majority of the key campaigners and political leaders and activists from the national to the local level in the period '76–'82 are presently supporters of Sinn Féin'.[151] When Thomas Power states that 'we were, on our own, numerically impotent, but that still didn't take away the principle of what we believed was the correct thing at the correct time',[152] the irony of the accusation they levelled at the People's Democracy stands out.

The group was certainly in need of a boost after the loyalist murders of Dr Miriam Daly in June and Ronnie Bunting, their most prominent Protestant member, and Noel Little in October 1980; 'those were bleak times'[153] for the movement. The IRSP did achieve some political success on the back of the H-Block campaign. The May 1981 local council elections saw them win two seats on Belfast City Council and 3,654 votes.[154] Although Ed Moloney has attributed this success to the lack of Sinn Féin candidates,[155] it would be unfair to completely dismiss the significance of the party's maiden electoral success. Indeed, Anthony Coughlan remarks that so strong was the political acumen he saw in Seamus Costello that he considered Costello's ascension to the Dáil inevitable.[156] After Costello's murder, the movement looked to Thomas 'Ta' Power for ideological guidance and were able to capitalise on the hunger strike period at a time when increasing leftist rhetoric from Sinn Féin cut off the republican socialist angle in Northern Ireland and the increased success of the Workers' Party in the South pressed the IRSP in the Republic:

> People just flooded to the group. The politics of it might have meant less in the emotion of the time . . . The INLA were on the streets . . . people remember that; people don't remember too many armed Provisionals on the streets – certainly in the Divis Flats, the New Lodge, Derry, the INLA [was] to the fore. What that does is it recruits young men into the military wing. Others might have been interested in politics, but really a hunger strike is that emotional it's really a rallying call for a military campaign because young men and women aren't going to say, 'Right, my neighbour is starving to death, I'm going to go out and sell a few papers or put posters up', they might do that as well, Ta Power did that during the day then fought British soldiers at night.[157]

While the INLA may have been attacking the security forces more frequently than the IRA during the hunger strikes,[158] there is no doubting which organisation was more deadly between 1 March, when Bobby Sands began the second hunger strike, and the death of Michael Devine on 20 August.[159] The IRA killed twenty-six during this period, including twenty-three current and former members of the security forces. During the same period, the INLA only killed UDR member Jack Donnelly on 16 April and RUC Constable Gary Martin on 27 April, losing three volunteers. They did kill prominent UDA man William 'Bucky' McCullogh on 16 October 1981, but the movement had been markedly less effective offensively than the IRA during the hunger strikes. The stuttering campaign raises a question of the calibre of recruit they were able to attract, with the political and military impetus resting firmly with the Provisionals. Some Provisional republicans did not see the INLA as rivals, good relations fostered during the prison protest undoubtedly contributing to the lack of ill-will towards an organisation that was otherwise highly volatile. This would change later in the decade.

Replenished with new recruits, as well as defections from PIRA, the INLA launched a wave of attacks throughout 1982 that would leave thirty-one dead. Eleven soldiers and six civilians were killed in an INLA bomb attack at the Droppin' Well bar in Ballykelly, County Derry on 6 December 1982. Although a town of moderate politics, the Army base nearby promoted Ballykelly as a suitable location for an attack on the security forces, the INLA announcing that 'we attacked soldiers who are occupying our country, who are using arms against our people. Ballykelly was an act of war.'[160] While the INLA in County Derry lacked the size and operational nous of the IRA, they were a tricky opponent for security forces, forming small operational units of two or three people who would often conduct operations on a spur-of-the-moment decision.[161] It was from this area that their most notorious leader emerged; Dominic 'Mad Dog' McGlinchey, who claimed responsibility for the planning of the Ballykelly bomb.[162]

Senior INLA members tended to be either former Official IRA men who sought to continue the armed struggle or former Provisional IRA volunteers who had fallen foul of the increasingly strict regime from the late 1970s onwards. McGlinchey fell into the latter category. Originally from Bellaghy, he was interned in 1971 and on his release teamed up with future hunger striker Francis Hughes to form a deadly IRA unit, the two pictured on a wanted poster issued by the RUC.[163] McGlinchey was jailed in the Republic between 1977 and 1982 and during this period defected to the INLA. Fra Halligan suggests that 'Dominic McGlinchey wouldn't have had any politics and wouldn't have had any problem saying [that] to you.'[164] Danny Morrison contends that 'the Republican Movement had really had an argument with him over his behaviour and so he wasn't disgruntled over politics, which . . . undermines this theory that they were a magnet for progressive and left wing ideologues',[165] although McGlinchey has been noted for reading left-wing literature while imprisoned.[166] It was not uncommon for prominent Provisionals to fall out with the leadership while imprisoned, Brendan Hughes recalling his own desire to defect to the INLA during his time in Long Kesh.[167]

The INLA would be an inconsistent thorn in the side of loyalist para-militaries. After the McCullogh killing, the INLA shot dead Red Hand Commando founder John McKeague in January 1982. Although the Droppin' Well bomb and the killings of McKeague and McCullogh may have suggested a more efficient paramilitary organisation, the eleven civilians who died at its hands in 1982 suggested otherwise; indeed, the INLA killed more civilians than any other organisation that year. Although it claimed that 'the Irish National Liberation Army are the only army in the north who have never attacked innocent civilians, nor carried out random bombings or shootings',[168] it was described in the press as 'badly organised and ill-equipped', with a membership of a 'mixture of extreme left-wing and young Catholics attracted by the prospects of violence'.[169] The IRSP's socialist Irish republic could hardly have seemed more distant.

The INLA's capacity for ruthlessness and recklessness was nowhere better represented than in its attack on Darkley Pentecostal Church in South Armagh on 20 November 1983. This attack was claimed by the 'Catholic Reaction Force', although the weapons used were INLA-owned.[170] Dominic McGlinchey was reported to have been dismayed by the incident, stating 'they were entirely innocent hillbilly folk who had done no harm to anyone. There is no justification for the incident',[171] even though he was widely believed to have been responsible for supplying the weapons used. Under the watchful eye of McGlinchey, considered a 'psycho killer' by RUC Special Branch's E4A unit, the INLA became more ruthless than the PIRA.[172]

Subordinated by the INLA, the IRSP embarked on a period of introspection which culminated with the September 1984 announcement of the formal adoption of the teachings of Marx, Engels and Lenin. The party's rhetoric from this period had a distinctly socialist feel to it, which is attributed to the influence of then party chairman Jim Lane, who had been active in the Irish Revolutionary Forces in the 1960s. Some party members left to form the Communist Party of Great Britain later in the decade.[173] The 1984 announcement was totally at odds with their line from nine years previously, where the party argued that 'they would not seek to import alien and mechanical formulas, whether by Lenin, Trotsky or anyone else'.[174]

With their new international socialist perspective now defined, the party attempted to form alliances with international socialist groups. On one occasion a sympathetic journalist set up a meeting between Republican Socialist representatives and a group of radical left-wing Frenchwomen. The representatives of the movement at the meeting were INLA men, based in Dublin, who travelled to Belfast to meet with the radicals. They decided to stop in a town on their journey north to rob a bank and proceeded to a bar to celebrate their crime. This led to their late and drunken arrival at the meeting, where the Frenchwomen had been kept waiting for a number of hours. Expecting a meaningful interaction with like-minded Irish socialists, they would certainly have been surprised and shocked to be greeted by drunken criminals who proceeded to chase them around the room, keen for further misadventures.[175] Needless to say, this potential alliance was thwarted before it began. Such recklessness was endemic in the INLA, even at organisational level. For Danny Morrison:

> It was noted by the Republican Movement that the INLA looked big for a short while and they were recruiting like mad and appointing people to powerful positions without them being tested, without any scrutiny . . . whereas the IRA was operating a much tighter recruiting policy and not letting everybody in who had been emotionally affected by the ten deaths . . . when the 'Supergrass' strategy was pursued by the Brits, the INLA suffered more than the IRA . . .[176]

The massive influx of volunteers who joined post-hunger strike, combined with the less-than-scrupulous recruitment policies of the organisation, exposed the INLA to informers. While the INLA's small operational unit structure reduced the chances of infiltration in rural areas, in larger urban areas they were more susceptible.[177] The INLA was 'riven by informers and criminal corruption',[178] and Thomas Power admitted that 'a number of highly placed informers . . . systematically brought the movement to its knees . . . by mid-1982 instability reigned'.[179] This was most sharply felt after the 1983 arrest of Harry Kirkpatrick. After confessing to the murder of Territorial Army member Hugh McGinn in 1980, Kirkpatrick implicated several members of the INLA, marking him as a 'supergrass'.[180] In 1985, twenty-seven INLA men were jailed on evidence supplied by Kirkpatrick, who received a reduced sentence.[181] In jail, Kirkpatrick was segregated from other republican prisoners and his wife was kidnapped by the INLA. Of the 120 total convictions during the supergrass era, sixty-eight were convicted on uncorroborated accomplice evidence, twenty-six of those on the word of Kirkpatrick.[182] Within a year of their convictions, all but three of the men were released, Gerard Steenson among their number.[183] The rapid abandonment of the policy emphasised its inherent flaws from a legal standpoint,[184] but the trials also fermented considerable distrust within Republican Socialism, leading to the emergence of three separate factions within the movement.

The political faction was led by John O'Reilly and Thomas Power and began to organise separately from the INLA, which itself had seen a splinter group led by Gerard Steenson emerge, labelling itself 'The Liquidators'.[185] Initially known as the INLA Army Council faction (distinct from the INLA General Headquarters faction), this splinter group became the Irish People's Liberation Organisation (IPLO). These divisions within the INLA reflected a new change of direction by the political wing of the movement. While it is true that 'from the outset, the INLA had problems with internal feuding',[186] the 1980s was a particularly volatile period in the movement's history, as frustration arising from the inability to capitalise on the prison campaign manifested itself in a series of clashes within the movement. Power himself supports this: 'the short history of this movement . . . has been plagued with inner turmoil and internal problems'.[187]

So it was that the IPLO emerged in late 1986 as part of, to borrow a phrase from Steve Bruce, 'a veritable "alphabet spaghetti" of smaller groupings'.[188] They announced their arrival with the killing of RUC Constable Derek Patterson on 10 November and INLA volunteer Thomas McCartan on 22 December. The IRSP declared the IPLO to be 'a collection of factions, who had previously resigned or been purged from the IRSM for criminal activity'.[189] Falling in with the pattern of republican splits, the natural successor to the split was the feud. For the IRSP:

> We do not regard what happened as feuding . . . There was a clear agenda to destroy the Republican Socialist Movement in order to pave the way for the final settlement of the Irish Question by the imposition of the two-state solution along so-called democratic lines to allow for further penetration by international capital.[190]

The motives of 'international capital' and how they might have been handled by Gerard Steenson remain unclear. For Fra Halligan, outside interference was a possibility:

> Was it the Provisional IRA? Was it the British government? You don't get out of bed one morning and say 'That's my friend, my comrade of the last ten years but I'm going to start a campaign against him.' I just haven't got to the root of it.[191]

The feud gathered pace during 1987 to the point that calls were made pleading for IRA intervention,[192] with the IPLO killing IRSP members Thomas Power and John O'Reilly in an attack near Drogheda on 20 January.[193] It was believed that a meeting had been arranged with a view to ending the feud before it significantly damaged the organisations. The IPLO had no interest in negotiating and arrived to shoot their former comrades, also injuring INLA Chief of Staff Hugh Torney. Before the end of the month Mary McGlinchey, wife of Dominic and a ruthless INLA volunteer herself, was shot dead at home. In response, Tony McCluskey received the dubious honour of becoming the IPLO's first 'fallen' member, tortured and killed by Dessie O'Hare, an INLA volunteer best known for the kidnapping and mutilation of Dublin dentist John O'Grady.[194] Gerry Adams declared to the INLA that it had 'become totally disorganised and anti-republican and its activities have become totally degenerate', and to the IPLO faction, 'Self-righteousness doesn't wash with anyone. You have no support either.'[195]

On 14 March, Gerard Steenson was killed, shot dead by the INLA on Springfield Avenue in West Belfast, with O'Hare allegedly involved.[196] Despite the loss of their most prominent member, the IPLO maintained their armed campaign over the remainder of the year, murdering two INLA members as well as Unionist councillor and UVF member George Seawright, a highly controversial figure prone to making extreme statements against both nationalism and Catholicism. They went on to kill Ulster Freedom Fighter Billy Quee, a close friend and accomplice of UDA racketeer Jim Craig, on 7 September 1988.[197] In their brief existence, the IPLO had proven themselves worthy adversaries for both the INLA and loyalism generally, but the reputation that both the INLA and IPLO were acquiring for reckless fratricidal conflict undoubtedly undermined their republican credibility. During this same period, the INLA's slide into criminality seemed unstoppable, with O'Hare in particular developing a fearsome reputation for lawlessness. The IPLO would continue its path of aimless violence, the nature of this violence represented by the fact that just under half of their victims were Catholics, exactly half were civilians and just under a third were INLA members.

The 1980s in the Irish Republican Socialist Movement were turbulent years. The bulk of the thirty-seven INLA volunteers who fell during the troubles died during these years, as did the majority of their 113 victims. So many deaths were attributable to internecine feuding that the movement posed almost as deadly a threat to its own members as it did to British security forces. Clearly the loss of key members had impacted on the ability of the movement to control itself and it was ironic that the Airey Neave killing should ultimately serve to undermine the movement, bringing with it increased security force attention and high expectations of violence that attracted new members. Equally, the movement gained little from the hunger strike period, reflecting that 'people who were there would have preferred that it didn't happen, they'd have rather had Patsy, Kevin and Mickey'.[198] The political success that it did achieve was quickly usurped under the stewardship of Dominic McGlinchey, during which the INLA became closely associated with mindless, often sectarian, violence, rather than any form of politics. What political action the movement was able to take would only serve to further marginalise them as they ensconced themselves in the radical far left. Nevertheless, the IRSP and INLA survived the decade and continued their struggle for the thirty-two-county socialist republic into a third decade as defiant as ever.

CONCLUSION

The hegemony of the Provisional republican movement was never seriously challenged by Republican Sinn Féin, The Workers' Party, Republican Socialists or any of the splinter groups emerging from the latter during the 1980s. The decade was defined by the hunger strikes of 1980 and 1981, the momentum from which was so successfully seized on by Provisional republicans, that some have accused the movement of manipulation and exploitation of its own volunteers. This certainly pushed forward the political struggle alongside the continuation of a relatively sophisticated military campaign against the British state. The Official republicans, despite the persistence of the Official IRA, continued to distance themselves from Provisional republicanism, changing the name of their organisation and enjoying relative political success despite their non-involvement in the prison protest and the associated mass movement. While this cost them support in Northern Ireland, where they were usurped by Sinn Féin before the decade was out, the Workers Party ended the decade as the fourth party in the twenty-sixth Dáil.

In sharp contrast to their former comrades, the Republican Socialist Movement was beset by factionalism and internecine violence throughout the 1980s, with the political credibility of the movement practically non-existent despite the modest success they enjoyed in the 1981 local elections. Any political success was ultimately overshadowed by reckless violence on the part of the INLA, their thirty-one murders of 1982 evidence of the deadly capabilities of the armed faction. The recklessness of the INLA was evident from their loose recruitment policies, a lack of discipline that would cost the movement dearly with a series of volunteers jailed on the word of a 'supergrass', which brought further division to the movement. Although the splintering of the INLA only fostered increasingly small groups, their predilection for violence would mark their existence as the national question took a firm back seat, ultimately prompting the Provisional IRA to rectify the problem in 1992.

Notes

1. English, *Armed Struggle*, pp. 187–237; O'Rawe, R., *Blanketmen* (Dublin: New Island, 2005); Beresford, *Ten Men Dead* (London: Grafton, 1987); Coogan, T. P., *On The Blanket: The H-Block Story* (Dublin: Ward River Press, 1980); Adams, G., *Cage Eleven* (Dingle: Brandon, 1990); McKeown, L., *Out of Time: Irish Republican Prisoners Long Kesh 1972–2000* (Belfast: Beyond the Pale, 2001); Morrison, D., *Then The Walls Came Down: A Prison Journal* (Cork: Mercier Press, 1999); Campbell, B., McKeown, L. and O'Hagan, F. (eds) *Nor Meekly Serve My Time: The H-Block Struggle 1976–1981* (Belfast: Beyond the Pale, 1994); Sands, B., *The Diary of Bobby Sands* (Dublin: Sinn Féin, 1981).
2. Richard O'Rawe, interview with author, Belfast, 15/2/2010. See also O'Doherty, *The Trouble with Guns*, p. 112; O'Malley, P., *Biting at the Grave: The Irish Hunger Strikes and the Politics of Despair* (Belfast: The Blackstaff Press, 1990), p. 238; English, *Armed Struggle*, p. 206.
3. Gerard Hodgins, interview with author, Belfast, 25/3/2010.
4. Tim Pat Coogan, *The IRA* (London: HarperCollins, 1995), pp. 415–18.
5. Moloney, *Voices*, pp. 238–40.
6. Gerard Hodgins, interview with author, Belfast, 25/3/2010.
7. Moloney, *Voices*, pp. 246–53.
8. Gerard Hodgins, interview with author, Belfast, 25/3/2010.
9. White, *Ruairí Ó Brádaigh*, pp. 276–8.
10. Gerard Hodgins, interview with author, Belfast, 25/3/2010.
11. *Hunger* directed by Steve McQueen, Icon Entertainment, Pathe Distribution (UK) 2008.
12. Rage Against The Machine, 'Rage Against The Machine', Sony Music Entertainment, 6 November 1992.
13. Gerard Hodgins, interview with author, Belfast, 25/3/2010.
14. O'Rawe, *Blanketmen*, pp. 172–83, 219.
15. Richard O'Rawe, interview with author, Belfast, 15/2/2010.
16. Gerard Hodgins, interview with author, Belfast, 25/3/2010.
17. Lord Dafydd Elis-Thomas AM, correspondence with author, 6/9/2010
18. Marian Price, interview with author, Belfast, 1/7/2010.
19. Moloney, *Voices*, pp. 77–8.
20. Adams, *The Politics*, p. 84.
21. Moloney, *Voices*, pp. 221, 251–3.
22. Adams, *The Politics*, pp. 78–9, Moloney, *Voices*, p. 229.
23. Eoin Ó Broin, interview with author, Belfast, 20/5/2005.
24. Adams, *Hope and History*, p. 28.
25. Adams, G., *The Politics*, pp. 58, 75–6.
26. *Observer* 14/10/1984.
27. Moloney, *Secret History*, pp. 550–8.
28. *TIP* Vol. XII No. 46 26/11/1983.

29. Ian Pearson MP, interview with author, Dudley, 2/9/2005.
30. English, *Armed Struggle*, p. 252.
31. 32CSM member, interview with author, Dublin, 26/3/2010.
32. Adams, *The Politics*, pp. 159–60.
33. Oppenheimer, *IRA*, pp. 164–5.
34. *Irish Press* 15/10/1986; *An Phoblacht/Republican News* 16/10/1986.
35. *BT* 15/10/1986.
36. Geraldine Taylor, interview with author, Belfast, 17/2/2010.
37. *AP/RN* 19/3/1987.
38. *AP/RN* 2/4/1987.
39. *AP/RN* 23/4/1987.
40. Cory Collusion Inquiry Report Lord Justice Gibson and Lady Gibson, 7/10/2003 http://cain.ulst.ac.uk/issues/collusion/cory/cory03gibson.pdf.
41. Chief of the General Staff, *Operation Banner: An Analysis of Military Operations in Northern Ireland*, Ministry of Defence, 2006.
42. Shanahan, T., *The Provisional Irish Republican Army and the Morality of Terrorism* (Edinburgh: Edinburgh University Press, 2009), p. 181.
43. *Sunday Times* 7/9/1986.
44. Cited in Moloney, *Voices*, p. 265.
45. *AP/RN* 14/5/1987.
46. Moloney, *Voices*, p. 266; English, *Armed Struggle*, p. 254.
47. Urban, *Big Boys' Rules*, pp. 224–7.
48. *Irish Press* 11/5/1987.
49. McKittrick et al., *Lost Lives*, pp. 1094–8.
50. *Sunday Times* 13/6/2010.
51. *AP/RN* 19/3/1987, *IN* 14/3/1987.
52. *AP/RN* 14/5/1987.
53. Marian Price, interview with author, Belfast, 1/7/2010.
54. Richard O'Rawe, interview with author, Belfast, 15/2/2010.
55. Former Provisional republican, interview with author, Belfast, 2/7/2010.
56. Marian Price, interview with author, Belfast, 1/7/2010.
57. Moloney, *Voices*, pp. 266–70; McIntyre, A., *Good Friday: The Death of Irish Republicanism* (New York: Ausubo Press, 2008), pp. 33–5.
58. Moloney, *Secret History*, pp. 306, 319.
59. Oppenheimer, *IRA*, pp. 189, 191, 193.
60. *The Phoenix*, 8/5/1987.
61. Former Provisional republican, interview with author, Belfast, 2/7/2010.
62. Lieutenant General Sir Alistair Irwin, interview with author, Aberlour, 16/2/2009.
63. Marian Price, interview with author, Belfast, 1/7/2010.
64. Ibid.
65. *BT* 29/3/1996.
66. White, *Ruairí Ó Brádaigh*, p. 298; *Saoirse* 154, February 2000.
67. Text of the motion on abstentionism (Resolution 162) as presented to the Sinn Féin Ard Fheis, Dublin (2 November 1986) http://cain.ulst.ac.uk/issues/politics/docs/sf/resolution162.htm.
68. Extract from Presidential Address by Gerry Adams, then President of Sinn Féin, on the issue of abstentionism (Resolution 162), Sinn Féin Ard Fheis,

Dublin (1 November 1986) http://cain.ulst.ac.uk/issues/politics/docs/sf/ga011186.htm.

69. Ibid.
70. Speech by Martin McGuinness, then Vice-President of Sinn Féin, on the issue of abstentionism (Resolution 162), Sinn Féin Ard Fheis, Dublin (2 November 1986), available at http://cain.ulst.ac.uk/issues/politics/docs/sf/mmcg021186.htm
71. Speech by Ruairí Ó Brádaigh, former President of Sinn Féin, opposing the motion on abstentionism (Resolution 162), Sinn Féin Ard Fheis, Dublin (2 November 1986) http://cain.ulst.ac.uk/issues/politics/docs/sf/rob021186.htm
72. Adams, Hope and History, p. 46.
73. Geraldine Taylor, interview with author, Belfast, 17/2/2010.
74. Ruairí Ó Brádaigh interview, IN 29/1/1990.
75. Toolis, Rebel Hearts, p. 320.
76. Saoirse No. 2 June 1987.
77. Ó Brádaigh, R., Dílseacht: The Story of Comdt. General Tom Maguire and the Second (All-Ireland) Dáil (Dublin: Irish Freedom Press, 1997), p. 3.
78. Thomas Maguire, speaking on 25/7/1987, quoted in Saoirse No. 106 February 1996.
79. Thomas Maguire, speaking in 1986, quoted in Ó Brádaigh, R., Dílseacht pp. 48–9.
80. Irish Press 5/1/1970.
81. White, Ruairí Ó Brádaigh, p. 295.
82. The Phoenix 21/11/1986.
83. Presidential Address from 1986 Sinn Féin Ard Fheis, Sinn Féin, The Politics of Revolution, p. 10.
84. Ruairí Ó Brádaigh interview, IN 29/1/1990.
85. Ruairí Ó Brádaigh, speaking in 1986, quoted in Bishop and Mallie, The Provisional IRA, p. 103.
86. Interview with Cathal Goulding, IN 31/1/1990.
87. Ruairí Ó Brádaigh interview, IN 29/1/1990.
88. Joe Cahill interview, IN 30/1/1990.
89. Marian Price, interview with author, Belfast, 1/7/2010.
90. Quoted in Sharrock and Devenport, Man of War, Man of Peace?, p. 245.
91. Adams, Hope and History, p. 18.
92. Republican News 18/10/1975, 29/10/1975 and 1/5/1976.
93. English, Armed Struggle, pp. 180–3; White, Ruairí Ó Brádaigh, pp. 257–8.
94. Lyons, P. and Sinnot, R., Voter Turnout in the Republic of Ireland (Dublin: University College Dublin Institute for the Study of Social Change, 2003).
95. White, Ruairí Ó Brádaigh, pp. 291–2.
96. AP/RN 26/2/1987.
97. Adams, The Politics, p. 151.
98. Interview with Joe Cahill, IN 30/1/1990.
99. TIP Vol. XIV No. 42 8/11/1986.
100. White, Provisional Irish Republicans, p. 150.
101. Guardian 28/1/1989.
102. Sunday Business Post 14/1/1996.
103. Geraldine Taylor, interview with author, Belfast, 17/2/2010.
104. Gerard Hodgins, interview with author, Belfast, 25/3/2010; also White, Ruairí Ó Brádaigh, p. 310.

105. Marian Price, interview with author, Belfast, 1/7/2010.
106. *Independent* 23/12/1986; *The Phoenix* 21/11/1986; *News Letter* 2/1/1987; *Sunday News* 4/1/1987.
107. Milotte, *Communism*, p. 278; White, *Ruairí Ó Brádaigh*, pp. 164–5; Roy Johnston, correspondence with author, 19/1/2008.
108. Marx, K., *Marx to Engels 2/11/1867*, in Marx, K. and Engels, F., *Ireland and the Irish Question* (Moscow: Progress Publishers, 1971), p. 144.
109. Berresford Ellis, *A History of the Irish Working Class*, p. 336.
110. Hanley and Millar, *Lost Revolution*, pp. 416–17.
111. *TIP* Vol. XI No. 18 8/5/1982.
112. Ibid., p. 425.
113. O'Hagan, *The Concept of Republicanism*, p. 19. LHLPC.
114. Hanley and Millar, *Lost Revolution*, p. 450.
115. Ibid., p. 493.
116. John Lowry, interview with author, Belfast, 9/8/2007.
117. *Magill*, April 1982.
118. *The Politics of The Workers Party*, undated, LHLPC (c. 1982).
119. Hanley and Millar, *Lost Revolution*, pp. 442–3.
120. Browne, V., 'The Secret World of SFWP', *Magill*, April 1982.
121. John Lowry, interview with author, Belfast, 9/8/2007.
122. Hanley and Millar, *Lost Revolution*, pp. 150, 188, 462.
123. Ibid., p. 535.
124. Holland and McDonald, *INLA*, p. 165.
125. Journalist A, interview with author, Belfast, 15/11/2004.
126. Moloney, *Voices*, p. 236.
127. Richard O'Rawe, interview with author, Belfast, 15/2/2010.
128. Fra Halligan, interview with author, Belfast, 25/2/2010.
129. John Redington and John Gilligan, Michael Devine Cumann IRSP Limerick, Address to Broad Front Conference, 22/11/1981, LHLPC.
130. *Guardian* 18/5/1981.
131. McDonald, H., *Gunsmoke and Mirrors: How Sinn Fein Dressed up Defeat as Victory* (Dublin: Gill and Macmillan, 2008), p. 104.
132. Holland and McDonald, *INLA*, p. 272.
133. *Starry Plough* 'Massive Tribute to Patsy O'Hara', June 1981 http://irsm.org/history/starryplough/patsy_ohara_01.html
134. Ibid.
135. Ibid.
136. Journalist A, interview with author, Belfast, 15/11/2004.
137. See Elections Ireland, 22nd Dáil – Waterford First Preference votes http://elections ireland.org/result.cfm?election=1981&cons=226.
138. Richard O'Rawe, *Blanketmen*, p. 190.
139. Kelley, *The Longest War*, p. 344, also *Guardian* 20/10/1982.
140. IRSP H-Block/Armagh Broad Front – An Assessment undated, LHLPC.
141. Gerry Ruddy, interview with author, Belfast, 24/11/2004.
142. John Redington, John Gilligan, Michael Devine Cumann IRSP Limerick, Address to Broad Front Conference, 22/11/1981, LHLPC.
143. Gerry Ruddy, interview with author, Belfast, 24/11/2004.

144. Eoin Ó Broin, interview with author, Belfast, 20/5/2005.
145. Danny Morrison, interview with author, Belfast, 24/1/2005.
146. Anthony McIntyre, interview with author, Belfast, 7/9/2005.
147. Robson, T., *The Broad Front*, undated, LHLPC.
148. O'Ruairc, L., 'The Legacy of Seamus Costello', in *The Blanket: A Journal of Protest and Dissent* October/November 2002 http://lark.phoblacht.net/scostello1.html
149. Redington, J. and Gilligan, J., 'Address to Broad Front Conference 22/11/1981', IRSP Box, LHLPC.
150. Danny Morrison, interview with author, Belfast, 24/1/2005.
151. Eoin Ó Broin, interview with author, Belfast, 20/5/2005.
152. Power, *The Ta Power Document*, 27/7/2004.
153. Fra Halligan, interview with author, Belfast, 25/2/2010.
154. See Northern Ireland Elections – Local Government Elections 1981 http://www.ark.ac.uk/elections/flg81.htm
155. Moloney, *Secret History*, p. 202.
156. Anthony Coughlan, interview with author, Dublin, 16/6/2010.
157. Fra Halligan, interview with author, Belfast, 25/2/2010.
158. *IT* 20/5/1981.
159. All information from McKittrick et al., *Lost Lives*, pp. 852–77.
160. *Observer* 12/12/1982; 'From the INLA to the People of England' 10/12/1982 http://www.irsm.org/statements/inla/821210.htm 21/6/2004.
161. Ex-Special Branch Officer, interview with author, Scotland, 30/7/2009.
162. *Independent on Sunday* Obituary, 12/2/1994 http://www.independent.co.uk/news/people/obituary-dominic-mcglinchey-1393697.html
163. McKittrick et al., *Lost Lives*, pp. 860–1.
164. Fra Halligan, interview with author, Belfast, 25/2/2010.
165. Danny Morrison, interview with author, Belfast, 24/1/2005.
166. Martin Dillon, *The Trigger Men* 2nd edn (Edinburgh, 2004) (1st edn 2003), pp. 121–2.
167. Moloney, *Voices*, p. 193.
168. *From the INLA to the People of England* 10/12/1982 http://www.irsm.org/statements/inla/821210.htm 21/6/2004.
169. *Guardian* 24/10/1982.
170. Holland and McDonald, *INLA*, p. 2.
171. *Guardian* 28/11/1983; see also McKittrick et al., *Lost Lives*, pp. 963–4.
172. Ex-E4A Officer, interview with author, Scotland, 28/7/2009.
173. Gerry Ruddy, interview with author, Belfast, 24/11/2004.
174. *IN* 2/1/1975.
175. Journalist A, interview with author, Belfast, 15/11/2004.
176. Danny Morrison, interview with author, Belfast, 24/1/2005.
177. Ex-E4A Officer, interview with author, Scotland, 28/7/2009.
178. Toolis, K., *An Anatomy of the INLA's Bloody Feuds*, Observer Report, undated, copy in LHLPC.
179. Power, *The Ta Power Document*.
180. McKittrick et al., *Lost Lives*, p. 844.
181. *Guardian* 20/12/1985; *Fortnight* 24/6/1985.
182. Jennings, T. and Greer, S., 'Final Verdict on Supergrass System', *Fortnight* 27/1/1986.

183. Greer, S., *Supergrasses: A Study in Anti-Terrorist Law Enforcement in Northern Ireland* (Oxford: Clarendon Press, 1995), p. 282.
184. Bonner, D., 'Combating Terrorism: Supergrass Trials in Northern Ireland', *Modern Law Review* Vol. 51 No. 1 January 1988, pp. 23–53, and Greer, *Supergrasses*, pp. 162–72, 198–204.
185. *Scotsman* 23/3/1987.
186. Geldard, I. and Craig, K., *IRA, INLA: Foreign support and International Connections* (London: Institute for the Study of Terrorism, 1988), p. 15.
187. Power, *The Ta Power Document*.
188. Bruce, S., *No Pope of Rome: Anti-Catholicism in Modern Scotland* (Edinburgh: Mainstream, 1985), p. 170.
189. IRSP, *The Irish Republican Socialist Movement – 20 Years of Struggle*, undated http://irsm.org/history/irms20yr.html
190. *The Plough*, Vol. 2 No. 5 17/9/2004.
191. Fra Halligan, interview with author, Belfast, 25/2/2010.
192. *Sunday News* 22/2/1987.
193. See http://www.irsm.org/fallen/power/ta_power.html 11/3/2009; McKittrick et al., *Lost Lives*, pp. 1059–60.
194. *Irish Independent* 15/12/2002; McKittrick et al., *Lost Lives*, pp. 1099–101.
195. *AP/RN* 5/3/1987.
196. McKittrick et al., *Lost Lives*, pp. 1065–6.
197. Ibid., p. 1145.
198. Fra Halligan, interview with author, Belfast, 25/2/2010.

CHAPTER 6

Irish-America in the 1980s

As violence in Northern Ireland peaked in 1972, so did interest in the conflict from the United States of America. Although commitment to the cause remained as strong as ever, Irish-American organisations found themselves squeezed by declining interest in Northern Ireland on the part of the communities and the increasingly sophisticated understanding of the Irish situation on the part of elected officials, the latter providing a channel through which those with genuinely peaceful aspirations for Ireland could pursue their interests in the Irish question.

As the republican struggle in Ireland became increasingly political, the American dimension began to centre on constitutional figures. The formation of the largely Democrat[1] Friends of Ireland congressional group, which included Edward Kennedy, saw understanding of the Irish situation develop under the influence of John Hume. His brand of constitutional nationalism gathered favour among figures such as Kennedy at the same time as his influence over Gerry Adams was increasing. As Irish republicanism turned towards politics, the dominance of the Provisional republicans was assured through carefully controlled strategic efforts domestically and internationally, with the United States of America again crucially important.

The onset of the prison campaign reinvigorated the American dimension of the republican campaign, as Noraid re-established itself as the dominant Irish republican organisation in the US and began to mould itself more closely in the image of its Irish counterparts; a younger leadership transitioning the movement towards acceptance of political participation. This created a rift that ultimately manifested itself in the form of a split.

168

The Prison Campaign and the USA

Just as it was the most significant development for Northern Ireland domestically, the prison campaign was also essential to the international dimension of the Northern Ireland conflict. In the United States, the divisiveness and high profile of the latter stages of the campaign, with the hunger strikes. In mid-1980 Congressman Hamilton Fish formed a committee on the judiciary which discussed the prison situation in Northern Ireland. Pace University Professor David Lowry presented a paper entitled 'The English System of Judicial Injustice in "Northern Ireland"', the use of quotation marks around 'Northern Ireland' high-lighting the confrontational nature of this presentation. He claimed that civil rights activists had 'tried the peaceful route towards reform', and that 'torture, inhuman and degrading treatment are integral compo-nents of [the British] strategy . . . when the victims of this system arrive in H-Block they meet conditions of indescribable squalor'.[2] Journalist Jack Anderson contextualised the Irish prison disputes for an American audience by comparing the H-Blocks to the tiger cages of Vietnam.[3] This comparison does not reconcile easily with the account of the Irish Embassy in London, who described conditions at Long Kesh as 'palatial'.[4]

Support for the first hunger strike had been strong, with thousands demonstrating in eighteen cities across the United States.[5] Noraid was aware of the opportunities that increased exposure of the protest could provide, noting that after the death of Frank Maguire, Sinn Féin might field an abstentionist candidate in the by-election to replace him, with the possibility of a hunger striker filling this role.[6]

With Noraid's links with the IRA formally recognised by the United States legal system,[7] the prison disputes invigorated Irish-American financial support for Irish republicanism; Noraid raised almost half a million dollars in the first half of 1981, raising more in the three months of the hunger strike than it did in most calendar years.[8] This was part of an overall donation of roughly $5 million since 1970.[9] The outcry in Irish-America following the deaths of Michael Gaughan and Frank Stagg during the 1970s had provided an indication of how emotive a hunger strike could be to the Irish in the United States,[10] and concerns were high at the possibility of a large-scale strike taking place. The Irish Embassy in Washington spoke in 1980 regarding the prospect of a hunger strike in Northern Ireland, asking, 'Could any civilised society, any humane

169

government, or any person with even a spark of humanity allow such a thing to happen?'[11]

Politically, the period created problems in the United States for the British. Although the Congressional Friends of Ireland, led by Senator Kennedy and Speaker O'Neill, had developed a more constitutional outlook on Northern Ireland, they wrote to Thatcher, questioning 'a posture of inflexibility that must lead inevitably to more senseless violence and more needless deaths in Northern Ireland',[12] and writing again in the wake of Bobby Sands' death, stating that, 'One Senior Irish Diplomat describes American Press Coverage of Ulster as "Disastrous". The IRA's American lobby is therefore "stronger than ever".'[13] Protests were widespread, with a large group descending on the British consulate in New York. The hunger strikes prompted the Massachusetts House of Representatives to offer the following resolution:

> the citizens of Massachusetts have long been anguished by the intransigence of the Government of Prime Minister Margaret Thatcher in refusing to grant political status to incarcerated Irish Republicans . . . The people of Massachusetts, in the light of the foregoing circumstances, view the British Consulate, situated in Boston, as persona non grata, an unwelcome representative of an unconscionable government who taxes the hospitality and toleration of their hosts most grievously . . . The Massachusetts House of Representatives insists that the State Department of the United States demand that the government of Prime Minister Margaret Thatcher of Great Britain recall and withdraw its local embassy, the consul located at Boston, until such a time as it shall accept the 5 demands propounded by the fasting IRA prisoners in Ulster, and to set a time table for the complete withdrawal of British troops.[14]

They also suggested 'imposing political and economic sanctions against the Empire of Great Britain'.[15] This resolution reflects how deeply Irish-America was affected by the deaths of the hunger strikers. British offices in New York City were forced to stop flying their national flag 'due to protesters . . . the British don't want to give the protesters a chance to tear it down'.[16] Capitalising on the momentum afforded, the Noraid publicity machine went into overdrive as Sands began his hunger strike. Former hunger striker Laurence McKeown wrote to *The Irish People*:

> before more young Irish men lay down their lives for the ideals they hold so dear, I implore you, the American people, to now, today, do something positive to help save them. Or must the cries of the Irish people and their imprisoned children once more go unheard? From an English prison camp on Irish soil, I send this desperate appeal to you.[17]

170

This was published alongside a letter from Martin Hurson who, by the time of publication, had already died. At what point he wrote this letter is unclear as most accounts of the strike note the fragile conditions of the strikers prior to their passing.[18] It read, 'I urge you to give active support in America and to let the British know that the hunger strikers and the blanket men do not stand alone in their just struggle.'[19] While McKeown's message was undoubtedly powerful, Hurson's message from beyond the grave overshadowed it considerably. Brendan Hughes also contributed: 'the impression we get, here on the blanket, is that American is England's weak spot . . . it is now we must demonstrate . . . the power of the Irish nation and her exiled children in America'.[20] Each letter represented as powerful a message as Irish republicanism could put out in the United States, particularly within Irish-America where Sands' election was celebrated as 'a stunning blow to the British establishment in North Ireland', even though the campaign was 'heavy with political intrigue and undertones of threatened violence'.[21] Noraid argued:

> Thatcher . . . claimed that they had no political support, but, before he died, Bobby Sands was elected to British Parliament by a greater majority than Thatcher had obtained in her constituency . . . Robert Sands, elected Member of Parliament, is dead. The English have murdered him . . . First and foremost, this is a time of anger, indeed rage, with the British regime that murdered Bobby Sands.[22]

The 1,447 majority Sands had over Harry West compared to Thatcher's 7,878 majority over Richard May in 1979 does not really bear out this assertion, but it is undeniable, in the words of George Harrison, that Sands 'awakened the conscience of the Irish American community'.[23] While his election undoubtedly gained significant coverage, his death was predictably plastered across the Irish-American newspapers. *The Irish People* carried the headline 'Murdered', with a lead article claiming that 'British politicians, who in life labelled him a criminal, have been indelibly branded as liars in the eyes of Americans and indeed of the world.'[24] This story was recycled nine times; following the death of Joe McDonnell, for example, it spoke of 'another British killing of a defenceless man who dared to stand up against aggression and terror'.[25]

The mainstream press assumed a position far more favourable to the British, with the *Washington Star* stating that 'Bobby Sands, a member of the IRA, was precisely not committed to a peaceful reconciliation of the Irish problem',[26] and the *New York Times* arguing that 'the Provisionals do not bring a solution closer; they bring on the unworkable politics of extremism. That is why it is so sickening to see their blackshirt tactics romanticized.'[27]

As the Adams leadership shifted the republican struggle towards the political arena, it was important to retain the support of Irish-America. This task was complicated; although a great deal of republican Irish-America followed mainstream Irish republicanism relatively blindly, Adams' brand of republicanism was carefully presented to the American audience. Although there was much evidence to link Sinn Féin with a socialist agenda, this was undesirable in a United States still in the midst of Cold War hostilities. *The Irish People* did reprint one of the 'Brownie' articles entitled 'Revolutionary Rules', which discusses 'collective leader-ship' and the 'national, political, social, cultural and economic liberation of the people'.[28]

To Irish-America, Adams' position was consistent: 'there is no Marxist influence within Sinn Féin, it simply isn't a Marxist organisation. I know of no-one in Sinn Féin who is a Marxist or would be influenced by Marxism.'[29] Adams' use of 'Marxist' rather than 'socialist' throughout is important. His ability to blur the picture by playing the 'green' card con-tributed to maintaining support from Irish-America. The prison struggle had brought the Irish issue to the forefront of international agendas, rally-ing support from myriad sources. Not all of this was necessarily beneficial to a movement that relied on the United States for much of its funding, notably the support of Fidel Castro, who commented that 'Irish patriots are writing one of the most heroic chapters in human history . . . How can such a cold and dramatic holocaust be tolerated?'[30] Such radicalism was evident within Irish-America. In 1982, George Harrison gave a talk to the Brooklyn Militant Forum where he said, 'While we support the fight for Irish freedom and the Argentine claims to the Malvinas, we also want a world free from the threat of nuclear holocaust. Therefore we must oppose the war politics of Reagan and Thatcher.'[31] Significant donations to the Centre for Cuban Studies further evidence the radicalism of one of Irish-America's central figures.[32] Libyan links were also problematic for Provisional republicans in the United States; Harrison's papers reveal defaced Irish American Defence Fund forms which refer to Libya.[33] The path towards republican politics was also hazardous in the US context.

As in the 1920s, with US support for partition based on the grounds that it was preferable to British control of the entire island, most Irish-Americans had little ideological investment in abstentionism. It was easy to downplay the socialist roots of republicans and *The Irish People* helped promote the 1982 local elections in which 'Sinn Féin hopes to show that large numbers of the six-county population reject the new Stormont.'[34] The transition towards politics was also observed by the mainstream American press, the *Baltimore Sun* arguing that 'the Sands affair is certain to help Protestant extremists in the coming local election, and possibly pro-IRA candidates as well'.[35] Certainly the two parties enjoying the largest increase in votes were the Democratic Unionist Party and Sinn Féin.[36] It was emphasised that 'Sinn Féin – the only Republican party – is complementing and reinforcing the Republican fight in the North.'[37] Not all Irish-American republicans agreed with the shift away from abstentionism and, as in Ireland, the movement ruptured.

IRISH-AMERICA: A PARTING OF THE WAYS

Tension was widespread within Irish-America throughout the early eighties. *The Irish People* detailed the 'ever widening chasm developing between Irish Northern Aid and the Washington based National Caucus', explaining how:

> The Washington Caucus differs radically . . . it has repeatedly denied the right of the Irish people to fight for national freedom, and has specifically condemned the Irish Republican Army . . . In a little more than one week a hunger strike will begin. We cannot afford to divide our energies into many different directions . . . Let us support the men of H-Block by support for the organization to which they themselves through their representatives in America call us. Let us support them through Irish Northern Aid.[38]

This contrasts with an earlier statement from Sean Walsh of the INC: 'I think it's proper to kill British soldiers.'[39] A chasm was developing within Irish-America and this occurred at the same time as the ascension of Martin Galvin to the Noraid leadership.[40] Galvin's role as the new editor of *The Irish People* gave him the platform to promote his views on the future for republicanism across the Atlantic, which began with the ending of abstentionism. Galvin would later side with the 32 County Sovereignty Movement, and contributed to their newspaper during the early twenty-first century.[41]

Despite their political differences, the old guard of Irish-America stood tall alongside the IRA. George Harrison, Michael Flannery, Tom Falvey, Paddy Mullens and Tommy Gormley were acquitted of charges of running guns to the Provisional IRA in 1982. They were successful with the highly irregular defence that they believed their actions had Central Intelligence

Agency approval.[42] Harrison commented, 'It was with pride that I stood trial in that courtroom because there in spirit stood with me some of Ireland's, America's and the world's most famous rebels . . . I, who's [sic] sole crime was to have believed that justice and freedom were worth fighting for.'[43] With such loyalty to republican tradition, it was inevitable that dissent would grow when the Provisional leadership embarked upon their reforms.

The importance of IRA support for the political developments in Sinn Féin for Irish-America was evident from reports of the 1986 Army Convention, which 'opened with a unanimous pledge of rededication to the armed struggle and confidence in the armed struggle as being the means of breaking the British connection and bringing about Irish independence'. Irish-America was assured that 'analogies to the past are invalid today because present Republicans will not abandon the fight for freedom',[44] even though internally, Sinn Féin felt that a 'tactical decision of the Irish Republican Movement should not be dictated by Americans' and Owen Carron was sent to America, confidently asserting that 'if Sinn Féin wants to come to power electorally, we must fight elections. There is no question that we are not committed to the ballot-box . . . Sinn Féin is not committed to the Armalite – the IRA in the north is, but Sinn Féin supports anyone who wishes to drive the Brits out of this country by what-soever means.'[45] Carron's associations with Bobby Sands were important here; even though his trip to the United States with Danny Morrison was cut short when both were arrested for attempting to enter the States illegally, the message was still powerful.[46]

Noraid support for the ending of abstentionism was obvious. *The Irish People* appealed, 'while we or our members may privately agree or disagree with the change in Sinn Féin tactics, we remain unequivocally committed to redouble our efforts to help the families of Irish political prisoners and to build moral support for the Irish Republican Army's struggle against British colonial occupation'.[47] A very real fear existed that the division in Irish republicanism could lead to a damaging split in Irish-America. As the hunger strikes became an increasingly diminishing memory, Irish-America faced the challenge of reinvigorating the Irish issue. With disunity endemic in the United States, this proved tricky.

'Out of concern for what they believed to be a betrayal of traditional Republican principles and values after the Sinn Féin convention was highjacked [sic] and the sitting leadership ousted',[48] Cumann na Saoirse, or the National Irish Freedom Committee, was formed by Flannery and Harrison in 1987. For Harrison, 'traditional republicans didn't fight and lay down their lives for a reformed Stormont, nor for a puppet government in Leinster House. They fought for a free and independent Irish social-ist republic and a thirty-two-county government.'[49] Flannery accused Gerry Adams of selling out republicans and announced that he would be sending money to Republican Sinn Féin,[50] but, as with their comrades in Ireland, the new organisation struggled to impose itself and became increasingly dominated by the Galvin-led Noraid, which remained loyal to the Gerry Adams leadership, although Galvin maintains he and Flannery enjoyed cordial relations even after this parting of ways.[51] Given the bloodless division that had occurred in Ireland, the split in the United States could more easily be framed as a parting of the ways, despite the rhetoric from the time. For Ruairí Ó Brádaigh, it 'was a proud moment for those present when Michael Flannery and General Tom Maguire met in support of Republican Sinn Féin in 1987 – the one the living link with the revolutionary All-Ireland Dáil of 1919–22 and the other the pillar of support from Irish-America for over 60 years.'[52]

Dáithí Ó Conaill exchanged letters with Harrison in the early months of 1987, remarking that in the Dáil election of February, in which Sinn Féin won only 1.8 per cent of first-preference votes:

> the performance of our former friends was a fiasco and has made a lot of members think again. John Joe McGirl lost his deposit for the first time ever. It is clear that two out of three solid Republican supporters did not vote for them. Adams blamed 65 years of abstentionism as the main cause for the disaster and said it should have been abolished 20 years ago. In other words the 1921 Treaty should have been accepted and we should have all joined Goulding in 69/70! So much for the hundreds of volunteers who died since! Adams has got very bitter since the elections.[53]

The Irish-American split proved to be relatively insignificant for two major reasons: Irish-America was sufficiently supportive of Provisional republican strategy, with loyalty to the twentieth-century convention of abstentionism relatively low-key among a community that had largely departed Ireland decades earlier; and the increasing dominance of consti-tutional politicians as pressure groups for Irish nationalism.

UNITED STATES POLITICIANS AND NORTHERN IRELAND

As Irish republicanism internationally shifted towards a more politicised position, the Friends of Ireland were becoming increasingly influential in the American Congress, a fact welcomed by Taoiseach Charles Haughey.[54] In order to undermine armed republican attempts to fundraise in the United States, they depended 'for their support on the good-will of a majority of Irish Americans who share their commitment to peace, non-violence and unity by agreement. However, this majority is neither organized nor vocal.'[55] Organising this demographic was an important task of those in America who opposed the IRA's armed struggle. Although the Friends of Ireland claimed that 'American support for the violence has declined',[56] the hunger strike period revitalised Irish-America and a strong publicity campaign, including speaking tours, aided fundraising efforts. Although convicted IRA members were unable to enter the United States, indeed the US Embassy states that an individual convicted of an offence 'may be permanently ineligible to receive a visa',[57] as Sinn Féin moved towards more peaceful methods, pressure grew on the American government to permit entry visas to republican leaders. The Irish American Bar Association of California invited Gerry Adams to address a group of attorneys in 1984,[58] marking an early attempt to bring Adams to the United States.

The visa issue became an integral part of US–UK relations during the late twentieth century. The question of the legality of British authority over Ireland was raised during the 1970s, with the United States government largely siding with the British; republicans were frequently denied entry to the United States.[59] The potential for increased donations prompted republicans to persist with their attempts to send IRA volunteers to the United States,[60] even though actually gaining entry to the United States proved a little trickier; Owen Carron's visa application was denied because of 'public statements in support of the legitimacy of violence and paramilitary efforts in Northern Ireland and the strong likelihood that he would be engaged in fund-raising activities on behalf of the Provisional Irish Republican Army while in the US',[61] even though Carron was at the time an MP. The National Council of Irish Americans described this as 'pure censorship' by President Reagan.[62] They also pointed out that Ian Paisley had been permitted a visa in spite of his arrests during the 1970s. Paisley's visa was subsequently invalidated by the State department.[63]

In the United Kingdom, The Prevention of Terrorism Act of 1984 'gives the Home Secretary the authority to exclude or prevent from entering Great Britain . . . anyone he believes may be connected with terrorism related to Northern Ireland'.[64] Martin Galvin was denied a visa for an attempted visit during 1984, because of the 'British Government seeking to suppress an open and free dialog on the issue of Northern Ireland among concerned individuals and organizations from the United States'.[65] Instead he travelled to the Republic and simply crossed the border in order to attend a republican rally. Appearing on stage, violence ensued when the police moved to arrest him. During the trouble, Sean Downes, who had been found guilty of IRA membership in 1977, was killed by a plastic bullet.[66]

Although prominent Irish republicans were unable to legally visit, the United States did become something of a safe haven for on-the-run volunteers. Discussions began between the British and American governments during the 1970s for the establishment of an extradition treaty.[67] Mayor of Boston Raymond Flynn claimed that the proposed Amendment 'would mean that the US is effectively intervening in the conflict in Northern Ireland – clearly on the British side . . . efforts directed at opposing terrorism in order to be successful must also take into account the terrorism of the forces of state, as well as the terror of paramilitary groups'.[68]

The existing extradition treaty did not extend to political crimes, the political nature of republican actions a point of contention for a number of years. The case of Joseph Doherty was highly symbolic of both the complicated constitutional relationship between the United States and United Kingdom as well as the increasing emphasis which republicans placed on the political motivations behind their actions. Doherty was convicted of the murder of SAS Captain Herbert Westmacott in 1980. Although most of his unit was jailed in 1981, Doherty managed to escape Crumlin Road jail the day before sentencing and fled to the United States, where he avoided capture until 1983.[69] On his arrest, a petition requesting his extradition was denied. The *New York Post* remarked:

> Terrorists the world over owe a vote of thanks to Manhattan Federal Court Judge John Sprizzo who refused to allow the extradition of an IRA assassin, Thomas Doherty, convicted of the ambush and murder of a British soldier. Judge Sprizzo has given aid and comfort to the cause of terrorists and their supporters everywhere. He has issued an open invitation to these killers to pursue their bloody work – after which they can flee to the US, where sympathetic judges are available to hear their pleas that their crimes were 'political.'[70]

The *Daily News* argued: 'It's a crazy ruling. Imagine the outcry if some foreign government refused to extradite a FALN bomber because it's a "political" struggle.'[71] Again the Irish struggle posed problems for the United States government. A Doherty campaign leaflet was circulated among potential supporters which drew analogy between the civil rights

177

struggles of African-Americans and Irish natives who 'under a harsh, brutal occupation [were] . . . subjected to slavery, poverty, starvation, and murder', also invoking romantic perceptions of Irish nationalism; while interned 'in the atmosphere of political and cultural resistance among the political prisoners, I began to find myself, and relate to my natural sense of Irishness . . . finding my roots again, my soul, which had been torn away by generations of English cultural murder'.[72] This certainly persuaded some in the United States, journalist Denis Hamill arguing that the story was 'a judicial obscenity . . . a car bearing five Special Air Service troops in plain clothes showed up and jumped out of the car firing Uzis. Doherty and the other IRA man returned fire in a typical battle of a political war.'[73]

The campaign to extradite Doherty dragged on for just under nine years until it was ultimately resolved in early 1992. The intervening period saw prominent politicians become involved, notably New York Mayor David Dinkins. While relatively senior elected officials felt able to intervene, the Public Papers of all presidents since Richard Nixon reveal a lack of reference to Northern Ireland which reflects the reluctance of American presidents to involve themselves in the affairs of the United Kingdom. The Reagan presidency marked the transition of the republican struggle towards the political arena with an increased number of statements on Northern Ireland, also reflecting the close relationship between Reagan and Margaret Thatcher. Typically, St Patrick's Day events were marked by such statements and Reagan used the occasion of the 1981 dinner to call for an end to violence,[74] also declaring that 'those who advocate or engage in violence and terrorism should find no welcome in the United States'.[75] Reagan was of the view that it was not the place of the United States to intervene in Northern Ireland,[76] choosing instead to support political initiatives that led to 1985's Anglo-Irish Agreement, which he described as 'a courageous move'.[77] Tip O'Neill had also lauded the agreement, remarking that he was:

> particularly pleased that these two neighbouring Western European democracies, so close in their ties of history and kinship to the United States but whose differences have been a cause of concern to many of their friends, should have found it possible to join in common purpose and chart out a path of hope and harmony in Northern Ireland.[78]

The Friends of Ireland declared the agreement 'an important step towards reconciliation'.[79] Ulster unionist hostility focused on the north south element of the Agreement, notably the controversial Maryfield secretariat in South Belfast, which would house southern officials. With the SDLP supportive of the Agreement, it is unsurprising that the Friends of Ireland should follow suit, just as Sinn Féin's opposition to the Agreement brought radical Irish-America along.[80]

After succeeding Reagan in 1989, George Bush, Sr was careful to note the considerable Irish influence on America, speaking of the 'millions of our people who share common ancestry form a bond between our nations which will never be broken'.[81] While the presidents of the United States during the 1980s were increasingly aware of the situation in Ireland and its importance to American people, their careful rhetoric on the subject reflects the position of neutrality and non-violence that the United States attempted to maintain throughout the decade. It was not until the election of William Clinton in 1993 that the president took an active role in Northern Ireland, effectively bookending the United States' involvement in Northern Ireland by heavily influencing the nascent peace process.

THE PUBLICITY WAR DURING THE 1980S

The relationship between Irish republicans and United States politicians during the 1980s was complicated. Although most officials in America were by now strong, and frequently outspoken, opponents of violence, relations with political representatives of the increasingly politicised republican movement were maintained to encourage the continuation of their political journey. Equally, the Irish republican leadership recognised that much of their support base was still broadly supportive of armed struggle. As in Ireland, in order to maintain support the IRA's campaign was considered necessary for fear of losing support in the event of a military split occurring in Ireland. The publicity campaign was therefore highly reminiscent of the previous decade, using claims such as that of Father Desmond Wilson that American donations were 'tiny ... the British propaganda line has been to inflate the importance of money coming from America and to pretend that it is being used for guns',[82] in an attempt to maintain support for the republican struggle.

Noraid remained prominent through the decade, but other organisations were formed, indicating both a reasonable level of interest in the Northern Ireland situation and the inability of Irish-American organisations to achieve any unity of purpose. The therefore ironically named Irish American Unity Conference was founded to support 'the political

179

reunification of Ireland, and, the right of its people to self determination'. It held a meeting in Chicago during 1983 which George Harrison attended. His handwritten notes suggest that British officials had been visiting the United States once a month in order to 'propagandize their view points', that the group would need to raise 'a minimum of $500,000/ year', and that it would use this money to influence 'the US government into pressurizing the British to immediately formulate a united Ireland solution to the problem'. The IAUC view was that Britain wanted to remain in Ireland because of 'the European Common Market, leverage over Irish economic and political affairs, oil in the North Sea, strategic goals involving NATO, benefits to be derived from supporting United States foreign policy in Europe'.[83] Anthony Coughlan also contends that 'the British wanted to stay in Ireland for strategic reasons because if the Cold War became a hot war, Ireland would be quite important';[84] the IAUC position was therefore rather more left-wing than was typical of Irish-American organisations.

The National Political Education Committee published a newsletter in late 1982 in which a Pace University professor wrote on the UDA, claiming that 'it is reliably estimated that its members have been responsible for over 600 of the 2,000 civilian deaths in the Province since 1972'.[85] Civilian deaths never reached two thousand and all loyalist paramilitary killings combined did not even reach six hundred during that period, but with access to accurate statistics scarce and such a claim being made by an academic, it was likely to have been believed. Equally concerning was the claim from a priest that the UDA exerted some influence over US government policy and that the UDA and KKK were co-organising guerrilla training camps in the United States.[86] The article quoted Sammy Duddy, a working- class loyalist who lived in a modest house in Rathcoole housing estate. He only acquired a passport in the latter years of his life and few loyalists enjoyed sufficient financial security to even take holidays, let alone embark on KKK training programmes in the American South.[87]

The American Irish Congress also made efforts to legitimise continued IRA violence, particularly against Protestant communities. It alleged that:

No Catholic is out at night for fear of being assassinated by Protestant death squads. There is a self-imposed curfew because of the terror reigned [sic] upon Catholic Belfast by the UDA and other Protestant paramilitary organizations . . . Driving on the Shankill at night . . . one sees small groups of men gathered at corner hangouts, openly drinking beer and behaving boisterously . . . One is immediately filled with a fear that our car might be targeted for harassment or intimidation of some sort, and we leave the area immediately.[88]

This tactic was less successful in the 1980s, as the American people became better informed on the Northern Irish situation. One letter from a reader after a report on Loughgall argued that 'the men of Loughgall whom you seek to glorify have made widows and orphans of Irish people on both sides of the religious divide'.[89] The editor of the newsletter responded that 'the misinformation contained in this letter is indicative of the mentality of the new Irish to our shores'.[90] It was also questioned: 'How can the loss of life sustained at Enniskillen be more deplorable than the loss of life of deliberately murdered Irish children by members of the British Army or RUC?',[91] the fact that the IRA killed more children than any security force organisation escaping the author.

The AIC struggled to achieve a prominent profile, discussion of Loughgall in the December 1988 newsletter, nearly eighteen months after the attack, being evidence of this fact. As early as mid-1982, the *New York Times* noted that Irish-American contributions had reduced following the end of the hunger strike, blaming IRA violence.[92] It was clear that violent nationalism, which was losing its appeal to the Irish republican leadership, was also beginning to hinder the development of Irish republicanism internationally.

Even though the armed struggle was being wound down in Northern Ireland, Irish-American republicans continued to justify the existence of the military wing of the movement. *The Irish People* claimed that 'the British have attempted to deflect world attention away from the ongoing torture and murder of Irish political prisoners by means of a label. That label is terrorism.'[93] It was also noted that 'the British also labelled as terrorists such people as George Washington, Mahatma Ghandi of India, Menachem Begin of Israel, and Eamon De Valera, the American-born Prime Minister'.[94] The newspaper continued to justify the armed campaign, boasting of 'attacks carried out with such surgical precision that no civilian was injured',[95] which was supported by Gerry Adams, who argued that 'armed struggle is a necessary and morally correct form of resistance in the six counties'.[96]

As the IRA campaign on the British mainland was escalated during the 1980s, vindication of republican violence was important, particularly with large volumes of American tourists visiting the United Kingdom throughout the 1980s; an average of 2.2 million tourists per year.[97] With support for Irish republicanism in the United States fleeting, it was crucial that the IRA be completely disassociated from indiscriminate violence that could pose a threat to Americans. After a December 1983 IRA bomb at Harrods store in London, a popular tourist destination, which killed six people and unable to distance the IRA from the attack, *The Irish People* reported the deaths despite 'a forty-five minute warning given to avoid civilian casualties . . . there will be no more repetition of this type of operation again . . . the claim of accident of war or miscalculation could not justify wilful resort to unprincipled tactics'.[98]

American Kenneth Salvesden was killed in the explosion, a fact that only underlined the counterproductivity of this attack. Letters between Thatcher and Reagan after the bomb emphasise the shared outrage between the two nations over the attack.[99] The two again shared correspondence after the 1984 Brighton bomb, an attack that targeted Thatcher personally. Reagan described the attacks as being 'increasingly indiscriminate and brutal, because acts such as the one last night are a growing threat to all democracies. We must work together to thwart this scourge against humanity.'[100]

After a bomb attack on London's busy Oxford Street, it was reported to *Irish People* readers that 'For the third week in succession the IRA have struck in England. The British reaction is predictable. It is out of contempt. It is almost as if such tactics are unfair . . . Let the British people take note that Irish children, the victims of plastic bullets fired by their soldiers, do not have the luxury of receiving warnings.'[101] Although several deaths and serious injuries resulted from the deployment of plastic and rubber bullets, it seems rather crass to justify planting a bomb in a busy shopping street on these grounds.

During his 1984 visit to the United States, Garret Fitzgerald made the important point that 'some are deluded to think there's a colonial war going on in Northern Ireland . . . They don't understand that four-fifths of those being killed by the terrorists are Irish people.'[102] Massachusetts-based newspaper *The Patriot Ledger* noted that 'even with the link between Noraid and the IRA now clear, the sponsors and those who contribute may hope that their money will be used to help the victims of the strife in Northern Ireland'.[103] Despite the clear presidential support for the British campaign against the IRA, in 1986 the *San Francisco Examiner* reported that three separate US Federal Court judges had ruled that the IRA was involved in a legitimate civil war and was not a terrorist organisation.[104] *The Irish People* seized on this, claiming that:

few would condemn the United States for sending arms to be used against Hitler
. . . it is difficult to consider the morality of providing arms for Irish Republican
Army soldiers in a dispassionate way . . . it is impossible for anyone who has personally seen British rule in Ireland firsthand, not to understand and sympathize
with those who would help the people of northeast Ireland end the occupation of
their country.[105]

The British Army was again easily cast in the role of colonial oppres-
sor. One of the more ludicrous allegations occurred after finding 'unarmed
explosives safely stored by the Irish Republican Army. Rather than simply
carrying the explosives away without damage or risk, the British chose to
detonate these materials. The homes of more than 300 people were cal-
lously and needlessly damaged by the British.'[106] The morality of storing
high volumes of explosives near to so many family homes was rather
conveniently overlooked and, in bizarre juxtaposition, an IRA bomb in
central Belfast was reported: 'In accordance with its strict regulations,
the soldiers of the Irish Republican Army gave no less than three warnings in more than adequate time to insure [sic] that no civilians would be
injured. The British deliberately refused to heed the warnings.'[107] Shortly
afterwards, those responsible for IRA bombs in Hyde Park and Regent's
Park were celebrated as 'one of the most professional active service units
ever to operate in Britain . . . civilian injuries were few and slight'.[108]
Those soldiers killed were cavalrymen on ceremonial duty and bandsmen
staging a concert. The bombs both contained a large number of nails and
their potential to injure and maim at least was large. A scientific officer
said that had the second bomb, concealed in a briefcase, been successfully planted under the bandstand, the audience would have been deci-
mated.[109]

Contributions from the Irish-American community also served a
purpose in the publicity campaign against the Army. One contributor
to *The Irish People*, claiming to have visited Northern Ireland in 1981
for his silver wedding anniversary, went to Joe McDonnell's funeral
and witnessed the violence that occurred: 'I watched a soldier aim at a
woman running with a baby in her arms . . . A young man lay next to me,
mortally wounded.'[110] Other reports included 'a British Army Saracen
intentionally knocked down and killed Hugh Maguire in Belfast . . . the
boy was nine years old . . . the Saracen deliberately swerved onto the
sidewalk . . .'[111] *The Irish People*'s source for this story was apparently a
nine-year-old boy. The Army claimed that he had been struck by an
iron bar which rebounded off the vehicle, allegedly thrown by a group

of youths near a filling station. According to the pathologist's report, his injuries were consistent with him having been hit on the head with an iron bar. A woman making similar claims to *The Irish People* was dismissed by the coroner, who said that 'no weight can be given to this woman's evidence. She is prepared to say anything that would incriminate the army.'[112] Attacks on the security forces were considered worthwhile as they 'tied down enemy personnel yet again for hundreds of wasted man hours. Hours when otherwise they might have been able to go about their normal business of brutalising and repressing the nationalist people.'[113]

Protestant figures were targeted during the 1980s as the IRA's armed struggle veered dangerously close to a sectarian campaign. *The Irish People* reported 'a series of spectacular raids last week, Irish Republican Army Volunteers . . . killed the Paisley-like hardline Loyalist MP Robert Bradford . . . he fed the sectarian supremacist ideology used by such Protestant paramilitary groups as the Ulster Defence Association and Ulster Volunteer Force'.[114] In 1982, the IRA shot dead the notorious Shankill Butcher, Lennie Murphy, an attack that, for *The Irish People* at least, 'illustrated the continued ability of the IRA to acquire military intelligence and to operate in Loyalist areas . . . Presumably this ability indicates the presence of Protestant members or supporters of the IRA living in these areas',[115] something at odds with other accounts of the murder, which suggest that fellow loyalists, fearful of the increasingly unstable Murphy, had conspired to arrange the murder.[116] The temptation to cite the apocryphal Protestant supporters of the IRA rather inaccurately framing the IRA as an army of the people was great, even when more constitutional figures such as Queen's University Belfast law faculty member and member of the 1982 Northern Ireland Assembly, Edgar Graham, were killed. *The Irish People* described him as 'a leading figure of the loyalist establishment and a prominent apologist for British Army terrorism'.[117] This has since been attributed to the restive Belfast Brigade of the IRA, which saw expulsions in the middle part of the decade because their actions were contrary to the aims of the movement at the time.[118]

CONCLUSION

The task of Irish-American organisations became increasingly complicated during the 1980s. The increased profile of the Northern Ireland conflict provided a platform from which they could reasonably expect to attract increased support, but the prison campaign also recaptured the interest of senior representatives such as Tip O'Neill and Ted Kennedy. With Sinn Féin moving towards a more politicised version of the republican struggle, it was natural that they should seek political allies. The more traditional republican armed struggle was maintained both at home and internationally as the movement attempted to balance the pragmatic with the long-established. This was necessary to ensure that the effects of the split that eventually occurred in 1986 were minimised. While the Irish-American media, most vociferously represented by *The Irish People*, returned to type, the publicity war was beginning to become rather tired and repetitive, much like the IRA's armed campaign itself. It was no longer simply enough to misreport events and justify IRA violence on rather tenuous grounds; the movement was in need of reinvigoration. The republican split of 1986 created a rift in the Irish-American support base, but the changed focus of Irish republicanism meant that figures like Michael Flannery and George Harrison were now viewed rather like Commandant Tom Maguire: important historical figures, but largely irrelevant in the contemporary context. Martin Galvin assumed control of Noraid during this decade, but it was towards the establishment figures that the Irish republican movement was now looking, their new political direction requiring validation from the highest level possible. This was realised the following decade as a new Irish-American president took office in the White House and immediately took issue with Northern Ireland.

NOTES

1. Memo on 'Friends of Ireland' organization, undated (c. 1981). KOD, BCBL.
2. Hamilton Fish Committee on the Judiciary, Congressional Record Proceedings and Debates of the 96th Congress, Second Session Vol. 126 No. 122, Washington 1/8/1980.
3. *The Bulletin* 29/10/1978; *Post* 29/10/1978.
4. Telex from Irish Embassy London to Washington, 7/5/1981. KOD, BCBL
5. *TIP* Vol. IX No. 48 29/11/1980 (labelled as 29/9/1980).
6. *TIP* Vol. VIII No. 4 27/1/1979; *TIP* Vol. X No. 11 21/3/1981.
7. Irish Northern Aid Briefing note, undated, NYUL, AIA 9, Box 1, Series A, Organizations.
8. Holland, *The American Connection*, p. 57.
9. *Staten Island Advance* 18/12/1985.
10. *TIP* Vol. III No. 24 15/6/1974.
11. Embassy of Ireland, Washington, DC, Press Release c. 1980. KOD, BCBL.

12. Letter from O'Neill, Kennedy, Carey and Moynihan to Margaret Thatcher, 6/5/1981. KOD, BCBL.
13. Telex, 'British Press Coverage of Today, 15 May 1981, of Prime Minister Thatcher's response to Telegram from Senators Kennedy and Moynihan, Speaker O'Neill and New York Governor Carey', 15/5/1981. KOD, BCBL.
14. Resolution offered by Representatives Marie Howe (D-Somerville), Charles Doyle (D-Boston) and John McNeil (D-Malden) Adopted Unanimously by the Massachusetts House of Representatives June 15, 1981 – Demanding the Recall and Withdrawal of the British Consulate. KOD, BCBL.
15. Ibid.
16. *New York Times* 2/5/1982.
17. *TIP* Vol. X No. 36 12/9/1981.
18. Beresford, *Ten Men Dead*.
19. *TIP* Vol. X No. 36 12/9/1981.
20. *TIP* Vol. IX No. 44 1/11/1980.
21. *TIP* Vol. X No. 15 18/4/1981.
22. Mid-Manhattan Irish Northern Aid statement c. 1982, NYUL, AIA 9, Box 1, Series A, Organizations.
23. *Newsday* 5/12/1982.
24. *TIP* Vol. X No. 18 9/5/1981.
25. *TIP* Vol. X No. 28 18/7/1981.
26. *Washington Star* 10/5/1981.
27. *New York Times* 10/5/1981.
28. *TIP* Vol. XI No. 25 26/6/1982.
29. *TIP* Vol. VIII No. 42 10/11/1979.
30. *Intercontinental Press* 12/10/1981.
31. *The Militant* 16/7/1982.
32. George Harrison Financial Papers, NYUL, AIA 9, Box 1 Series A, Personal Papers.
33. Defaced IADF form, undated, NYUL, AIA 9, Box 13, Series B, Organizations.
34. *TIP* Vol. XI No. 38 25/9/1982.
35. Baltimore *Sun* 5/5/1981.
36. Northern Ireland Assembly Election 1982 http://www.ark.ac.uk/elections/fa82.htm
37. *TIP* Vol. XI No. 6 13/2/1982.
38. *TIP* Vol. IX No. 42 18/10/1980.
39. *Washington Star*, 19/11/1975.
40. *Staten Island Advance* 18/12/1985.
41. *The Sovereign Nation: The Republican Voice*, October–November 2006.
42. *Irish Echo*, 'Guns and Roses: Twenty Years On, Acquitted IRA Gunrunners Still Celebrate' http://www.irishecho.com/newspaper/story.cfm?id=12401 24/2–2/3/2010.
43. Harrison-Falvey Defence Committee, Press Release from Harrison 18/11/1982, NYUL, AIA 9, Box 5, Series B, Prisoners.
44. *TIP* Vol. XIV No. 40 25/10/1986.
45. *TIP* Vol. XI No. 11 20/3/1982.
46. *New York Post* 13/10/1983.
47. *TIP* Vol. XIV No. 43 15/11/1986.

48. National Irish Freedom Committee, 'Founding Members' http://www.irishfreedom.net/NIFC/NIFC%20Background%20folder/Founding%20members.htm
49. Quoted in English, *Armed Struggle*, p. 316.
50. *Independent* 11/12/1988.
51. Martin Galvin, correspondence with author, 21/6/2010.
52. Quoted in Ó Brádaigh, *Dilseacht*, p. 49.
53. Letter from Dáithí Ó Conaill to George Harrison, NYUL, AIA 9, Box 13, Series B, Organizations.
54. Statement by Mr Charles J. Haughey, TD, Taoiseach (Prime Minister of Ireland) in response to the announcement of proposed Friends of Ireland Group in the US Congress, 16/3/1981. KOD, BCBL.
55. Memo on 'Friends of Ireland' organization, undated (c. 1981). KOD, BCBL.
56. Friends of Ireland Joint St Patrick's Day Statement 1981. KOD, BCBL.
57. See Embassy of the United States, London, UK, 'Additional Administrative Processing' http://www.usembassy.org.uk/cons_new/visa/niv/add_crime.html
58. The Irish American Bar Association of California letter to Gerry Adams, 2/4/1984, NYUL AIA 9, Box 1, Series A, Organizations.
59. Danny Morrison, interview with author, Belfast, 13/7/2007.
60. Moloney, *Voices*, pp. 270–1.
61. Letter from Richard Fairbanks, Assistant Secretary for Congressional Relations, Department of State to O'Neill, 21/10/1981. KOD, BCBL.
62. Letter from Michael McLoughlin, Director Massachusetts Chapter of National Council of Irish Americans, 29/11/1981. KOD, BCBL.
63. *Boston Globe* 23/12/1981.
64. The Prevention of Terrorism (Temporary Provisions) Act 1984 (The Stationery Office).
65. Congressional Record Proceedings and Debates of the 98th Congress, Second Session, Vol. 130 No. 113, Washington, 12/9/1984, NYUL, AIA 9, Box 5, Series B, Prisoners.
66. McKittrick et al., *Lost Lives*, pp. 993–4.
67. *Irish Times* 21/10/1982.
68. Remarks of Mayor Raymond L. Flynn Before the US Senate Foreign Relations Committee, 18/9/1985, NYUL, AIA 9, Box 5, Series B, Prisoners.
69. Bowyer Bell, *The Secret Army*, pp. 487–8; McKittrick et al., *Lost Lives*, pp. 827–8; *Sunday Tribune* 22/4/1984.
70. *New York Times* 18/12/1983.
71. *Daily News* 16/12/1984.
72. Doherty, J., 'The Destruction and Revival of Irish Culture', February 1986, NYUL, AIA 9, Box 5, Series B, Prisoners.
73. *Newsday* 10/10/1986.
74. Toast at a St Patrick's Day Luncheon Hosted by the Irish Ambassador, 17/3/1981. Public Papers of the Presidents of the United States – Ronald Reagan 1981 (Washington, DC: United States Government Printing Office, 1982), p. 258.
75. Thatcher, *The Downing Street Years*, pp. 322–5; Public Papers of the Presidents of the United States – Ronald Reagan 1983 (Washington, DC: United States Government Printing Office, 1984), p. 405.
76. Interview with Brian Farrell of RTE Television, Dublin, Ireland on Foreign Issues,

25/5/1984. Public Papers of the Presidents of the United States – Ronald Reagan 1984 (Washington, DC: United States Government Printing Office, 1985), p. 751.

77. Public Papers of the Presidents of the United States – Ronald Reagan 1986 (Washington, DC: United States Government Printing Office, 1988), p. 359.

78. Suggested Elements for a Statement by the Speaker in Support of an Anglo-Irish Agreement c. 1985. KOD, BCBL.

79. Friends of Ireland Statement on the successful conclusion of the Anglo-Irish Summit, undated. KOD, BCBL.

80. American Irish Congress Newsletter, December 1986.

81. Remarks at a St Patrick's Day Ceremony with Deputy Prime Minister Brian Lenihan of Ireland, 16/3/1990. Public Papers of the Presidents of the United States – George Bush 1990 (Washington, DC: United States Government Printing Office, 1991), p. 377.

82. British Occupation in the North of Ireland: Two Priests Speak Out, undated, NYUL, AIA 9, Box 5, Series B, Prisoners.

83. Irish American Unity Conference meeting, 15–17 July 1983, Chicago, IL, notes by Harrison; American Irish Unity Conference Memo to Members, 19/7/1985, NYUL, AIA 9, Box 1, Series A, Organizations.

84. Anthony Coughlan, interview with author, Dublin, 15/6/2010.

85. Bartlett, A., 'Britain's other Army', *National Political Education Committee National Newsletter*, December 1982/January 1983 Vol. 7 No. 6.

86. Dougherty, R., 'Northern Ireland Loyalist Death Squads', *National Political Education Committee National Newsletter*, October/November 1984 Vol. 9 No. 5.

87. Sammy Duddy, interview with author, Belfast, 21/1/2005.

88. American Irish Congress Newsletter, December 1986.

89. Ibid.

90. Ibid.

91. Ibid.

92. *New York Times* 2/5/1982.

93. *TIP* Vol. X No. 21 30/5/1981.

94. *TIP* Vol. X No. 18 9/5/1981.

95. *TIP* Vol. XI No. 31 7/8/1982.

96. *TIP* Vol. XII No. 46 26/11/1983.

97. VisitBritain Long-Term Trends http://www.visitbritain.org/Images/ips%20trends%20since%201979_tcm139-170410.xls 25/6/2010.

98. *TIP* Vol. XII No. 50 24/12/1983.

99. Reagan letter to Thatcher, 19/12/1983; Thatcher letter to Reagan, 21/12/1983, Reagan Library: NSA Head of State File (Thatcher: Cables [4]) Box 35 http://www.margaretthatcher.org/search/results.asp?ps=500&w=MTRR

100. Reagan letter to Thatcher, 12/10/1984, Reagan Library: NSA Head of State File (Box 36) http://www.margaretthatcher.org/archive/displaydocument.asp?docid=109351

101. *TIP* Vol. X No. 42 31/10/1981.

102. *Rocky Mountain News* 18/03/1984.

103. Editorial, *The Patriot Ledger* Vol. 148 No. 54 10/03/1984.

104. *San Francisco Examiner* 21/10/1986.

105. *TIP* Vol. XI No. 20 3/7/1982.

106. *TIP* Vol. XI No. 27 10/7/1982.

107. *TIP* Vol. XI No. 27 10/7/1982.
108. *TIP* Vol. XI No. 30 31/7/1982.
109. McKittrick et al., *Lost Lives*, pp. 908–10.
110. *TIP* Vol. XI No. 9 6/3/1982.
111. *TIP* Vol. IX No. 8 23/2/1980.
112. McKittrick, D. et al., *Lost Lives*, pp. 820–1.
113. *TIP* Vol. XI No. 25 26/6/1982.
114. *TIP* Vol. X No. 45 21/11/1981.
115. *TIP* Vol. XI No. 47 27/11/1982.
116. Dillon, M., *The Shankill Butchers* (London: Hutchinson, 1989).
117. *TIP* Vol. XII No. 49 17/12/1983.
118. Moloney, *Secret History*, pp. 243, 317.

CHAPTER 7

Changed Priorities: The 1990s

The trend towards politics that was established during the 1980s continued during the 1990s as the Provisional republican movement made its final move away from violence with two major ceasefires in the middle years of the decade. The republican militarist tradition proved durable as a series of splinter groups emerged for a variety of reasons. Factionalism occurred as a result of both ideological and personal differences as Northern Ireland moved closer to peace, the involvement of mainstream republicanism stimulating the military prerogatives of a significant minority.

Important again in the affairs of Northern Ireland during this decade was the United States of America. The transition of Irish-America from military support to political intervention was completed as President Bill Clinton took an active interest in the nascent peace process in Northern Ireland and exerted considerable influence on wider republican attitudes to the peace process. The political direction adopted by the Provisional republican movement during the 1980s was highly influential during this decade, with support for politics over armed struggle boosted by the growing perception that the IRA could not actually defeat the British security forces. While the political transition of Sinn Féin is a topic well covered,[1] this chapter will aim to consider how this influenced further division that occurred within republicanism as the peace process developed.

THE OFFICIAL REPUBLICANS IN THE 1990S

Although the 1990s saw the twentieth anniversary of the Official IRA ceasefire, and the movement's evolution to the Workers' Party had jettisoned as much republican baggage as was possible, the movement was not able to rid itself of the distinctly republican tendency for disagreement and division. With the fall of the Berlin Wall in November 1989, the Workers' Party was forced into a period of introspection. While Proinsias De Rossa argued that a more democratic socialism would emerge from the ashes of international communism, the truth was that the group was in deep ideological trouble.[2] In 1990, Eoghan Harris published *The Necessity of Social Democracy*, his personal reflections on the new situation that faced the movement which was deeply critical of the political left. An internal squabble ensued which ultimately prompted Harris to leave the party, precipitating the more serious division that took place in 1992. Roy Johnston later admitted that 'the culture-gap between our attempted Marxist analysis of the situation and the then Irish political environment was huge'.[3]

They were also troubled by allegations that 'Group B', the Official IRA, had been involved in extortion, racketeering and other criminal pursuits. The issue highlighted the geographical division in the movement; in the North, Tom French stated that 'I can say clearly that there is no place in the ranks of the Workers' Party for anyone who has links with any paramilitary group',[4] whereas Joe Ruddock, the Workers' Party representative for Dun Laoghaire, argued that 'the reality is that the dogs in the street know the Official IRA exists and that members of the Workers' Party are involved in it. These people are bringing the party into disrepute.'[5] *The Irish News* claimed that the Official IRA were not only in existence, but were armed and ready to strike with roughly a hundred members.[6]

The fact that the Official IRA had not only persisted but had retained such a significant membership nearly two decades after its ceasefire emphasises the complicated structure of the Workers' Party. While the movement was unable to completely jettison the military wing of the movement, it could not reasonably expect full political credibility and the party had struggled the previous decade because of OIRA activity. The 1972 decision to refer to the Official IRA as Group B was ostensibly for legal reasons,[7] but there were also important strategic and ideological reasons for this: there was no real reason to refer to the political party as 'Group A' for very long given the legality of the party and the rapid

191

acquisition of political acceptance; and the symbolism of 'B' being subordinate to 'A' established a hierarchy within the movement. The inability to completely rid the movement of what Derry Kelleher referred to as 'its mediocre elements',[8] was exacerbated by, for Roy Johnston, the 'disorientation and confusion of both the Marxist left and the republican left'.[9] Dessie O'Hagan and John Lowry note the impact of international events at the time and how this forced the party into developing a new long-term strategy which, in turn, would require an increase in funding to enable the group to carry out important tasks such as recruiting.[10] It was arguably the inability to achieve this refinancing that really damaged the movement; with legal means of fundraising proving insufficient to sustain the movement, alternative measures were required.[11] The activities of the Official IRA undoubtedly helped to sustain the movement, providing an outlet for the criminal aspirations of some and ideological justification for others. Regardless, these activities served to undermine the political credibility of the Workers' Party.

In 1991 it was claimed that the Workers' Party did not exist as a political party, rather as a group led by Seamus Lynch, John Lowry and Mary McMahon with approximately fifty thugs below them in the organisation's hierarchy. Furthermore, it was alleged that the OIRA continued to be involved in petty crime, extortion and protection rackets, with criminals offered allegiance to the movement in an effort to strengthen the movement numerically.[12] Television documentaries in both Britain and Ireland detailed OIRA criminal activity and shone light on an area of organisational activity that the political leadership would have preferred to ignore.[13]

While the party enjoyed considerable political success in the Republic, a growing rift between the northern and southern membership troubled the organisational integrity. The distinct political situations north and south of the border manifested themselves with the northern membership consistently supportive of the revolutionary party position while the southern faction was increasingly keen to distance itself from the weighty baggage of Official IRA violence. John Lowry points out that 'we basically were following a common agenda, which was directed towards political agitation, heightening of social and economic agitations'.[14] Seamus Lynch's election as the chair of a council committee in Belfast in the summer of 1991 was tempered by the growing consensus that the Workers' Party was unable to achieve its goals in Northern Ireland and the southern membership had largely lost interest in the North.[15] Conscious of an imminent southern General Election, it was important that the credibility of the party be rehabilitated, particularly after the resignation of Charles Haughey as Taoiseach. The Workers' Party leadership moved quickly with the intention of acting before their internal opponents were able to organise. A special Ard Fheis was called in February 1992, which would dissolve and reconstitute the party, engineered towards removing the opponents of the parliamentary party.[16] The problem of the Official IRA was also significant and the proposed reconstitution would have allowed the leadership to purge members suspected of paramilitarism; opposition to paramilitary activity evident in Proinsias De Rossa's incredible faux pas that he was in favour of the reintroduction of internment to combat paramilitary activity.[17]

Moves towards reconstitution of the party were led by both southern chairman De Rossa and Belfast chairperson Seamus Lynch, although a majority of northern members opposed the move. South of the border, support was almost total within the party's TDs, with only Tomás Mac Giolla refusing to declare his intentions ahead of the Ard Fheis. After two recounts it transpired that the motion had only won 241 votes with 133 votes against; this was just short of the two-thirds majority required for the motion to pass. In a further blow to De Rossa, Mac Giolla refused to support the motion, leaving those in favour of reconstitution with only five TDs, one short of the six required to be considered a Dáil group and to be eligible for the associated £100,000 in state funding.[18] The movement was irrevocably divided and shortly afterwards the De Rossa faction formed a group initially called New Agenda, which quickly became the Democratic Left. As noted by Roy Foster, this group retained 'some of the leftist ideology of its parents in 1960s Sinn Féin, but not enough to make it uncomfortable company in the Dáil'.[19]

This split was particularly untidy, with each branch of the Workers' Party divided between loyalty to the party and to De Rossa. Although most of the elected officials departed with De Rossa, the majority of Workers' Party veterans remained, with Garland and Mac Giolla prominent. The reaction of the southern electorate to the split was complicated: Mac Giolla was defeated, finally removing the Workers Party from the Dáil, and Democratic Left TDs Joe Sherlock, Pat McCartan and Eric Byrne all failed to be re-elected, although Liz McManus's success in Wicklow was noteworthy. North of the border neither group enjoyed much success, with the Workers' Party achieving 4,359 votes, just over double the figure attained by the candidates standing under the New Agenda banner.

193

During the election campaign, his 1987 appeal to Moscow for support troubled De Rossa to the extent that he launched libel proceedings against the *Sunday Independent*, a case which he would eventually win with a record payout.[20] The accusations levelled at De Rossa were not costly to the Democratic Left, who found themselves in government by the end of 1994. The twenty-seventh Dáil was a coalition of Fianna Fáil and the Labour Party, with Albert Reynolds as Taoiseach. Following a series of scandals in 1994, notably over the issue of child abuse among members of the Catholic clergy, the Labour Party left the government and formed the twenty-fourth Government of Ireland with their traditional coalition partners, Fine Gael, and the Democratic Left. This coalition lasted from December 1994 until June 1997, when it was succeeded by the Fianna Fáil–Progressive Democrats coalition.

De Rossa was named as the Minister for Social Welfare and his personal transition from his 1950s internment was complete.[21] The Workers' Party became marginalised during the peace process negotiations, which fermented resentment within the movement and a further split with a group self-titled the Official Republican Movement emerging in late 1997 and early 1998. For Anthony McIntyre:

> The Workers' Party started off Provisional IRA, Official IRA, Republican Clubs, Sinn Féin The Workers' Party then The Workers' Party, then the Democratic Left, then the Irish Labour Party and they have just become totally happy in the political establishment . . . I think what happens is when radicals go into institutions which are not radical, the institutions subordinate the radical soul.[22]

After losing two of its six seats in the 1997 General Election, Democratic Left merged with the Irish Labour Party in 1999. Significant was the decision to exclude the Northern Irish branch of the Democratic Left from this merger; the Labour Party was a sister organisation of the SDLP in the North, but this move left Dungannon councillor Gerry Cullen stranded with a mandate but no party.[23] The decision was a result of the combined vote of the two parties dropping to 13 per cent in the 1997 election, an indication that two left-wing parties might be stretching the viable support for the left among the Irish electorate.[24]

Cullen's isolation was particularly interesting in light of the relative failure of the Workers' Party during the 1997 local council elections in Northern Ireland. Although they achieved quadruple the total votes of the Democratic Left, who only fielded one candidate, they were the most popular party not to achieve representation in the elections. The following year, they achieved fewer than two thousand votes in the

Assembly elections, their vote again dropping to 1,421 in the 2001 Local Government elections, roughly 0.2 per cent of the vote.

THE IRSP AND INLA IN THE 1990S

Entering the decade mired in a feud, the cycle of violence for the Republican Socialist Movement continued during the early years of the 1990s. Any political aspirations that were held within the movement were suppressed by the overwhelming danger for anyone declaring allegiances to any group associated with the movement. The INLA had dominated the movement almost since its inception and while the peace process was gathering momentum across Northern Ireland, the most striking aspect of Republican Socialist violence during the early 1990s was the speed with which former comrades turned their guns on each other. Although the movement continued to fracture, with the majority of republicans now in the business of peace, the cycle of reckless internecine violence could not be allowed to continue.

Predictably, the IPLO began the decade mired in violence, losing one of its more active members on 16 August 1991 when Martin O'Prey, believed to have been involved in the George Seawright murder, was killed by the UVF.[25] In histories stained with blood, the final weeks of 1991 stand out as some of the most violent in the relatively short history of the INLA and IPLO. One death that had serious ramifications for the peace process in Northern Ireland was that of Colm Mahon, a Catholic doorman, who was shot by the IPLO after a disagreement outside Frames snooker club in central Belfast on 15 December 1991. Christopher McWilliams had been ejected from the bar following a fight and returned to shoot Mahon, a crime for which he was later imprisoned.[26] McWilliams, who died of cancer in 2008, had previously been jailed in 1984 for his part in the shoot-out that killed an RUC sergeant. After his initial release, he joined the IPLO but became ostracised after the Mahon murder.[27] Keen to reintegrate himself with the INLA in prison, McWilliams eventually won favour with the INLA by leading the operation to kill loyalist Billy Wright in late 1997.

While the Mahon murder had the hallmarks of a particularly counter-productive killing, it could scarcely be argued that much IPLO activity served any real purpose. On 20 December, Patrick McDonald of the IPLO was shot in Dublin, possibly by a Dublin-based criminal gang,[28] and the following day the IPLO killed two Protestants in the Donegall

Arms public house in the Village area of South Belfast.[29] The IPLO did stand out for its ability to create terror, thanks to a reckless campaign of violence that continued into 1992.

On 17 February, the IPLO shot dead Andrew Johnson, who had been working in a video library in North Belfast. They claimed that it was a response to nationalists being shot dead, the SAS having killed four IRA men the previous night in an ambush.[30] The UVF killed Johnson's suspected killer, Conor Maguire, in late April and the IPLO reacted by shooting Protestant pensioner Billy Sargent on 5 May. The endless cycle of seemingly pointless violence inevitably brought further division and during the summer of 1992 the IPLO itself split into two factions, styled as the IPLO Army Council and IPLO Belfast Brigade.[31] It is significant that both groups were so keen to maintain the IPLO brand, the organisation having done more to divide republicanism in its short existence than arguably any other group. Following the divide, the IPLO began to turn its guns on its own members; Jimmy Brown was killed by the IPLO-BB faction on 18 August 1992, with retaliatory killings taking place over the following month before the spiral of violence was finally cut short by the intervention of the Provisional IRA. On 31 October 1992, the PIRA shot dead Samuel Ward, the leader of the IPLO Belfast Brigade, and wounded ten others. This 'night of the long knives'-style attack sent out a very clear message across republicanism: the Provisional IRA would no longer tolerate futile republican feuding. In the absence of the IPLO, the Republican Socialist Movement could attempt to reasset itself on the militant left wing of republicanism.

Still in charge of the INLA was Dominic McGlinchey. Having been refused permission to attend the funeral of his wife in 1987, he resumed control of the INLA upon his release from prison in 1993. Following allegations that the UVF had become involved with Irish criminals, he survived an assassination attempt by Mid-Ulster UVF leader Billy Wright.[32] The threat on his life made McGlinchey rather fatalistic, commenting with reference to his nickname, 'What do you do with a Mad Dog except put it down?'[33] His fears were realised on 10 February in Drogheda. His son, who had witnessed the murder of his mother, also witnessed his father being gunned down. It was alleged that his killers were members of the UVF, although the number of enemies that the McGlinchey family had accrued over the years makes any such assertion nearly impossible.[34] His nickname was adopted by loyalist Johnny Adair, who would later collaborate with Wright's Loyalist Volunteer Force faction. Adair remarked that, 'The difference between me and McGlinchey is that he killed policemen but I kill taigs.'[35]

His former comrades claimed that 'Dominic could be likened to that other great revolutionary, O'Donnovan [sic] Rossa',[36] and, in a bizarre twist, Bernadette McAliskey, who had left the IRSP because of her opposition to militarism, called him the greatest republican of his generation,[37] also claiming that 'this man never in the whole of his life dishonoured the cause he believed in'.[38]

Retaining much of its propensity for violence even post-McGlinchey, the INLA continued to sporadically target alleged loyalist paramilitaries, perpetuating the cyclical violence that tarred the late 1980s and early 1990s in Northern Ireland. In deliberately targeting loyalist paramilitaries, the INLA cast themselves in a mirror-image role to loyalist paramilitaries, a pseudo-vigilante movement that claimed to protect its community but in reality fed its members thirst for violence. Neither side carried out this role particularly effectively, with the INLA killing forty-one civilians and ten of its own volunteers relative to five loyalists. Meanwhile, loyalist paramilitaries killed 546 civilians compared to thirty-one republican paramilitaries.

In killing civilians during 1994, the INLA attempted to justify their actions by claiming their victims to have been paramilitary members.[39] A summer attack on the Shankill Road killed UVF volunteers Colin Craig, Trevor King and David Hamilton. Given the UVF's inevitably reckless response, which included a gun attack on the Heights Bar in Loughinisland during a Republic of Ireland football match which killed six, including eighty-seven-year-old Barney Green, the judiciousness of such operations is questionable. If the purpose of INLA violence was to remind republicans how counterproductive it could be, it certainly succeeded.

The cycle of violence again served to divide the INLA, with another internal feud robbing the movement of Chief of Staff Gino Gallagher, shot dead on 31 January 1996 by members of his own organisation as he visited the social security office on the Falls Road. Fra Halligan recalls that 'Hugh Torney and that lot were court-martialled and were dismissed with ignominy from the INLA. They then bought a gun off a drug dealer and got a drug dealer and his friends to murder Gino, so they were planning this for two years.'[40] Torney, a former Chief of Staff, was murdered by the INLA as part of a year of violence that also claimed the life of nine-year-old Barbara McAlorum in March, in an attack allegedly directed at her

197

elder brother Kevin. His life was ended, in turn, when he was shot dead while dropping his child at Oakwood Integrated Primary School in mid-2004.[41] The movement was also troubled by criminal associations during the 1990s, particularly after member John Morris was shot dead by Gardaí in Dublin during a robbery.[42] The INLA's propensity for violence was emphasised by their opposition to the peace process, with strong political objections to 1998's Good Friday Agreement also noteworthy. Ironically, the INLA contributed, unintentionally or otherwise, to the peace process with their murder of Billy Wright inside the Maze prison on 27 December 1997, an action that has since attracted a great deal of controversy.

After the dust had settled on the paramilitary ceasefires of the mid-1990s, the INLA and LVF remained the only two active organisations. The imprisonment of members of either group in the same H-Block, separated by only a short corridor, fuelled conspiracy theories after Wright was murdered by an INLA unit led by Christopher McWilliams, who was attempting to integrate himself with the group after his conviction for the Colm Mahon murder.

Using a gun smuggled into the prison, the INLA prisoners crawled through a hole in the wire fence, ran across the roof of the H-Block, jumped down into the yard and shot Wright who was sitting in a prison van waiting to be transported to the visitors' area. The two other LVF prisoners in the van were unharmed. Journalist Chris Anderson's book *The Billy Boy* poses many questions as to the controversy of the killing, such as why renegade republican Christopher McWilliams was transferred to the Maze prison; where the INLA obtained wire cutters from; why the INLA prisoners were informed of which LVF prisoners were receiving visits on 27 December; and why the watchtower over H6 was unmanned along with the malfunctioning security camera over the same H-Block.[43]

Such issues brought allegations that Britain had colluded with the INLA in order to kill the troublesome and maverick Wright. As part of an investigation into controversial killings in Northern Ireland, retired Canadian Supreme Court judge Peter Cory conducted an inquiry that recommended a full investigation into the killing of Billy Wright, as well as those of Lurgan solicitor Rosemary Nelson, Belfast solicitor Pat Finucane and Portadown man Robert Hamill. The Billy Wright enquiry opened in November 2005, with former Assistant Chief Constable Sam Kincaid claiming that intelligence had indicated an attempt to kill Wright was likely.[44]

Perhaps the most significant aspect of these allegations was the notion that an Irish republican paramilitary group could collude with their sworn enemy, regardless of the purpose of the collusion. The IRSP contend that they were the victims, rather than the beneficiaries, of collusion:

> Let's say Costello, Ronnie Bunting and Dr Miriam Daly weren't killed. From '74 to '87, with two councillors elected in '79–'80, that would have been a party to be reckoned with, one hell of a political force fighting for the working class. Yes, it would have been attacked, it had to be attacked . . . Down the line Whitehall has absolutely no gumption about executing people, they did so themselves when they let the likes of Robin 'the Jackal' Jackson, Billy Wright do it. So they were quite happy to dirty their hands but probably more happy to let someone else do it for a few quid.[45]

The IRSP argued that 'the INLA can hardly be accused of collusion if they simply took advantage of failures on the part of the authorities'.[46] While the INLA was capable of well-planned operations, indicated by the 1979 murder of Airey Neave, it had struggled to maintain this capacity for violence and was better associated for reckless actions, such as the murder for which McWilliams was himself imprisoned. Certainly, the mid-Ulster UVF unit had proven themselves to be a sufficiently troublesome unit to merit their expulsion from the mainstream organisation and their propensity for violence was further indicated by the actions of the LVF post-split. Following the killing of Wright, the LVF and INLA lashed out wildly at each other as tit-for-tat violence spiralled out of control. Ten further killings took place in the aftermath of Wright's murder as apolitical violence plagued the province during the early months of 1998.[47]

In the midst of this violence, reports emerged that a ceasefire was being debated within the movement in light of the Good Friday Agreement.[48] The ceasefire was confirmed in August 1998, with the group stating that 'there is no political or moral argument to justify a resumption of the campaign'.[49] The INLA ended the decade with a statement that read:

> The Good Friday Agreement is a failed and flawed agreement. The Northern Ireland State is a failed political entity . . . However the INLA does not see a return to armed struggle as a viable alternative at this time. Accordingly we have encouraged our membership and supporters to become actively involved in the day-to-day struggles of ordinary people. Such political involvement is following the example of our founder Seamus Costello. A revolutionary army without a clear base of political understanding and activity is no longer a revolutionary Army. The INLA is part of and acts in the interests of the Irish working class . . . Five years on from our ceasefire there is still a role for the INLA. We will remain vigilant in defence of working class communities but we will not take offensive action.[50]

199

Quite what the purpose of the INLA's struggle during the 1990s was remains unclear. Rather than bringing the struggle for Irish unity to the fore, the group served to emphasise the problems of disunity with their almost constant involvement in feuding. The group allowed itself to become a home for unsavoury elements of a struggle that frequently bordered on the nasty because of their associations with violence. The strong personalities that the lack of structured recruitment policy allowed into the movement inevitably clashed and turned their guns on each other. Even the intervention of the Provisional IRA in 1992 could not end the internecine feuding that beset the IRSM. The group did attain some notoriety with the Billy Wright killing, which in many ways was undermined by the unit that carried out the killing. Christopher McWilliams had proven his apolitical, criminal credentials with the Colm Mahon murder. That the peace process did not destroy the IRSM was remarkable and spoke to the commitment of a membership that would be tested as it attempted to redefine Republican Socialism for peace-time Ireland in the new century.

REPUBLICAN SINN FÉIN AND THE CONTINUITY IRA

Perhaps rather predictably, Republican Sinn Féin remained in the shadows of Sinn Féin during the 1990s. The majority of republicans had declined to join the new party, evidence that few modern republicans were tied to the policy of abstentionism. The abandonment of this tenet of republican policy was better received than the perceived abandonment of the armed struggle, which became increasingly apparent with the onset of the Provisional IRA ceasefires, moves which boosted the Continuity IRA, an armed wing that had ostensibly formed in 1986 but only emerged during the 1990s. Opposition to electoral participation had not manifested itself in a significant rupture and, as agitation grew with the apparent decline of the IRA's armed campaign, Republican Sinn Féin was not in a position to capitalise on this dissent because it lacked a viable armed wing.

Republican Sinn Féin suffered major losses during the 1990s. The passing of Dáithí Ó Conaill on New Year's Day 1991 robbed the movement of one of its most talented members, still only in his fifties. Ó Brádaigh described him as having 'the ablest mind in the Republican Movement for over 20 years'.[51] Geraldine Taylor called him 'a very astute man, very clever man. He was a great loss to the Republic and to Ireland itself'.[52] The group then mourned the loss of its patron Tom Maguire in mid-1993. One opportunity provided at Maguire's funeral was for the Continuity IRA to announce themselves, the group having been dormant since their apparent formation in 1986.

The armed struggle had proven problematic to Republican Sinn Féin, who continued to refer to the Provisional IRA as their own army during the late 1980s.[53] Dáithí Ó Conaill had noted:

It's very difficult to reconcile the two – the constitutional and the unconstitutional. In the Northern Context it is understood, and where you have good military operations it generally enhances one's prospects in election. In the Southern context, however, it can be the other way around, unless you have, for instance, a good strike against the British army – that can have a good effect. But the shooting of a few UDR men can have a negative effect, and the further south you go the greater the negative effect. So you are caught in a bind in that sense, in that we are trying to combine two forms of action – military action and political action – which at times work against each other. It makes our task more difficult.[54]

With the southern base of Republican Sinn Féin, a campaign against the security forces was problematic given IRA General Order number eight which prohibited action against southern security forces. As 1994 progressed and it became apparent that the Provisional IRA was readying itself for a ceasefire, calling 'a complete cessation of military activities' as of midnight on 31 August,[55] Republican Sinn Féin reacted, declaring that 'The Provisionals have now taken several historic and irrevocable steps: 1. Accepting the 26-County; 2. Accepting the so-called "Northern Ireland" Statelet; and 3. The war of national liberation, as far as they are concerned, has been stopped.'[56]

The emergence of the Continuity IRA was described by Republican Sinn Féin newspaper, *Saoirse*, as 'a dramatic public announcement'.[57] Although slightly over-stated, the emergence of the group was important as it established the context in which contemporary dissident republicanism would operate: opposition to the ceasefires, a fundamental tenet of support for armed struggle.[58] *Saoirse* carefully noted that 'the stated objectives appear to be the same as those of Republican Sinn Féin but of course as a military body it would be working for those by different means. For its party Republican Sinn Féin, as a political organisation, works solely by political means.'[59] With continuity important to the movement, the presence of four out of the seven members of the first Provisional Army Council on the first Continuity Army Council[60] gave the movement strong republican credentials but emphasised the outdated strategy that the movement as a whole pursued.

The first act of the Continuity IRA was to serve as the firing party during the funeral of Commandant General Tom Maguire. A statement from the Irish Republican Publicity Bureau declared that 'a firing-party of Volunteers of Óglaigh na hÉireann – the Irish Republican Army – loyal to the principles of the late Comdt-General Tom Maguire rendered military honours at his grave in Cross, Co. Mayo'.[61] Sought out to act as consul for republicans at various junctures of the campaign, the mysticism around Maguire was somewhat lost on former IRA volunteer and author Eamon Collins, who remarked cynically:

> What will Sands-McKevitt and Ó Brádaigh do now that the old general has passed away? If they had his body mummified they could wheel it on during rallies, and if they have a tape of him supporting the Provisionals they could always change it to 'Continuity' or '32 County Sovereignty' . . . It is either that or join forces as one 'Real/New IRA' and go on an archaeological dig to discover a new more powerful oracle of republican truth.[62]

George Harrison took over as patron of Republican Sinn Féin until his death in 2004 when he was, in turn, succeeded by Dan Keating, the last survivor of the Irish War of Independence, who died in 2007.

The Continuity IRA returned to the shadows until 1996, causing serious damage to the Killyhevlin hotel in Enniskillen in July with a car bomb which injured seventeen. Other than this their struggle of the 1990s is marked with small bombings and minor reports of shootings.[63] Their next noteworthy attack was in November 1997 when a large bomb exploded in Markethill, County Armagh. It was dismissed in some quarters as 'a small group with a limited paramilitary capability',[64] and 'made up of at most two dozen volunteers',[65] although reports of co-operation between the dissidents drew concern.[66] Through collaboration, allegations emerged of defections to and from the Real IRA.[67] The seemingly easily permeable borders between the dissident republican organisations emphasises the apolitical nature of these groups, with members simply transferring their allegiance to the organisation most likely to provide them with an outlet for their desire for violence. Although *Saoirse* criticised the INLA on the ground that 'the history and activities of that organisation show that not all of its members have been ideologically motivated',[68] one could easily question the ideological motivations of Continuity IRA recruits.

Republican Sinn Féin contested local elections during the 1990s, with Sean Lynch successfully elected to Longford County Council in both

1991 and 1999, but with little other success to note. Politically, the group criticised Sinn Féin's involvement in the peace process, Ó Brádaigh arguing that 'Bobby Sands and his comrades did not die for a few cross-border bodies traded against the definition of the nation contained in the 1937 constitution.'[69] The hunger strike proved a handy propaganda tool, if less convincing over time. As Eoin Ó Broin notes, 'people use and reinterpret [republican history] . . . in ways that suit them'.[70] Certainly the Republican Sinn Féin interpretation proved a durable, if not entirely popular, form of republicanism through the 1990s.

PROVISIONAL POLITICAL STRATEGY

In 1973, Ruairí Ó Brádaigh had appealed to northern republicanism to continue to support Sinn Féin once the role of the IRA had started to diminish.[71] The IRA went on to dominate the republican struggle for another eight years, and remained an integral part of the movement for another twenty, but the challenge of maintaining support for the republican movement as it sought political credibility for Sinn Féin while the IRA continued to commit acts of violence proved difficult, particularly during 1993. In April 1992, Gerry Adams lost the West Belfast seat at the General Election. The SDLP reclaimed the seat under Dr Joe Hendron, who had only lost to Adams by two thousand votes in 1987. It was claimed that Hendron had succeeded thanks to roughly three thousand votes from loyalists,[72] an assertion partially supported by the reduction in Ulster Unionist Party votes from 7,646 in 1987 to 4,766. The idea that loyalists might have some favour for the constitutional nationalists was quickly dispensed with as the UFF launched a series of bomb attacks at the homes of three SDLP members.[73] That republican violence had sufficiently strong opposition to motivate people to vote in such a manner was considerably more likely.

Many IRA operations during the 1990s were remarkable for their sheer counterproductivity. The introduction of proxy bombs, whereby the IRA forced civilians to deliver bombs to targets, was especially so. On 24 October 1990, Patsy Gillespie, who worked on an army base near Derry, had his family kidnapped and was ordered to drive a bomb to an Army checkpoint on the border, at which point the bomb detonated, killing Gillespie and five soldiers.[74] Peter Brooke described this attack as reaching 'new depths in IRA evil', and the *Irish Times* reflected that the use of proxy bombs had a 'devastating effect on the IRA's image'.[75] This was exacerbated by attacks such as the January 1992 bombing of a minibus near Teebane in County Tyrone which killed eight Protestant workers. Loyalist reaction was inevitable and took the form of a gun attack on a bookmaker's shop on the Ormeau Road in Belfast which killed five. The publication of Sinn Féin's *Towards a Lasting Peace in Ireland* at their Ard Fheis of mid-February could scarcely have seemed more bitterly ironic.

As if to drive the point home, the IRA then attacked the Baltic Exchange in London in April, causing £800 million damage. Ill-advised operations in Northern Ireland were sharply at odds with ruthlessly effective operations in England and point to an organisation lacking unity of purpose. Attacks such as Teebane were contrary to contemporary republican strategy and suggest a demand for action among IRA militants. Each side appeared content to merely flex their paramilitary muscles and, once again, the conflict took on a sinister, sectarian tone. Marian Price contends, 'some of the events were very much designed to turn people off the armed struggle',[76] and indeed, it seemed the only beneficiaries of these attacks were those who sought an end to conflict.

To this end, two IRA attacks of 1993 dramatically undermined the credibility of the republican movement. On 20 March, the IRA planted two bombs in the Cheshire town of Warrington. One attack was on a gasworks, creating a spectacular explosion but causing no fatalities. The second attack involved two bombs in the town centre, killing three-year-old Johnathan Ball instantly. Five days later, twelve-year-old Timothy Parry, who had been seriously injured in the bombing, had his life-support machine switched off.[77] Widespread outrage at the bombings provoked republican accusations that they had given adequate warnings for the bombings, blaming police intransigence for the loss of life. An IRA volunteer claimed in an interview with *The Independent* that he felt 'horror. Exactly the same emotion as went through the minds of the volunteers who planted the bombs. I am furious that there are those within the British authorities who have played this cynical game for almost 12 months.' Although 'a warning was given half-an-hour before', it failed to mention where the bomb was planted.[78] Such claims were reminiscent of the most far-fetched Irish-American reports of the 1970s and 1980s where the people unable to locate IRA bombs were apportioned more blame than those who actually planted the devices. The tragedy of the day was heightened when it was reported that Ball had been in the city centre to purchase a Mother's Day card and Parry to purchase new football gear.[79] Ball's mother later died after suffering from severe depression following the death of her son.[80]

While only the IRA's fiercest enemy would accuse the movement of deliberately targeting children, it cannot be overlooked that the indiscriminate nature of a bombing campaign comes with implicit recognition that anyone could fall victim to such an attack. Attempts to devolve responsibility had no purchase, particularly in a town that could hardly be claimed to have any strategic or tactical importance for the IRA. A bomb in Warrington, a soft target without the symbolic power of an attack on London, served to create terror, reminding the British of how dangerous Provisional republicans could be, while simultaneously undermining the IRA campaign. Over one hundred killed on the British mainland had only strengthened British resolve against the IRA, rather than pushing Irish unity any closer.[81] Bombs in England, while having a stronger propaganda effect than bombs in Ireland, also served to remind loyalists that the IRA's ideological enemy was the British state, not the Protestants of Ireland. A joint statement from Adams and John Hume emphasised this, calling for the right of self-determination for the Irish people. Two weeks later, the IRA caused £1 billion worth of damage in a large-scale bomb attack on the city of London.[82]

Sectarian violence was still on the agenda as the IRA targeted the UDA offices in the mid-Shankill Road in October 1993. A bomb was planted below the offices in Frizzell's fish shop on a Saturday morning, when it was believed that the UDA inner council was conducting a meeting. While the intention was allegedly to clear the building of civilians before it detonated, leaving the loyalist hierarchy trapped above the explosion, fate conspired against the IRA: not only was the UDA office empty, but the bomb exploded prematurely, killing nine Protestant civilians and the bomber, Thomas Begley, as well as injuring almost sixty people. Retrospective reports of the bomb merely having an eleven-second fuse suggest a distinct ambivalence to the safety of Shankill residents.[83] Begley's co-conspirator Sean Kelly later stated:

> The fact innocent people died is something I will have to live with for the rest of my life. While we did go out to kill the leadership of the UDA, we never intended for innocent people to die. It . . . was an accident and if I could do anything to change what happened, believe me I would do it.[84]

Gerry Adams' appearance as one of Begley's pallbearers was an appalling sight to the Protestant communities of Northern Ireland. Although Adams had often fulfilled such a role for deceased IRA volunteers and had to be particularly careful not to distance himself from the IRA with the peace process still in a very fragile condition, his motivations for assuming a position of prominence at this funeral were particularly ambiguous. Having been deposed as West Belfast MP the previous year by Shankill voters, who supported the SDLP, there could be no more defiant an act for Adams than to carry the coffin of a man who brought the war back to the heart of that very community.[85]

In the Republic, the bombing was widely condemned. Irish Taoiseach Albert Reynolds spoke of his 'abhorrence at the appalling death and injury inflicted on defenceless people on the Shankill Road last Saturday'.[86] Fine Gael leader John Bruton considered, 'Perhaps they are under such pressure from the security forces that they cannot adopt the targeted activities they adopted in the past and we are seeing an organisation under severe pressure because of increased intelligence being deployed against them.'[87] Predictably outspoken against the Provisional republicans, the Democratic Left, through Dun Laoghaire TD Eamon Gilmore, spoke of:

> The hypocritical statements of regret on the part of the IRA leadership and the phoney expressions of concern on the part of Gerry Adams . . . despite the attempts by themselves, and others, to impart an artificial aura of political respectability on their organisation, the IRA is just another sectarian murder gang.[88]

The goal of peace was certainly damaged by the attack. Worshippers were warned against lingering outside their chapel after Mass that night, such was the fear that the UFF might attack innocent Catholics by way of retaliation, reports later substantiated by Johnny Adair, the supposed target of the IRA bomb.[89] A series of retaliatory gun attacks by loyalists left four dead before the UFF attacked the Rising Sun bar in Greysteel, on the eastern edge of Londonderry, on Halloween. Gunmen burst into the bar and one called out 'trick or treat' before opening fire on the hundreds who had congregated to watch a band perform, killing eight. The sectarian death toll of the year ended with twenty-eight Catholics murdered by the UFF, eleven by the UVF and twenty-two Protestants killed by the IRA. Of the eighty-eight people killed that year, sixty-one were civilians.

The IRA made a commitment to peace on 6 April 1994, calling a three-day ceasefire which was followed up by a cessation of military activities on 31 August. Comparisons with the old IRA were invoked, one Sinn Féin member noting that 'twenty years ago . . . we used to look at the leadership of the republican movement and say "they haven't the bottle for the fight". Now I see young volunteers in their teens and early 20s and I wonder are they looking at us and saying the same thing.'[90] It was also pointed out that 'it is highly ironic that an organisation that owed its very foundation to a rejection of politics now appears almost certain to opt for the same route'.[91] The most significant difference this time around was that the Adams leadership had a far tighter grip on the movement than had the Goulding leadership in the 1960s. Although 'there was majority support in the IRA at the end of 1969, under the leadership of Cathal Goulding, for switching to political action',[92] this ignores the fact that many republicans had exiled themselves from the movement in protest at Goulding's politicisation programme. Adams was adamant that 'there will be no Republican split',[93] and there was good reason for this: his political programme had been secured from its very outset with the successes of the hunger strike elections. From this point on, no republican could reasonably argue that politics was not good for the republican movement. Adams had also been careful to 'reassure sceptics that they retain the capacity for "Armed Struggle" if the peace process does not yield republican advances . . . better for the IRA to continue in this way than to allow discontent to grow and encourage undisciplined splinter groups to develop'.[94]

The following year, the publication of the Framework Documents by the British and Irish governments in the midst of continuing peace discussions was an important constitutional step in the peace process. With US politicians sufficiently convinced that Adams was committed to peace, he was permitted entry to the United States to fundraise for Sinn Féin and attended a St Patrick's Day reception at the White House. The back and forth of the peace process well in swing, the publication of an IRA document which used the acronym TUAS raised concerns, with debate raging as to whether it stood for 'Totally UnArmed Strategy' or 'Tactical Use of Armed Struggle'.[95] Concerns were further raised by Adams' August comment that the IRA 'haven't gone away, you know'.[96] The need for transparency became ever greater and the issue of decommissioning of paramilitary weapons would remain a sensitive subject for much of the next fifteen years. Fears for peace proved well founded when a group using the cover name 'Direct Action Against Drugs' committed a series of murders over the winter of 1995. The following year, the IRA re-emerged.

The ceasefire was broken in spectacular fashion, with a half-ton bomb in London's Canary Wharf in February killing two and another bombing in Manchester in June also causing massive destruction. The scale of the London bomb and the fact that Manchester was playing host to a European Championship football match the following day provided the IRA with the international publicity it sought. Again, these attacks served to emphasise the IRA's capacity for destruction and the threat posed if Sinn Féin was not accepted as a credible political partner but with minimal loss of life. Perhaps more significantly, from an internal perspective:

> The Army Executive had to be re-elected at the Army Convention of 1996 and Adams needed to make sure that his supporters retained their majority on the Executive so they orchestrated Canary Wharf and Manchester to try and convince the Army that the ceasefire was just a tactic . . . In particular, they had to convince Brian Gillen to make sure that the IRA in Belfast was kept onside.[97]

The murder of Garda Jerry McCabe on 7 June 1996, killed during an attempted robbery in West Limerick, was particularly troubling. IRA General Order number eight forbade any military action against security forces in the Republic and the direct contravention of this order, in addition to the criminal aspect of the robbery, highlighted the growing disillusionment with the peace strategy in the republican movement. The PIRA killed its last British soldier on 12 February 1997, when Stephen Restorick was shot by a sniper in South Armagh.

The UK General Election of 1 May was hugely significant for Sinn Féin. Tony Blair's Labour government had several MPs with nationalist sympathies, notably Clare Short, whose uncle owned a bar in Crossmaglen.[98] Adams regained the West Belfast seat and Martin McGuinness was successful in Mid-Ulster; the party also managing to outpoll the DUP by nearly twenty thousand votes. The renewal of the ceasefire was now inevitable and on 20 July 1997 it was reinstated. The IRA claimed that:

> The potential of the peace process to deliver real and lasting peace lies in its ability to bring meaningful change, to remove the injustices which created the conflict and to end the conflict itself. If the political will exists, the peace process contains the potential to resolve the conflict and deliver a durable peace.[99]

The ambiguity of the term injustices is important; in reality, the injustices referred to had merely created the circumstances into which the conflict emerged, not the conflict itself. This had been created and perpetrated for entirely different reasons on the whole, although the Provisional IRA version did attract some adherents. Ideologically, the injustice of the British presence in Ireland continued and the lack of armed struggle to resolve this 'injustice' meant that, as predicted three years previously by Michael Flannery, the ceasefire precipitated further division in the movement.[100]

The Real IRA and the Return to Violence

The 32 County Sovereignty Movement was formed in late 1997 by Irish Republicans who were increasingly concerned with the ideological retreat within Republicanism preceding the signing of the Belfast Agreement in April 1998 . . . The 32 County Sovereignty Movement are the only effective organisation challenging British interference in Ireland today, and we call on all Republicans and anti-imperialists to support our efforts through the United Nations . . . The objectives of the 32 County Sovereignty Movement are – (a) The Defence of the Irish National Sovereignty. (b) To seek to achieve unity among the Irish people on the issue of restoring National Sovereignty and to promote the ideals of Revolutionary Republicanism and to this end involved itself in resisting all forms of colonialism and imperialism. (c) To seek the immediate and unconditional release of all Irish Republican Prisoners throughout the world.[101]

The emergence of the Continuity IRA during the 1990s was evidence that the Provisional IRA's transition away from violence would not be entirely smooth. Following the 1997 ceasefire, the IRA held an Army Convention in County Donegal in October. Leading opposition to the ceasefire was Quartermaster General Michael McKevitt and his wife, Bernadette Sands-McKevitt, the younger sister of Bobby Sands. When the convention declared its support for the ceasefire, the pair led a breakaway group that labelled itself Óglaigh na h Éireann. It became known as the Real IRA after a member described it as such during an illegal roadblock in South Armagh:[102] 'a few of the lads were making a propaganda video and having a bit of a laugh, telling people that they were the "real" IRA . . . it's just a sound bite . . . the group has always been Óglaigh na hÉireann'.[103]

That the IRA quartermaster should oppose the involvement of the peace process was both unsurprising and ominous. When the movement split in 1922 over the Anglo-Irish Treaty, the IRA's Director of Munitions' opposition was problematic to the movement. Jonathan Powell commented that 'McKevitt was the biggest challenge to Adams and McGuinness . . . he was a credible figure.'[104] No member of the movement possessed more information about the movement's weaponry, and ideological justification for Real IRA claims to Provisional IRA weaponry existed on the basis that the Provisional movement was no longer active in the armed struggle against Britain. Indeed, with much of this weaponry of Libyan origin,[105] imported to fortify the armed struggle, the ceasefire suggested a betrayal on the part of the leadership.[106]

The 32 County Sovereignty Movement, the political wing of the movement, had strong republican credentials: in addition to several long-serving PIRA volunteers, Sands-McKevitt brought real ideological power. The Provisional movement 'really fears her, because, while they can threaten other dissidents, they couldn't touch a hair on the head of the sister of a dead hunger-striker'.[107] She readily invoked the memory of her brother during peace discussions: 'Bobby did not die for cross-border bodies with executive powers. He did not die for nationalists to be equal British citizens within the Northern Ireland state.'[108] While such claims are inherently speculative, coming from Sands' sister, they did carry ideological weight. Eoin Ó Broin notes that:

> there's obviously an issue . . . for today, which is how the legacy of the hunger strikes is remembered and is mobilised in the present political context . . . I'm sure there are views . . . that Sinn Féin mobilises the memory and the politics of the hunger strike in the service of where Sinn Féin is at present and absolutely we do and we make no apologies for that because we see it as part of a continuity of political struggle.[109]

Further support came from Marian Price. Price, arguably the most prominent female IRA volunteer, had impeccable republican credentials; from a republican family, she took part in early PIRA bomb attacks on London, was imprisoned and force-fed while on hunger strike.[110]

The 32CSM sent a delegation to the United States in April 1998, taking the unique step of lodging and legitimising their quarrel with the British presence in Ireland by submitting a document with the United Nations.[111] The capital necessary for funding a guerrilla campaign was no longer available from the United States, which was now almost exclusively behind the political campaign led by President Clinton, and the Real IRA was forced to raise funds from alternative sources. Early involvement in criminality cost Ronan MacLochlainn his life on 1 May 1998 when he was shot by the Garda as he took part in an attempted robbery in County Wicklow.

The Real IRA's opposition to the ceasefire took the form of action. After a series of relatively small-scale bomb attacks had indicated that 'people were ready for action',[112] the group bombed the County Tyrone market town of Omagh in August 1998 with disastrous consequences. On the fifteenth of that month, a 500 lb bomb was planted in the centre of the town during a busy Saturday afternoon and two telephone warnings were placed, warning of a bomb outside the courthouse. Police cleared the crowds of shoppers down the hill a quarter of a mile away from the court-house. The warning was woefully inaccurate and instead of shepherding civilians away from the bomb, they were guided towards it. Twenty-nine died in the largest single loss of life to occur during the troubles. The Real IRA stated, 'It was a commercial target, part of an ongoing war against the Brits. We offer apologies to the civilians.'[113] Marian Price: 'I had spoken to people who were in the Real IRA at the time and I remember one of them saying to me, "Who the hell picked Omagh as a target? Sure, that's a nationalist town . . . ", and that was just from a strategic point of view.'[114]

The Omagh bomb proved to be a watershed moment in the Northern Irish troubles in a number of ways. Gerry Adams stated, 'I am totally horrified by this action. I condemn it without any equivocation whatsoever.'[115] The Provisional IRA declared that the Real IRA had no right to exist[116] and ordered them to disband within two weeks under the threat of violent action.[117] Sands-McKevitt spoke of 'the disgraceful use of a tragedy, such as Omagh, as a whipping stick to serve a particular political agenda . . . The 32 County Sovereignty Movement . . . believe it is only when the whole truth about the Omagh tragedy is uncovered that our position will be vindicated.'[118] So counterproductive was the attack that a view has developed that it was state-directed, with the intention of completely undermining republican violence. Price questions:

> Why when the bomb warning was given, why did the police allow busloads of school children into the centre of Omagh? Normal procedure would be to stop all traffic going into the centre of the town. From what I gather there was a fairly adequate warning given that basically was messed up and I think that it's very telling that of all the people killed in Omagh, there wasn't a policeman or soldier injured, not even by flying shrapnel . . . I think Omagh stinks to high heaven and I think that it's one of the reasons why there will never be an international enquiry, there are too many secrets there.[119]

What had become obvious to the Provisional republican movement was that the general public was tired of violence. Shifting its bombs from Northern Ireland to England had created additional exposure for their struggle but the tragedy at Warrington had emphasised the fact that little support could be garnered by explosions. In planting a bomb in a town that was almost two-thirds Catholic,[120] the Real IRA was seen to be attacking its own community, an act that could hardly be seen to be in the interests of Irish nationalism. Graffiti on the Springfield Road in West Belfast served as evidence of popular opinion on the movement: 'Bernadette! Bobbie's [sic] turning in his grave. RIP.'[121] Francie Mackey claimed that the attack meant that 'it took people longer to reach a point of understanding what our business was and what our argument was. It delayed that process. But it didn't come close to breaking up the structure of the committee.'[122] Although the structure of the committee may have remained intact, the support for the group plummeted,[123] money from the US 'before Omagh would have been negligible: after Omagh there would be nothing at all',[124] and the Real IRA, clearly dismayed by either their own inefficacy or the mass of criticism and condemnation, quickly suspended military operations and declared a ceasefire in September. A 32CSM member admits that it was 'a loose operation, criminally loose . . . but if I phone in a warning and you plant the bomb, how am I supposed to know you've put it where you were supposed to?'[125]

The Northern Ireland Affairs Committee published a report in March 2010 on the Omagh bomb, raising questions as to how preventable the bomb was. The government refused to share intelligence on the subject, claiming reasons of national security. The report suggested that the bomb could have been prevented by taking action against those guilty of bomb attacks earlier in 1998. Questions were also raised about why no convictions were pending over the attack, with answers as to whether those responsible were actually known to the security forces.[126]

With his condemnation of the attack, Gerry Adams' move away from violence was almost complete.[127] The group ended the decade on ceasefire. As Danny Morrison noted, 'the bulk of the Republican Movement did not join the Real IRA but stayed in the peace process'.[128] Without significant republican mandate to justify its campaign, the future appeared bleak for the 32CSM. The new century would see renewed efforts to re-establish the armed struggle as the development of the peace process facilitated disillusion across republicanism.

SPLITS IN LOYALISM: THE LVF

As the peace process developed, so did opposition to it. This opposition occurred on either side of the sectarian divide. Heavily dependent on republican paramilitarism to justify their own existence, the involvement of the Provisional republican movement in peace talks rather undermined the continued existence of loyalist paramilitary groups. It was therefore predictable that divisions should occur.

Loyalist dissent was led by Billy Wright. Wright had commanded the Mid-Ulster brigade of the UVF, joining the organisation in response to the IRA Kingsmills massacre of 1976, a fact that underscores the folly of sectarian attacks on the part of the IRA. In this role he directed many sectarian killings, although one notable success against the IRA was the UVF attack of 3 March 1991 which killed three IRA volunteers along with one Catholic civilian in a bar in Cappagh, County Tyrone.[129]

Around this time, the Combined Loyalist Military Command was established to co-ordinate loyalist activities. Under the auspices of this umbrella group, a loyalist ceasefire was called on 13 October 1994 in response to the Provisional IRA ceasefire that had been called two weeks previously. Although ostensibly a unified loyalist front, Ian Wood has shown how each organisation was keen to assert its dominance on the CLMC.[130] Such personality clashes have shaped the history of loyalism. The co-operation between the two organisations quickly unravelled as mistrust grew over the high profile of the UVF-aligned Progressive Unionist Party.

From his home base of Lurgan, County Armagh, *Sunday World* journalist and former Workers' Party member[131] Martin O'Hagan had begun writing about Wright and his UVF gang, which labelled itself the 'brat pack'. O'Hagan satirically renamed them the 'rat pack', with Wright christened 'King Rat', a nickname he despised. Reports linked the UVF bombing of the *Sunday World* offices in Belfast with the growing tensions between Wright and O'Hagan.[132] O'Hagan was exiled to the Republic for his own safety and Wright's unit took keen interest in the developing stand-off at Drumcree over the annual Portadown Orange Order march. Following objections to the march on the part of the nationalist community of the Garvaghy Road, the 1995 parade eventually passed but tension resurfaced the following year. The 1996 parade was banned and the UVF ordered Wright not to intervene; he, in turn, criticised the UVF leadership for not supporting the Orangemen, a folly Wright's unit saw fit to rectify with the killings of Michael McGoldrick on 8 July 1996 and James Morgan on 24 July 1997. These unauthorised attacks led to Wright's dismissal from the UVF. Although discipline has never been a hallmark of loyalist paramilitaries, the military structures inherent in the UVF have often manifested themselves in the form of strict procedure. His response was to found the Loyalist Volunteer Force and the group quickly developed a formidable reputation for violence, even though his tenure at the helm of the group was to be brief.

Wright was resident in the Corcrain estate, located a short walk from Obins Street, the original route for the Portadown Orangemen before their diversion to the nearby Garvaghy Road. His interest in the Portadown march was therefore long-standing and his identification with the Orange Order manifested itself in his rhetoric in the aftermath of the foundation of the LVF, what Susan McKay has labelled 'old-style Protestant fundamentalism'.[133] Although Wright was critical of UVF leaders for their socialist rhetoric, the location-specific nature of the vast majority of LVF operations – one-third of their killings were in County Armagh – suggests an element of local consciousness on the part of Wright and his comrades.

Wright's murder in the Maze prison in late 1997 robbed the movement of its enigmatic leader. They killed nine people over the course of 1998 before calling a ceasefire, although the reality of this ceasefire was merely a scaling back of their military campaign. They threw their support behind the anti-Agreement stance of the Democratic Unionist Party during negotiations towards the Good Friday Agreement.[134] To legitimise their stance, a ceasefire was called on 15 May, one week before the referendum. The group's ceasefire statement finished with a tribute to Wright, 'murdered by republican scum'.[135] The group's ceasefire made LVF prisoners eligible for parole under the prisoner release programme of the Good Friday Agreement, meaning that Wright could have been eligible for release less than a year after he was killed. The LVF responded to the release of its prisoners by offering arms to the Independent International Commission on Decommissioning.[136] The LVF were arguably the most enigmatic loyalist paramilitary group; in their short existence, they had committed acts of reckless sectarian violence, abruptly ended their campaign and quickly decommissioned weaponry. Then, as quickly as they had disarmed, they resumed hostilities with their former comrades in the UVF early in the twenty-first century and the Secretary of State declared their ceasefire over in 2001.

Two other notable loyalist factions emerged in the latter years of the decade. The Red Hand Defenders became active in 1998, opposed to the Good Friday Agreement. The last two deaths of 1998 were both attributed to the organisation, with Catholic RUC Constable Frank O'Reilly and Catholic civilian Brian Service killed by the group. The following year, the organisation was responsible for a series of pipe-bomb attacks which targeted Catholic families across Northern Ireland. In March, they claimed their most prominent victim, Catholic lawyer Rosemary Nelson, killed by a bomb under her car. Two days later, RHD member Frankie Curry was killed by rival loyalists. They remained active for the rest of 1999 before a hiatus that lasted until early 2001.

The Orange Volunteers appeared around the same time and carried out a series of attacks on Catholic property. It was suggested that the OV and the RHD shared the same membership pool. Ian Wood noted that the RHD 'began to act as a magnet for young disaffected and ruthless members of both the UDA and UVF'.[137] That disaffected and ruthless UVF members also found solace in the LVF is significant and would prove especially so in the early years of the following decade.

The peace process also brought political division to loyalism, as the United Kingdom Unionist Party split in 1998 over claims that leader Robert McCartney was to take the party out of the Assembly if Sinn Féin was allowed to join the Executive. These dissidents formed the Northern Ireland Unionist Party, taking four of UKUP's Assembly members and leaving McCartney isolated.[138]

American Involvement in the Northern Ireland Peace Process

The tale of Irish-American involvement in the Northern Irish troubles is neatly bookended by the prominent role that American figures played in securing peace for the troubled province during the 1990s. John Hume had played an integral role in bringing major political actors in the United States towards a position of support for peace, and the accession of Bill Clinton to the White House in 1992 was also crucial. While the Irish issue had become important for all presidents after Jimmy Carter, Clinton announced that 'the United States stands ready to do whatever we can to help in bringing peace to Northern Ireland . . . I want to underscore my strong support for that important goal.'[139]

Although he highlighted that 'the people that have to resolve this are the Irish and the British',[140] Clinton took an active role in promoting peace. One of his first acts was to grant a visitor visa to Gerry Adams. Prime Minister John Major was reportedly furious at Clinton's decision to grant the visa, as he struggled with perceived concessions to republicans by the governments of both the United States and the Irish Republic.[141] For Clinton, provided there were 'no overwhelming evidence that he was connected to terrorists, if he was a duly elected Member of Parliament in a democratic country, we should have real cause before denying him a visa'.[142]

While Adams was no longer an MP and his prominent role at the

Begley funeral provided compelling evidence that he was indeed connected to IRA violence, he still achieved over sixteen thousands votes in the 1992 election, losing to Dr Joe Hendron by fewer than a thousand. This still suggested a considerable political mandate for Adams and Sinn Féin in general, who achieved 78,291 votes across the province, 10 per cent of the vote. With the British prime minister remarking, 'If the implication . . . is that we should sit down and talk with Mr Adams and the Provisional IRA, I can say only that that would turn my stomach',[143] it was obvious that the Clinton administration granting Adams a visa would rankle with the British government. Even with secret discussions ongoing with the IRA leadership, dependence on Ulster unionist support meant that Major had to maintain an aggressive policy with regard to Irish republicans, particularly after the high-profile IRA attacks on the British mainland of the early 1990s. Clinton was careful to highlight his 'good relationship . . . with Prime Minster Major' and that 'this whole business about weapons decommissioning is, obviously, critical to the completion of the process'.[144]

Clinton justified allowing Adams into the country, arguing, 'I think when he came here, he saw that the Irish in America want peace. They want him to be a part of the peace process.'[145] Clinton's diplomatic skills would be thoroughly tested during this period. Also integral to the Adams visa campaign was Senator Ted Kennedy. Kennedy had been convinced of the merits of providing Adams with a visa during a visit to Ireland over the winter of 1993 when he met with his sister Jean Kennedy Smith, the American ambassador in Dublin, and Taoiseach Albert Reynolds, who also declared his support. Kennedy recalled, 'Jean was convinced that Adams no longer believed that continuing the armed struggle was the way to achieve the IRA's objective of a united Ireland. He was in fact working to convince the IRA's more aggressive members to end the violence and pursue the political path', also citing the influence of John Hume.[146]

Hume had also spoken with Kennedy at the funeral of mutual friend Tip O'Neill in January 1994 and convinced him to support Adams' application for a visa.[147] Kennedy gathered the support of a further fifty members of Congress. Perhaps over-egging the issue, Kennedy's website makes much of the granting of the Adams visa: 'President Clinton granted Mr Adams the visa and, in August 1994, the IRA called an historic cease-fire, an event that Mr Adams has said would not have transpired had he not been granted the visa. Six weeks later, Protestant paramilitaries announced their own cease-fire';[148] Adams' skills as a statesman were clearly to the fore.

In 2009, Senator Edward Kennedy was awarded an honorary knight-hood by Queen Elizabeth II.[149] This announcement prompted consid-erable criticism across the United Kingdom. Lord Tebbit stated, 'This honour is wholly inappropriate . . . It cheapens the whole honours system',[150] and Andrew Roberts of the *Daily Mail* described the honour as 'Britain at its most masochistic, New Labour at its most cynical and Kennedy at his most hypocritical'.[151] His controversial position in the 1970s, reinforced by his support for the Adams visa, was well remembered by his opponents.

Adams visited the United States in early 1994 in a huge publicity coup for Sinn Féin. In March, the IRA was involved in a series of mortar attacks on Heathrow airport, acts that would undoubtedly have gar-nered significant concern within the United States with roughly fifteen million passengers travelling to and from the US in 1994 and the major-ity using Heathrow airport.[152] Clinton met with Taoiseach Reynolds on St Patrick's Day and later declared, 'I think that Sinn Féin ought to renounce violence and ought to join the peace process',[153] also highlight-ing the importance of domestic agreements, such as the framework docu-ments, which he believed laid 'the foundation for all-party talks among the British and Irish governments and the political parties in Northern Ireland . . . The benefits of peace are obvious to all, and I urge the parties to seize this opportunity.'[154]

While the United States had largely been an opponent of IRA violence for a number of years, the Oklahoma City bomb of April 1995 offered a new context in which Americans could understand the IRA armed struggle. The 168 dead in a single attack was higher than the death toll for most years in Northern Ireland, but the experience of domestic terror underlined the importance of the peace strategy. On Adams, Clinton remarked that 'as long as he continues to renounce terrorism and as long as they continue on the progress that they – the path that they have set, including the willingness to talk about weapons decommission-ing, then I think we re doing the right thing'.[155] The publication of the 'TUAS' document four days later left the IRA's stance on peace rather ambivalent, the continuation of violence, through Direct Action Against Drugs, along with Adams' continuing dialogue with a variety of political figures, emphasising this. The decision to end the IRA ceasefire with a series of spectacular attacks on commercial targets in England may have been a prudent decision from an Irish republican perspective, but in the United States, the Docklands bomb only served to remind Americans of Oklahoma. Clinton was quick to state that 'all Americans join Hillary and I in our outrage at the bomb explosion today in London. I condemn in the strongest possible terms this cowardly action . . . I am deeply concerned by reports that the Irish Republican Army has announced an end to the cease-fire.'[156] Clinton was concerned that the bomb could 'plunge Northern Ireland into a senseless spiral of violence',[157] evidence of the tension of the time, with all governments wary of the upcoming Drumcree Orange march. Clinton's rhetoric of the time was careful, noting after the death of Stephen Restorick in early 1997 that 'the loyalists and their leaders have shown great courage and restraint in not allowing themselves to be drawn into an escalating spiral of violence. I urge them to remain steadfast'.[158] He did, however, note that the 'decision to suspend Sinn Féin from the Northern Ireland peace talks shows that the UK and Irish governments are committed to an inclusive process but one that reaffirms that it is unacceptable to mix politics and violence'.[159] Clinton's ability to maintain a conciliatory stance was integral to the success of the peace process. At the 1998 Sinn Féin Ard Fheis, Adams noted the influence of Irish-America in general and Clinton in particular,[160] an indication of the significant political journey Sinn Féin had been on.

Significant funds were still being raised – Doirse Dochais raising over $100,000 the previous year[161] – but Noraid was now considerably less vocal on the Irish question. The Irish American Unity Conference attempted to fill this void, their newsletter reporting a landmine attack in which four UDR soldiers were killed: 'Hundreds of pounds of explosives, skilfully packed in the culvert for maximum upward effect, were detonated under the car . . . four lives that might have been lived for an Ireland with justice and peace for all its people. Instead, they chose the course of oppression.'[162] However, the audience for such material was considerably reduced and even though the IAUC claimed that it 'played an important part in working with politicians on all sides to bring the "Good Friday Peace Agreement" to where it stands today',[163] the reality of the situation was that pro-republican Irish-American organisations had begun their journey into obsolescence.

As the IRA campaign wound down in Ireland, the legalities of American involvement centred on the case of Joe Doherty. Doherty was ultimately deported on 19 February 1992, but a strong campaign against his extradition was ongoing throughout the decade, even carried in *People* magazine.[164] Doherty supporters wrote to George Bush, protesting the decision,[165] one claiming that 'there is absolutely no difference in the way Mr Mandela fought apartheid in South Africa than Joe Doherty fights British injustice in North Eastern Ireland'.[166] The campaign to free Doherty had gathered some prominent supporters, notably New York City Mayor David Dinkins. Dinkins, the first African-American mayor of New York, wrote to Doherty in jail in early 1993, later verbalising his support during a visit to Ireland. This latter statement prompted comment from British Consul-General Alistair Hunter:

> I was surprised and disappointed to hear you say that the next time you visited Ireland you would like to visit Joe Doherty in prison. I find it surprising, particularly in the light of this city's current preoccupation with terrorist incidents, that you should wish to call on a known terrorist. Mr Doherty is a convicted murderer; he has been found guilty of carrying explosives in a hi-jacked car; and he has admitted taking hostages. It seems to me that, by offering support to Mr Doherty in this way, and by making public your wish to see him, you are undermining our joint efforts to combat the terrorist threat.[167]

For Dinkins, however, 'I believe that Mr Doherty suffered a terrible injustice in this country . . . It is unfortunate that, often, when Americans speak out about the situation in Northern Ireland they are accused of supporting violence',[168] although it seemed as though the accusation was more that Dinkins was condoning, rather than supporting, violence. Important to recall was the fact that Doherty was, by this stage, a prisoner at the Maze, where he remained until his release under the Good Friday Agreement in 1998. Dinkins involvement in the issue, although unpleasant for the United Kingdom, ultimately served little purpose other than to reach out to the Irish community in New York during his unsuccessful campaign for re-election in 1994.

CONCLUSIONS

The 1990s were dominated by the peace process, a process which was carefully manipulated by the Provisional IRA; planting bombs when it was felt prudent to remind the world of their power and reining in renegade republicans when internecine violence became a problem. Their partners in Irish-America were almost unanimous in their support for peace, particularly in the light of acts of domestic terrorism and the prominent role President Clinton assumed in peace discussions. The careful choreography of Provisional republicanism managed to keep potential dissidents onside for sufficiently long to ensure that there would be no major split in the movement. This was crucial to prospects for peace, as dissidents not only had access to considerable weaponry but still believed in the merits of armed struggle. Where the Continuity and Real IRA were ideologically motivated, splits in loyalism had a sinister criminal undertone, albeit with some ideological purpose. The breakaway factions would prove problematic for the security forces in Northern Ireland the following decade.

NOTES

1. Feeney, *Sinn Féin*; Maillot, *New Sinn Féin*; Rafter, K., *Sinn Féin: In the Shadow of Gunmen* (Dublin: Gill and Macmillan, 2005); Bean, K., *The New Politics of Sinn Féin* (Liverpool: Liverpool University Press, 2008).
2. Hanley and Millar, *Lost Revolution*, p. 547.
3. Johnston, *Century of Endeavour*, p. 310.
4. *IN* 29/2/1992.
5. *Sunday Press* 16/2/1992.
6. *IN* 29/2/1992.
7. Hanley and Millar, *Lost Revolution*, p. 262.
8. Kelleher, *Irish Republicanism*, p. 316.
9. Johnston, *Century of Endeavour*, p. 310.
10. Dessie O'Hagan and John Lowry, interview with author, Belfast, 9/8/2007.
11. Hanley and Millar, *Lost Revolution*, p. 406.
12. Confidential Republican Source. Official IRA Box, LHLPC.
13. Hanley and Millar, *Lost Revolution*, pp. 530–1, 570.
14. John Lowry, interview with author, Belfast, 9/8/2007.
15. Hanley and Millar, *Lost Revolution*, pp. 574–5.
16. Ibid., p. 583.
17. *IN* 7/2/1992; *IT* 17/2/1992.
18. Hanley and Millar, *Lost Revolution*, p. 587.
19. Foster, R. F., *Luck and the Irish*, p. 96.
20. Hanley and Millar, *Lost Revolution*, pp. 592–3.
21. *An Phoblacht/Republican News* 16/1/1997; Hanley and Miller, *Lost Revolution*, p. 12.
22. Anthony McIntyre, interview with author, Belfast, 7/9/2005.
23. Northern Ireland Elections, 'Dungannon Borough Council, 1993 and 1997' http://www.ark.ac.uk/elections/lgdungannon.htm
24. King, S., 'Steven King on Thursday', *BT* 17/12/1998.
25. McKittrick et al., *Lost Lives*, pp. 1196–7, 1202–3, 1241, 1246.
26. Ibid., p. 1262.
27. *Irish Examiner* 22/10/1998.
28. McKittrick et al., *Lost Lives*, p. 1262.
29. Ibid., p. 1263.
30. Ibid., pp. 1280–1.

31. *Independent* 22/8/1992.
32. *Argus* 1/2/2007.
33. *Guardian* 14/2/1994.
34. McKittrick et al., *Lost Lives*, pp. 1346–9.
35. Quoted in Lister, D. and Jordan, H., *Mad Dog: The Rise and Fall of Johnny Adair and C Company* (Edinburgh: Mainstream, 2003), p. 148.
36. *IRSP Greeting to IRSC*, 23/3/1984 http://www.irsm.org/statements/irsp/archive/840323.html 22/6/2004
37. Holland and McDonald, *INLA*, p. 230.
38. *Scotsman* 14/2/1994.
39. McKittrick et al., *Lost Lives*, pp. 1350, 1355–6, 1358.
40. Fra Halligan, interview with author, Belfast, 25/2/2010.
41. *Independent* 17/3/1996; *An Phoblacht* 10/6/2004.
42. Fallen Comrades of the IRSM – John Morris killed in action on 5 June 1997 http://irsm.org/fallen/morris/
43. Anderson, C., *The Billy Boy: The Life and Death of LVF Leader Billy Wright* (Edinburgh: Mainstream, 2002).
44. 'Inquiry hears plan to kill Wright', BBC Online 24/3/2009 http://news.bbc.co.uk/1/hi/northern_ireland/7961612.stm 24/3/2009.
45. Fra Halligan, interview with author, Belfast, 25/2/2010.
46. *The Plough*, No. 33 2/4/2004.
47. McKittrick et al., *Lost Lives*, pp. 1420–33.
48. *IT* 5/5/1998.
49. *Independent* 22/8/1998.
50. INLA Statement on 5th Anniversary of INLA Ceasefire 22 August 1999 http://www.irsm.org/statements/inla/030822.html
51. *Saoirse*, No. 45, Jan 1991.
52. Geraldine Taylor, interview with author, Belfast, 17/2/2010.
53. Republican Sinn Féin speeches, Pat Ward at Bodenstown, 1987 http://www.rsf.ie/boden87.htm
54. O'Malley, P., *Uncivil Wars* (Belfast: The Blackstaff Press, 1983), pp. 274–5.
55. IRA Ceasefire Statement, 31/8/1994 http://www.cain.ulst.ac.uk/events/peace/docs/ira31894.htm
56. *Saoirse*, No. 133, May 1998.
57. *Saoirse*, No. 106, February 1996.
58. Former Continuity IRA volunteer, interview with author, Belfast, 2/7/2010.
59. *Saoirse*, No. 106, February 1996.
60. White, *Ruairí Ó Brádaigh*, p. 310.
61. Quoted in Ó Brádaigh, *Dilseacht*, p. 52.
62. *IN* 23/5/1998.
63. *IN* 11/11/2000.
64. Boyne, S., 'The Real IRA: After Omagh, What Now?' http://www.janes.com/regional_news/europe/news/jir/jir980824_1_n.shtml 11/6/2002, dated 24/8/1998.
65. *Guardian* 24/8/1998.
66. *BT* 11/8/1998.
67. *IN* 9/12/1998.
68. *Saoirse*, No. 126, October 1997.

69. *IN* 9/11/1998.
70. Eoin Ó Broin, interview with author, Belfast, 20/5/2005.
71. White, *Ruairí Ó Brádaigh*, p. 199. White also notes that in 1985, wary of being undermined by Sinn Féin, the IRA attempted to oust Adams, p. 296.
72. 'Westminster election 1992', Northern Ireland Elections http://www.ark.ac.uk/elections/fw92.htm.
73. 'Loyalist terrorists in bomb attacks on SDLP politicians', *Independent* 21/7/1993.
74. *Independent* 25/10/1990; McKittrick et al., *Lost Lives*, pp. 1214–15.
75. *Independent* 25/10/1990; *IT* 14/4/1991.
76. Marian Price, interview with author, Belfast, 1/7/2010.
77. McKittrick et al., *Lost Lives*, pp. 1314–15, 1317.
78. *Independent* 23/3/1993.
79. 'Warrington bomb victims centre opens', BBC News, 20/3/2000 http://news.bbc.co.uk/1/hi/uk/683087.stm
80. *Liverpool Echo* 12/12/2009.
81. McGladdery, G., *The Provisional IRA in England*, p. 168.
82. BBC, 'IRA bomb devastates City of London' http://news.bbc.co.uk/onthisday/hi/dates/stories/april/24/newsid_2523000/2523345.stm; also 'The Bishopsgate Bomb: Toll of injured rises to 51', *Independent* 26/4/1993.
83. *Guardian* 5/8/2000.
84. *Guardian* 5/8/2000.
85. *AP/RN* 24/4/1997.
86. Dáil Éireann, Vol. 435, 27 October 1993, Parliamentary Debates, 'Northern Ireland: Statements' http://historical-debates.oireachtas.ie/D/0435/D.0435.199310270136.html
87. Ibid.
88. Ibid.
89. *IN* 21/10/2003; Adair, J., *Mad Dog* (London: John Blake, 2007), pp. 80–156.
90. *IT* 1/9/1994.
91. *BT* 31/8/1994.
92. Ibid.
93. *Time* 1/8/1994.
94. *Observer* 30/10/1994.
95. *Sunday Tribune* 23/4/1995.
96. *Guardian* 22/11/2007.
97. 32CSM member, interview with author, Dublin, 26/3/2010.
98. Harnden, *Bandit Country*, p. 56.
99. Easter Statement by the Irish Republican Army, 31 March 1999 http://www.cain.ulst.ac.uk/events/peace/docs/ira31399.htm
100. *Independent* 2/9/1994.
101. *TSN* October–November 2006.
102. Harnden, T., *Bandit Country*, pp. 429–31.
103. 32CSM member, interview with author, Dublin, 26/3/2010.
104. Powell, *Great Hatred*, p. 113.
105. *IT* 27/6/2000.
106. 32CSM member, interview with author, Dublin, 26/3/2010.
107. Breen, S., article in *Magill*, undated.

108. Quoted in Hennessey, T., *The Northern Ireland Peace Process: Ending the Troubles* (Dublin: Gill and Macmillan, 2000), p. 112.
109. Eoin Ó Broin, interview with author, Belfast, 20/5/2005.
110. Marian Price, interview with author, Belfast, 1/7/2010.
111. 32CSM 'United Nations Submission' http://www.32csm.info/UNsubmission.html
112. 32CSM member, interview with author, Dublin, 26/3/2010.
113. *Independent* 19/8/1998.
114. Marian Price, interview with author, Belfast, 1/7/2010.
115. McKittrick et al., *Lost Lives*, p. 1442.
116. *BT* 8/9/1998.
117. *IT* 3/9/1998.
118. *IN* 6/9/2000.
119. Marian Price, interview with author, Belfast, 1/7/2010.
120. Northern Ireland Census 2001, Key Statistics http://www.nisranew.nisra.gov.uk/Census/pdf/Key%20Statistics%20ReportTables.pdf
121. Photograph in *Ireland on Sunday* 23/8/1998.
122. *BT* 28/2/2000.
123. *Sunday Tribune* 13/9/1998; Tonge, J., '"They Haven't Gone Away, You Know". Irish Republican "Dissidents" and "Armed Struggle"', pp. 671–93, in *Terrorism and Political Violence*, Vol. 16 No. 3 Autumn 2004, p. 688.
124. *Magill*, September 1998.
125. 32CSM member, interview with author, Dublin, 26/3/2010.
126. 'Downing Street defends Omagh bomb intelligence move', BBC News, 16/3/2010 http://news.bbc.co.uk/1/hi/northern_ireland/8569651.stm
127. *Scotland on Sunday* 10/5/1998.
128. http://dannymorrison.ie/articles/what-really-happened.php 18/05/2006.
129. Harnden, *Bandit Country*, p. 140.
130. Wood, *Crimes of Loyalty*, pp. 148–9, 237.
131. Hanley and Millar, *Lost Revolution*, pp. 172, 191, 513.
132. McKay, S., 'Faith, hate and murder', *Guardian* 17/11/2001.
133. Ibid.
134. *Irish Examiner* 9/3/1998.
135. Loyalist Volunteer Force ceasefire statement, 15/5/1998 http://cain.ulst.ac.uk/events/peace/docs/lvf15598.htm
136. RTE News, 'LVF begins decommissioning', 18/12/1998 http://www.rte.ie/news/1998/1218/lvf.html
137. Wood, *Crimes of Loyalty*, pp. 232–3.
138. BBC News, 'NI Unionists and UK Unionist parties' http://news.bbc.co.uk/news/vote2001/hi/english/parties/newsid_1179000/1179165.stm 6/7/2010.
139. Remarks at a St Patrick's Day Ceremony with Prime Minister Albert Reynolds of Ireland and an Exchange with Reporters, 17/3/1993. Public Papers of the Presidents of the United States – William J. Clinton 1993 (Washington, DC: United States Government Printing Office, 1994), pp. 314–17.
140. Remarks Announcing the Nomination of Deval L. Patrick to be Assistant Attorney General for Civil Rights and an Exchange with Reporters, 1/2/1994. Public Papers of the Presidents of the United States – William J. Clinton 1994 (Washington, DC: United States Government Printing Office, 1995), p. 161.

141. Powell, *Great Hatred*, pp. 78, 84–5.
142. The President's News Conference Public Papers of the Presidents of the United States – William J. Clinton 1993 (Washington, DC: United States Government Printing Office, 1994), p. 663.
143. 'House of Commons Hansard Debates for 1 Nov 1993' http://www.publications. parliament.uk/pa/cm199293/cmhansrd/1993-11-01/Debate-2.html
144. Remarks at a Saint Patrick's Day Ceremony with Prime Minister John Bruton of Ireland and an Exchange with Reporters, 17/3/1995. Public Papers of the Presidents of the United States – William J. Clinton 1995 (Washington, DC: United States Government Printing Office, 1996), pp. 368–9.
145. Remarks at a Saint Patrick's Day Ceremony with Prime Minister Albert Reynolds of Ireland and an Exchange with Reporters, 17/3/1994. Public Papers of the Presidents of the United States – William J. Clinton 1994 (Washington, DC: United States Government Printing Office, 1995), p. 480.
146. Kennedy, *True Compass*, pp. 460–1, 463.
147. *Time*, 'Northern Ireland Remembers Ted Kennedy, the Peacemaker', 28/8/2009; also 'Providing a leading voice for human rights and democracy around the globe' http:// tedkennedy.org/service/item/foreign_policy 5/12/2009.
148. Senator Edward Kennedy, 'Providing a leading voice for human rights and democracy around the globe' http://tedkennedy.org/service/item/foreign_policy
149. BBC News, 'In Full: Brown's Speech to Congress' http://news.bbc.co.uk/1/hi/ uk_politics/7924332.stm
150. *Daily Mail* 4/3/2009.
151. *Daily Mail*, 5/3/2009.
152. Parliamentary Office of Science and Technology, 'Statistical information on air passenger numbers and characteristics' http://www.parliament.uk/documents/post/ e3.pdf
153. Interview with Gavin Esler of the British Broadcasting Corporation, 27/5/1994. Public Papers of the Presidents of the United States – William J. Clinton 1994 (Washington, DC: United States Government Printing Office, 1995), p. 997.
154. Statement on the Peace Process in Northern Ireland, 22/2/1995. Public Papers of the Presidents of the United States – William J. Clinton 1995 (Washington, DC: United States Government Printing Office, 1996), p. 242.
155. The President's News Conference, 23/5/1995. Public Papers of the Presidents of the United States – William J. Clinton 1995, p. 738.
156. Statement on the Terrorist Attack in London, United Kingdom, 9/2/1996. Public Papers of the Presidents of the United States – William J. Clinton 1996 (Washington, DC: United States Government Printing Office, 1997), p. 199.
157. Statement on Multiparty Talks on the Future of Northern Ireland, 13/1/1997. Public Papers of the Presidents of the United States – William J. Clinton 1997 (Washington, DC: United States Government Printing Office, 1998), p. 33.
158. Statement on the killing of a British Soldier in Northern Ireland, 13/2/1997. Public Papers of the Presidents of the United States – William J. Clinton 1997, p. 157.
159. Statement on the Northern Ireland Peace Process, 20/2/1998. Public Papers of the Presidents of the United States – William J. Clinton 1998 (Washington, DC: United States Government Printing Office, 1999), p. 262.

160. Presidential Address by Gerry Adams to Sinn Féin Ard Fheis, 18 April 1998 http://www.cain.ulst.ac.uk/events/peace/docs/ga18498.htm
161. Doirse Dochais Cash Flow statement, 31/3/1991, NYUL, AIA 9, Box 5, Series B, Prisoners.
162. Irish American Unity Conference New Jersey Region Newsletter, May 1990.
163. IAUC National Newsletter, July/August 1998, NYUL, AIA 9, Box 1, Series A, Organizations.
164. *People* 6/1/1991.
165. Letter from Anthony Philbin to President Bush, 16/10/1992, NYUL, AIA 9, Box 5, Series B, Prisoners.
166. Letter from Thomas Enright to President Bush, 6/10/1992, NYUL, AIA 9, Box 5, Series B, Prisoners.
167. Letter from HM Consul-General Alistair Hunter to Mayor Dinkins c. May 1993 Re: Dinkins' comments at Shannon Airport, NYUL, AIA 9, Box 5, Series B, Prisoners.
168. Letter from Mayor David Dinkins to the Honourable Alistair Hunter, HM Consul-General, 10/8/1993, NYUL, AIA 9, Box 5, Series B, Prisoners.

CHAPTER 8

The Twenty-first Century

The peace that existed at the dawn of the twenty-first century was uneasy. Although the final year of the previous century had only seen eight deaths, three of these in particular appeared to challenge the conventional wisdom that the peace process was fostering reconciliation between the two communities: former IRA man Eamon Collins beaten to death near his home in Newry, seemingly by former comrades; and two murders attributed to the Red Hand Defenders which pointed towards loyalist opposition to the peace process. Collins had been an outspoken critic of the republican movement since his departure and had provided evidence against Thomas 'Slab' Murphy in a civil trial after *The Sunday Times* had named Murphy as the IRA's Northern Commander.[1]

The close association between violence and politics was especially apparent during the early part of the new century as implementation of key criteria of the Good Friday Agreement caused unrest. This centred on decommissioning. While largely a symbolic act, with each organisation capable of re-equipping relatively quickly, it remained important. As the LVF began decommissioning in 1998, hopes for total paramilitary involvement in the process were high; in return, the LVF became eligible for the prisoner release programme that was implemented under the Agreement. Particularly divisive during these years was the Portadown Orange march, the loyalist perception that concessions to republicans were beginning to impinge on their culture fuelling violence province-wide.

REPUBLICANISM IN THE NEW CENTURY

The early years of the decade saw much progress associated with the Good Friday Agreement. By the middle of 2000, the last paramilitary prisoners were released and moves towards reconciliation were underway with the establishment of the Saville Inquiry into the events of Bloody Sunday in 1972. State commitment to the Good Friday Agreement was indicated by announcements that security bases were to close, but such moves only served to highlight the fact that the most important paramilitary group, the Provisional IRA, had yet to make a definitive commitment to decommissioning. Newspaper reports highlighted the low-level activity that continued to be attributed to the group,[2] but events taking place over the winter of 2004 really raised concerns that the Provisional IRA was not only decommitting from the peace process, but readying itself for a return to military action.

Meanwhile, the Official republican movement also achieved a level of exposure. Sean Garland, who had been behind Cathal Goulding's controversial proposal that outlined the ending of abstention prior to the 1969–70 split in the movement, was involved in the production of counterfeit United States dollars, something US officials alleged was to the benefit of North Korea. The USA applied to the United Kingdom to have him extradited and he was arrested in Belfast in October 2005. Eoghan Harris noted the contradiction in American politicians who welcomed Provisional IRA leaders but who 'would pursue a sick old man who led the Official IRA to a ceasefire in 1972 for the bloodless crime of forgery'.[3] The Sean Garland campaign is being fought with vigour from all sides: a pressure group was formed and gathered signatures protesting his extradition.[4] Garland, recently replaced as Workers' Party president by Mick Finnegan, an active trade unionist from West Dublin,[5] had been suffering from cancer and diabetes and was supported by figures in the Irish Senate.[6] The campaign is, at the time of writing, ongoing.

THE NORTHERN BANK ROBBERY

On 20 December 2004, an estimated £25 million was stolen from the Northern Bank in central Belfast. The previous night, a group of armed, masked men captured the families of two Northern Bank officials, ordering the two officials to carry out their day's work as normal before admitting the kidnappers into the bank at the close of business. With Northern

Bank notes constituting half of the haul, the bank recalled £300 million of its currency from the market and reissued redesigned currency in an attempt to minimise potential money laundering. The thieves were hindered by the fact that £10 million of the stolen Northern Bank notes were unused and therefore eminently more traceable, not to mention the problems inherent in attempting to launder Northern Irish banknotes outside of Northern Ireland.

Media reports were quick to blame the Provisional IRA, claiming that few other organisations would have had the wherewithal to actually conduct such an operation.[7] A former NIO minister noted that 'robberies like . . . the Northern Bank must have been sanctioned at Provisional Army Council level . . . so Adams and McGuinness must have known about that'.[8] Explanation for the robbery was less clear, with even Danny Morrison, while no longer a member of the republican movement, surely still in the intelligence loop, struggling. Certainly Morrison's initial feeling, that the robbery was to send a message to the British government,[9] is persuasive, but others have argued that Tony Blair, along with his chief negotiator Jonathan Powell, should shoulder some of the blame for turning a blind eye to previous IRA crimes.[10] For his part, Powell recalled, 'I felt like a complete idiot coming over for talks with Adams and McGuinness when the IRA had been planning a major crime like this.'[11] The apparent consensus that the Sinn Féin leadership knew of the robbery in advance rather suggests that they either were prepared to allow it to take place, or that they were powerless to stop it.

Although a portion of the money was recovered in 2004, before a Cork financier was found guilty of laundering £3 million,[12] the fact that the majority of the haul has, at the time of writing, yet to be accounted for, highlights the criminal capabilities of the IRA. While the Northern Bank robbery represented all that was sophisticated and disciplined about the IRA, that the organisation had been unable to rid itself of its lesser elements was in evidence mere weeks after its most famous heist.

THE ROBERT MCCARTNEY MURDER

On 30 January 2005, Short Strand resident Robert McCartney was drinking in Magennis's bar on May Street in central Belfast with his friend Brendan Devine. A group of IRA men had returned from a Bloody Sunday rally in Derry and were also drinking in the bar. Devine was accused of insulting a female and his refusal to accept this or apologise led to a fight breaking out. McCartney, attempting to defend Devine, was attacked with a broken bottle before being dragged into the street and stabbed repeatedly.[13]

Although shocking in its own right, the murder drew increased controversy with allegations of a Sinn Féin cover up. The police were unable to investigate the crime scene because of a riot that broke out in the area. Sinn Féin's Alex Maskey claimed, 'It appears the PSNI is using last night's tragic stabbing incident as an excuse to disrupt life within this community, and the scale and approach of their operation is completely unacceptable and unjustifiable.'[14] Although Maskey was attempting to utilise long-standing distrust of the police to deflect attention from the specific issue, Judge John Gillen noted that one witness 'may have been influenced or even directed by the IRA. At the very least there must be a real possibility that his evidence has been through a sieve orchestrated by this unlawful organisation.'[15] While there were an estimated seventy people in the bar, not one came forward as a witness.[16] The suspensions of twelve Sinn Féin members and the expulsions of three IRA members have been tied to the murder.[17] The IRA stated that they planned to shoot the killers of McCartney, indication of their 'complete incomprehension of how obsolete their methods had become'.[18] For Anthony McIntyre, the Provisional IRA 'treated Bert McCartney with the same inhuman disdain that Lenny Murphy would have been proud of'.[19]

Gerry Adams, although outspoken in his claims that no republican was involved, did not actively call on witnesses to provide information to the police after the murder. Two years later, once 90 per cent of voters at the 2007 Ard Fheis had voted to support policing in Northern Ireland, he made a rather belated plea for information.[20] With the only individual charged in connection with the murder released in 2008, any information that may have been forthcoming was not decisive. Despite raising the profile of the case internationally, the McCartney sisters had failed to achieve justice for their brother. After meetings with world leaders proved futile, they publicly stated that 'the person who we believe ordered it is high up in the IRA . . . This person is bigger than the IRA, he's bigger than the whole movement.'[21] What purpose the IRA might have with ordering the murder of a man with whom they had no apparent quarrel is unclear. The murder bore all the hallmarks of a typical bar-brawl, the macho culture endemic in paramilitary groups perhaps costing McCartney his life for having the audacity to stand up to an IRA man. The image of the educated republican paramilitary, certainly an image encouraged by Provisional republican leaders, took a severe hit after the McCartney murder as the IRA was cast as an undisciplined organisation that not only permitted its members to commit acts of murder, but apparently condoned them. Marian Price, well familiar with the masculine culture of republican paramilitarism, notes, 'there always has been a degree of bullying . . . people have been joining the IRA for the wrong reasons, so they can go down the Falls Road with their chest out'.[22]

The discipline of the wartime IRA and the outlet for aggression that the troubles provided were sorely absent in Magennis's bar. While the asset value of such volunteers had diminished as the armed campaign wound down, the leadership had to carefully manage them for fear of losing them to dissident paramilitary groups.

The Northern Bank robbery and Robert McCartney murder also had implications in the United States. On St Patrick's Day 2005, Senator Kennedy met with McCartney's sisters in Washington. Significant about this meeting was that it coincided with his snub for Adams, whom he refused to meet because of the increased IRA activity of the period. Kennedy called on the IRA to disband following his meeting with the sisters, and Senator Hillary Clinton argued that the peace process 'cannot go forward unless there is a complete reckoning with the demand for justice in the murder of Robert McCartney'.[23] Kennedy's website argues that his 'consistently tough message, coupled with a decision not to see Gerry Adams on St Patrick's Day in 2005, contributed to the decision of the IRA to disarm in September of 2005'.[24] As the leadership struggled to come to terms with how to deal with issues relevant to 2005, a new challenge emerged.

RICHARD O'RAWE AND REPUBLICAN REVISIONISM

The centrality of the hunger strikes to both the popular appeal of the Provisional republican movement and the political wing of Provisional republicanism is undoubted. The natural progression from the stimulus of Britain's criminalisation policy of 1976 through the blanket and dirty protest to the hunger strikes and the associated elections to the ending of abstention and the developing political credibility of Sinn Féin had remained an unchallenged aspect of conventional wisdom about the path of modern republicanism; it would not be an exaggeration to say that the hunger strikes were the foundations on which Provisional republican politics rested. In 2005, these foundations were severely and credibly challenged as former IRA prisoner Richard O'Rawe published his memoir of the hunger strike period, *Blanketmen*.

O'Rawe was a fairly typical IRA volunteer, coming from republican stock and joining the movement in early 1971. With no ostensible reason for dissenting from the movement, his claim that the republican leadership had deliberately allowed hunger strikers to die in order to publicise their electoral campaigns had credibility. His claim was that, prior to the death of fifth hunger striker Joe McDonnell, an offer was forthcoming from the British government that would have ceded to four of the prisoners five demands, with only free association withheld; in O'Rawe's own words, 'Can you imagine if we'd have had our own clothes, if we'd said to our people, "Send us our own clothes next week"? In the eyes of the world, we'd have broken Maggie Thatcher.'[25]

Such a claim was immediately refuted by the republican leadership. Brendan 'Bik' McFarlane, Bobby Sands' successor as prison OC, flatly denied O'Rawe's account.[26] O'Rawe was not the first republican to make such a claim, Republican Sinn Féin having argued in 1987 that 'the Republican Movement was hijacked by political opportunists during the H-Block Hunger Strike, people who saw in our tragedy and grief a convenient platform, an ideal bandwagon, which could convey them and their fellow travellers to the parliamentary woolsack'.[27] Anthony McIntyre believes that over time O'Rawe's position has only been strengthened,[28] and *Blanketmen* has effectively reopened debate on republican strategy as far back as the 1970s: every move made by the Adams leadership is now retrospectively analysed in the context of Sinn Féin's ascension to power. So protective of the legacy of the hunger strikes – or wary of the ramifications of such revelations – was the Sinn Féin leadership that O'Rawe was warned off writing his memoir by several republicans and his motivation for writing the book was brought into question by former comrades. He recalls:

> I'd always been unhappy right from the word go that the prisoners had been overruled and as a result six of our guys died . . . I'd see Gerry Adams talking about IRA men, kissing hunger strikers' mothers and hugging them and it sickened me because in my mind, he had an opportunity to save the hunger strikers' lives . . . The cynicism . . . and the sheer hypocrisy turned my gut . . . As far as I'm concerned, six very brave men – whether you believed in their war or their politics is irrelevant – gave their lives for what they believed to be right and that is an awful noble thing. If loyalists had have done that I would have admired them. It was wrong that their history wasn't being recorded accurately or properly and it was just as wrong that they had been cynically exploited. People were living lies

and very comfortable with those lies, hugging mothers and kissing their sisters, knowing all the time that they played a part in their deaths . . . when they could have saved them, they didn't.[29]

McIntyre, himself something of an opponent to contemporary Provisional republicanism, recalls O'Rawe 'giving off on the matter for years'.[30] Also disillusioned with his experiences in the IRA was senior Belfast volunteer Brendan 'The Dark' Hughes, who passed away in February 2008. During the early years of the new century, he agreed to take part in an oral history project under the auspices of Boston College, with the understanding that his account would be sequestered until after his death. Finally published in 2010, *Voices From The Grave* was revelatory, describing Gerry Adams' oft-denied role in the IRA, detailing in particular his role in the Bloody Friday attacks as well as the highly controversial 'disappearance' of mother-of-ten Jean McConville. Unintentionally, Hughes became a symbol for opposition to the Adams leadership. Hughes' account challenged the republican leadership because of his centrality to the Belfast IRA throughout the troubles and, as became Provisional republican policy in the light of such allegations, it was denied vehemently. Living alone in the Divis Tower that looms over the foot of the Falls Road, Hughes had been troubled by ill health and alcohol problems in his later years. The implications of Adams' statement that 'he wasn't well and hadn't been for a very long time, including during the time he did these interviews',[31] could hardly have been clearer: Hughes was an unreliable source. For Marian Price:

> Brendan Hughes was an exemplary republican . . . I know his name has been dragged down by members of Sinn Féin, who say he was just a drunk. Yes, Brendan did drink, but he drank to dull the pain that he felt because he felt that everything he worked for, everything he watched his friends and comrades die for, had been abandoned . . . he was very disappointed in former comrades who he felt had been bought off . . . I have read his book and his book is the absolute truth.[32]

Of course, the republican leadership could hardly completely cast one of their most prominent volunteers aside and after he died Adams commented that 'although he disagreed with the direction taken in recent years, he was held in high esteem by all who knew him'.[33]

Whether or not Adams would appear at Hughes' funeral was uncertain, so vast had the divide between the two developed. Marian Price: 'When Brendan said that he would have taken a bullet for Adams, he meant it, and when he said, "I should have put one in him" he also meant it. I think Brendan was very disappointed in what Adams turned out to be.'[34] That

Adams not only attended, but, according to his opponents, seized on the funeral as an opportunity for publicity, served to antagonise many republicans: 'it was as if the King had arrived',[35] one noted. Other republicans commented on how Adams defied even Catholic convention to appear outside the chapel before anyone else, even the priest.[36] The suggestion that Adams, who had visited Hughes during his final days, had made peace with his former colleague was refuted by Hughes' brother, who said that Hughes had lapsed into a coma and was unconscious during Adams' visits.[37]

Consensus began to develop around the view that Gerry Adams had carefully orchestrated the republican campaign from as early as the 1970s and that the IRA had been deliberately and consistently undermined. Unsurprisingly, this contributed to an increasing culture of dissent.

BRITISH SECURITY CONCERNS AND DISSIDENT IRISH REPUBLICANS: THE RIRA AND CIRA

On 28 July 2005, the Provisional IRA formally declared its war to be over. Within two months, it was confirmed by General John de Chastelain, the head of the decommissioning body, that all IRA arms had been put beyond use.[38] The lack of trust inherent in such a peace process was evident, with it claimed that the IRA still had access to weaponry and had continued to gather intelligence.[39] While the likelihood that the IRA no longer had access to any weaponry was slim, the allegations of intelligence gathering were particularly troubling. In 2002, it was revealed that the IRA had been gathering intelligence at Stormont, a revelation that led to the collapse of the Northern Ireland Assembly.[40] There were also issues within republicanism, with Martin McGuinness reluctant to begin IRA decommissioning for fear of the opportunity it would provide dissident republicans.[41] In formally ending their war, the PIRA was perceived to have relinquished their right to the title of Óglaigh na hÉireann.

All contemporary republican groups claim rightful ownership of the title, *The Sovereign Nation* reporting on 'Óglaigh na hÉireann (whom the media refer to as the Real IRA)',[42] and a jailed Continuity IRA man shouting 'Up Óglaigh na hÉireann' as he was led from the dock.[43] With the PIRA ceasefire, the quest for republican legitimacy had begun a new phase.

RIRA

The Real IRA had declared a ceasefire in the aftermath of the Omagh bomb – 'we had to shut it down and reboot'[44] – and it issued a call to arms in 2000. The campaign was relaunched with a series of small bombings across Northern Ireland as well as a missile attack on the headquarters of MI6 in London, using an RPG launcher never before seen in the UK.[45] Volunteer Joseph O'Connor was shot dead in the Ballymurphy area of Belfast in October, an act that saw former Provisional IRA prisoner Anthony McIntyre threatened for publicly blaming the Provisional IRA. McIntyre argued that 'the Provisional IRA who killed Joseph O'Connor sent out a message. That message is that the use of the gun to sort out political disputes is still legitimate post-Good Friday. This message reinforces the intellectual pool from which armed republicans drink.'[46]

In early 2001, the Real IRA continued its campaign in England, launching bomb attacks in London, including a notable attack at BBC headquarters.[47] The pattern of small-scale bomb attacks continued throughout 2001 and 2002. At the end of 2002, Real IRA prisoners in Portlaoise prison called on the Army Council of the organisation to stand down, troubled by criminality within the movement. They argued that 'this Army leadership's financial motivations far outweigh their political commitment to our struggle . . . We believe that the current Army leadership has forfeited all moral authority to lead the (Real) IRA.'[48]

This statement was directed at Michael McKevitt, who was arrested in March 2001 'because he talked to the FBI agent, had him round his house and everything'.[49] The FBI agent in question was David Rupert, involved in an elaborate sting operation. McKevitt enjoyed support in the campaign for his freedom, but it was limited to his wife, who had also been arrested initially before being released without charge, her sister, Marcela, and Father Desmond Wilson.[50] Outwith this small circle of support, he was described as 'a seriously inept terrorist leader',[51] and after an apparent attempt to hang himself in prison in early 2006, he was placed on suicide watch.[52] He became increasingly isolated in prison, the 'badmouthing' of his colleagues only expediting his fall.[53]

During this period it was suggested that the lines of demarcation between the dissident paramilitary organisations had become rather blurred. Some claimed that Omagh had been a joint RIRA–CIRA operation,[54] an allegation the latter vehemently denied, complaining of a 'sustained campaign of denigration. Spurious charges of the most outrageous kind have been levelled against [the Continuity IRA] by sections of the media which are pliant in the hands of the establishment.'[55] A 32CSM member admitted that there had been CIRA involvement in the operation,[56] but this was because of the complicated nature of dissident republicanism during the late 1990s; others noted that 'people drift between the two'.[57] Indeed, Colm Murphy, the only man to be jailed for the Omagh bombing in 2002 before his conviction was quashed in 2008,[58] had been involved with the INLA during the 1970s and had alleged connections with the CIRA.[59] Was it therefore the case that volunteers were simply transferring their allegiance from one group to another depending on which group was more likely at any given time to feed their hunger for violence, or perhaps that no real demarcation existed between the groups who essentially selected their operatives from a single pool of volunteers? The 32CSM has been outspoken on their proposals for a 'Republican Unity Initiative', which 'has the capabilities to promote debate, discussion and formulate republican strategy based on democratic principles, agreement and decision'. It claims:

> Republicanism divided into factions only assists those who are content to ignore us. They refuse to challenge our analysis, our position leaves them uncomfortable so they have to retreat to ignore us in the hope we will go away. That is not going to happen, we in the 32CSM know that with debate and understanding across the republican base, republicans will come together just as they did in 1916 and that with such unity the republican position cannot be ignored.[60]

Gerry Kelly commented, 'It's patently ludicrous for them to call for republican unity, since they made an attempt to split the IRA and create disunity. They do not have support in republican areas and putting a prefix in front of IRA will not make it any more real for republicans.'[61] The 32CSM does note that 'armies cannot merge or rely on each other',[62] even though in 2007 it stated:

> The speculation . . . that Óglaigh na hÉireann . . . have agreed to renounce armed struggle in conjunction with the INLA and Continuity IRA is completely without foundation . . . It is our opinion that such stories have been deliberately planted in the media in order to cause divisions among the Republican organisations . . . This project has at its core the concept of Republicans working initially on areas of agreement rather than continuing to focus on areas of disagreement. It is our hope that following a period of practical co-operation, Republicans could unite upon agreed areas of strategy and policy in order to build a much more effective challenge to Britain's illegal occupation of the north of Ireland.[63]

Ideologically, there is little separating the groups, both sharing the belief that 'armed struggle is a perfectly legitimate form of resistance to the British presence in Ireland'.[64] The initiative has prompted like-minded republicans to reach out to each other, particularly evident when Marian Price noted the passing of Christopher 'Crip' McWilliams[65] at Bodenstown in 2008. The visit of Ian Paisley to Cork in April 2008 saw a protest under the banner of republican unity, Price commenting that 'Paisley was greeted by a unified republican voice'.[66] The associated photograph in the newspaper showed fourteen people active in the protest. Geraldine Taylor states that 'we are the republican movement therefore we don't believe in broad fronts . . . Those other groups [have] a right to exist [but] we have the legitimacy and have been recognised as a legitimate government of the Republic.'[67] Price believes that the only difference between those who joined CIRA and RIRA was 'timing, that's all . . . There's no great political difference between them, it just took them a while to realise that they were being sold out.'[68]

After Provisional IRA decommissioning in 2005, a dissident 'recruitment drive in west Belfast . . . fell flat on its face'.[69] The lack of recruitment was visible in the small-scale operations of 2005 to 2007, which included a hoax bomb alert at Down Royal Racecourse, disrupting a race festival, and a series of small bombs planted around border regions. The border counties, traditionally a strong republican base, represented opportunities for recruitment across the minority republican groups, particularly in South Armagh, where bomb attacks in the wake of the Provisional IRA ceasefire had preceded the Omagh bomb. After their campaign had appeared to have fizzled out, the Real IRA embarked on a period of introspection and reorganisation, although small-scale attacks persisted, most likely in an attempt to keep recent recruits onside.[70]

CIRA

The early twenty-first century was equally unproductive for the Continuity IRA. The foundation of the Independent Monitoring Commission in 2004 tasked the non-state organisation with keeping track of all paramilitary groups. In 2007, it noted that the CIRA had 'sought to recruit members . . . and to develop a youth wing; it has attempted to acquire weapons, and it may have tested home-made explosives; it has made efforts to see that involvement in Republican Sinn Féin (RSF) did not divert members from paramilitary activity; and it has sought to raise finance.'[71] This review, contrasted with those of the INLA and RIRA, suggested that the Continuity IRA posed the most significant threat to the peace process, an implication that did not sit easily with the evidence of the previous decade.

The Continuity IRA demanded that the Provisional IRA disband in 2000 and hand over their weapons to an organisation that was prepared to perpetuate the armed struggle.[72] This version of the armed struggle took the form of a series of small-scale bombings and the murder of former UDA member Charles Folliard in Strabane. The CIRA campaign was escalated somewhat during 2003, but this was more of a numerical escalation which took its toll on CIRA resources and undermined the prospects of a significant campaign in 2004. The Real IRA's hiatus of 2005–7 was mirrored by the CIRA, with only a few operations attributed to the movement. For the two main dissident republican organisations to share an extended period of inactivity immediately after the Provisional IRA decommissioned is not coincidental. After the debacle of the Omagh bomb a far more careful strategy had to be put in place, not to mention the considerable threat posed by the Provisional IRA pre-decommissioning; the IPLO had learned how ruthless the PIRA could be when it was deemed necessary to use violence for the promotion of the peace strategy that the movement had been committed to for several years.

BACK TO WAR?

The hiatus did the dissidents good, as indicated by a summer 2008 landmine and rocket-propelled grenade attack on police in County Fermanagh.[73] The July 2007 withdrawal of the British Army had left the Police Service of Northern Ireland solely responsible for security, with only a residual Army presence to provide specialised ordnance disposal and support for public order. This, along with the decade of relative peace since the 1997 ceasefire, had left police officers rather vulnerable to attack and CIRA volunteers had attempted to lure police officers into dangerous situations.[74] MI5 also noted that dissident republican groups 'continue to be actively involved in low-level campaigns . . . improvised explosive device and incendiary attacks against infrastructure and commercial targets'.[75] The rising threat of the CIRA and RIRA was indicated by a 2008 report that British security agencies were more concerned with the activity of republicans than with Islamic extremists.[76]

The 32 County Sovereignty Movement admitted that they were 'attracting disillusioned and disenfranchised Republicans right across

Ireland and further afield as are other Republican organisations'.[77] The IMC noted that 'RIRA has made efforts to enhance the organisation's capability',[78] efforts which contributed to the reactivation of their campaign against the British state in March 2009.

On 7 March, Sappers Mark Quinsey and Patrick Azimkar, two soldiers from the 38 Engineer Regiment, were shot dead outside Massareene barracks in Antrim town while collecting a pizza delivery in an attack that was claimed by the Real IRA.[79] The pizza delivery workers were also injured in the attack, a fact justified by the movement: 'In delivering the pizza, they were serving the British state occupation of Ireland. If they [the soldiers] want pizza, then why can't they make it themselves? It's like at Teebane',[80] comparing the attack to the 1992 PIRA bombing which killed eight Protestant workmen who had been working on an Army base. Although militant republicanism never enjoyed widespread popular support, the tactic of targeting workers who happened to be assigned maintenance work on security force property, while effective in ensuring such property existed in a poor state of repair, damaged the popular credibility of a movement deliberately targeting civilians. At a time when Sinn Féin was desperate for political credibility, the tactic could hardly have been more counterproductive. The 32CSM remains unconcerned about popular perception; having been universally criticised since Omagh, they consider that 'the media are going to say negative things about us anyway', and therefore do not consider bad publicity a negative consequence of their actions.[81] The pair were the first soldiers to die in Northern Ireland since Lance Bombardier Stephen Restorick was killed in South Armagh in 1997. For Anthony McIntyre, 'Years ago this type of news would rally the spirit. Now it just dampens the mood and feeds into despair, the strategic futility of it all every bit as debilitating as the political failure it constitutes.'[82]

Two days later, in what appeared to be a co-ordinated attack, Police Service of Northern Ireland Constable Stephen Carroll, a Catholic, was shot dead by the Continuity IRA in Craigavon.[83] In killing a Catholic officer, the dissidents had followed through on their long-standing threat to Catholics who chose to accept the forces of British justice in Ireland.[84] Lurgan had also been the location for the murders of constables Roland Graham and David Johnston, the last police officers to die, in 1997. At the suggestion that the attacks had been co-ordinated, the 32CSM comment that 'Lurgan was a case of the "Contos" going "Oh shit, we'd better do something, oh look there's a cop car, let's shoot at it"';[85] therefore part of a dissident campaign of one-upmanship rather than part of a synchronised dissident offensive.

Deputy First Minister Martin McGuinness declared those responsible to be 'traitors to the island of Ireland'.[86] In one statement, McGuinness had unintentionally summarised the massive contradiction inherent in modern republicanism; Provisional IRA violence, which had claimed over 1,700 lives, including nearly a thousand security force members, was somehow distinguishably different from that of the Real and Continuity IRA. The PIRA had criticised the Official IRA for their non-violent strategy that was adopted in the 1970s, but now could somehow reconcile their previous adherence to the armed struggle with their new non-violent campaign. For McGuinness, one of the most visible former IRA commanders in Sinn Féin, to have made the statement provoked serious comment across the political spectrum.[87] The 32 County Sovereignty Movement commented that 'Mr McGuinness and his party are avid supporters of the British presence in Ireland. As he stood shoulder to shoulder with the head of Unionism and the most senior figure in the British colonial police in Ireland and condemned the actions of Republicans in targeting the British Army he displayed how there are no real political differences between any of these three men.'[88]

Criticism from McGuinness now considered a badge of honour, commentators reflected that the absence of powerful PIRA figures such as Brian Keenan, who died of cancer in early 2008, had contributed to the rise of the dissidents.[89] The credibility that Keenan enjoyed across republicanism, having helped bring in the Libyan weaponry in the 1970s before becoming a notable convert to Adams' 1990s strategy,[90] was sorely absent after his death. The 'outing' of senior republican Denis Donaldson as a British informer in late 2005 was particularly damaging given the prominent role he had assumed in Sinn Féin.[91] After it was revealed that Donaldson had served as a British agent for two decades,[92] he went into hiding and was found shot dead in a cottage in a remote area of County Donegal.[93] The issue had emerged two years previously when IRA informer 'Stakeknife' was alleged to have been Freddie Scappaticci, the head of the IRA's internal security.[94] A former PIRA volunteer recalled being approached by members of the security force and offered money in exchange for future co-operation, passing the information on to the internal security department, 'but of course it went to Scap, who said "leave it with me, I'll look into it", when in fact he probably didn't do a thing'.[95] The 32CSM commented:

One would think such a key department in the IRA, internal security, would of necessity be headed by the most trustworthy and incorruptible of Irish republicans. But under the direction of the Provisional leadership we find it was staffed by one known British agent and an ex-member of the British Special Forces . . . It is now apparent to basically everyone on this island that the Adams and McGuinness clique was not only riddled with British agents but that this clique managed over decades to seize total power within the movement by strategic stealth and cunning.[96]

These revelations have fuelled allegations that the Provisional republican movement had been controlled by the British from an early stage and was now actively policing former comrades. Republican Sinn Féin believe that 'it's very dangerous for those lads at this time because the Provos are informing on the Continuity IRA . . . they know all the ins and outs and how to fight a war in this area and those lads could be arrested at any time'.[97] This is echoed by the 32CSM, who question that 'Martin McGuinness calls Irish Republicans "traitors" and asks people to go to the regurgitated RUC, a sectarian "Police" force, and give information about Republicans which could result in their deaths?'[98]

All republican leaders were now the topic of speculation as to their role in the IRA, McGuinness at the centre of claims that he had been British agent J118.[99] Marian Price believes that infiltration was 'huge' and began during the early 1970s. 'Procedures within the army became lax. When you were joining the army you had to go through certain procedures and I think that was kind of thrown to the side in the early 70s . . . with the whole community backing you, any person who came and said they wanted to join the IRA it was "come on ahead".'[100] McGuinness's comments in March 2009 prompted the Real IRA to declare:

Let us remind our former comrade of the nature and the actions of a traitor. Treachery is collaborating with the enemy, treachery is betraying your country. Let us give our one time comrade an example. Denis Donaldson was a traitor and the leadership of the Provisional movement, under the guidance of the British government, made provisions for Donaldson to escape republican justice in the same manner as Freddie Scappaticci. It fell to the volunteers of Óglaigh na hÉire-ann to carry out the sentence and punishment demanded in our Army Orders and by the wider republican family.[101]

Interestingly, when read to the crowd at the City Cemetery in Derry, the last sentence was omitted.[102] The implication was that the movement was uncertain whether or not to claim responsibility for the Donaldson murder. The full statement had appeared the previous day in the main-stream media, and again in *The Sovereign Nation*, but the omission was noteworthy, particularly so when one considers that a previous edition of the movement's newspaper had debated the murder and who had been responsible. Although it noted that 'as is the case with any informer, Donaldson could expect no pity from Republicans',[103] it stopped short of claiming responsibility for the killing. Had the Donaldson assassin joined the movement during the intervening period? Had the new-found self-belief from the Antrim murders given the movement the confidence to declare itself Donaldson's assassin? The group appeared to have considerable momentum behind it:

> Actions by the volunteers of Óglaigh na hÉireann in the last year have proved that the Tactical Use of Armed Struggle can, and does, bring results. As was witnessed in Antrim, British soldiers and the colonial police will continue to lose their lives as long as the issue of national sovereignty remains unresolved. Óglaigh na hÉireann will continue to strike at the British occupation forces wherever and whenever we decide.[104]

This statement is interesting, seeming to take credit for both the Massareene and Lurgan operations. Although the statement exudes self-confidence, it does rather ignore the reality that killing three security force members was still a considerable distance from uniting Ireland. Declaring that it would act whenever it saw fit also provided a caveat to explain future lack of action and implied a relatively small capacity for violence. Despite the relatively complicated attack on the soldiers, the murder of PC Carroll was particularly cowardly and bore similarity to attacks on the Northern Ireland Fire and Rescue Service after hoax emergency calls.[105] The killings marked the beginning of a concerted campaign of violence.

The Real IRA staged a roadblock in South Armagh towards the end of the summer, a classic republican show of strength in an area where the PSNI was particularly vulnerable.[106] The group was also attempting to purchase arms in the former Soviet Union. These attempts turned to farce with Michael Campbell arrested and charged with attempting to buy weapons in Lithuania's first-ever terrorist trial. 'He did not conceal that the arms and explosives were meant for the Real IRA and were to be used against the authorities, like blowing up police armoured vehicles', said Deputy Chief Prosecutor Irmantas Mikelinions.[107] The 32CSM complained that 'Irishman, Michael Campbell, is still being held without charge in barbaric prison conditions 14 months after being arrested.'[108]

Although this mission had proven unsuccessful, the evidence of Real IRA operations since Massareene indicates that the movement possesses a considerable arsenal. Over the remainder of 2009, a series of bombs were planted across Northern Ireland, notably a 600 lb bomb discovered at Forkhill in County Armagh,[109] and a 400 lb bomb left outside the Policing Board's Belfast Headquarters in November 2009.[110] They continued to target Catholic PSNI officers, Peader Heffron having his leg amputated after a bomb exploded under his car in Randalstown on 8 January 2010.[111] Using an operational base of the border regions of Northern Ireland, the Real IRA continued their campaign with a bomb at Newry courthouse planted in late February 2010 before the body of Kieran Doherty was found on the outskirts of Londonderry on 24 February 2010. He was alleged to have been a Real IRA volunteer by MI5, who had attempted to recruit him as an informer.[112] Perhaps in response to this, the Real IRA planted a car bomb outside Palace Barracks in Hollywood.

In 2007, the British Army concluded Operation Banner, its long-running campaign in Northern Ireland. Responsibility for security now fell on the PSNI, whose major security concern remained dissident republicans. After the March attacks, its ability to launch Operation Dissent on 18 September 2009 was indicative of the small scope of dissident republicans. Where the PIRA was able to employ a variety of offensive tactics, the main dissident threat has been bomb attacks. The lack of gun attacks, which are considerably easier to organise, suggests that either the dissident arsenal is low on weaponry, or that few volunteers are prepared to actively engage security forces. This was evident in many PIRA operations from the 1980s onwards, as the destructive capabilities of the bomb were deployed in favour of the riskier tactic of shooting at security officers.

Even with Provisional republican co-operation in identifying members of dissident organisations, the consistent and large-scale incidents of 2010 have damaged long-term prospects for peace. For Army General Andrew Graham, they have developed into 'a gnat that happens to have a big stick'.[113] Equally concerning has been the continued schismatic tendency that is evident from IMC reports. Although it considered that the Real IRA appeared to have divided into two factions, one labelled Óglaigh na hÉireann, it observed other groups emerging, such as the Irish Republican Liberation Army and Saor Uladh.[114]

These reports clash with the views of republicans: the IRLA was a tiny group that was expelled from the CIRA after threatening Republican Sinn Féin members during 2007, following allegations that IRLA members Ed Burns and Joe Jones had been murdered by the Continuity IRA after a row over missing weapons and stolen cash.[115] In reality, once these individuals had died, the IRLA was effectively out of existence.[116] It is worth noting that 'the IRA has always historically been Óglaigh na hÉireann, IRA members don't swear allegiance to the IRA, they swear allegiance to Óglaigh na hÉireann'.[117] In May 2008, the IMC discussed the group separately from both RIRA and CIRA, noting an increase in activity and 'the murder of Andrew Burns (also a local member) in County Donegal on 12 February 2008 – the first murder attributable to ONH'.[118] The recent tendency for dissidents to declare themselves 'Óglaigh na hÉireann' has served to confuse the picture.

The 32CSM does claim to be enjoying increased support across Northern Ireland, not just Newry and Derry where the strength of the movement is apparent because 'that's where people are getting killed'. What is apparent is that the areas where the movement is gathering support are those areas with a reputation for militant republicanism, notably the border regions and East Tyrone.[119] Richard O'Rawe considers the current republican landscape:

> There are genuine republicans amongst these guys and they believe that they need that support to keep the flame lit, that some time in the future the conditions might be there for a more vigorous armed struggle that might perhaps succeed – I don't think that will ever happen – but they do think that. I've met people in Fermanagh who are very committed republicans, who genuinely believe that Sinn Féin have sold out and who believe that armed struggle is a viable means of political activity. I've also met some guys in Belfast who are members of these organisations and they're taking a tax from drug dealers and are exercising their authority through the tyranny of the streets, they fight personal vendettas through these organisations. There are good republicans amongst the Belfast dissidents, but there are also people who are a corruption, nothing more than thugs and gangsters.[120]

The scale and scope of Real IRA attacks during 2009 and 2010 have indicated that, although the organisation claims not to be concerned with collateral damage, keeping casualties to a minimum is a factor in dissident operations. The likelihood of innocent civilians being killed in a midnight attack on an Army barracks relative to a Saturday afternoon attack in a busy town centre is considerably lower. The increasingly publicised political agenda of the 32CSM is evident from their newspaper, and the movement was outspoken in its opposition to the 2007 Lisbon Treaty, as well as on a variety of Middle Eastern issues.

The political agenda of Republican Sinn Féin is less obvious. Certainly, the movement has been marked throughout its existence by the advanced age of many of its members. Geraldine Taylor notes:

243

It's been an uphill struggle. In 1986, I was practically on my own here in Belfast because of course Adams was the man of the moment. Most of my own comrades stopped speaking to me. We got out and sold papers. I've seen changes since in former comrades who recognise that they were wrong . . . they're not prepared to become involved because they've been so let down, sold out, disappointed, afraid to commit themselves again because of all that . . . They would support us, buy our papers and various things like that and I would say it would take something major to happen to bring them back into the fold, at the moment they're too disillusioned . . . In the most recent years we've seen young people coming on board. We are growing, our paper sales are going up – we're getting more support from the people and we're getting there slowly but surely. A lot of support in Ardoyne, a lot of support in the New Lodge, Ballymurphy's not too bad . . . I'm sure there's a hell of a lot more support out there for us. We realise ourselves that we haven't the membership to cover all those other areas yet. Newry are doing really well, Lurgan has done extremely well, Armagh is doing extremely well, Derry not so much at the moment but Fermanagh and Tyrone are doing very well, Donegal around there, Bundoran, we're doing very well up there.[121]

While Sinn Féin seeks support outside the areas it has traditionally relied on, Republican Sinn Féin, along with other republican groups, is focused on republican strongholds. They maintain a relatively credible political movement with their visible presence on the Falls Road in Belfast as well as their Dublin office. The agenda may not have changed – Dessie O'Hagan comments, 'Republican Sinn Féin still think this is the 1950s . . . or even the 1920s'[122] – but the small Belfast office is remarkably busier in 2010 than it was in 2007 and the influx of younger members is obvious from even a brief visit. Nevertheless, an attempted coup in May 2010 was of concern to hopes of unity even within the organisation.[123] Ruairí Ó Brádaigh said, 'I am part of a tradition of dissenters who feel that philosophy was lost then, and if Sinn Féin get sucked into the constitutional line, who else is there to speak up?'[124] That is a philosophy shared across the organisation:

After the split in 1986, I cried sore hard tears and I made myself a promise and it was the only thing that kept me going: that I could not let down those men and women, boys and girls who paid the supreme sacrifice, buried in Milltown cemetery . . . I gave a promise to them that I would keep going, until it was built up again and that they would not have died in vain.[125]

INLA

After their largely counterproductive campaign of the 1990s, the INLA remained relatively quiet during this period, with the group apparently committed to peace. During early 2002, notorious INLA gunman, Dessie 'The Border Fox' O'Hare, had begun to attract attention to the group as he campaigned to be released from prison. Rumoured to have killed in excess of thirty people,[126] O'Hare was granted temporary release on a series of occasions, although the PSNI's Historical Enquiries unit have refused to rule out further investigation into his alleged crimes.

Even in the absence of feuding, which had beset the movement throughout its history, the killing of Kevin McAlorum as he dropped his children off at school in Derriaghy on the outskirts of Belfast served as a reminder of the movement's troubled past. McAlorum was alleged to have been the assassin of INLA Chief of Staff Gino Gallagher in 1996.[127] The INLA's reputation for vengeance, established at an early stage of its existence, was still strong. It did, however, remain relatively quiet for much of the decade before it launched a series of attacks on drug dealers during 2009.[128] The IMC had noted that 'INLA retains a capacity for extreme violence; we cannot rule out its becoming more dangerous in future; and in the meantime it is largely a criminal enterprise.'[129] The contradiction of both attempting to tackle anti-social behaviour and criminality and yet having a substantial criminal element within the organisation prompted the standing down of the entire INLA Dublin brigade in March 2009.[130]

The INLA announced a formal end to its armed campaign on 11 October 2009 during an oration at the graveside of Seamus Costello.[131] *The Irish Times* commented that 'legitimacy has been in short supply with the INLA down the years. Even now it remains a ruthless and dangerous organisation that is up to its neck in criminality.'[132] It then followed up this announcement, a matter of days before the legislation allowing the IICD to operate ended, by decommissioning its weapons.[133] The INLA had ventured far down the path of non-violence and their act of decommissioning represented the end of armed struggle for the Republican Socialist Movement. Anthony McIntyre noted that 'in the early days, the IRSP would have been nothing without the INLA, it would have been just another name . . . overall I think the INLA has done a great disservice to Republican Socialism by continuously infighting and feuding'.[134] Eoin Ó Broin added:

the INLA's activity . . . has been hugely detrimental to any political aspirations that the IRSP would have and the INLA's involvement in a number of particularly unpopular actions in the Ardoyne area has meant that, while there may have been an opening for political support for an organisation to the left of Sinn Féin, for example, clearly it's, in my view, damaged its own prospects of ever capitalising on that . . . My own sense is that the IRSP doesn't really exist as an organisation any more, there are collections of individuals who are desperately trying to hold this entity together, some of them very genuine and committed people, others who I would have more question marks over . . . [135]

IRSP Ard Chomhairle member John Murtagh admits that 'we have a long way to go to reassure the Irish working class that republican social-ists are deserving of their support'.[136] The organisation has previously confidently stated that 'Republican Socialism is not an old fashioned and time-warped ideology. It is a belief whose time is coming.'[137] Fra Halligan notes:

I would say that although the political landscape has changed, it has changed, for the IRSP, for the better . . . It's an interesting time, a time of very hard work. Some have said this is our last attempt, we have to do it now or else we might just wrap up and shut shop . . . We're looking to youth, we're looking at the kids that are standing on the corners on the Falls Road saying 'We've no future', and that's a sad, sad thing for a seventeen-year-old to say . . . We've a lot of work internally to do, we've a lot of structures to put back in place and we've a lot of hard work ahead of us. We'll push to a position when we're ready that we will go for council elec-tions and we will be challenging these people and we'll try to educate the working class and get that mass movement going where you say 'You don't have to live like this' . . . After thirty years some of us are tired, but these kids are bouncing. As long as we stay within the parameters left by Ta Power, Gino Gallagher, Miriam Daly and Ronnie Bunting, we can't go wrong.[138]

Revered IRSP figure Thomas 'Ta' Power noted that the road to hell is paved with good intentions,[139] and after nearly thirty-five years, the IRSP finds itself with a very strong CV of them.

ÉIRÍGÍ

From the Irish for 'rise', this group was founded as a socialist republican group in Dublin in April 2006, coinciding with the ninetieth anniver-sary of the Easter Rising, and registered as a political party in Ireland in 2009. Their stated aim is 'ending the British occupation of the six coun-ties and the establishment of a thirty-two county Democratic Socialist Republic'.[140] Its chosen symbol of a green star with the name of the group displayed in orange is important, reflecting both the republican and the socialist tendencies within the movement. The idea of a republican broad front appeals to éirígí, stating that 'it will be part of such a coali-tion, working on shared projects with other progressive individuals and groups in Ireland'.[141] Commentators highlight the decision by Sinn Féin to recognise the legitimacy of the PSNI as integral to the formation of éirígí.[142]

The group contains some powerful personalities. General Secretary Brendan McKenna (Breandán Mac Cionnaith) served as the spokesman for the Garvaghy Road Residents Coalition and his prominence during the Drumcree dispute during the late '90s and early 2000s brought some publicity to éirígí, as did Colin Duffy and Dominic McGlinchey, son of the former INLA leader.[143] The three were all prominent in protests against British involvement in Iraq and Afghanistan, the party protesting against 'the hypocrisy of British war-criminal Tony Blair claiming to be a "man of peace" in Ireland, while simultaneously directing the brutal occupations of Iraq and Afghanistan'.[144] Their involvement in such protests represents an act of ideological opportunism, the natural position of a republican against the British Armed Forces allowing the group to latch on to the increasingly powerful protest movement against operations in the Middle East.

Duffy had narrowly avoided death in 1990; leaving Lurgan RUC station having signed bail conditions, he and Sam Marshall were shot at. Duffy survived, Marshall did not. The incident brought allegations of state complicity, with claims that only the police knew the time of the signing. When Duffy was later jailed for the murder of a UDR member, it was revealed that a key witness in the trial was Lindsay Robb, a convicted UVF gun-runner.[145] In 1997, he was accused of murdering two RUC officers, although it was claimed that a dozen witnesses could place him elsewhere at the time of the killings. In this case, he was represented by solicitor Rosemary Nelson, who was murdered by a loyalist bomb in 1999. The charges were dropped before the case came to trial. Each case fuelled allegations of the existence of a conspiracy to imprison Duffy, allegations that also served to enhance his republican credentials. His association with éirígí was seemingly brief, ending just before he was arrested in connection with the murder of sappers Quinsey and Azimkar in March 2009.[146] His arrest prompted éirígí to claim that it 'is an open, independent, democratic political party which is not aligned to, or supportive of, any armed organisation'.[147] Duffy's association with the group served to undermine its political credibility, and the republican legitimacy that is often associated with small republican groups because of their membership was notably absent. Instead, Duffy's presence had brought éirígí unwanted attention from the security forces. The 32CSM are rather condescending about the group, opining that 'no-one wants to get in trouble . . . as soon as he got arrested, they got rid of him',[148] questioning the membership's stomach for the republican struggle.

In the run-up to the 2009 elections, éirígí launched a poster campaign entitled 'Spot the difference', where photographs of the leaders of Ireland's nine largest political parties were set side by side in an attempt to contend that the nine were politically offering the same programme for Ireland.[149] It is worthwhile to note that éirígí has two councillors, although neither was elected on the éirígí ticket; Dungannon councillor Barry Monteith and Dublin city councillor Louise Minihan both defected to the organisation from Sinn Féin.[150]

LOYALIST FEUDS

Loyalism was in a particularly fractured state at the end of the 1990s. The Combined Loyalist Military Command had overseen the ceasefire, but the co-operation that was a tenet of this organisation was notable by its absence during the early years of the new century as the UDA and UVF feuded, with seven murders taking place in late summer 2000. Although the total number of killings for 2000 and 2001 was small when compared with the worst years of the troubles, now thirty years in the past, these must be considered in the context of worsening sectarian confrontations across Northern Ireland. At the centre of this was the UDA,[151] with their C Company of the lower Shankill Road omnipresent throughout the period under the stewardship of Johnny Adair. Adair was the poster boy for loyalism during this period, a self-cultivated image borne of a diet of weight-lifting and steroids during his time in jail. He was the figure that the IRA had sought in October 1993 in its fateful bomb attack on a fish shop. After the 1997 ceasefire, loyalist paramilitary groups were deeply troubled by the need for a cogent enemy against which they could justify their continued existence. The culture of personality, partially fostered by the news media and their partiality for giving the loyalist characters of which they wrote catchy nicknames, drove wedges between those whose comradeship was essential to the integrity of their respective movements. For Billy McQuiston:

> Splits within loyalism in my view are not about ideology. Basically, they're about gangsterism . . . The split that developed within the UVF for instance, that was a group that was involved in drugs and criminality that pulled away from the UVF but they used ideology as a smokescreen, saying they didn't agree with the Good Friday Agreement and the way the organisation was going. If you look at the split

that developed within the UDA, the UDA at that time were involved in basically cleaning up the organisation and the transition of the organisation to basically leave the stage. There were people who didn't want the organisation to leave the stage because that would take away the cover they were using for criminality.[152]

From his lower Shankill power-base, Adair had forged links with the LVF. In early 2000 the murder of UVF commander Richard Jameson in Portadown provoked serious violence, with two teenagers murdered in retaliation; their only crime was a tenuous association with Billy Wright. Johnny Adair and John White's arrival at the funeral of one was followed by a UDA call for peace before a gable wall in the lower Shankill, Adair's heartland, was adorned with Wright's image. Adair increased his public profile during the Drumcree dispute of 2000, notably present during an LVF firing party.

A show of strength, loosely disguised as a Loyalist festival of culture, in August 2000, complete with firing party, spilled into trouble as the homes of UVF families were attacked, as was the Rex bar on the mid-Shankill Road, not too far from the reconstructed fish shop. The bar was targeted after drinkers reacted to the sight of an LVF flag, a clear act of provocation. Adair's centrality to so much of the violence of this period led to Peter Mandelson, then Secretary of State for Northern Ireland, revoking Adair's early release licence and returning him to jail, Adair's attempts to declare support for the Belfast Agreement falling on deaf ears.[153]

The Red Hand Defenders firmly established the link between the Adair faction and the LVF after the murder of Martin O'Hagan, the only journalist to die in the troubles. He was shot dead as he walked home from his local pub in Lurgan on 28 September 2001. Although O'Hagan had been involved with the Official IRA during the early 1970s and had been interned prior to spending five years in prison on an arms charge,[154] his killing was for personal reasons, having made himself an enemy of renegade loyalists. Around the same time, the RHD claimed responsibility for the death of William Stobie, the UDA man who had been charged with the murder of solicitor Pat Finucane in 1989. The RHD, by now a recognised cover name for the UDA, struck again, killing postman Daniel McColgan in 2002.[155] The group's activity was phased out as it was either brought into the fold of the UDA, or aligned itself with the organisation as the UDA's structure began to disintegrate as a result of the descent into criminality. The O'Hagan and Nelson murders marked the RHD as a joint UDA–LVF cover name, Lurgan being a noted LVF stronghold and Billy Wright's successor at the helm of the LVF, Mark Fulton, was revealed to

249

have been responsible for the Nelson murder.[156] The coalescence of the LVF with the increasingly narcissistic Adair was 'an unholy alliance, you had the LVF broken away from the UVF because of gangsterism and they wanted to continue their own profit-making activities and you've got Adair who was basically looking to take over loyalism, but not for any idealistic purpose or reason. I think his idea was to build a super-criminal gang.'[157]

As the LVF struggled, Fulton committing suicide in Maghaberry prison, so too did Adair. He was again released from prison in 2002 and was quickly expelled from the UDA. Adair's inability to fully embrace peace-era Northern Ireland led to his return to prison in early 2003, but resentment at his expulsion from the UDA continued to manifest itself in violence, and South East Antrim Brigadier John Gregg was murdered on 1 February.

Gregg cast a formidable figure, tall, heavy-set and covered in tattoos, and had begrudgingly supported the peace process as a means to an end; with peace, his comrades would be released from prison.[158] Ironically, his death was a result of the internecine violence that the absence of a tangible republican enemy had fostered. Gregg's murder has been attributed to the increasing criminal element that assumed control of areas of North Belfast, linked to Adair.[159] Before Gregg was buried, the Adair faction fled Northern Ireland, settling in Bolton where they were joined by Adair himself on his release from prison in 2004. The group struggled to settle into their unfamiliar surroundings, Alan McCullogh returning to Belfast where he was shot dead in retaliation for Gregg's murder.[160] Adair's eldest son, Jonathan, became involved in criminality and was jailed for five years for selling drugs.[161] Adair later moved to Troon, Ayrshire.[162] Adair's claims that his war was over have been substantiated by the fact that he continues to live in a town with relatively easy access for grudge-bearing loyalists.

The rise of gangsterism plagued loyalists during the early years of the twenty-first century, notably among the UDA. This organisation has had considerable problems in the North Belfast–South East Antrim area, personified in the Shoukri brothers. *Sunday World* editor Jim McDowell wrote a book on the two most prominent brothers, Andre and Ihab, who involved themselves in the Johnny Adair-led C Company during the 1990s. The *Sunday World* had been on a long-running quest against Ulster paramilitaries, and its staff had been deeply unpopular with paramilitary figures for a number of years. In 1984, Jim Campbell narrowly avoided death after being shot by UVF figures.[163] Seventeen years later, Martin O'Hagan was less fortunate. The paper's crusade against the rising gangster culture led to numerous death threats being placed on its staff, with editor McDowell the victim of a vicious attack in December 2009.[164]

The Shoukri brothers, labelled 'ceasefire soldiers' because of their appetite for violence in post-conflict Northern Ireland,[165] led a renegade faction of the UDA from their North Belfast base, with criminality high on their agenda. Billy McQuiston noted, 'The Shoukris were basically protégés of Adair. Adair put them there in order to further his own ambitions . . . When Adair went they were next in line.[166] While Andre was imprisoned in 2006, the two were expelled from the organisation and Andre was forced to leave the UDA wing of Maghaberry prison.'[167] The brothers association with criminality did not fit the vision the UDA had for itself, led by prominent South Belfast leader Jackie McDonald. As a loose conglomerate of vigilante groups from its inception, the UDA had always had a looser structure than the UVF, and once the groups began to move beyond violence, UDA members felt less obliged to follow the party line. Ian Wood has noted that the UVF retained discipline under its long-serving overall commander John Graham but still carried a perceived threat thanks to a long history of violence.[168] The increasing political credibility of the Progressive Unionist Party was a result of the close ties fostered between it and the UVF.[169] With Andre imprisoned for nine years on charges of intimidation and blackmail, his brother Ihab died in late 2008 from what was believed to have been a drug-related seizure.[170] In the absence of its key personalities, the Shoukri faction was rather weakened and ultimately gave up its arms in early 2010.

Although the threat of the renegade UDA faction persisted, it joined with the mainstream group to announce it was decommissioning its weaponry in 2009, an indication that the internal conflict had indeed ended. The IMC noted that the LVF, although now a very small faction, was a 'deeply criminal organisation' and largely apolitical.[171] In their most recent report, the IMC had little comment for the LVF other than to note that people with LVF associations were involved in serious crime. The UDA had apparently gathered intelligence on dissident republican groups, but their decommissioning offered encouragement for prospects of peace.

The ceasefire era posed problems for loyalist paramilitaries. Ostensibly formed to protect their communities from the threat of the IRA, the dissident republicans had not proven to be as capable an enemy as the

Provisionals and had offered little threat to loyalist communities.[172] Although their raison d'être no longer existed, the privileged position that so many enjoyed was not easily relinquished. It is unsurprising that many attempted to prolong their careers by making the relatively simple transition into criminality. The murder of Kevin McDaid in Coleraine in May 2009 seemed to involve both UDA and UVF men, but the circumstances of the murder seem to suggest a mob attack rather than a paramilitary operation. McDaid was killed after a group of Glasgow Rangers supporters had entered a Catholic area of the Heights estate following a match in which the team sealed the Scottish Premier League title.[173]

Although the incessant feuding that plagued the early part of the new century can be partially attributed to the vacuum left by the Provisional IRA, it is important to note that loyalist paramilitaries had proven to be their own worst enemy: ninety-three loyalists were killed by other loyalists, almost double the fifty-five killed by republicans. Indeed, loyalists only killed forty-one republicans, although the 870 civilians who died at the hands of groups such as the UDA and UVF attest to the violence they were capable of.

It is not surprising that many similarities exist between recent splits in republicanism and loyalism. The perceived esteem enjoyed by paramilitaries would not be renounced without a struggle. The cult of personality played a significant role in loyalist factionalism during the early part of the twenty-first century, manifested in a series of feuds and personified by Billy Wright and the Shoukri brothers. The two factions highlight a key difference between the UVF and UDA. Wright's ideological objection to the role that the PUP had taken in discussions that led to the organisation's ceasefire contrasted sharply with the seemingly criminal aspirations of the Shoukri brothers. The relative ease with which loyalist groups have shifted towards decommissioning in the light of the IRA making the same move emphasises their lack of concern at the threat posed by dissident groups. Although decommissioning has been an integral aspect of the peace process, it should not be overlooked that arms acquisition has never proven particularly tricky for groups so inclined, and the fact that loyalist paramilitary organisations seem to be without weaponry in early 2010 does not necessarily mean they will remain as such.

CONCLUSION

There is much irony in the use of the term 'dissident' in the context of Irish republicanism. Inherent in its use is the, however tacit, implication that the Provisional brand of Gerry Adams is true Irish republicanism. Because of this, to the bulk of Adams' opponents, 'dissident republican' is no longer a pejorative term. The mass of revelation about how the Adams leadership conducted its business at least during the second half of the troubles has justified the distance that individual republicans and their movements have created between themselves and the Provisional republicans. Indeed, those defined as dissidents do not see their existence on those terms; their struggle remains as it ever was, therefore why should they be considered to have dissented? Republican Sinn Féin are consistent on this issue; their first Ard Fheis following their split with Provisional Sinn Féin was considered their eighty-third.

The rioting that followed the Orange marches of 12 July in both 2009 and 2010 served as evidence of Sinn Féin's less than steady grip on the community. Even though the Provisional republican programme was recognised as being 'well organised [with] a brand of community politics which has involved many young people',[174] the inability of party representatives to stop the violence was telling. While Gerry Kelly, the MLA for Belfast North, could reasonably claim that his support had increased, after achieving nearly four thousand extra votes in the 2010 General Election compared to 2005, his protestations at the violence fell on deaf ears. Kelly and Sinn Féin no longer have a mandate over such protesters; these individuals are more inclined to support groups defined as dissidents.[175]

One former Provisional and Continuity IRA volunteer comments that membership of minority republican organisations is personality driven: 'It's about who you know and what group they are with', which suggests that politics, a major issue during earlier republican division, is less of a factor. He continues, 'I still believe in the armed struggle',[176] a fundamental part of the 'dissident' programme. Crucially, despite what appears to have been the best attempts of the Provisional IRA to totally decommission, sufficient weaponry still exists to allow for the continuation of republican violence. Of the estimated six tonnes that the IRA received from Libya during the 1980s, two tonnes was handed over as part of the final act of decommissioning.[177] Losing the man responsible for all IRA weaponry during the late 1990s undoubtedly facilitated significant loss of armaments to dissidents, and the complicated relationship between RIRA, CIRA and INLA during the early years of post-Good Friday Northern Ireland meant that weapon-sharing would have been highly likely.

As Northern Ireland attempts to move beyond the conflict, the issue of reconciliation has become divisive. Those seeking justice for victims of the troubles have been countered by those who query the wisdom of reopening emotional wounds. The most significant enquiry, costing almost £200 million and lasting twelve years, was the Saville Enquiry into Bloody Sunday. For some, this was a watershed moment as all the victims of Bloody Sunday were exonerated and soldiers from the Parachute Regiment were accused of acting with murderous intent. For others, however, notably Gregory Campbell, the DUP MP for East Londonderry, the enquiry was wasteful and achieved little: former Prime Minister John Major admitted in 1992 that those shot 'should be regarded as innocent of any allegation that they were shot whilst handling firearms or explosives'.[178] A loyalist viewpoint was that 'the report is being cherry-picked and the real losers are not the army, but Protestants again ... all this dealing with the past thing is nonsense ... The peace process is biased in favour of republicanism.'[179] The perception exists among loyalists that republicans have been granted access to political power in exchange for little more than the cessation of violence. The loyalist ceasefire did not see loyalist political groups ascend to power in Northern Ireland and the disillusion felt is rapidly increasing.

The first decade of the twenty-first century has proven that the dissident threat, while considerably lower than that of the Provisional IRA at the height of their campaign, is very real. Calls for unity between minority republican groups have yielded little success outside the occasional co-operation between the men of violence. The increased support that groups outside mainstream republicanism enjoy is obvious: politically from the presence of young members at the Republican Sinn Féin office on the Falls Road or at IRSP meetings; militarily from the increased activity by groups claiming the title Óglaigh na hÉireann. When the 32CSM states that 'volunteers are currently planning more operations in both Ireland and in England',[180] the threat is starkly obvious. While they note that 'probably only one operation in ten actually takes place',[181] the fact remains that they only need to be lucky once.

The most crucial aspect of republican division is that it has occurred in stages. The inability of these groups to coalesce has hindered minority

republicanism and prompted calls for unity among republicans. In disunity, these groups cannot hope to influence the path of Irish history. For
Richard O'Rawe:

> I find it difficult to believe that anyone, after the ferocity of the IRA campaign
> and the vigour with which it was pursued and the commitment that was given
> to it, seriously accepts or credibly believes that armed struggle is the way forward
> as a tactic . . . If the IRA couldn't bring about the condition under which the
> British could have been forced to withdraw, ten, fifteen, twenty or a hundred guys
> who don't seem to be anywhere near as committed as the IRA was are not going
> to do it. There's an immorality about fighting a war when you know you can't
> win.[182]

Marian Price argues:

> republicanism and republicans are not geared for a long war and that's why in
> the past IRA campaigns have probably lasted six years maximum because what
> happens is . . . people are killed, people go to prison, families become burnt out so
> the movement has to call halt because resources dry out, we're not designed for a
> long war we're designed for a short sharp hit and then retreat so the whole concept
> of a long war is a nonsense . . . Gerry Adams is long credited with masterminding
> the so-called long war and I don't believe that for a minute. I think what Gerry
> Adams was orchestrating was the long peace process.[183]

The irony of modern Northern Ireland is that a vote for Sinn Féin is
effectively a vote for peace, or, for Anthony McIntyre, a vote against the
IRA.[184] The reality is that, despite the revelations about how the Adams
leadership manoeuvred the republican movement throughout the duration of his leadership, the vast majority of people in Northern Ireland
have become tired of violence. Even though it may offend their ideological principles, the majority of republicans continue to support the Adams
programme, however begrudgingly, because the alternatives are considerably less appealing.

NOTES

1. Collins, E., *Killing Rage* (London: Granta Books, 1997).
2. *Irish Examiner* 12/3/2005.
3. *Times* 5/2/2009.
4. See 'Stop the Extradition of Sean Garland' http://www.seangarland.org/index.html
5. 'Trade Union and workers' rights activist Mick Finnegan elected' http://www.
   workerspartyireland.net/id163.html
6. 'Support for Sean Garland in the Senate' http://www.seangarland.org/seanad.html
7. *Daily Telegraph* 26/12/2004; *Guardian* 22/12/2004.
8. Ian Pearson MP, interview with author, Dudley, 2/9/2005.

9. 'An exchange between Charles Moore and Danny Morrison' http://www.danny morrison.com/wp-content/dannymorrisonarchive/021.htm 10/7/2010.
10. *Times* 22/9/2005.
11. Powell, *Great Hatred*, p. 262.
12. *Guardian* 19/2/2005; *Irish Times* 27/3/2009.
13. *Sunday Tribune* 13/2/2005.
14. BBC News, 'Arrest after stabbing victim dies' http://news.bbc.co.uk/1/hi/northern _ireland/4221599.stm 9/7/2009.
15. *Sunday Times* 28/6/2008.
16. *Guardian* 9/7/2008.
17. *Irish News* 27/1/2006.
18. Powell, *Great Hatred*, p. 267.
19. McIntyre, *Good Friday*, p. 158.
20. 'Sinn Féin votes to support policing', BBC News 28/1/2007 http://news.bbc.co.uk/1/ hi/northern_ireland/6308175.stm; 'Adams backs PSNI McCartney probe', BBC News, 31/1/2007 http://news.bbc.co.uk/1/hi/northern_ireland/6317565.stm
21. 'McCartney "killer" plans US move', BBC News, 22/12/2005 http://news.bbc. co.uk/1/hi/northern_ireland/4551468.stm
22. Marian Price, interview with author, Belfast, 1/7/2010.
23. *Daily Mail* 17/3/2005.
24. 'Providing a leading voice for human rights and democracy around the globe' http:// tedkennedy.org/service/item/foreign_policy
25. Richard O'Rawe, interview with author, Belfast, 15/2/2010
26. *Irish News* 12/3/2005.
27. Pat Ward, speaking on 14/6/1987, quoted in *Saoirse*, No. 3 July 1987.
28. The Pensive Quill, *Victory to the Blanketmen* http://thepensivequill.am/2009/09/ victory-to-blanketmen.html; Cllr McIvor: Sinn Féin 'allowed' no one to die on hunger strike http://www.longkesh.info/2009/10/10/cllr-mcivor-sinn-Féin-%E2% 80%98allowed%E2%80%99-no-one-to-die-on-hunger-strike/; Bobby Sands Trust, *Documents Still Withheld* http://www.bobbysandstrust.com/archives/1115; *Irish News* letters page, 9/4/2009.
29. Richard O'Rawe, interview with author, Belfast, 15/2/2010.
30. McIntyre, *Good Friday*, p. 84.
31. 'Sinn Féin's Gerry Adams denies McConville death claims', BBC News, 29/3/2010 http://news.bbc.co.uk/1/hi/northern_ireland/8591844.stm
32. Marian Price, interview with author, Belfast, 1/7/2010.
33. *Guardian* 19/2/2008.
34. Marian Price, interview with author, Belfast, 1/7/2010.
35. 32CSM member, interview with author, Dublin, 26/3/2010.
36. *TSN* May–June 2008; Marian Price, interview with author, Belfast, 1/7/2010.
37. Moloney, *Voices*, p. 297.
38. 'IRA "has destroyed all its arms"', BBC News, 26/9/2005 http://news.bbc.co.uk/1/hi/ northern_ireland/4283444.stm
39. *Guardian* 1/2/2006.
40. *Daily Telegraph* 6/10/2002.
41. Powell, *Great Hatred*, pp. 147–8.
42. *TSN* July–August 2007.

43. *Irish News* 1/6/2001.
44. 32CSM member, interview with author, Dublin, 26/3/2010.
45. *Independent* 23/9/2000.
46. *Observer* 5/11/2000.
47. 'Real IRA bombers jailed', BBC News, 9/4/2003 http://news.bbc.co.uk/1/hi/uk/2930957.stm
48. Real IRA Statement 20/10/2002 http://cain.ulst.ac.uk/othelem/organ/ira/rira201002.htm
49. 32CSM member, interview with author, Dublin, 26/3/2010.
50. Sands, M., 'The Framing of Michael McKevitt', *The Blanket* 22/6/2006.
51. *Belfast Telegraph* 7/8/2003.
52. *Sunday World* 22/1/2006.
53. 32CSM member, interview with author, Dublin, 26/3/2010.
54. *Guardian* 25/6/2003.
55. *Saoirse*, No. 197 September 2003.
56. 32CSM member, interview with author, Dublin, 26/3/2010.
57. *Sunday World* 1/9/2002.
58. *Scotsman* 16/1/2002; *Irish Times* 28/1/2008; *Times* 21/12/2007.
59. *Scotsman* 23/1/2002.
60. *TSN* May–June 2008.
61. Undated Sinn Féin statement, c. 1998, available in LHLPC.
62. 32CSM member, interview with author, Dublin, 26/3/2010.
63. *TSN* July–August 2007.
64. Ibid.
65. *TSN* August–September 2008.
66. Ibid.
67. Geraldine Taylor, interview with author, Belfast, 17/2/2010.
68. Marian Price, interview with author, Belfast, 1/7/2010.
69. *Sunday World* 5/3/2006.
70. *Tyrone Herald* 7/2/2008.
71. Independent Monitoring Commission (IMC) (2007). Seventeenth Report of the Independent Monitoring Commission (HC 18), (7 November 2007), London: The Stationery Office (TSO), pp. 11, 12, 14.
72. *Irish News* 11/5/2000.
73. 'PSNI officers survive landmine attack', RTE News, 16/6/2008 http://www.rte.ie/news/2008/0616/fermanagh.html; 'Dissident republican in rocket attack on police in Northern Ireland', *Guardian* 18/8/2008.
74. Independent Monitoring Commission (IMC).(2008). Twentieth Report of the Independent Monitoring Commission (HC 1112), (10 November 2008), London: The Stationery Office (TSO), p. 6.
75. MI5 'Dissident Irish Republicans' http://www.mi5.gov.uk/output/dissident-irish-republicans.html 16/6/2009.
76. *Daily Telegraph* 28/7/2008.
77. *TSN* August–September 2008.
78. Independent Monitoring Commission (IMC) (2007). Seventeenth Report of the Independent Monitoring Commission (HC 18) (7 November 2007), London: The Stationery Office (TSO), pp. 11, 12, 14.

79. 'Real IRA was behind army attack' http://news.bbc.co.uk/1/hi/northern_ireland/7930995.stm 10/3/2009.
80. 32CSM member, interview with author, Dublin, 26/3/2010.
81. Ibid.
82. 'Massareene', *The Pensive Quill*, 8/3/2009 http://thepensivequill.am/2009/03/massereene.html
83. 'Continuity IRA shot dead officer', BBC News, 10/3/2009 http://news.bbc.co.uk/1/hi/northern_ireland/7934426.stm
84. *Daily Telegraph* 28/7/2008.
85. 32CSM member, interview with author, Dublin, 26/3/2010.
86. *Times* 11/3/2009.
87. *Times* 13/3/2009.
88. *TSN* May–June 2009.
89. *Times* Online, 24/3/2009 http://www.timesonline.co.uk/tol/comment/columnists/guest_contributors/article5962357.ece 16/6/2009; 'Paramilitaries still a threat in Nth Ireland: Experts', in *Brisbane Times* 10/3/2009 http://www.brisbanetimes.com.au/news/world/paramilitaries-still-a-threat-in-nth-ireland-experts/2009/03/10/1236447188908.html 11/3/2009.
90. Moloney, *Secret History*, pp. 446, 453, 470–1; Powell, *Great Hatred*, p. 2.
91. See BBC report 'Sinn Féin expels "British Agent"' http://news.bbc.co.uk/2/hi/uk_news/northern_ireland/4535774.stm 16/6/2009.
92. *Times* 29/5/2006.
93. BBC report, 'Sinn Féin British agent shot dead' http://news.bbc.co.uk/2/hi/uk_news/northern_ireland/4877516.stm 16/6/2009.
94. *Guardian* 19/8/2003.
95. Former Provisional republican, interview with author, Belfast, 2/7/2010.
96. *TSN* February–March 2006.
97. Geraldine Taylor, interview with author, Belfast, 17/2/2010.
98. *TSN* May–June 2009.
99. *Observer* 4/6/2006.
100. Marian Price, interview with author, Belfast, 1/7/2010.
101. *TSN* May–June 2009.
102. *Belfast Telegraph* 14/4/2009.
103. *TSN* October–November 2006.
104. *TSN* May–June 2009.
105. 'Minister sets out legislation to protect fire fighters', The Department of Health, Social Services and Public Safety, 21/7/2005 http://archive.nics.gov.uk/hss/050721a-hss.htm
106. *Irish Independent* 30/8/2009.
107. *Times* 19/8/2009.
108. *TSN* May–June 2009.
109. 'Bomb "was left to kill officers"', BBC News, 8/9/2009 http://news.bbc.co.uk/1/hi/northern_ireland/8244138.stm
110. '400 lb Bomb left at Policing Board', BBC News, 22/11/2009 http://news.bbc.co.uk/1/hi/northern_ireland/8372713.stm
111. 'Murder bid Police Officer moves out of Intensive Care', BBC News, 20/2/2010 http://news.bbc.co.uk/1/hi/northern_ireland/8525838.stm

112. See 'Family of Shot Man Criticise MI5', BBC News, 27/2/2010 http://news.bbc.co.uk/1/hi/northern_ireland/8540110.stm and 'Real IRA admits to border killing', BBC News, 26/2/2010 http://news.bbc.co.uk/1/hi/northern_ireland/foyle_and_west/8535731.stm

113. Lieutenant General Andrew Graham CBE, interview with author, Shrivenham, 29/1/2010.

114. Independent Monitoring Commission (IMC) (2009). Twenty-First Report of the Independent Monitoring Commission (HC 496) (7 May 2009), London: The Stationery Office (TSO), p. 11.

115. Sunday Tribune 25/3/2007; Belfast Telegraph 18/3/2007.

116. Former Continuity IRA volunteer, interview with author, Belfast, 2/7/2010.

117. Marian Price, interview with author, Belfast, 1/7/2010.

118. Independent Monitoring Commission (IMC) (2008). Eighteenth Report of the Independent Monitoring Commission (HC 496) (1 May 2008), London: The Stationery Office (TSO), p. 4.

119. 32CSM member, interview with author, Dublin, 26/3/2010.

120. Richard O'Rawe, interview with author, Belfast, 15/2/2010.

121. Geraldine Taylor, interview with author, Belfast, 17/2/2010.

122. Dessie O'Hagan, interview with author, Belfast, 10/8/2007.

123. IN 27/5/2010, 10/6/2010.

124. Belfast Telegraph 29/3/1996.

125. Geraldine Taylor, interview with author, Belfast, 17/2/2010.

126. Irish Independent 15/12/2002.

127. Independent, 4/6/2004.

128. Breen, S., 'INLA Claims Responsibility for murder of Derry Drug Dealer' http://www.tribune.ie/news/home-news/article/2009/feb/15/inla-claims-responsibility-for-murder-of-derry-dru/ 15/2/2009; 'INLA Say They Shot Father of Three', Derry Journal http://www.derryjournal.com/journal/INLA-say-they-shot-fatherofthree.5576249.jp 21/8/2009.

129. Independent Monitoring Commission (IMC) (2007). Seventeenth Report of the Independent Monitoring Commission (HC 18) (7 November 2007), London: The Stationery Office (TSO), pp. 11, 12, 14.

130. Breen, S., 'INLA Claims to have Ceased its Operation in Dublin', Sunday Tribune http://saoirse32.blogsome.com/2009/03/09/inla-claims-to-have-ceased-its-operations-in-dublin/ 8/3/2009.

131. Irish Times, 12/10/2009.

132. Irish Times 12/10/2009.

133. Kearney, V., Northern Ireland INLA Paramilitaries Dump Terror Cache http://news.bbc.co.uk/1/hi/northern_ireland/8501929.stm 6/2/2010.

134. Anthony McIntyre, interview with author, Belfast, 7/9/2005.

135. Eoin Ó Broin, Interview with author, Belfast, 20/5/2005.

136. The Plough, Vol. 2 No. 42 27/6/2005.

137. Easter Statement from IRSP leadership, 2/4/1999.

138. Fra Halligan, interview with author, Belfast, 25/2/2010.

139. Power, T., The Ta Power Document http://irsm.org/history/tapowerdoc.html 27/7/2004.

140. éirígí: For a Socialist Republic http://www. eirigi.org/about_us/faq.htm

141. Ibid.
142. *Guardian* 1/9/2008.
143. Ibid.
144. éirígí: For a Socialist Republic http://www. eirigi.org/campaigns/index.htm; *Belfast Telegraph* 2/11/2008.
145. McKittrick et al., *Lost Lives* pp. 1192–3, 'Friends of Colin Duffy' http://friendsofcolin duffy.com/default.aspx.
146. 'Who is Colin Duffy', BBC News, 27/3/2009 http://news.bbc.co.uk/1/hi/northern _ireland/7967680.stm.
147. *Daily Telegraph* 14/3/2009.
148. 32CSM member, interview with author, Dublin, 26/3/2010.
149. éirígí: For a Socialist Republic http://www.eirigi.org/campaigns/spot_difference.html
150. *Irish News* 1/8/2009.
151. Wood, *Crimes of Loyalty*, p. 266.
152. Billy McQuiston, interview with author, Belfast, 1/7/2010.
153. Wood, I., 'Loyalist Paramilitaries and the Peace Process', pp. 181–204, in Barton, B. and Roche, P. J., *The Northern Ireland Question: The Peace Process and the Belfast Agreement* (Basingstoke: Palgrave Macmillan, 2009), p. 194.
154. 'Faith, hate and murder', *Guardian* 17/11/2001.
155. Wood, *Crimes of Loyalty*, p. 275.
156. 'Killer of Rosemary Nelson is named', *Sunday Herald* 16/6/2002.
157. Ibid.
158. Wood, I., 'Loyalist Paramilitaries and the Peace Process', p. 194.
159. Billy McQuiston, interview with author, Belfast, 1/7/2010.
160. McKittrick et al., *Lost Lives*, p. 1521.
161. *Independent* 20/3/2004.
162. *Observer* 19/2/2006.
163. *Press Gazette* 16/11/2007.
164. *Belfast Telegraph* 8/12/2009.
165. Wood, 'Loyalist Paramilitaries', p. 199.
166. Billy McQuiston, interview with author, Belfast, 1/7/2010.
167. *Times* 25/6/2006.
168. Wood, 'Loyalist Paramilitaries', p. 186.
169. Edwards, A., 'Abandoning Armed Resistance? The Ulster Volunteer Force as a case study of Strategic Terrorism in Northern Ireland', pp. 146–66, in *Studies in Conflict and Terrorism* Vol. 32 No. 2 2009, p. 153.
170. *Belfast Telegraph* 24/11/2008, 'Paramilitary Shoukri group gives up final arms', BBC News, 3/3/2010 http://news.bbc.co.uk/1/hi/uk_politics/8547504.stm
171. Independent Monitoring Commission (IMC) (2006). Twelfth Report of the Independent Monitoring Commission (October 2006), London: The Stationery Office (TSO), p. 7.
172. Independent Monitoring Commission (IMC) (2009). Twenty-Second Report of the Independent Monitoring Commission (HC 1085) (4 November 2009), London: The Stationery Office (TSO), pp. 15–20.
173. *Times* 26/5/2009.
174. Ian Pearson MP, interview with author, Dudley, 2/9/2005.
175. *IN* 6/11/2002.

176. Former Continuity IRA volunteer, interview with author, Belfast, 2/7/2010.
177. Oppenheimer, *IRA*, pp. 85, 193.
178. *Independent*, 11/6/2010.
179. Communication from loyalist source, Belfast, 17/6/2010.
180. 32CSM member, interview with author, Dublin, 26/3/2010.
181. Ibid.
182. Richard O'Rawe, interview with author, Belfast, 15/2/2010.
183. Marian Price, interview with author, Belfast, 1/7/2010.
184. Anthony McIntyre, interview with author, Belfast, 7/9/2005.

Bibliography

Manuscripts/Archives

Boston Public Library, Boston MA, USA – Public Papers of the Presidents of the United States.

Burns Library, Boston College, Boston MA, USA –Irish Manuscripts Collection, Irish Political Pamphlets, Charitable Irish Society Records, Thomas P. O'Neill Papers.

Linen Hall Library Political Collection, Belfast – IRSP/INLA Box, Holland and McDonald Box, Hunger Strikes Boxes, Workers' Party Box, Loyalism Boxes, Provisional IRA Boxes, IRA (CIRA, RIRA) Box, IRA (Provisional) Boxes, Peace Process Boxes, UDA Boxes, Loyalist Workers' Movement Press Cuttings, Republican Clubs Press Cuttings, IRSP Press Cuttings, INLA Press Cuttings, Supergrass Trials Press Cuttings, Bernadette Devlin Press Cuttings, IRA Press Cuttings, Sinn Féin Press Cuttings.

National Archive, Kew – Foreign and Commonwealth Office Files, Ministry of Defence Files.

National Archive of Ireland, Dublin – Taoiseach Papers, Department of Foreign Affairs Papers, Jack Lynch Papers.

Papers in Private Possession – Papers in personal possession of Ian S. Wood.

Public Records Office of Northern Ireland – Cabinet Files, Central Secretariat Files, Northern Ireland Constitutional Convention Files, Office of the Executive Files, Northern Ireland Office Files, Community Relations Files, Paddy Devlin Papers.

Tamiment Library and Robert F. Wagner Labor Archives, Elmer Holmes Bobst Library, New York University, New York NY, USA – The Archives of Irish-America, George Harrison Papers, Irish Republicanism Collection.

The American Catholic History Research Center and University Archives, Catholic University of America, Washington, DC, USA – Thomas J. Shahan Papers, National Catholic War Council (NCWC) Papers, Muldoon-Burke Files,

Chairman's Files, National Catholic Welfare Conference Papers, Organizations: Secular 1921 66 Papers, Office of the General Secretary (OGS)/Executive Department Consultant on International Affairs and Inter-American Bureau Papers.

University College Dublin Archives, UCD Library, Dublin Sighle Humphreys Papers, Moss Twomey Papers.

Interviews and Correspondence

Journalist, Belfast, 15/11/2004.

Gerry Ruddy, Irish Republican Socialist Party, Belfast, 24/11/2004.

Sammy Duddy, Ulster Political Research Group North Belfast Spokesman, Belfast, 21/1/2005, 10/11/2006.

Danny Morrison, former Sinn Féin Director of Publicity, Belfast, 24/1/2005, 13/7/2007.

Eoin O'Broin, Director of European Affairs, Sinn Féin, Belfast, 20/5/2005.

Ian Pearson, Member of Parliament, former Northern Ireland Office minister, Dudley, 2/9/2005.

Anthony McIntyre, former IRA prisoner and writer, Belfast, 7/9/2005.

John Lynn, CBE, former Chairman, Northern Ireland Milk Marketing Board, Coleraine, 19/2/2006.

Tom Boyle, Irish American Heritage Center, Chicago, IL, USA, 10/4/2007.

Sean McKeown, former Workers' Party member, Belfast, 10/7/2007.

Geraldine Taylor, Vice-President, Republican Sinn Féin, Belfast, 8/8/2007, 17/2/2010.

John Lowry, General Secretary, The Workers' Party, Belfast, 9/8/2007.

Des O'Hagan, Central Executive, The Workers' Party, Belfast, 9/8/2007.

Roy Johnston, author and commentator, 4/3/2008.

Ex-E4A officer, Scotland, 28/7/2009.

Ex-Special Branch officer, Scotland, 30/7/2009.

Lieutenant General Sir Alistair Irwin, former General Officer Commanding, Northern Ireland, Aberlour, 16/2/2009.

Lieutenant General Andrew Graham, CBE, former Commander 39 Brigade, Shrivenham, 29/1/2010.

Richard O'Rawe, former IRA volunteer and author, Belfast, 15/2/2010, 25/3/2010.

Fra Halligan, IRSP Ard Comhairle, Belfast, 25/2/2010.

Gerard Hodgins, former IRA volunteer, Belfast, 25/3/2010.

32 County Sovereignty Movement member, Dublin, 26/3/2010.

Anthony Coughlan, former Connolly Association member, Dublin, 15/6/2010.

Martin Galvin, prominent Irish-American activist, 21/6/2010.

Billy McQuiston, Ulster Political Research Group West Belfast, Belfast, 1/7/2010.

Marian Price, republican commentator, Belfast, 1/7/2010.

Former Provisional republican, Belfast, 2/7/2010.

Former Continuity IRA volunteer, Belfast, 2/7/2010.
Loyalist source, Belfast, 17/6/2010.
Lord Dafydd Elis-Thomas AM, 6/9/2010.

Newspapers and Journals

An Phoblacht; *An Phoblacht/Republican News*; *Belfast Morning News*; *Belfast Telegraph*; *Boston Evening Globe*; *Boston Globe*; *Boston Sunday Globe*; *Chicago Sun-Times*; *Daily Express*; *Daily Mirror*; *Daily Telegraph*; *Durham Morning Herald*; *Evening Herald*; *Fortnight*; *Guardian*; *Hibernia*; *Intercontinental Press*; *International Herald Tribune*; *Irish Echo*; *Irish Independent*; *Irish News*; *Irish Political Studies*; *Irish Press*; *Irish Republican Observer*; *Irish Times*; *Marxism Today*; *New York Times*; *News Letter*; *Newsweek*; *Observer*; *Pegasus: The Journal of the Airborne Forces*; *Philadelphia Daily News*; *Randolph Herald*; *Rocky Mountain News*; *San Francisco Examiner*; *Salt Lake Tribune*; *Saoirse Irish Freedom*; *Socialist Review*; *Staten Island Advance*; *Sunday Business Post*; *Sunday Independent*; *Sunday Life*; *Sunday Mirror*; *Sunday News*; *Sunday Press*; *Sunday Tribune*; *Sunday World*; *Terrorism and Political Violence*; *Time*; *The Argus*; *The Armagh Observer*; *The Boston Herald American*; *The Irish People*; *The Journal of Communist Studies*; *The Militant*; *The Pilot*; *The Star-Ledger*; *The Sun (Baltimore)*; *The Sunday Times*; *The Sunday Tribune*; *The United Irishman*; *The Washington Star*; *The Weekender and Press, Cambridge (MA)*; *The Weekender and Supplement to Watertown (MA)*; *Troops Out*; *Village Voice*; *Workers' Press*.

Books

Adair, J., *Mad Dog* (London: John Blake 2007).

Adams, G., *The Politics of Irish Freedom* (Dingle: Brandon 1986).

— *Cage Eleven* (Dingle: Brandon 1990).

— *Hope and History: Making Peace in Ireland* (Dingle: Brandon 2003).

Adams, J., *The Financing of Terror* (Sevenoaks: New English Library 1986).

— with Morgan, R., Ambush: *The War Between the SAS and the IRA* (London: Macmillan 1988).

Anderson, C., *The Billy Boy: The Life and Death of LVF Leader Billy Wright* (Edinburgh: Mainstream 2002).

Anderson, W. K., *James Connolly and the Irish Left* (Blackrock: Irish Academic Press 1994).

Bambery, C., *Ireland's Permanent Revolution* (London: Bookmarks 1986).

Bartlett, T. (ed.), *The Life of Theobald Wolfe Tone* (Dublin: The Lilliput Press 1998).

Barton, B. and Roche, P. J. (eds), *The Northern Ireland Question: The Peace Process and the Belfast Agreement* (Basingstoke: Palgrave Macmillan 2009).

Bean, K., *Recent Developments in Irish Republican Ideology and Strategy* (Liverpool:

University of Liverpool Institute of Irish Studies Occasional Papers 1994).

— *The New Politics of Sinn Féin* (Liverpool: Liverpool University Press 2007).

Berresford Ellis, P., *A History of the Irish Working Class* 2nd edn (London: Pluto Press 1985) (1st edn 1972).

Bew, P., Gibbon, P. and Patterson, H., *Northern Ireland 1921/2001 Political Forces and Social Classes* (London: Serif 2002).

— and Patterson, H., *Sean Lemass and the Making of Modern Ireland* (Dublin: Gill and Macmillan 1982).

Bishop, P. and Mallie, E., *The Provisional IRA* (London: Heinemann 1987).

Bowman, J., *De Valera and the Ulster Question 1917–1973* (Oxford: Oxford University Press 1989) (1st edn 1982).

Bowyer Bell, J., *The Secret Army: The IRA* (Dublin: Poolbeg 1997) (1st edn 1970).

Bradley, A. K., *History of the Irish in America* (Secaucus: Chartwell Books 1986).

Bradley, G., with Feeney, B., *Insider: Gerry Bradley's Life in the IRA* (Dublin: The O'Brien Press, 2009).

Brady, C. (ed.), *Historical Revisionism 1938–1994* (Dublin: Irish Academic Press 1994).

Brannigan, J., *Brendan Behan: Cultural Nationalism and the Revisionist Writer* (Dublin: Four Courts Press 2002).

Bruce, S., *No Pope of Rome: Anti-Catholicism in Modern Scotland* (Edinburgh: Mainstream 1985).

— *The Red Hand: Protestant Paramilitaries in Northern Ireland* (Oxford: Oxford University Press 1992).

Burton, F., *The Politics of Legitimacy: Struggles in a Belfast Community* (London: Routledge and Kegan Paul Ltd 1978).

Byman, D., *Deadly Connections: States that Sponsor Terrorism* (Cambridge: Cambridge University Press, 2005).

Byron, R., *Irish America* (Oxford: Oxford University Press, 1999).

Campbell, B., McKeown, L. and O'Hagan, F. (eds), *Nor Meekly Serve My Time* (Belfast: Beyond the Pale Publications 2006) (1st edn 1994).

Clark, D., *Irish Blood: Northern Ireland and the American Conscience* (London: Kennikat Press Corp. 1977).

Clarke, G., *Border Crossing: True Stories of the RUC Special Branch, the Garda Special Branch and the IRA Moles* (Dublin: Gill and Macmillan 2009).

Clarke, L. and Johnston, K., *Martin McGuinness: From Guns to Government* 2nd edn (Edinburgh: Mainstream 2003) (1st edn 2001).

Clifford, B., *Against Ulster Nationalism* (Belfast: Athol Books 1992).

Coakley, J. and Gallagher, M., *Politics in the Republic of Ireland* 4th edn (London: Routledge 2005) (1st edn, PSAI Press 1992).

Collins, E., *Killing Rage* (London: Granta Books 1997).

Communist Party of Ireland *Armed Struggle* (Dublin: A Communist Party Pamphlet 1988).

Connolly, R. E., *Armalite and Ballot Box: An Irish-American Republican Primer* (Fort Wayne: Cuchullain Publications 1985).

Coogan, T. P., *The IRA* (London: HarperCollins 2000).

Coombes, A. E., *History after apartheid: Visual Culture and Public Memory in a Democratic South Africa* (Durham, NC, Duke University Press, 2003).

Corrigan, P., *Soldier U: SAS Bandit Country* (Rochester: 22 Books 1995).

Coughlan, A., *C. Desmond Greaves, 1913–1988: An Obituary Essay* (Dublin: Irish Labour History Society 1990).

— *The Northern Crisis: Which Way Forward?* (Dublin: Dublin University Press Ltd 1969).

— *Fooled Again? The Anglo-Irish Agreement and After* (Dublin: The Mercier Press 1986).

Cox, M., Guelke, A. and Stephen, F., *A Farewell to Arms? Beyond the Good Friday Agreement* (Manchester: Manchester University Press 2006) (1st edn 2000).

Crawford, C., *Inside the UDA: Volunteers and Violence* (London: Pluto Press 2003).

Cronin, M., *The Blueshirts and Irish Politics* (Dublin: Four Courts Press 1997).

Cronin, S., *Washington's Irish Policy 1916–1986: Independence, Partition, Neutrality* (Dublin: Anvil Books 1987).

Cummins, I., *Marx, Engels and National Movements* (London: Croom Helm 1980).

Cusack, J. and McDonald, H., *UVF* 2nd edn (Dublin: Poolbeg 2000) (1st edn 1997).

Davis, H. B., *Nationalism and Socialism: Marxist and Labor Theories of Nationalism to 1917* (London: Monthly Review Press 1967).

De Baroid, C., *Ballymurphy and the Irish War* revised edn (London: Pluto Press 2000) (1st edn 1989).

Devlin, B., *The Price of My Soul* (London: Pan Books 1969).

Dezell, M., *Irish America Coming into Clover: The Evolution of a People and a Culture* (New York: Doubleday 2001).

Dillon, M., *The Trigger Men* (Edinburgh: Mainstream 2004).

— *Killer in Clowntown: Joe Doherty, The IRA and the Special Relationship* (London: Hutchinson 1992).

— and Lehane, D., *Political Murder in Northern Ireland* (Harmondsworth: Penguin 1973).

Dobson, C. and Payne, R., *The Terrorists: Their Weapons, Leaders and Tactics* (New York: Facts on File Inc. 1982).

Doherty, P. and Hegarty, P., *Paddy Bogside* (Cork: Mercier Press 2001).

Doorley, M., *Irish-American Diaspora Nationalism: The Friends of Irish Freedom, 1916–1935* (Dublin: Four Courts Press 2005).

Dudley Edwards, O. and Pyle, F. (eds), *1916 – The Easter Rising* (London: MacGibbon and Kee 1968).

Dunnigan, J. P., *Deep-Rooted Conflict and the IRA Cease-Fire* (Lanham: University Press of American Inc. 1995).

Dunphy, R., *The Making of Fianna Fail Power in Ireland 1923–1948* (Oxford: Clarendon Press 1995).

Dupuy, T. N., *Understanding War: History and Theory of Combat* (London: Leo Cooper 1992).

English, R., *Armed Struggle: The History of the IRA* (London: Pan MacMillan 2003).

— *Radicals and the Republic* (Oxford: Clarendon Press 1994).

Edwards, A., *A History of the Northern Ireland Labour Party: Democratic Socialism and Sectarianism* (Manchester: Manchester University Press 2009).

— 'Abandoning Armed Resistance? The Ulster Volunteer Force as a case study of Strategic Terrorism in Northern Ireland', pp. 146–66, in *Studies in Conflict and Terrorism* Vol. 32, No. 2, 2009.

Faul, D. and Murray, R., *The Sleeping Giant: Irish Americans and Human Rights in N. Ireland* (no publisher, no date).

Feeney, B., *Sinn Féin: A Hundred Turbulent Years* (Dublin: Poolbeg Press 2002).

Fisk, R., *The Great War for Civilisation: The Conquest of the Middle East* (London: Harper Perennial, 2006) (1st edn 2005).

Flackes, W. D. and Elliott, S., *Northern Ireland: A Political Directory 1968–88* (Belfast: The Blackstaff Press 1989).

Flynn, B., *Soldiers of Folly: The IRA Border Campaign 1956–1962* (Cork: The Collins Press 2009).

Foley, G., *Ireland in Rebellion* (New York: Pathfinder Press 1971).

Foster, R., *Modern Ireland 1600–1972* (London: Penguin 1988).

— *Luck and the Irish: A Brief History of Change, 1970–2000* (London: Penguin 2007)

Foy, M. and Barton, B., *The Easter Rising* (Stroud: Sutton 1999).

Frampton, M., *The Long March: The Political Strategy of Sinn Féin 1981–2007* (London: Palgrave Macmillan 2009).

Gailey, I. B., Gillespie, W. F. and Hassett, J., *An Account of the Territorials in Northern Ireland 1947–1978* (Belfast: Territorial, Auxiliary and Volunteer Reserve Association for Northern Ireland 1979).

Garland, R., *Gusty Spence* (Belfast: The Blackstaff Press 2001).

Garvin, T., *The Evolution of Irish Nationalism* (Dublin: Gill and Macmillan 2005) (1st edn 1981).

Geldard, I. and Craig, K., *IRA, INLA: Foreign Support and International Connections* (London: Institute for the Study of Terrorism 1988).

Gilmour, R., *Infiltrating the IRA: Dead Ground* (London: Little, Brown 1998).

Greaves, C. D., *Northern Ireland: Civil Rights and Political Wrongs* (Dublin: Communist Party of Ireland 1969).

— *Reminiscences of the Connolly Association* (London: Connolly Association 1978).

Greer, S., *Supergrasses: A Study in Anti-Terrorist Law Enforcement in Northern Ireland* (Oxford: Clarendon Press 1995).

Guelke, A., 'The American Connection to the Northern Ireland Conflict', in *Irish Studies in International Affairs* Vol. 1, No. 4, 1984, pp. 27–39.

Hanley, B., *The IRA 1926–1936* (Dublin: Four Courts Press 2002).

— 'The Politics of Noraid', in *Irish Political Studies* Vol. 19, No. 1, Summer 2004, pp. 1–17.

— and Miller, S., *The Lost Revolution: The Story of the Official IRA and the Workers' Party* (Dublin: Penguin 2009).

Harnden, T., *Bandit Country: The IRA and South Armagh* (London: Hodder and Stoughton 1999).

Hayden, T., *Irish on the Inside: In Search of the Soul of Irish America* (New York: Verso 2001).

Henderson, L., Miller, D. and Reilly, J., *Speak No Evil: The British Broadcasting Ban, the Media and the Conflict in Ireland* (Glasgow: Glasgow University Media Group 1990).

Hennessey, T., *A History of Northern Ireland 1920–1996* (London: Palgrave 1997).

Henry, R. M., *The Evolution of Sinn Féin* (Dublin: The Talbot Press Limited 1920).

Her Majesty's Stationery Office, The Compton Report: Report of the enquiry into allegations against the Security Forces of physical brutality in Northern Ireland arising out of events on the 9th August, 1971 http://www.cain.ulst.ac.uk/hmso/compton.htm

Holland, J., *The American Connection: U.S. Guns, Money and Influence in Northern Ireland* (New York: Penguin 1987).

— *Too Long a Sacrifice: Life and Death in Northern Ireland Since 1969* (New York: Dodd, Mead 1981).

— and McDonald, H., *INLA: Deadly Divisions* (Dublin: Torc 1994).

Howell, D., *A Lost Left: Three Studies in Socialism and Nationalism* (Manchester: Manchester University Press 1986).

Irish Republican Army *With the IRA in the Fight for Freedom 1919 to the Truce* (Tralee: The Kerryman 1955).

— *In the 70s The IRA Speaks* A Repsol Pamphlet No. 3 Undated.

Irish Republican Socialist Movement, *Aims, Principles, and Politics* http://www.irsm.org/history/costello/seamus03.html

— *Twenty Years of Struggle* http://irsm.org/history/irsm20yr.html.

— *Republicans and the Protestant Working Class: A Discussion Document* http://www.irsm.org/statements/irsp/current/030502.html

— *Seamus Costello: Political Biography* (The Seamus Costello Memorial Committee 1979).

— *H-Block/Armagh Broad Front – An Assessment* (undated).

Irwin, T., 'Prison Education in Northern Ireland: Learning from our Paramilitary

Past', in *The Howard Journal of Criminal Justice* Vol. 42, Issue 5, pp. 471–84.

Johnston, R. H. W., *Century of Endeavour: A Biographical and Autobiographical view of the Twentieth Century in Ireland* (Dublin: The Lilliput Press 2006) (USA: Academica/Manusel 2003).

Keane, E., *Sean MacBride: A Life* (Dublin: Gill and Macmillan 2007).

Kearney, C., *The Writings of Brendan Behan* (Dublin: Gill and Macmillan 1977).

Kearney, R., *Postnationalist Ireland: Politics, Culture, Philosophy* (London: Routledge 1997).

Kelleher, D., *Irish Republicanism: The Authentic Perspective* (Greystones: Justice Books 2001).

Kelley, K., *The Longest War: Northern Ireland and the IRA* (London: Zed Books 1983).

Kennedy, E. M., *True Compass* (New York: Twelve Books 2009).

Keogh, D., *The Rise of the Irish Working Class* (Belfast: The Appletree Press 1982).

Lee, J. J. and Casey, M. R. (eds), *Making the Irish American: History and Heritage of the Irish in the United States* (New York: New York University Press 2006).

— and Ó Tuathaigh, G., *The Age of de Valera* (Dublin: Ward River Press 1982).

Lenin, V. I., *Lenin Collected Works* (Moscow: Progress Publishers 1965).

Lister, D. and Jordan, H., *Mad Dog: The Rise and Fall of Johnny Adair and C Company* (Edinburgh: Mainstream 2003).

MacEoin, U., *The IRA in the Twilight Years 1923–1948* (Dublin: Argenta Publications 1997).

MacStiofain, S., *Memoirs of a Revolutionary* (Edinburgh: Gordon Cremonesi 1975).

Manning, M., *The Blueshirts* (Dublin: Gill and Macmillan 2006).

Marx, K. and Engels, F., *Ireland and the Irish Question* (Moscow: Progress Publishers 1971).

Maillot, A., *New Sinn Féin: Irish Republicanism in the Twenty-First Century* (London: Routledge 2005).

McAuley, J., *The Politics of Identity: A Loyalist Community in Belfast* (Aldershot: Avebury 1994).

McCaffrey, L. (ed.), *Irish Nationalism and the American Contribution* (New York: Amo Press 1976).

— *The Irish Diaspora in America* (London: Indiana University Press 1996).

McCann, E., *War and an Irish Town* (Harmondsworth: Penguin 1974).

McCann, S., *The Fighting Irish* (London: Leslie Frewin Publishers 1972).

MacDermott, E., *Clann na Poblachta* (Cork: Cork University Press 1998).

McDermott, J., *Northern Divisions: The Old IRA and the Belfast Pogroms 1920–22* (Belfast: Beyond the Pale 2001).

McDonald, H. and Cusack, J., *UDA: Inside the Heart of Loyalist Terror* (Dublin: Penguin 2004).

McDonald, H., *Colours: Ireland From Bombs to Boom* (Edinburgh: Mainstream 2004).

— *Gunsmoke and Mirrors: How Sinn Féin Dressed up Defeat as Victory* (Dublin: Gill and Macmillan 2008).

McElrath, K., *Unsafe Haven: The United States, the IRA and Political Prisoners* (London: Pluto Press 2000).

McEvoy, K., *Paramilitary Imprisonment in Northern Ireland: Resistance, Management and Release* (Oxford: Oxford University Press 2001).

McGarry, F., *Irish Politics and the Spanish Civil War* (Cork: Cork University Press 1999).

— *Eoin O'Duffy: A Self-Made Hero* (Oxford: Oxford University Press 2005).

— *The Rising Ireland: Easter 1916* (Oxford: Oxford University Press 2010).

McGladdery, G., *The Provisional IRA in England: The Bombing Campaign 1973–1997* (Dublin: Irish Academic Press 2006).

McGuire, M., *To Take Arms: A Year in the Provisional IRA* (London: Macmillan 1973).

McKeown, L., *Out of Time: Irish Republican Prisoners Long Kesh 1972–2000* (Belfast: Beyond the Pale 2001).

McKittrick, D.; Kelters, S.; Feeney, B.; Thornton, C.; McVea, D., *Lost Lives* (Edinburgh: Mainstream 2004) (1st edn 1999).

McIntyre, A., *Good Friday: The Death of Irish Republicanism* (New York: Ausubo Press 2008).

McMichael, G., *Ulster Voice: In Search of Common Ground in Northern Ireland* (Dublin: Roberts Rinehart Publishers 1999).

McNamee, P. and Lovett, T., *Working Class Community in Northern Ireland* (Belfast: Ulster People's College 1987).

Meagher, T., *The Columbia Guide to Irish American History* (New York: Columbia University Press 2005).

Metscher, P., *Republicanism and Socialism in Ireland* (Frankfurt: Verlag Peter Lang 1986).

Milotte, M., *Communism in Modern Ireland: The Pursuit of the Workers Republic since 1916* (Dublin: Gill and Macmillan 1984).

Moloney, E., *A Secret History of the IRA* (London: Penguin 2002).

— *Voices From The Grave: Two Men's War in Ireland* (London: Faber and Faber 2010).

Mooney, J. and O'Toole, M., *Black Operations: The Secret War against the Real IRA* (Ashbourne: Maverick House 2003).

Morgan, A. and Purdie, B., *Ireland: Divided Nation, Divided Class* (London: Ink Links 1980).

Morris, C. R., *American Catholic: The Saints and Sinners Who Built America's Most Powerful Church* (New York: Vintage Books 1997).

Morrison, D., *Ireland: The Censored Subject* (Belfast: Sinn Féin Publicity Department 1989).

— *Then The Walls Came Down: A Prison Journal* (Cork: Mercier Press 1999).

Mulholland, M., *The Longest War: Northern Ireland's Troubled History* (Oxford: Oxford University Press 2002).

Munck, R., *The Difficult Dialogue: Marxism and Nationalism* (London: Zed Books 1986).

Murray, G. and Tonge, J., *Sinn Féin and the SDLP: From Alienation to Participation* (Dublin: The O'Brien Press 2005).

Myers, K., *Watching the Door: Cheating Death in 1970s Belfast* (London: Atlantic Books 2006).

Nic Dháibhéid, C. and Reid, C. (eds), *From Parnell to Paisley: Constitutional and Revolutionary Politics in Modern Ireland* (Dublin: Irish Academic Press 2010).

O'Ballance, E., *Terror in Ireland: The Heritage of Hate* (Novato: Presidio Press 1981).

Ó Brádaigh, R., *Dilseacht: The Story of Comdt. General Tom Maguire and the Second (All-Ireland) Dail* (Dublin: Irish Freedom Press 1997).

— *Our People Our Future* (Dublin: Sinn Féin Lower Kevin St 1973).

O'Brien, R. B. (ed.), *The Autobiography of Theobald Wolfe Tone* (London: T. Fisher Unwin undated).

O'Carroll, J. P. and Murphy, J. A. (eds), *De Valera and His Times* (Cork: Cork University Press 1986).

O'Casey, S., *The Story of the Irish Citizen Army* (New York: Oriole Editions 1919).

O'Connor, T., *The Boston Irish: A Political History* (Boston: Back Bay Books 1995).

O'Doherty, M., *The Trouble with Guns: Republican Strategy and the Provisional IRA* (Belfast: The Blackstaff Press 1998).

O'Donnell, P., *Proud Island* (Dublin: The O'Brien Press 1975).

O'Drisceoil, D., *Peader O'Donnell* (Cork: Cork University Press 2001).

O'Hagan, D., *The Concept of Republicanism* (Dublin: The Workers' Party undated).

O'Hanlon, R., *The New Irish Americans* (Niwot: Roberts Rinehart Publishers 1998).

O'Hearn, D., *Nothing But An Unfinished Song: Bobby Sands, The Irish Hunger Striker Who Ignited a Generation* (New York: Nation Books 2006).

O'Loughlin, M., *Frank Ryan: Journey to the Centre* (Dublin: Raven Arts Press 1987).

O'Malley, P., *Biting at the Grave: The Irish Hunger Strikes and the Politics of Despair* (Belfast: The Blackstaff Press 1990).

O'Neill, T. P., Jr with Novak, W., *Man of the House: The Life and Political Memoirs of Speaker Tip O'Neill* (New York: Random House 1987).

O'Rawe, R., *Blanketmen* (Dublin: New Island 2005).

O'Ruairc, L., 'The Legacy of Seamus Costello', in *The Blanket: A Journal of Protest and Dissent* October/November 2002 http://lark.phoblacht.net/scostello1.html

O'Sullivan, P. (ed.), *The Irish World Wide: History, Heritage, Identity*, 6 volumes (Leicester: Leicester University Press 1992–7).

Official Republican Movement *Internal Official Republican Movement document relating to Structure of Movement* August 1973.

— *An Important Message to the Voters of Waterford* (undated).

Oppenheimer, A. R., *IRA The Bombs and Bullets: A History of Deadly Ingenuity* (Dublin: Irish Academic Press 2009).

Parker, J., *Death of a Hero: Captain Robert Nairac, GC and the undercover war in Northern Ireland* (London: Metro 1999).

Patterson, H., *Class Conflict and Sectarianism: The Protestant Working Class and the Belfast Labour Movement 1868–1920* (Belfast: The Blackstaff Press 1980).

— *The Politics of Illusion: A Political History of the IRA* (London: Serif 1997).

Porter, N. (ed.), *The Republican Ideal: Current Perspectives* (Belfast: The Blackstaff Press 1998).

Powell, J., *Great Hatred, Little Room: Making Peace in Northern Ireland* (London: The Bodley Head 2008).

Power, T., *The Ta Power Document* Irish Republican Socialist Movement http://irsm.org/history/tapowerdoc.html

Prince, S., *Northern Ireland's '68: Civil Rights, Global Revolt and the Origins of the Troubles* (Dublin: Irish Academic Press 2007).

Provisional IRA *Freedom Struggle* (London: Red Books 1973).

Public Papers of the Presidents of the United States:

— Ronald Reagan 1981 (Washington, DC: United States Government Printing Office 1982).

— Ronald Reagan 1983 (Washington, DC: United States Government Printing Office 1984)

— Ronald Reagan 1984 (Washington, DC: United States Government Printing Office 1985)

— Ronald Reagan 1986 (Washington, DC: United States Government Printing Office 1988)

— George Bush 1990 (Washington, DC: United States Government Printing Office 1991)

— William J. Clinton 1993 (Washington, DC: United States Government Printing Office 1994)

— William J. Clinton 1995 (Washington, DC: United States Government Printing Office 1996)

Purdie, B., *Politics in the Streets: The Origins of the Civil Rights Movement in Northern Ireland* (Belfast: The Blackstaff Press 1990).

— *Ireland Unfree* (London: International Marxist Group Publications 1972).

Rafter, K., *Sinn Féin: In the Shadow of Gunmen* (Dublin: Gill and Macmillan 2005).

Ransom, B., *Connolly's Marxism* (London: Pluto Press 1980).

272

RECON, *Inside the IRA: Interviews with Cathal Gouling Chief of Staff IRA* (Philadelphia: RECON Publications 1974).

Reeve, C. and Reeve, A. B., *James Connolly and the United States: The Road to the 1916 Irish Rebellion* (Atlantic Highlands, NJ: Humanities Press 1978).

Redmond, S., *Desmond Greaves and the Origins of the Civil Rights Movement in Northern Ireland* (London: Connolly Publications 2000).

Regan, J. M., *The Irish Counter-Revolution 1921–1936: Treatyite Politics and Settlement in Independent Ireland* (Dublin: Gill and Macmillan 1999).

Robson, T., *The Broad Front* (Belfast: Irish Republican Socialist Party undated).

Ross, F. S., *Smashing H-Block: The rise and fall of the popular campaign against criminalisation, 1976–1982* (unpublished PhD Thesis, Queen's University, Belfast 2008).

Rowan, B., *Behind the Lines: The Story of the IRA and Loyalist Ceasefires* (Belfast: The Blackstaff Press 1995).

Rumpf, E. and Hepburn, A. C., *Nationalism and Socialism in twentieth-century Ireland* (Liverpool: Liverpool University Press 1977).

Ryan, M., *War and Peace in Ireland: Britain and the IRA in the New World Order* (London: Pluto Press 1994).

Ryan, P., *The Birth of the Provisionals – A Clash between Politics and Tradition* CAIN web service http://cain.ulst.ac.uk/othelem/organ/docs/ryan01.htm

Sands, B., *The Diary of Bobby Sands* (Dublin: Sinn Féin 1981).

Shanahan, T., *The Provisional Irish Republican Army and the Morality of Terrorism* (Edinburgh: Edinburgh University Press 2009).

Shannon, W. V., *The American Irish: A Political and Social Portrait* (New York: Macmillan 1966) (1st edn 1963).

Sharrock, D. and Devenport, M., *Man of War, Man of Peace? The Unauthorised Biography of Gerry Adams* (London: Macmillan 1997).

Sinnerton, H., *David Ervine: Uncharted Waters* (Dingle: Brandon 2002).

Sluka, J. A., *Hearts and Minds, Water and Fish: Support for the IRA and INLA in a Northern Irish Ghetto* (London: JAI Press Inc. 1989).

Smith, M. L. R., *Fighting for Ireland: The Military Strategy of the Irish Republican Movement* (London: Routledge 1995).

Staunton, E., *The Nationalists of Ireland 1918–1973* (Dublin: The Columba Press 2001).

Stewart, A. T. Q., *The Narrow Ground: Aspects of Ulster 1609–1969* (Belfast: The Blackstaff Press 1997) (1st edn 1977).

Stone, M., *None Shall Divide Us* (London: John Blake 2003).

Swan, S., *Official Irish Republicans 1962 to 1972* (lulu.com 2007).

Taylor, P., *Loyalists* (London: Bloomsbury 1999).

— *Brits: The War Against the IRA* (London: Bloomsbury 2002).

Theoharis, J. and Woodard, K., *Freedom North: Black Freedom Struggles Outside the South, 1940– 1980* (New York: Palgrave Macmillan 2003).

The Workers' Party, *Cathal Goulding: Thinker, Socialist, Republican, Revolutionary 1923–1998* (Dublin: The Workers' Party of Ireland 1999).

— *The Politics of The Workers' Party* (undated).

Toolis, K., *Rebel Hearts: Journeys Within the IRA's Soul* (London: Picador 1995).

Townshend, C., *1916: The Irish Rebellion* (London: Allen Lane 2005).

Ua Corbaidh, P., *Irish Democracy, Republicanism, Nationalism and Socialism* (self-published 1982).

Ulster Defence Association *A Brief History of the UDA/UFF* (undated).

— *Devolution – The Road to Progressive Democracy* (UDA: Belfast 1987).

— *A Brief History of the UDA/UFF in Contemporary Conflict Northern Ireland 1969–1995* (Belfast: UDA undated).

Ulster Political Research Group *Common Sense: Northern Ireland – An Agreed Process* (Belfast: Ulster Political Research Group 1987).

Urban, M., *Big Boys' Rules: The Secret Struggle against the IRA* (London: Faber and Faber 1992).

Walker, G., *A history of the Ulster Unionist Party: Protest, pragmatism and pessimism* (Manchester: Manchester University Press 2004).

Walsh, P., *Irish Republicanism and Socialism: The Politics of the Republican Movement 1905–1994* (Belfast: Athol Books 1994).

White, R. W., *Irish Republicans: An Oral and Interpretive History* (London: Greenwood Press 1993).

White, R. W., *Ruari O'Bradaigh* (Bloomington: Indiana University Press 2006).

Wilson, A. J., *Irish America and the Ulster Conflict 1968–1995* (Belfast: The Blackstaff Press 1995).

Wood, I. S., *Crimes of Loyalty: A History of the UDA* (Edinburgh: Edinburgh University Press 2006).

Woods, A., *Ireland: Republicanism and Revolution* (London: Wellred Books 2005).

Index